EXPLORATIONS

CENTENARY ESSAYS

MARY IMMACULATE COLLEGE
LIMERICK

EXPLORATIONS

CENTENARY ESSAYS

MARY IMMACULATE COLLEGE
LIMERICK
1898 - 1998

LIAM IRWIN
EDITOR

Comóradh Céad Bliain

1898 1998

1898 - 1998
Centenary

First published in 1998 for Mary Immaculate College, Limerick.

© Mary Immaculate College and in

the individual essays, the author 1998

ISBN 1 900146 35 5

Printed by Colour Books Ltd., Dublin.

CONTENTS

History

Philosophy

Geography

Gaeilge

Media Studies

Acknowledgments

For their permission to reprint material I am grateful to the following publishers and journals: *Edwin Mellen Press* for chapter 2; *Travaux de Littérature* for chapter 3; *Oxford University Press* for chapter 4; *North Munster Antiquarian Journal* for chapter 7; *History of Education* for chapter 8; *Studies* for chapter 11; *Doctrine and Life* for chapter 12; *Irisleabhar Mhá Nuad* for chapter 17; *Irish Communications Review* for chapter 23.

CONTRIBUTORS

Úna Ní Bhroiméil	Léachtóir, Roinn na Staire
Pádraic Breathnach	Léachtóir, Roinn na Gaeilge
Kieran R. Byrne	Vice Pres., Univ. of Limerick
Gareth Cox	Lecturer, Music Dept.
Maura Cronin	Lecturer, History Dept.
Michael Culhane	Lecturer, Religious Studies
Eilís Ní Dheá,	Léachtóir, Roinn an Oideachais
Gerry Dukes	Lecturer, English Dept.
Úna Nic Éinrí	Léachtóir, Roinn na Gaeilge
John Eustace	Assistant Librarian
John Hayes	Head, Philosophy Dept.
Liam Irwin	Head, History Dept.

Susan Liddy	Lecturer, Women's Studies
Des McCafferty	Head, Geography Dept.
Deirdre McMahon	Lecturer, History Dept.
Áinéad Ní Mhuirthile	Ceann, Roinn na Gaeilge
Stiofán Newman	Léachtóir, Roinn na Gaeilge
Eugene O'Brien	Lecturer, Communications
Díóg O'Connell,	Lecturer, Media Studies
Jo O'Donovan	Head, Religious Studies
Darach Sanfey	Lecturer, French Dept.
Stephen Thornton	Lecturer, Philosophy Dept.

Foreword

I agreed, early in 1997, to chair a committee for the organisation of academic events, one of a number of such bodies set up around that time to plan appropriate celebrations for the Centennial of the foundation of Mary Immaculate College in 1898. During one of our relaxed preliminary meetings a seemingly innocuous suggestion was made that it might be appropriate to arrange publication of a volume of essays which would reflect scholarship in the College, one hundred years after its establishment. My approval of this idea was expressed with what was, in hindsight, an unwise enthusiasm. I had envisaged a truly spirited competition among my numerous fellow committee members for the privilege of transforming this noble aspiration into a hardbacked and securely bound reality. Despite having proved in my personal life the untruth of a famous dictum, it was clearly felt by my colleagues to be a truth universally acknowledged that such an enthusiastic chairman must be in search of a book to edit. And thus it came to pass that I undertook the planning, editing and production of the work that now, my dear reader, presumably lies open before you.

I have implemented the original suggestion as closely as possible. No overall theme was imposed and no area of research has been excluded. All faculty in the College, full time, contract or part time were invited to contribute and all material received has been included. Individual departments were not approached nor were particular topics suggested or commissioned. The volume provides simply a snapshot of the range of academic research and writing currently being conducted, or recently published, by the staff of Mary Immaculate College. While it has used a wide angle lens, it does not reflect the entire research profile of the College though any lacuna in this regard arises from the choices made by individual faculty and not from any editorial preconditions or decisions.

I have dispensed with the usual introduction format of providing a descriptive commentary on each chapter. The various disciplines represented here are quite clearly indicated and in most instances the titles of the individual chapters are a key to their contents. Where this may not be the case the author clearly intended to create a certain mystique and I do not wish to spoil that effect.

I have neither the competence nor the arrogance to offer opinions on the ideas and arguments presented in such a wide variety of papers and feel sure that those who consult this work are not, in any case, very interested in editorial comments or interpretations. Having thus eliminated the main point of having an introduction, this section has been designated as a foreword in the confident expectation that this is a sufficiently vague concept to accommodate what I do wish to say.

I am grateful to all the contributors, whose professionalism, cooperation and patience are deeply appreciated. The President, Sr. Angela, and the College authorities provided both encouragement and financial support for the undertaking. Eileen Madden supplied secretarial assistance, Sheyla Ryan answered my word processing queries, Gerry Byrne gave me technical advice and Úna Nic Éinrí was a benign gadfly for the completion of the task. It has been a lengthier than anticipated process and the final details were only completed with the kind indulgence of the History Department faculty at the University of St. Thomas in Houston, where I am, ostensibly, fully engaged in informing their students about the Irish past.

A final word to the original committee. I am now, as Miss Austen might put it, ever sensible of the warmest gratitude towards those persons who by bringing me into this enterprise have been the means of my deriving much satisfaction.

Liam Irwin,
Houston, Texas,
September 1998.

ENGLISH

1

THREE IN A ROW:A FABLE OF URBAN REDEVELOPMENT

GERRY DUKES

The First Saturday

It begins in deep dreamlessness many layers down from the sublunary. Sweet sleep holds me tenderly in the downy duvet. A faint stir, the trembling of a feather on a lip and I begin to float upward through zones of desire and preference. First a sun-stunned deserted beach in Barcares, lapped by weak warm waves. Then in the beach-bound car straining to read the faded road sign, *marquage efface au sol*. Damn that whining mosquito. Groping now for a weapon, ungluing the eyelids and preparing for the barred Mediterranean blaze lancing through the shutters. Upright at last, open-eyed, vigilant.

- Where is it? Bloody hell, it's Dame Street!

The bloodshot eye of the clock-radio blinks 7.05 and the whine grows louder. What in the name of..? Out of the bed and over to the window, the tender foot stepping on the business end of an abandoned toy excavator. Jerk aside the curtains, nurse that foot and stare. Down outside City Hall in the bleak dawn a man is carefully cutting along a yellow chalkline with a tungsten power saw. As he relaxes from his forward drive the blade spins faster, the whine rising to a higher pitch. Oh, Valéry, thou shouldst be living at this hour: the throbbing foot and suffering ears conspire to produce a total derangement of the senses. If the saw comes can the drill be far behind?

The eight o'clock pips are going as the boring nemesis thumps into life. To cacophony is added vibration, the thuds perceptible through the interior springing. No chance now for the routine rhythm of a normal Saturday; the leisurely lie-in, the stroll to the shop for a newspaper and hot croissants, cup after cup of strong sweet coffee. After a while a syncopated rhythm breaks in on the local disturbance. They are digging at Essex bridge too. When the motorists get going chaos will be loosed.

This time it is the traffic lights. At various times over the last two years it was the gas, the electricity, the telephone, the water, the sewers. Each time a designated crew had arrived, dug their hole, fixed whatever needed fixing, put back the surface and departed. Each time the integrity of the street was further compromised with bumps and hollows. My young son thinks that the whole world is a redevelopment site, crawling with dumpers, diggers, bulldozers and cranes. His joy at the beach is in the demolition of sandcastles with his earthmoving machines. Nurture has triumphed over nature and he is as casual about parking the gear as any of the contractors in Temple Bar.

On the street the noise is colossal, an assault on the fragile flesh, the flayed nerves. Not only are they digging the street but they are excavating around the base of each of the three sets of traffic lights. This time there is a duet of pneumatic drills, their coloratura voices figured against the throbbing bass of two compressors. The dust rises gently, sticking to the still tacky paint of the expensive redecoration, nestling with static cling to the window panes on all four floors, clogging the breath, choking the spirit. Still to come is the excavator to lift the rubble, the truck to take it away. I forehear the grinding scrapes, the rush of thuds as the bucket releases its load on the flatbed cunningly constructed to achieve maximum amplification.

All afternoon, from his site at the window, my son keeps me posted on the work in progress. He joyously re-enacts the

activities in the street with his little yellow toys. I haven't the heart
to tell him where his excavator is. My literary excavations have
long since ground to a halt; a rising tide of noise drowns all boasts.

- *Dad, tá an steamroller ag teacht anois.*
- *Cloisim é.*
- *Tá sé beag bídeach agus buí.*

The little yellow taratantara comes scuffling up the street, loose
grit squealing under thunderous rollers. At least it signifies the end
of operations for today. With a bit of luck the cut-backs will not
allow for Sunday working. The manic horn blowing at lane
closures will be pastoral bliss compared to what has gone on
throughout the day.

The Second Saturday

The drunken cones, the painted rusting barrels, the tattered
plastic tape had all been removed by Monday but the holes around
the bases of the lights were still raw. Prognosis? Further surgery.
First cut of the day came at 7.30. The tungsten scalpel was being
wielded with a vengeance, tearing the heart out of the street,
probing the lining of my sensorium. Duvet and pillow provided no
defence. It is not hospital I need, it's asylum. Nothing for it but get
up and out. The banal Christmas musak at the shopping-centre
with its Mobius loop of Como and Bennett may soothe the savage
beast within. He gets a fillip as I remove the ticket from under the
wiper and stuff it in the glove box to join its extended family.
Peace on earth (please, Jesus) and goodwill to all, that's the drill.
    Surveying the battlefield after the twilight truce had been
declared I saw that this week B had been connected to C. Last
week it had been A to B. The lights at A and C had new bases but
B remained gaping. No bother, I thought, a little filling, mere
dentistry. Fool, fool. I had forgotten the hypotenuse.

A Digression Concerning Sunday

Crashing to the surface, gasping at 7.45.

- *Christ! It's a new noise!*

- Mn?
- It's a different noise. They're doing something else.
- Mn. It's a chain-saw. Go back to sleep.

She was right. Outside, a lorry laden with two Christmas trees had drawn up in front of City Hall. Beside it, its appendages locked in the down position, wheels clear of the ground, a mobile crane to hoist the trees into place. The crew was already busy with the chain-saw, tailoring the trees for the twin niches. Heigh ho, heigh ho, it's off to work they go, these displaced lumberjacks. Had the foreshortened dwarfs looked up their eyes would have met those of an anguished fool i' the urban forest, grinding his snow-white molars and his gleaming axe, swearing vengeance on the City Fathers, mothers to a man.

The Third Saturday

The same shattering noise, the dust, the fumes, the vibrations, the exhaust and the standard Saturday exhaustion. Yes, Didi. Habit is a great deadener. I can handle it; commuting a thousand miles a week, truncated sleep, clapped-out buses, spiteful car alarms, the confetti of parking tickets. It's a breeze. Stick another cigarette up your nose and relax, there's nothing more they can do to you. Guess again, Punch. They can shatter your nights too.

Divide the hypotenuse AC at its mid-point, say X. Under no circumstances must we stop the vital traffic flow. Rip up A to X with as much violence as you can conjure. Do whatever is to be done and close up the trench. Break for lunch and consider the next move because it will be dark soon. Right, Mick, start her up and we'll make short work of X to C. Oh, ecstasy, ecstasy. The last lap. Soon it will be over and what passes for silence will steal back, tiptoeing on its delicate hob-nails.

Shut her down, Mick....SHUT HER DOWN, MICK. It's too dark to finish off. Packie and the lads are coming with the plates and we'll just anchor them with a bit of the black stuff. Grand job.

But they had forgotten to level the plates. Every time a car crossed them they boomed, lugubrious, mournful and loud. They boomed all night, all Sunday and in to Monday. And BOOM that weekend BOOM the motorised Dubs were BOOM out in force

BOOM BOOM.

What sights and sounds the nighttown has to offer the insomniac! At 2.30 a rumpus brought me to the window. Down in the Millennium Park a drunken transvestite was roaring macho obscenities because he had laddered his tights. His companion was on his hands and knees in a flowerbed being extravagantly sick. Around 3.00 an unusual car pulled up (slow double boom) at the flats opposite. Each one of its ten doors was viciously slammed. Judging by the voices, its disgorged cargo was strictly male, strictly heterosexual. They roused their putative hostess by liberal use of the horn (the car's, that is). She left them in no doubt as to where they should go and what they should do to themselves. She even suggested that they should try doing it to each other or, failing that, to the beer bottles they were carrying. After a couple of rounds of neighbourly banter the ten doors were re-slammed and the boys took off in search of less recalcitrant flesh. I seem to remember looking at the clock sometime after 4.00 and then I slept.

I Have A Dream

My son and I alight from the tram at the Olympia theatre. We watch admiringly as it pulls noiselessly away on balloon tyres, the trolley hissing faintly in the darkness. We turn hand-in-hand down Sycamore Street, the child's dumper truck clattering along behind.

- *Dad, an bhfuilimid ag dul go dtí an gluaistean?*
- *Níl. Tá atógáil ar siúl sa car park faoi láthair. Tá an gluaistean in áit eile ag bailiú ticéidí.*

At the gate of my former car park there is a large hole dug in the new cobbled surface. A pristine yellow digger bestrides the pile of rubble like a fat toad squatting on her multitudinous spawn. Its baleful yellow eye pulses rhythmically. I recognize the driver asprawl in his seat because he and all the other workmen standing about chatting and smoking are masked with my face. Around the edge of the hole men are kneeling, like mourners at a funeral. They are dressed in identical grey suits, blue shirts and discreet floral ties. They seem to be praying.

We go nearer, straining to hear. I catch snatches - formulas for the calculation of the increase in traffic flow given certain economic parameters, for the gauge of steel to reinforce concrete, for the width of sewers to transport so many tons of waste given specific housing density. Each man speaks to himself alone, there is no communication. I know them now, architects, surveyors, engineers, planners, investment managers, bankers, solicitors, speculators. Good, good.

- *Dad, tá na cinn eile agam anseo.*

I look down and see him stacking the spare clips neatly in his dumper. I have no idea when he let go my left hand nor what it is I am grasping firmly. I lift it slowly. The big Browning gleams fitfully in the yellow light. Tenderly, I fit the patented silencer.

2

TOWARDS A JOYCEAN ETHICS OF IRISH IDENTITY

EUGENE O'BRIEN

In the *Cyclops* chapter of *Ulysses*, the absorptive tendencies of the advanced nationalist ideology are parodied mercilessly. The hyperbolic and surreal humour of the passage is obvious, but its epistemological import has received comparatively little attention. This passage comes as an interpolation in the opening of the chapter, where the citizen, an ultra-essentialist nationalist, is seen as a mythical Irish hero. The resonances with the Celtic and Gaelic revivals are obvious, as the urban, twentieth century Irishman is metamorphosed into a figure analogous to that of Cuchulain or Fionn or any of the Celtic heroes of the revival pantheon. The passage begins with a description of this heroic figure:

> The figure seated on a large boulder at the foot of a round tower was that of a broadshouldered deepchested stronglimbed frankeyed redhaired freelyfreckled shaggybearded widemouthed largenosed longheaded deepvoiced barekneed brawnyhanded hairylegged ruddyfaced sinewyarmed hero.[1]

The use of the adjective-noun construction lends an epic air to the description, combining an archaic word form with a hint of the

Anglo-Saxon kenning, which created a descriptive picture in the form of an adjective-noun construction. The giant is then described in terms of his gigantic physical measurements, his clothing, ox-hide, deerskin and 'a girdle of plaited straw and rushes'.[2] From this girdle, hung 'a row of seastones' and on these were inscribed with 'rude yet striking art the tribal images of many Irish heroes and heroines of antiquity'.[3]

Thus far, the imagery, diction and general tone are in keeping with a revivalist portrayal of heroic ur-Irishness, and one expects the ensuing list of 'Irish heroes and heroines' to resound with the names that were associated with the heroic tales of Standish O'Grady; however, the list in question defeats this expectation with a mixture of bathos and humour. It begins in the manner expected, detailing real and imaginary figures from the Celtic and Gaelic pantheons: 'Cuchulin, Conn of hundred battles, Niall of nine hostages, Brian of Kincora, the ardri Malachi, Art MacMurragh, Shane O'Neill, Father John Murphy, Owen Roe, Patrick Sarsfield, Red Hugh O'Donnell, Red Jim MacDermott, Soggarth Eoghan O'Growney, Michael Dwyer, Francy Higgins, Henry Joy M'Cracken'.[4] So far, we would appear to be in the familiar generic territory of the revivalist project. A list of figures, both mythical and historical, is generated through their association with a particular vision of Ireland. It is from the next name on that the essentialist appropriation of past history into an ethnocentric socio-cultural narrative is parodied in a manner which undercuts through hyperbole the assimilative and absorptive tendencies of the Celtic and Gaelic revivalist ideologies:

> Goliath, Horace Wheatley, Thomas Conneff, Peg Woffington, the Village Blacksmith, Captain Moonlight, Captain Boycott, Dante Alighieri, Christopher Columbus, S. Fursa, S. Brendan, Marshal MacMahon, Charlemagne, Theobald Wolfe Tone, the Mother of the Maccabees, the Last of the Mohicans, the Rose of Castile, the Man for Galway, The Man that Broke the Bank at Monte Carlo, The Man in the Gap, The Woman Who Didn't, Benjamin Franklin, Napoleon Bonaparte, John L. Sullivan, Cleopatra, Savourneen Deelish, Julius Caesar, Paracelsus, sir Thomas Lipton, William Tell, Michelangelo Hayes, Muhammad,

the Bride of Lammermoor, Peter the Hermit, Peter the Packer, Dark Rosaleen, Patrick W. Shakespeare, Brian Confucius, Murtagh Gutenberg, Patricio Velasquez, Captain Nemo, Tristan and Isolde, the first Prince of Wales, Thomas Cook and Son, the Bold Soldier Boy, Arrah na Pogue, Dick Turpin, Ludwig Beethoven, the Colleen Bawn, Waddler Healy, Angus the Culdee, Dolly Mount, Sidney Parade, Ben Howth, Valentine Greatrakes, Adam and Eve, Arthur Wellesley, Boss Croker, Herodotus, Jack the Giantkiller, Gautama Buddha, Lady Godiva, The Lily of Killarney, Balor of the Evil Eye, the Queen of Sheba, Acky Nagle, Joe Nagle, Alessandro Volta, Jeremiah O'Donovan Rossa, Don Philip O'Sullivan Beare.[5]

This list of 'Irish heroes and heroines of antiquity' is an example of a specific form of writing: that of a 'catalogue verse' wherein a list of entities is used to show progression, generation or, in this case, commonality. The genre can be traced back to two of Western civilization's canonical works: the genealogical list in the *Book of Genesis* and the list of Trojan War heroes in Homer's *Iliad*. In *Ulysses*, this catalogue is placed in the *Cyclops* chapter wherein Irish nationalism, in the *persona* of the monocular 'citizen', and by extension, the essentialist nationalist ideology of Irish identity, is being placed under critique. That this critique is phrased in humorous terms in no way negates its power, in fact, I would argue that the impact is heightened through the ironic exfoliation of the 'Irishness' of the heroes and heroines involved.

Here, alterity breaks through such essentialism, as Joyce achieves a double purpose. Firstly, he is mocking the absorptive desire to subsume diverse historical and cultural patterns into a sameness of identity. In this sense, he is anticipating the thought of Levinas who asks 'how can the opposition of the Same and the Other not lead to the triumph of the Same?'[6] This sameness is very often constituted by the placement of the present within the frame or *parergon* of the past. Such a notion is central to the politicized nationalism that derived from the Gaelic and Celtic revivals. The past, or at least a version of the past, is hypostasized or reified so that it becomes the grounding moment for definitions. As a centre, an unmoved mover, it becomes a conduit for the duplication of sameness at the expense of alterity. Given the complete lack of connection with any notion of Celticity in, for example, Goliath, Velasquez, Captain Nemo, Napoleon Bonaparte, the first Prince of Wales, or Thomas Cook and Son, the motivated nature of these choices gradually exfoliates in the satire as we are forced to expand our definition of the Irishness involved.

Secondly, Joyce is including alterity within sameness, he is creating an identity that is different from itself and also reconstructing the paradigms through which cultural nationalism was constituted. He is providing a classic example of what Derrida sees as the necessity for 'opening, uncloseting, destabilizing foreclusionary structures so as to allow for the passage toward the other'.[7] By placing people who are demonstrably *not* part of 'tribal images of many Irish heroes and heroines of antiquity' in this catalogue, Joyce is reinventing the definitions of Irishness, and by extension, of identity as we know it. He creates, through a protreptic discourse, an *Auseinandersetzung*, which brings out the alterity that is central to a negative definition of Irishness as he hopes to express it. The very fact that the English language is being used as a form of expression demonstrates an alterity that inhabits the core of what is seen as essentialist rhetoric. It is through English that most Irish people have knowledge of these multi-cultural figures in the Joycean pantheon. Through this linguistic *protrepsis*, Joyce is presaging a cultural one, wherein the English language is not seen as a colonial imposition, but rather, as an ethical imperative towards alterity which frees Irishness from the prison-house of sameness and monological essentialism.

As examples of this negative definition of identity, three figures from the above catalogue stand out, namely, 'Patrick W. Shakespeare, Brian Confucius, Murtagh Gutenberg'. The identity that is encapsulated in these proper names allows for the expression of an Irishness that is plural, and certainly far from the sublating absorption that is part of the essentialist project. Thus, while such juxtapositions are quite comic in themselves, they do make a serious point. The whole nature of identification is oppositional, in that to be Irish is not to be English, or to be French is not to be German. Following logically on this thread is the desire to differentiate through language, culture *et al* so that it becomes clear on which side of a particular opposition the individual belongs. Over a period of time, such differentiations take root in the epistemology of the culture in question, and become reified. Their differential status is etiolated, and instead there is a Heideggerian *Versammlung* (gathering) of such qualities in favour of an ethnocentric valorization which make the *Volk* the *Volk*.[8] This privileging of a form of reified sameness is, for Joyce as for Derrida, the very antithesis of what identity should be. Derrida, speaking at Villanova University in 1994, made the point that this privilege which is granted to 'unity, to totality, to organic ensembles, to community as a homogenized whole' can be seen as a 'danger for responsibility, for decision, for ethics, for politics.[9] Making the point that cultural identity is not the 'self-identity of a thing', he goes on to say that 'the identity of a culture is a way of being different from itself', adding that a 'culture is different from itself' and that 'language is different from itself'.[10]

It is this 'difference from itself' that Joyce is foregrounding in his three emblematic figures, 'Patrick W. Shakespeare', 'Brian Confucius' and 'Murtagh Gutenberg'. These names open up the centralities of Irishness by defining them in terms of other cultures. All three perform this function, but given the historical antipathy between Ireland and England, perhaps the most significant of these is 'Patrick W. Shakespeare'.

In terms of the exfoliation of English culture throughout the British empire, the teaching of the works of Shakespeare was of seminal importance; indeed, the proper name 'William Shakespeare' functions as a transcendental signifier, as synecdoche for all things English and cultural. The subtle political message that is to be found especially in the tragedies, namely that those who upset the hierarchy of institutionalized power do so at their own and their societies' peril, was not lost on colonized peoples. Macbeth, Claudius, Regan and Goneril, Oswald, politically, and Othello, racially, demonstrate the fate that befalls such resistance to the given socio-political order, both for the individual microcosm and the socio-political macrocosm.

13

However, here the trope of naming is used to create a different effect as 'William Shakespeare' becomes 'Patrick W. Shakespeare'. Here, the bard is appropriated into a new cosmos of identification as name is transformed into trope, with a 'turning away' (the original meaning of trope) from colonial associations. That the proper name of Shakespeare undergoes a chiasmic transformation in the ongoing process of transcultural anglicization that has taken place in Ireland during British rule is symbolic of Joyce's project; namely the redefinition and pluralization of Irish identity. Joyce posits the notion of reciprocal interchange between cultures: just as Irish language and culture became Anglophone, so English, both the language and culture, was likewise altered by the interaction with Ireland. The *hauntological* imbrication of the two cultures is enacted in the name of 'Patrick W. Shakespeare', a name which will force a redefinition of both Irishness and Englishness as essences, standing outside the historical processes. In this name, the figures of *gnomon* and parallelogram,[11] or pointer and shadow interfuse, so that it is hard to know which is which. Clearly such a process is analogous to negative dialectics in that it 'reflects its own motion'.[12] For Joyce, the juxtaposition of Shakespeare, that classic synecdoche of Englishness, with 'Patrick', the classic nominal synecdoche of Irishness, is not a dialectical fusion, an *Aufhebung* in the Hegelian sense or a *Versammlung* in the Heideggerian one, rather is its logic one of 'disintegration'.[13] In fact, it is a perfect example of what we have termed protreptic discourse, in that this neologistic name embodies a 'calling and answering while yet remaining preliminary to the circumstances of its fulfilment'.[14] Here, self and other exist mutually in terms of an identity that is complex and differential.

The transformation of 'William' to 'Patrick W.' could, at first be seen as a classic postcolonial reversal – the reappropriation of the synecdoche of Englishness through juxtaposition with a synecdoche of Irishness. However, the other non-Irish names in the list of heroes would seem to undercut this reading. In fact, the catalogue verse in the *Cyclops* chapter functions as an *antiphrasis*,[15] with the Irish and non-Irish heroes interrogating each other. This economy displaces the Irish/English and colonial/post-colonial binarisms, the

14

central defining factors of Irish identity, and instead places the names of both nations in a broader world catalogue verse, where they *gnomonically* redefine each other. This catalogue emphasizes the emancipatory function of 'Patrick W. Shakespeare' with respect to essentialist notions of identity: this troped name will validate neither imperial Englishness nor nationalist Irishness; rather will it usher in reciprocality and plurality in terms of political identities.

Joyce sees the nominal troping of 'Patrick W. Shakespeare' as a liberation from that sterile essentialism of contemporary Irish and English political ideologies. In *Finnegans Wake* he refers to Shakespeare as 'Shikespower.....Anonymoses'[16] and later in the telling line 'all the rivals to allsea, shakeagain, O disaster! shakealose'.[17] Here the name of Shakespeare is being invoked to empower the shaking loose (again) of the nets that Joyce feels Stephen must fly by, namely those of 'nationality, language, religion'.[18] Through this classic microcosmic example of protreptic discourse Joyce, like Stephen, will attempt to 'fly by those nets'.

Ironically, Shakespeare, as the almost universal figure of Englishness would seem to be an unusual symbolic choice in this quest, but the 'mirror-minded' man of *Finnegans Wake* figures largely in Joyce's work.[19] The changed name of Shakespeare will allow Joyce to shake up and shake lose the influences of Irish nationalism and British imperialism; in other words, the troped name of Shakespeare will introduce an ethical force into Joyce's writing, a force which will liberate notions of Irish identity from the essentialist vision of the citizen, and instead introduce a European and world-based negative view ('anonymoses') of Irish identity. The composite name of 'Patrick W. Shakespeare', an example of *Finnegans Wake*'s view of the bard's ability, as 'Great Shapesphere puns it',[20] allows him to reshape the sphere of national identity, and hence is a constituent factor in the political dimension of Joyce's work. The cultural appropriation of Shakespeare is very much within the *Weltanschauung* of *Ulysses*, and of Joyce's overall attitude towards identity.

In *Ulysses*, Stephen makes the point that history 'is a nightmare from which I am trying to awake'.[21] I would argue that the particular ideology of history from which Stephen wishes to escape is the monocular one of the citizen, who sees Ireland as identical with Gaelic, Catholic, and nationalist viewpoints. This ideological position is stated a number of times in this chapter with the following sardonic passage being a typical example. Here, in the parodic genre of newspaper reportage, the attitudes of the green wing of nationalism are given expression. The usual conflation of real and imaginary details are to be found with the 'panceltic' Finn MacCool invoked to add a note of authenticity:

> After an instructive discourse by the chairman, a magnificent oration eloquently and forcibly expressed, a most interesting and instructive discussion of the usual high standard of excellence ensued as to the desirability of the revivability of the ancient games and sports of our ancient Panceltic forefathers. The well-known and highly respected worker in the cause of our old tongue, Mr Joseph M'Carthy Hynes, made an eloquent appeal for the resuscitation of the ancient Gaelic sports and pastimes, practised morning and evening by Finn MacCool, as calculated to revive the best traditions of manly strength and prowess handed down to us from ancient ages.[22]

Here are all the familiar trappings of monological identity, predicated on the past and self-valorization, with no room for alterity. It is a process summarized by Levinas in his essay 'Transcendence and Height', as he notes that the 'Same or the I surmounts diversity and the Non-I, which stands against it, by engaging in a political and technical destiny'.[23] Here, there can be no other course of action than the 'revivability' of ancient Irish games so as to endorse the sameness of identity.

In contradistinction to this neo-revivalist perspective, much of the rest of the book posits a negative notion of Irish identity; the book as a whole features Leopold Bloom, a Hungarian Jewish hero, Molly Bloom, a British heroine born in Gibraltar, and Stephen Dedalus, Irish, but whose name certainly betokens a pluralist vision of identity in itself, as we have seen. The organizing myth is Greek, and Bloom's comments on Irish Catholic rituals, themselves synecdoches of centripetal identity, are certainly those

16

of a *spectator ab extra*;[24] while the structural parallel with Homer's classical *Odyssey* foregrounds the identificatory perspective of Joyce. His book is paralleled with one of the first great books of Western civilization; he is placing Ireland, and the subject matter of Ireland squarely in the ambit of European culture, against which Irishness will be defined negatively. The troped name of 'Patrick W. Shakespeare' brings this ethical definition of identity as an openness to alterity into focus, but I would argue that this is not confined to this passage in *Ulysses*. In fact, the Shakespearean spectre is to be found haunting many different portions of Joyce's writings, and this imbrication of Shakespeare and Joyce will have the effect of transforming them both.

Some literary detective work will demonstrate the place of Shakespeare in the literary politics of Joyce and this detective work begins with *A Portrait of the Artist as a Young Man*. The name of 'Shakespeare' is not to be found anywhere in this novel. However. Don Gifford has detected a ghostly Shakespearean presence in the genesis of Stephen Dedalus's aesthetic theory. Stephen's aesthetic theory is underpinned by Victor Hugo's *Préface* to his play *Cromwell*. Hugo lays out a tripartite division of art in a manner similar to that of Stephen, in his aesthetic theory. In this theory, Stephen states:

> These forms are: the lyrical form, the form wherein the artist presents his image in immediate relation to himself; the epical form, the form wherein he presents his image in mediate relation to himself and to others; the dramatic form, the form wherein he presents his image in immediate relation to others...[and where] he or she assumes a proper and intangible esthetic life... The esthetic image in the dramatic form is life purified in and re-projected from the human imagination. The mystery of esthetic, like that of material creation, is accomplished. The artist, like the God of creation, remains within or behind or beyond or above his handiwork, invisible, refined out of existence, indifferent, paring his fingernails.[25]

Stephen's highest form – the dramatic where each person 'assumes a proper and intangible esthetic life' – is associated by Hugo with the poetry of 'Shakespeare, Dante and Milton'.[26] This Shakespearean-inspired aesthetic is in direct opposition to the 'old man' in a mountain cabin met by John Alphonsus Mulrennan, who embodies insularity and reactionary nationalism: 'there must be terrible queer creatures at the latter end of the world'. The fact that this man speaks Irish is important: English, which can be seen as the symbol of colonial oppression, can, by a chiasic twist, also be seen as a world language, and the gateway to European and world literature through translation. Indeed, translation is a possible name for the change from 'William Shakespeare' to 'Patrick W. Shakespeare'.

Here, Shakespeare as trope is a figure of hybridity and syncretization; he symbolizes an embrace of world literature and also the emancipatory aspects of the English language as spoken in Ireland. The poetry of Milton, and translations of the poetry of Dante, would not be so readily available to an Irish writer were it not for colonization, and the process of linguistic change that was coterminous with it. In this sense Stephen's flight to Europe at the end of *A Portrait of the Artist as a Young Man* can be seen as inspired by the ghostly presence of Shakespeare, or as he is significantly termed in *Finnegans Wake* 'that favourite *continental* poet, Daunty, Gouty and Shopkeeper'.[27] The troped name of 'Patrick W. Shakespeare' symbolizes the possibilities that arise between the transactional intersections of England and Ireland in terms of language and identity. It is important to note the transformative drive at work here. Shakespeare as British national bard has been transformed into what is beautifully termed in *Finnegans Wake* 'clasp shakers (the handtouch which is speech without words)'.[28] Here is the *hauntological* power of language that is pure speech, or in Levinasian terms, pure saying, as opposed to said. As he puts it, language as 'saying is ethical sincerity', it is 'an ethical openness to the other',[29] and this speech without words in *Finnegans Wake*, especially in this Shakespearean context, makes the point that such an ethicity of language has not yet come into full being; Joyce is involved in creating such a language which is 'different from itself'[30] and which creates the conditions for a negative notion of Irishness.

The name is the clasping of two cultures together, and the result of this clasping is to shake the essentialist notions of both cultures 'Shikespower'. This troped name is both an image of implied potential and a ghostly figure redolent of the past. This ghostly Shakespearean presence in Joyce's *oeuvre* is further discussed in Stephen Dedalus's theory of Shakespeare in *Ulysses*. As Buck Mulligan observes: '[i]t's quite simple. He proves by algebra that Hamlet's grandson is Shakespeare's grandfather and that he himself is the ghost of his own father'.[31] That the Shakespearean presence in *A Portrait of the Artist as a Young Man* is mediated through the theoretical comments of Hugo foregrounds the macrocosmic placement of Irish political identity in the Joycean aesthetic. It also refers proleptically to the catalogue verse at the beginning of this section where the list of 'Irish heroes and heroines' contains a macrocosmic definition of Irishness, with many of the works being available only through English trans-lations, ghosts of the originals, analogous to the *hauntological* presence of Shakespeare in *A Portrait of the Artist as a Young Man*. Like the vision of the artist in the final chapter, the presence of Shakespeare remains 'within or behind or beyond or above' the text 'invisible, refined out of existence', as a metonym of the *gnomonic* definition of Irishness which Joyce is expressing.

In terms of Shakespeare as a signifier of a plural form of identity, there is an interesting passage in the *Scylla and Charybdis* chapter of *Ulysses*, where there is reference to a French production of *Hamlet*. This reference raises yet more issues about identity and nationality:

> *Hamlet*
> *ou*
> *Le Distrait*
> *Pièce de Shakespeare*
> He repeated to John Eglinton's newgathered frown:
> *Pièce de Shakespeare*, don't you know. It's so French. The
> French point of view. *Hamlet ou...*[32]

Once again Shakespeare is mediated through a continental influ-ence, this time Mallarmé, once more demonstrating the protean power of 'Patrick W. Shakespeare' as an avatar of a macrocosmic placement of Irish identity. The verb *'distraire'* has the following meanings: 'to distract, amuse, separate, set aside' with the added connotation of 'absent minded'. The separation of Shakespeare from his position as national bard, the 'setting aside' of the criteria of essentialist identity, the distraction from Englishness, and the transformation into 'Patrick W. Shakespeare', spectral presence over Joyce's pluralization of Irish identity, proceeds apace with that terminal *'ou'* ('or') which leaves the way open for polysemic connotations in terms of meaning. The ghostly presence in *A Portrait of the Artist as a Young Man* has become a *hauntological* image of the transforming of essentialist notions of Englishness into polysemic and negative images of Irishness. Is Mallarmé's *Hamlet* French or English; is Victor Hugo's conception of Shakespeare French or English; are Irish performances of Shakespeare English or Irish, what nationality is the Akira Kurisawa's Japanese production of *Macbeth*. For that matter, what is the language of Joyce's *Finnegans Wake*?

Joyce's interrogation of essentialist attitudes to culture and nationality reaches a climactic point in Leopold Bloom's answer to the question asked in *Ulysses*, a question with strong echoes of a similar one which began this study. However, if the question is similar, then the answer is very different:

> What is your nation if I may ask? says the citizen. Ireland, says Bloom. I was born here. Ireland.[33]

This is the ultimate emancipatory aim of the invocation of *Patrick W. Shakespeare*: the pluralization of identity which allows a Hungarian Jew to claim Irish identity as almost an accident of birth. The troped name allows the dissemination of the singular, colonial image of 'Shakespeare' into the polylinguistic and multi charactered image of pluralism and difference. When Mr Deasy in *Ulysses* asks '[b]ut what does Shakespeare say?' and then answers his own question, '[p]*ut but money in thy purse*', Stephen makes this very point by murmuring 'Iago'.[34] There is not one Shakespeare but rather, as Joyce notes in *Finnegans Wake*, 'myriads of drifting minds',[35] and these drifting minds, these polysemic characters, allow for a new politics of Irish identity as epitomized by Leopold Bloom's assertion of Irishness. What is necessary here is that, if Bloom is to be Irish, then the definition of Irishness must be revised so as to include him. Any notion of a reified identity is now destroyed, and the future becomes a future determined by the synchronic present, as opposed to the diachronic past. The language of Joyce points towards the 'absolute future of what is coming';[36] while it does refer to the past, there is extensive mediation of that past so as to ensure that an oversimplistic pseudomorphosis between a particular narrated past and the present and future cannot be created – indeed, for Adorno, a resistance to such a premature fusion is a point in common with both art and philosophy.[37]

Bloom equates such pluralistic identity with a certain view of language, prefiguring the postnationalistic language of *Finnegans Wake*, and he again cites Shakespeare as a source of such a view: '[b]ut then Shakespeare has no rhymes: blank verse. The flow of the language it is'.[38] This flow of language, inhabited by the spectral figure of 'Patrick W. Shakespeare', is dialectical in operation and ethical in direction, and is the precise opposite of what has been valorized in the name of 'Saxon' Shakespeare.[39] This view of Shakespeare as some kind of monological transcendental figure embodying Englishness is the opposite side of the same coin from which was minted the Irish revival, and the image of the spectre, as negative trope of such identificatory fundamentalism, is further developed in terms of Stephen Dedalus's theory of Shakespeare, in *Ulysses*, where the spectrality of the bard is again discussed:

> It is the ghost, the king, a king and no king, and the player is Shakespeare who has studied *Hamlet* all the years of his life which were not vanity in order to play the part of the spectre....Is it possible that that player Shakespeare, a ghost by absence, and in the vesture of buried Denmark, a ghost by death, speaking his own words to his own son's name (had Hamnet Shakespeare lived he would have been prince Hamlet's twin).[40]

Here, Shakespeare as ghost symbolizes the power of literature as genre to undermine essentialism and provoke polysemy and heterogeneity. The blurring process whereby the author, his son, and his character all blend and merge tends to foreground a negative aspect of personal, and by extension, societal identity.

This process of the spectralization of Shakespeare culminates in *Finnegans Wake*. Here Shakespeare functions as a database of the language which the Joycean virus will infect and then turn from text to hypertext. Each word becomes a jumping-off point for a linguistic voyage as signifier leads to signifier and meanings, like histories and identities, become plural in 'a commodius vicus of recirculation'.[41] This book cuts the umbilical chord between language and nationalistic insularity by freeing the Irish reader from the feelings of alienation in English experienced by Stephen in the funnel/tundish episode: '[h]is language, so familiar and so foreign, will always be for me an acquired speech'.[42] Given the ironic portrayal of Stephen in this book, one wonders how deeply Joyce himself felt such a sense of linguistic alienation in English? Hence, the book embodies the funeral wake of a nationalist linguistic ideology, and an awakening to the possibilities of language as a gateway to pluralism and heterogeneity: through narration from nation to inter-nation and thence to international.

There are numerous exfoliations of the troped name of Shakespeare in *Finnegans Wake*, exfoliations in which spectral negative identity is constantly foregrounded through transactional signifiers. These transformations *hauntologically* embody his notion of Irish negative identity.[43] We see such transformations as 'Shikespower' (47,19);[44] 'bacon or stable hand' (141, 21); 'shakeagain' (143, 21); 'shakealose' (143, 22); 'Chickspeer' (145, 24); 'Bragspeer' (152, 33); 'shakespill and eggs' (161, 31); 'clasp shakers' (174, 9); 'slowspiers' (174, 28); 'Shakhisbeard' (177, 32); 'Shake hands' (248, 23); 'as Shakefork might pitch it' (274, Left margin, note 4); 'As great Shapesphere puns it' (295, 3-4); 'the curly bard' (465, 28); 'Shivering William' (507, 35); the list goes on, reinforcing the epistemological foundation underlying both this list and the Joycean conception of identity. This epistemology involves the *gnomonic* definition of Irishness against that of Europe, England,

and the English language. The spectralization of Shakespeare throughout the Joycean *oeuvre* signifies this protreptic openness to the other which involves the shaking lose, and shaking again, of essentialist notions of the politics of Irish identity.

By placing the conception of Irishness *gnomonically* against all sorts of other cultures, and othernesses, Joyce is defining identity in terms of what Adorno, borrowing from Benjamin, would term a constellatory manner. His *hauntological* frame of reference places Irishness within a constellation wherein the essentialisms of the past are denuded of their reified ontology, and instead are spectralized in terms of the other. This alterity, and the whole Joycean project, is predicated towards the future, or more correctly, towards a future wherein there will be 'absolute hospitality', as embodied in the final affirmation of *Ulysses*. Molly's famous cry of 'yes I said yes I will Yes'[45] points towards what Derrida, in *Specters of Marx*, calls 'the "yes" to the *arrivant(e)*, the "come" to the future that cannot be anticipated'.[46] This notion of a future as defined negatively, in a constellatory manner, may seem, as Joyce puts it, 'a strange wish for you, my friend, and it would poleax your sonson's grandson utterly';[47] but this would only be true if the future generations held to the same essentialism that we have seen in some advanced nationalist and Gaelic revivalist ideological positions. Joyce sees a future where Irishness is a constellation of identities, and where the sonson's grandson can say, as he does two lines later '[c]hee chee cheers for Upkingbilly'.[48] Irishness as *gnomonic* constellation would be defined in terms of Adorno's formulation that:

> Cognition of the object in its constellation is cognition of the process stored in the object. As a constellation, theoretical thought circles the concept it would like to unseal, hoping that it may fly open like the lock of a well-guarded safe-deposit box: in response, not to a single key or a single number, but to a combination of numbers.[49]

In Joyce's case, much of his work can be seen as creating a constellation of Irish identity, and the circular thought proceeds to create a *Zentrum* of Irishness which is not defined logocentrically, or *ab initio*, by some kind of unmoved mover. Rather is it created through the *hauntological* negative dialectics of Joyce's epistemology of language, for, as Adorno has put it, by 'gathering around the object of cognition, the concepts potentially determine the object's interior'.[50] I would suggest that this is precisely what Joyce has done in these passages. He has refused essentialism and embraced a polyglossic negative definition of Irishness. Bloom's reply to the citizen argues for a redefinition of identity. Just as Shakespeare is transformed in *A Portrait of the Artist as a Young Man, Ulysses,* and *Finnegans Wake,* from a monological symbol of Englishness into a *hauntological* series of symbols of plurality and alterity, so Bloom's reply transforms the essentialism of MacMorris into the ethics of the future. His notion of Irishness is necessarily negative in that it must leave *gnomonic* space for an Irishness, like his own, which is to come. Such Irishness is indefinable as a set of fixed presences; rather is it a series of traces, traces like the spectre of Shakespeare in the writings of Joyce. The Joycean notion of a community is Levinasian in that at its centre is 'an empty place, the anarchy of an absence at the heart of a community'.[51] Such an emptiness is a negative form of identity which serves as a space within which alterity can be accommodated, and from which a new Irishness can be defined.[52]

Such a definition is ethical in a very real sense; it is open to the differences from the self that are creative of a form of Irishness that embraces alterity. This ethical affirmation achieves its apotheosis in that famous soliloquy of Molly Bloom, with the anaphoric use of 'yes' which serves as a mantra for the affirmation of alterity in Joyce. As Derrida has noted, the relationship of a *'yes* to the Other, of a *yes* to the other and of one *yes* to the other *yes,* must be such that the contamination of the two *yes*es remains inevitable'.[53] Here affirmation involves a dialectical transaction of difference, which, while contaminating the edges, never fully blurs the two 'yeses' together. The relationship is *hauntological* and *gnomonic,* and it is a relationship that is embodied by the notion of emigration as trope.[54]

Bloom, Molly, Daedalus and Stephen are all emigrants of one form or another. Joyce himself lived the majority of his life as an emigrant. *Finnegans Wake* could be seen as a language of emigration in that the safe an *Heimlich* shores of interpretation and reference are left behind in favour of an *Unheimlich* language of traces and alterity. 'Patrick W. Shakespeare' has been troped into an emigrant, a position which is analogous to that of the initial interrogator of this discussion, his character, MacMorris. MacMorris looked for transcendental categories of the political and national as he answered his own question; Joyce also looks towards a notion of transcendence, but in a manner analogous to that cited by Simon Critchley in his discussion of the writings of Philippe Lacoue-Labarthe and Jean-Luc Nancy. Writing about their notion of the withdrawal of the political, by which he means any sense of the withdrawal of the transcendental perspective which has led to 'immanentism', Critchley points to the need to restore some form of transcendental perspective. He notes that:

> The *retreat* of the political is the complete withdrawal of the transcendence or alterity of the political in an immanentist society, and the re-tracing of the political is therefore an attempt at a re-inscription of the transcendence of the political. However, this re-inscription does not aim at restoring transcendence by founding the political on the transcendental signified of God, man, history, or destiny; rather, it is necessary to rethink the political without nostalgia for a lost plenitude of presence.[55]

Here we see the *aporia* facing those who would attempt to construct a sense of Irish identity. Without some level of trans-cendental perspective, as Adorno has pointed out, a community is immanent, and this immanence can result in a narrow *Weltansch-auung* which reifies the central categories of identity and becomes hostile to alterity in any form which might interrogate its own immanent perspective. Here then, some notion of the transcend-ental can serve as a regulative guard against the worst excesses of essentialist nationalism which sees all subjects as either the same, or in need of transformation into that sense of sameness. However, as our discussion of the Gaelic and Celtic revivals has shown, transcendental signifieds of identity can have a similar reifying and hypostasizing effects on identificatory constructions, valorizing one

25

set of criteria at the expense of another, in search of this 'lost plenitude of presence'. The effect can be the same, with alterity being absorbed or obliterated under such a hypostasized trans-cendental rubric. Critchley, aware of such a problematic, offers a different definition of the transcendental:

> Thus, the task of re-tracing the transcendence of the political is not a matter of bringing the political out of its withdrawal or of founding the political in a new act of instauratio; it is rather a matter of focusing the question of the political precisely around this withdrawal, where the transcendence of the political is, it could be said, the alterity of an absence.[56]

I would suggest that this is exactly the perspective adopted by Joyce in his notion of emigration as trope. Here, transcendence is predicated upon absence, it is a negative notion of Irishness, which allows space for alterity such as that of Leopold Bloom. For Bloom to be Irish, then Irishness must be redefinable in such a manner as to include him. In other words, the space in a *gnomon* that looks to be filled in so as to make a parallelogram is the space that is left for alterity in Joyce's epistemology of language.

NOTES

[1] James Joyce *Ulysses*, edited by Hans Walter Gabler, Wolfhard Steppe and Claus Melchior; first published 1922, London, 1989, p. 243.

[2] *Ibid.*

[3] *Ibid.*, p. 244.

[4] *Ibid.*

[5] *Ibid.*

[6] Emmanuel Levinas, *Emmanuel Levinas: Basic Philosophical Writings*, edited by Adrian T. Peperzak, Simon Critchley, and Robert Bernasconi, Bloomington, 1996, p. 16.

[7] Jacques Derrida, *Acts of Literature*, edited by Derek Attridge, London, 1992, p. 341.

[8] For a thorough discussion of Heidegger's use of this term, and of its philosophical and ethical implications, see *Specters of Marx*, pp 23-30.

[9] Jacques Derrida, *Deconstruction in a Nutshell: A Conversation with Jacques Derrida*, edited with a commentary by John D. Caputo, New York, 1997, p. 13.

[10] *Ibid.*

[11] In the opening story of *Dubliners*, Joyce uses the term '*gnomon*' in his revised opening paragraph. This term denotes a parallelogram from one corner of which a smaller parallelogram has been removed. I argue that this shape, which is not a parallelogram, but which is necessarily defined in terms of a parallelogram is a paradigm of the epistemology of language enunciated by Joyce in his works. For a further exploration of this theme, see my *Towards an Ethics of Irish Identity in the Writings of W. B. Yeats and James Joyce*, New York, (Edwin Mellen Press) 1998, chapter 4.

[12] Theodore Adorno, *Negative Dialectics*, translated by E. B. Ashton, London, 1973, p. 141.

[13] *Ibid.*, p. 145.

[14] Gabe Eisenstein, 'The Privilege of Sharing: Dead Ends and the Life of Language', in *Dialogue and Deconstruction: The Gadamer-Derrida Encounter*, edited by Diane P. Michelfelder, and Richard E. Palmer, New York, 1989, p. 275.

[15] The ironic use of a word to indicate the opposite of its lexical meaning.

[16] James Joyce, *Finnegans Wake*, first published 1939, London, 1975, p. 47, 19.

[17] *Ibid.*, p. 143, 21-2.

[18] James Joyce, *A Portrait of the Artist as a Young Man*, edited by R. B. Kershner, first published 1916, Boston, 1993, p. 216.

[19] Joyce, *Finnegans Wake*, p. 576, 24.

[20] *Ibid.* p. 295, 4.

[21] Joyce, *Ulysses*, p. 28.

[22] *Ibid.*, p. 260.

[23] Levinas, *Emmanuel Levinas: Basic Philosophical Writings*, p. 15.

[24] The *Hades* chapter in *Ulysses* is a comic masterpiece of this type of commentary.

[25] Joyce, *A Portrait of the Artist as a Young Man*, p. 187.

[26] Don Gifford, *Joyce Annotated: Notes for 'Dubliners' and 'A Portrait of the Artist as a Young Man'*, second edition, revised and enlarged, first published in 1967, Berkeley, 1982, p. 254.

[27] Joyce, *Finnegans Wake*, p. 539, 5-9.

[28] *Ibid.*, p. 174, 9-10.

[29] Emmanuel Levinas, *Ethics and the Infinite*, in *States of Mind: Dialogues with Contemporary Continental Thinkers*, Richard Kearney, Manchester, 1995, pp 193-4.

[30] Derrida, *Deconstruction in a Nutshell*, p. 13.

[31] Joyce, *Ulysses*, p. 15.

[32] *Ibid.*, pp 153-4.

[33] *Ibid.*, p. 272.

[34] *Ibid.*, p. 25.

[35] Joyce, *Finnegans Wake*, p. 159, 7.

[36] Jacques Derrida, *Specters of Marx: The State of the Debt, the Work of Mourning & the New International*, translated from the French by Peggy Kamuf, introduction by Bernd Magnus and Stephen Cullenberg, London, 1994, p. 90.

[37] Adorno, *Negative Dialectics*, p. 15.

[38] Joyce, *Ulysses*, p. 125.

[39] *Ibid.*, p. 152.

[40] *Ibid.*, *Ulysses*, p. 155.

[41] Joyce, *Finnegans Wake*, p. 3, 2.

[42] Joyce, *A Portrait of the Artist as a Young Man*, p. 166.

[43] In terms of the spectralization of Shakespeare, it is interesting to note that Vincent Cheng has found some forty seven echoes in *Finnegans Wake* of the injunction of the ghost of Old Hamlet to his son to 'List, list O list', *Shakespeare and Joyce: 'A Study of 'Finnegans Wake'*, pp 202-3. This book features a comprehensive list of correspondences between Joyce's work and Shakespeare. Vincent J.Cheng, *Shakespeare and Joyce: 'A Study of 'Finnegans Wake'*, Pennsylvania, 1984.

[44] As all of the following are sourced from *Finnegans Wake*, for the purpose of brevity, the citations of each of these terms will refer to the page and line of the book.

[45] Joyce, *Ulysses*, p. 644.

[46] Derrida, *Specters of Marx*, p. 168.

[47] Joyce, *Finnegans Wake*, p. 53, 32-3.

[48] *Ibid.*, p. 53, 36.

[49] Adorno, *Negative Dialectics*, p. 163.

[50] *Ibid.*, p. 162.

[51] Simon Critchley, *The Ethics of Deconstruction: Derrida and Levinas*, Oxford, 1992, p. 228.

[52] Critchley, in this quotation, is actually speaking about the Levinasian notion of God, as opposed to my own discussion on identificatory categorizations. However, whether speaking about God, or nationality, the epistemological thrust is similar. Transcendence is not seen as a hovering presence, but rather as an absence within a grouping which leaves a place for alterity.

[53] Derrida, *Acts of Literature*, p. 304.

[54] This notion of emigration has been further developed by Seamus Heaney, at the end of his book *North*, where, pulled by different notions of identity, he denies that he is either an 'internee' or an 'informer' he sees himself as an 'inner émigré, grown long-haired/And thoughtful', *North*, page 73 (Internment was a policy of imprisoning those who were known to have sympathies with terrorist organizations, both republican and loyalist, which was introduced into Northern Ireland on August 9th, 342 people were arrested,

mostly republicans, and such a process loomed very large in the Catholic psyche at this time.) In this poem, *Exposure*, Heaney defines his vision of Irish identity as a form of inner emigration, with parallels to the generation of Russian *émigré's* who flooded Western Europe after the Russian revolution. There are strong affinities between Heaney's notion of Irishness, and those of Yeats and Joyce

[55] Critchley, *The Ethics of Deconstruction*, p. 217.
[56] *Ibid.*

FRENCH

3

L'ATTRIBUTION DE LA LETTRE CXLIV DES *LETTRES PERSANES*

DARACH SANFEY

Le texte des *Lettres persanes* a depuis toujours suscité auprès de ses éditeurs nombre d'hésitations, de réflexions, et de doutes. Toutes les éditions critiques, depuis celle d'Henri Barckhausen, en dessinent l'histoire et l'évolution à travers les éditions A et B de 1721, C de 1754 et D, posthume, de 1758.[1] Histoire fascinante et parfois compliquée, dont nous ne retiendrons ici que les éléments susceptibles d'éclairer directement notre discussion. Par souci d'économie et de clarté, nous avons donc décidé de reproduire en appendice une version légèrement modifiée du tableau des manuscrits proposé autrefois par Paul Vernière.[2] Ce tableau suffit à illustrer très clairement le problème dont il sera ici question: l'attribution interne de la lettre CXLIV, soit à Usbek, soit à Rica. Notre discussion fera intervenir à la fois l'état matériel des manuscrits et la tradition éditoriale (les choix et arguments des successifs éditeurs des *Lettres persanes*); elle mettra également en jeu des questions portant, d'une part, sur les 'logiques internes' du texte (personnages, temporalité, organisation et structure du roman) et, d'autre part, sur la signification des lectures (ou interprétations) possibles de cette lettre particulière.

On sait, depuis Barckhausen, le rôle des *Cahiers de corrections* dans l'histoire parfois dramatique des ultimes modifications apportées par Montesquieu à son ouvrage.[3] En 1751, l'abbé Gaultier avait publié *Les* Lettres persanes *convaincues d'impiété*. Désireux de défendre son livre, et de se disculper des accusations de «légèreté», Montesquieu prépara très patiemment, pour l'édition que lui demandait le libraire Huart, d'une part un certain nombre de corrections, d'autre part un *Supplément* de onze lettres (les trois nouvelles de l'édition B et huit inédites, dont notre lettre CXLIV), enfin l'avertissement intitulé: «Quelques réflexions sur les *Lettres persanes*».[4] C'est l'édition C du tableau placé en annexe, qui fut publiée, nous le verrons, dans des circonstances longtemps méconnues.

L'auteur, à moitié aveugle, continua ce travail de révision jusque dans les derniers mois de sa vie. Sur son lit de mort, il confia ses cahiers de corrections à Mme la duchesse d'Aiguillon et à Mme Dupré de Saint-Maur, qui les transmirent par la suite à Jean-Baptiste de Secondat, fils de Montesquieu. C'est ce dernier, et l'avocat de la famille Richer, qui donn-èrent en 1758 l'édition définitive des *Œuvres complètes* de Montesquieu, d'après le manuscrit que l'auteur «avait confié de son vivant aux libraires». Or, comme l'ont constaté plusieurs éditeurs et commen-tateurs, Richer n'a pas repris systématiquement toutes les variantes suggérées par les cahiers de corrections. Celles-ci sont en grande majorité des révisions d'ordre stylistique, mais dans un certain nombre de cas, elles tendent à atténuer les audaces de l'œuvre de jeunesse. Pour reprendre les termes de Paul Vernière,

> l'étude des variantes révèle en effet, non seulement les doutes du styliste, mais les affres de conscience d'un homme dont on fait le siège jusqu'au lit de mort [...]. La duchesse d'Aiguillon, qui l'assista à ses derniers moments, en février 1755, écrivait à Maupertuis: 'Les Jésuites le pressant de leur remettre les corrections qu'il avait faites aux Lettres persanes, il me remit et à Mme Dupré son manuscrit en nous disant : Je veux tout sacrifier à la raison et à la religion, mais rien à la société (de Jésus). Consultez avec mes amis et décidez si ceci doit paraître'.[5]

D'emblée, l'on comprend le statut ambigu de ces cahiers, du moins pour ce qui est des 'repentirs' qu'ils contiennent. Les éditeurs de 1758, à qui il faut tout de même reconnaître d'avoir agi dans la meilleure foi possible, ont profité de la liberté que leur laissait l'auteur mourant, et l'on constate avec plaisir que, si les prescriptions qui ne concernent que le style ont presque toutes été respectées par Richer et Secondat fils, les 'audaces' juvéniles, au contraire, ces 'traits trop hardis' que Montesquieu avait pu souhaiter faire oublier à un certain moment, ont été maintenues. Décision à la fois courageuse et judicieuse, car rien ne prouve en fait que Montes-quieu aurait finalement opéré tant de sacrifices.[6] Le bien-fondé de ce choix semble être confirmé lorsqu'on observe les principes d'édition suivis par les éditeurs ultérieurs des *Lettres persanes*.

Henri Barckhausen, à qui revient la découverte des cahiers, a décidé pour son édition de 1897 de tenir compte de toutes les indications qu'ils donnent: il a même estimé devoir en exclure la lettre CXLV, sous prétexte qu'elle ne figure dans aucun des cahiers. Le texte ainsi établi par Barckhausen (et repris en 1913 dans la série des *Textes français modernes*) a été suivi par Elie Carcassonne (Belles Lettres, 1929) et Roger Caillois («Bibliothèque de la Pléiade», 1949). Mais depuis que le 'dossier de la Brède', contenant entre autres les cahiers de corrections, et inaccessible depuis Barckhausen, a été enfin mis à la disposition générale, l'on voit se dessiner une préférence unanime pour le texte de l'édition Richer.[7] D'abord chez André Masson, pour l'édition des *Œuvres* publiée sous sa direction entre 1950 et 1955, et qui reproduit en facsimilé le texte de 1758; mais aussi, par la suite, chez Antoine Adam, Paul Vernière, Jean Starobinski et Laurent Versini, qui reprennent tous comme point de départ le texte D, en consignant d'une part les variantes ABC, et d'autre part ces corrections ou repentirs des cahiers de 1754 qui ne sont pas maintenus dans l'édition Richer de 1758. Cinq éditions 'modernes', donc, établies sur les mêmes bases, et dont on serait en droit d'attendre qu'elles présentent un texte à peu près identique.

Or, dans le cas de la lettre CXLIV, on a pu déceler entre elles une incohérence qui n'est pas sans importance. Un coup d'œil sur le tableau-appendice déjà mentionné révèle — chose bien curieuse — que cette lettre a été attribuée, selon l'édition, à deux correspondants différents: si la plupart des éditeurs suivent fidèlement le texte de l'édition D et gardent donc la suscription «Usbek à Rica», trois d'entre eux intervertissent ces deux noms pour attribuer la lettre à Rica.

Une telle interversion serait de moindre portée s'il s'agissait ici d'un trait de mœurs, d'une lettre philosophique ou satirique à portée générale, ou si le 'contenu' de la lettre pouvait être rapporté, plus ou moins indifféremment, à la perspective de l'un ou de l'autre de nos épistoliers persans. C'est à peu près le cas pour d'autres lettres, et d'ailleurs, nous montrerons plus loin que Montesquieu ne s'est point privé de changer quelques attributions, sans apporter d'autres modifications significatives aux textes. Mais le cas de la lettre CXLIV est autrement problématique.

Elle comprend, tout d'abord, un *hapax* assez frappant: bien que la lettre soit adressée à Rica (dans C et D), Usbek s'y adresse curieusement à lui-même:

> «Oh! mon cher Usbek, que la vanité sert mal ceux qui en ont une dose plus forte que celle qui est nécessaire à la conservation de la nature!»

On peut supposer que c'est pour 'corriger' cette apparente anomalie que Roger Caillois et Paul Vernière ont interverti le nom du destinateur et celui du destinataire, mais ils ne proposent aucune note explicative qui nous permettrait de le savoir avec certitude.[8] Laurent Versini fait de même, en justifiant sa démarche dans une note:

> La lettre CXLIV manque dans A et B et est la septième du *Supplément* de C; elle porte dans C et D la suscription «Usbek à Rica», *par inadvertance puisque l'épistolier s'y adresse à «mon cher Usbek»* (§3).'(C'est nous qui soulignons).[9]

D'autre part, la lettre en question prend, par sa datation, une valeur très spéciale dans l'économie des *Lettres persanes*. Datée «De Paris, le 22 de la lune de Chabban [novembre], 1720», elle ouvre la séquence des trois dernières lettres du roman — non, certes, du point de vue de l'ordonnance-ment typographique, mais du point de vue de l'ordre chronologique.

Pierre Testud,[10] et plus récemment Jean-Paul Schneider,[11] sont parmi les commentateurs qui ont souligné avec le plus de netteté le soin avec lequel Montesquieu a joué sur la distribution temporelle des lettres de son roman.[12] On s'était déjà aperçu du 'décroche-ment' chronologique assez spectaculaire que représentent les quinze dernières lettres, celles qui font la chronique des événements dramatiques aboutissant à la désagrégation et à l'effondre-ment final du sérail; mais avant Testud, on s'était contenté d'applaudir l'adresse de Montesquieu à conserver à son dénouement sa force dramatique, qui eût été perdue pour le lecteur si ces lettres avaient été intégrées dans le texte aux dates de leur réception, comme c'est le cas pour presque toutes les autres missives. C'est le mérite de Pierre Testud d'avoir eu l'idée de replacer ces lettres dans l'ordre chronologique, aboutissant ainsi à des révélations assez étonnantes sur la cohérence dont est pourvu ce chef d'œuvre du genre épistolaire avant Laclos. Il nous faut, à ce point-ci, renvoyer le lecteur aux études de Testud et de Schneider déjà citées. Renvoi un peu brutal, certes, auquel nous sommes toutefois contr-aints, les limites de ce travail nous imposant de renoncer à résumer ici les arguments qui y sont développés, et qui sont pourtant indispensables à la discussion qui suivra.[13]

En effet, les longs silences d'Usbek à partir de 1718, ainsi que le ton lugubre qui caractérise beaucoup de ses lettres, ne se comprennent que lorsqu'on met en relation les deux séries de lettres identifiées par Schneider — celles qu'Usbek reçoit d'Ispahan, à des intervalles réguliers, et celles qu'il écrit lui-même sous le coup des nouvelles troublantes contenues dans les premières.[14] Peut-être serait-il à propos de souligner aussi la manière dont Montesquieu, de façon très ironique, rend encore plus sensible la 'fatalité' de la situation d'Usbek.

Usbek reçoit donc, au début du mois de février 1718, la lettre du grand eunuque l'informant des graves désordres du sérail. Il y répond immédiate-ment, envoyant ses ordres le 11 février 1718, par la lettre CXLVIII. Son esprit, dès lors, est trop accaparé par le drame qui se joue loin de lui pour pouvoir s'intéresser à autre chose, et entre le 5 janvier (lettre CVIII) et le 4 octobre (lettre CXI) il n'écrit plus aucune lettre. Puis, les mois passant sans que parviennent du sérail de nouvelles lettres, Usbek peut croire que l'ordre, peu à peu, se rétablit. Il se rassure et reprend sa correspondance en octobre et novembre, dissertant notamment, à l'usage de Rhédi, sur un problème très général: la dépopulation du globe (lettres CXIII — CXXII). Mais en décembre arrive l'explication de cette apparente quiétude du côté d'Ispahan, avec la lettre CXLIX de Narsit en date du 5 juillet: «Le Grand eunuque vient de mourir, magnifique seigneur [etc.]». Une fois encore, Usbek répond immédiatement, le 25 décembre 1719, sur un ton bien plus pressant, et donne des «ordres sanglants» à Narsit — mais cette lettre, «surprise» en route, ne parviendra pas non plus à son destinataire (*cf.* lettres CLI et CLII). Dès lors, c'en est fait de la tranquillité d'esprit d'Usbek: en 1719, il n'écrira qu'une seule lettre 'philosophique' — lettre sévère et désabusée, qui se termine de façon significative par l'éloge de la puissance paternelle, «de toutes les puissances, celle dont on abuse le moins» (lettre CXXIX, du 4 août). Cette année-là et en 1720, Rica le rem-place visiblement dans son rôle d'observateur du monde occidental: c'est lui, cette fois, qui écrit une série de lettres consécutives, ce parallélisme soulignant la démission intellectuelle d'Usbek: en 1720, en effet, Usbek ne se manifeste que trois fois, le 22 et le 26 octobre et le 11 novembre.

Or, comme l'a déjà montré Schneider, la séquence des lettres CXLIV-CXLV-CXLVI acquiert sous ce jour une importance capitale. Ce sont les toutes dernières lettres d'Usbek, écrites à un moment où l'on peut supposer qu'il a reçu la lettre CLXI de Roxane déclarant au maître sa révolte de toujours, la destruction des eunuques et le choix libre d'un suicide héroïque qui lui a même fait échapper enfin au chatiment. Les lettres constitueraient donc l'unique témoignage sur l'état d'esprit d'Usbek *après* le drame d'Ispahan.

Il faut tout de suite signaler que, si la démarche ingénieuse de Testud a ouvert la voie à des interprétations interéssantes, son étude ne saurait soutenir directement notre analyse de la lettre CXLIV, et pour une raison très simple. Ecrivant en 1966, Testud s'est naturellement servi de l'édition la plus récente des *Lettres persanes*, c'est-à-dire celle de P. Vernière; édit-ion qui jouissait par ailleurs — et à juste titre — d'une grande estime de la part des critiques comme de celle du public.[15] Or, on l'a déjà constaté, cette édition attribue la lettre CXLIV à Rica, et non à Usbek: les remarq-ues de Testud sur la séquence finale se bornent donc aux seules lettres CXLV et CXLVI.

Jean-Paul Schneider, dans son analyse extraordinairement minutieuse des rapports de temps entre le *récit* et l'*histoire* des *Lettres persanes*, et des jeux de sens qui s'en dégagent, revient avec une attention particulière sur ces trois lettres. A la différence de Testud, Schneider a utilisé pour son analyse l'édition établie par Antoine Adam. Pour lui, donc, ces trois lettres sont bien d'Usbek, et constituent une sorte de conclusion 'morale' aux *Lettres persanes*, qui répondrait à la conclusion 'romanesque' de la lettre CLXI. Schneider n'a pas été inattentif non plus à l'incohérence dont il est ici question: il note[16] la décision prise par certains éditeurs d'intervertir les noms d'Usbek et de Rica. Mais l'auteur ne pousse pas plus loin cette constatation, se contentant de rappeler que l'édition d'Adam ne signalait aucune variante qui eût autorisé cette inversion. De plus, pour étayer sa thèse d'une 'conclusion double', Schneider s'appuie surtout sur le contenu de la lettre CXLVI. Celle-ci a certes l'avantage de nous représenter l'état final des réflexions amères qui assiègent Usbek, mais il est regrettable que Schneider ne se soit pas intéressé davantage à la lettre CXLIV: c'est là qu'on peut lire, 'à chaud' pour ainsi dire, les réactions presque imméd-iates[17] d'un tyran puni de son propre aveuglement, d'un chef de harem trompé — où plutôt *détrompé* — par sa femme préférée, bref, d'un homme qui se sait désormais condamné à la solitude. Qu'on relise en effet cet 'examen de conscience'. Dans la première partie de la lettre, Usbek résume, avec une ironie sèche, une conversation qu'il a entendue entre deux 'savants'. Puis, il s'interrompt et s'exclame (c'est évidemment nous qui soulignons):

«Oh! mon cher Usbek, *que la vanité sert mal ceux qui en ont une dose plus forte que celle qui est nécessaire pour la conservation de la nature!* Ces gens-là veulent être admirés *à force de déplaire.* Ils cherchent à être supérieurs, et ils ne sont pas seulement égaux. Hommes modestes [....], quand je vous compare dans mon idée avec *ces hommes absolus que je vois partout, je les précipite de leur tribunal,* et je les mets à vos pieds.»

De Paris, le 22 de la lune de Chabban, 1720.

Est-il vraiment abusif, dans ces conditions, de vouloir discerner dans ces phrases des propos à double entente? Pas plus, sûrement, que pour les phrases des lettres CXLV et CXLVI que citent Schneider et Testud. D'une façon générale, ce genre de lecture un peu 'poussée', relevant sans doute plus des mentalités du XXe siècle que de celles du XVIIIe, ne convaincra pas tous les lecteurs de Montesquieu. Mais c'est précisemment dans le fait d'avoir suscité une telle diversité de lectures et d'interprétations que réside une grande partie du génie de ce livre remarquable. Que l'on prête foi, ou non, à ces hypothèses de lecture, la question de savoir si la lettre CXLIV émane d'Usbek ou de Rica ne perd point de son intérêt. Car il va de soi que l'identité de l'auteur de cette lettre est d'une importance primordiale pour le sens qu'on peut lui attribuer.

A supposer que Rica en soit l'auteur et Usbek le destinataire, cette lettre devient alors — dans le contexte que nous avons brièvement esquissé — un commentaire incisif, mais plutôt mal à propos pour ce qui est des sensibilités d'Usbek à ce moment très douloureux. Ce qui n'est nullement exclu: n'oublions pas qu'en juillet 1720, c'est à dire à mi-chemin exactement entre l'envoi de la lettre CLXI de Roxane et la réception de celle-ci par Usbek, Rica lui avait adressé la lettre CXLI contenant l'*histoire d'Ibrahim et d'Anaïs.* Cette histoire, Rica l'avait relatée à l'intention d'une dame de la cour, «belle, digne des regards de notre monarque, et d'un rang auguste dans le lieu sacré où son cœur repose. [....] Il me parut que la vie du sérail n'était pas de son goût, et qu'elle trouvait de la répugnance à voir un homme partagé entre dix ou douze femmes. Elle ne put voir, sans envie, le bonheur de l'un; et sans pitié, la condition des autres». Rica apprend alors à Usbek qu'il lui avait envoyé, quelques jours après, «...un conte persan. *Peut-être seras-tu bien aise de le voir travesti».* C'est toujours nous qui soulignons, inutilement bien sûr, car l'ironie de Montesquieu n'est nulle part plus visible que dans ce conte, reflet hyperbolique d'un sérail dont l'ordre établi, injuste, vient à être bouleversé par une force à laquelle rien ne saurait résister. D'une part, la vengeance d'une femme martyre de la vertu et de sa détermination à dire la vérité, d'autre part le désir de liberté et d'amour de «la superbe Roxane», âme sœur de Zuléma, qui «joignait à tant de connaissances un certain caractère d'esprit enjoué, qui laissait à peine deviner si elle voulait amuser ceux à qui elle parlait, ou les instruire». Nous ne pouvons nous empêcher de rapprocher ces propos de ceux de Roxane dans la lettre CLXI: «...tu as longtemps eu l'avantage de croire qu'un cœur comme le mien t'était soumis: nous étions tous deux heureux; tu me croyais trompée, et je te trompais», et ensuite, de relire dans la lettre XXVI l'étonnante naiveté et l'étroitesse de vision dont Usbek fait preuve lorsqu'il évoque avec nostalgie «les chastes scrupules» et la «pudeur vertueuse» qui firent résister si longtemps Roxane à «la fureur de [son] amour». L'on a souvent affirmé que l'ironie de Montes-quieu était moins acerbe que celle, par exemple, d'un Voltaire ou d'un Diderot: il conviendrait, selon nous, d'accorder plus d'attention à cet égard à la partie 'romanesque' des *Lettres persanes.*

Pour tenter de dépasser cette ambiguïté des logiques de l'œuvre, qui autoriserait à lire la lettre ou dans l'ironie de Rica ou dans le pathétique d'Usbek, on peut recourir à une tout autre démarche et ressaisir la difficulté par l'histoire externe du texte et de sa genèse. On connait l'étude consacrée aux cahiers de corrections de Montesquieu par Madeleine Laurain-Portemer, ancien conservateur des manuscrits à la Bibliothèque Nationale.[18] Cette étude exhaustive, d'une admirable minutie, a montré que, même après le travail préalable fait par André Masson,[19] les cahiers nous réservaient encore quelques surprises (*cf.* l'article de Mme Laurain-Portemer, dont nous résumerons d'abord les conclusions les plus pertin-entes à notre objet).

Mme Laurain-Portemer a pu montrer qu'il existe trois 'étapes' dans les corrections:

1e étape: révision générale et premières corrections. Montesquieu reprend son texte sur l'édition de 1721, ajoute quelques lettres nouvelles et « Quelques réflexions ». Ce travail est recopié sur le grand cahier; c'est l'état α, sans ratures ni surcharges.

2e étape: nouvelles corrections. Le grand cahier est relu et retravaillé. Beaucoup des premières variantes sont supprimées. Enprésence des multiples modifications/ratures, Montesquieu fait recopier son texte sur un 'petit cahier' intitulé «nouvelle copie» (état β).

3e étape: dernières corrections. Montesquieu reprend l'examen du grand cahier, y porte de nouvelles ratures ou corrections, change même complètement la rédaction de certain-es lettres ajoutées, comme par exemple la lettre LXXVII et, notamment, le début de CLX (voir, plus loin, notre note 22). C'est l'état γ qui comprend à la fois les passages non raturés du grand cahier et les différences qui subsistent entre le grand cahier et le petit cahier.

L'étude de la chronologie des variantes, désormais possible sur ces nouvelles bases, a mené Mme Laurain-Portemer à une 'découverte' très surprenante: l'examen, fait ligne par ligne, des additions de l'édition C aboutit à constater que celles-ci tiennent compte de toutes les modific-ations apportées dans les cahiers (y compris quelques 'inattentions'). Seule conclusion possible: le texte du *Supplément* de C est en fait postérieur aux cahiers de corrections.[20] De ce fait, le grand cahier se présente comme un véritable manuscrit de travail.

Dans le petit cahier, la lettre CXLIV (folios 114v[o]-115) porte la suscription: «Rica à Usbek, à *** », mais dans le grand cahier, une correction l'attribue à Usbek: de la chronologie établie, il résulte nécessairement que Montesquieu a interverti les noms de Rica et d'Usbek au cours de l'étape finale des corrections (passage de l'état β à l'état γ). Cela explique pourquoi la lettre CXLIV nous a paru être aussi facilement 'attribuable' à Rica — Montesquieu la lui avait de fait attribuée, à l'origine, pour ensuite changer d'idée.

Mais cette ultime modification est-elle bien, comme le propose Laurent Versini, une 'inadvertance' de la part de Montesquieu? Hypothèse plausible, et même compréhensible, compte tenu des

Hypothèse plausible, et même compréhensible, compte tenu des conditions difficiles dans lesquelles travaillait l'auteur, presque aveugle, et harcelé jusqu'à son lit de mort par le jésuite irlandais Routh. Cependant, nous croyons pouvoir apporter quelques arguments pour soutenir un point de vue opposé.

J. P. Schneider fait allusion[21] à la supériorité, sur le plan de l'esthétique, de cette «conclusion en triptyque» que constituent les lettres CXLIV-CXLV-CXLVI: cet argument, en soi assez fort, paraît être confirmé par d'autres modifications structurelles. Les dates des lettres CXLV et CXLVI furent en effet changées en 1754 (au moment où Montesquieu introduisit pour la première fois notre lettre CXLIV), de façon à les faire 'coller' dans la chronologie du roman:

> (i) CXLV : ne paraît pas dans A; dans B, elle est datée du «10 Zilcadé [= janvier], 1715»; mais dans C et D elle est transportée au «26 Chabban [=octobre], 1720».

> (ii) CXLVI : portait dans A la même date; dans B elle a été reportée en arrière, au «11 Gemmadi II [= juillet], 1720»; mais dans C et D elle est à nouveau datée du «11 Rhamazan [= novembre], 1720».

Ces mises au point semblent bien indiquer qu'en 1754, Montesquieu était, effectivement, très attentif à la datation des lettres et à leur cohérence chronologique, ce qui justifie en quelque sorte la démarche des commen-tateurs comme Schneider. Une autre lettre subissant un changement de date est la lettre CXXIX d'Usbek. Elle est transportée de 1715 (A, B, et C) pour devenir la seule lettre qu'il écrit en 1719 (voir *infra*, pp 5-6).

Ces constations semblent inviter au moins à pousser plus loin l'hypoth-èse d'une correction 'voulue' par Montesquieu: une certaine cohérence structurelle, sur le plan de la datation; et du côté de l'esthétique, l'heureuse création d'un dernier témoignage d'Usbek sous forme d'un triptyque de lettres dont le sens ironique ne se découvre que dans une sorte de lecture seconde.

Toutefois, la possibilité d'une inadvertance n'est toujours pas exclue: si la conclusion «en triptyque» postulée par Schneider

43

elle ne présente pas de lien étroit avec la plausibilité — ou non — d'une inversion des noms qui reste, sous plusieurs aspects, assez étonnante. D'abord parce que, si vraiment Montesquieu a voulu — tout à la fin — que nous prenions cette lettre CXLIV comme un témoignage d'Usbek, nous sommes dès lors conduits, aussi bien par le 'contenu' que par le ton de celle-ci, à faire le constat d'une modification importante dans l'impression qu'il a voulu nous laisser du caractère d'Usbek: son personnage principal.[22].

Mais qu'est-ce qui autoriserait à discerner la pensée précise de l'auteur mourant devant la création littéraire très complexe et très contradictoire qu'est Usbek? Pour résumer quelques arguments avancés par d'autres commentateurs,

— On a déjà constaté que la voix d'Usbek se fait plus rare dans la seconde moitié du roman, pour la raison déjà indiquée des accidents et des incertitudes du courrier venu d'Ispahan.

— On a souvent souligné, également, le ton de pessimisme et d'abbattement croissants qui caractérise la plupart de ces lettres, dont surtout les lettres CXXIX, CXLV, CXLVI, et, plus frappante encore, la très belle et très sombre lettre CLV.

Sur le plan de la probabilité stylistique, on ne peut, à vrai dire, rien tirer de concret. Certes, le style de notre lettre, comme a bien voulu nous l'indiquer M. Versini, fait penser à la lettre LII de Rica (on pourrait le rapprocher aussi de celui de la lettre LIX); c'est qu'à l'origine, les cahiers nous l'ont montré, cette lettre était effectivement 'née' de la plume de Rica. Or, on nous accordera au moins qu'il n'est nullement *interdit* de la lire comme émanant d'Usbek, malgré l'étrangeté de cette phrase un peu spectaculaire: «Oh! mon cher Usbek...». Après tout, cela n'a évidemment pas trop choqué la grande majorité des éditeurs, y compris Richer, ni les commentateurs comme Schneider.[23] Par ailleurs, on trouve plusieurs exemples, dans les *Lettres persanes*, d'interruptions semblables sous forme d'aparté (ou de 'monologue interne' si l'on veut), comme par exemple dans la lettre LII de Rica («Portrait de vieilles coquettes»): «Ah! bon Dieu, dis-je en moi-même, ne sentirons-nous jamais que le ridicule des autres», ou encore, de la plume d'Usbek, «Ah! bon Dieu, dis-je en moi-même...[etc.]» (Lettre LXXIV, à laquelle on reviendra plus loin). Ces sortes

(Lettre LXXIV, à laquelle on reviendra plus loin). Ces sortes d'élans se produisent surtout à des moments d'émotions fortes: ainsi, dans la célèbre lettre CLV d'Usbek à Nessir: «Malheureux que je suis! je souhaite de revoir ma patrie, peut-être pour devenir plus malheureux encore ! Eh ! qu'y ferai-je? [etc.]». C'est justement là, aux yeux de Montesquieu, l'une des qualités les plus précieuses du roman par lettres, «qui réuss[it] ordinairement, parce que *l'on rend compte soi-même de sa situation actuelle; ce qui fait plus sentir les passions*, que tous les récits qu'on en pourrait faire» («*Quelques réflexions*», §2. C'est nous qui soulignons).

Mais pour rendre plus plausible notre *lectio difficilior* de la lettre CXLIV, nous nous appuierons sur deux aspects particuliers de la révision finale des *Lettres persanes*:

1. L'effet de l'adjonction des huit 'nouvelles' lettres du *Supplément* de 1754 (trois des onze lettres — CXI, CXXIV et CXLV [datée de 1715 dans B] — figuraient déjà dans B).

2. Les autres occasions où Montesquieu semble considérer comme 'interchangeables' ses épistoliers persans. Il y a quatre exemples de ce phénomène, ce qui nous apprend des choses surprenantes sur la conception du 'personnage' épistolaire chez Montesquieu.

Les huit 'nouvelles' lettres (y compris CXLIV) nous proposent des perspectives supplémentaires sur la vie de sérail, ou du moins sur la vie en Perse; et presque toutes, d'une façon ou d'une autre, enrichissent et 'problématisent' notre impression du sérail d'Usbek, impression déjà composite et à perspectives multiples. Nous exclurons d'abord deux de ces lettres, que nous croyons pouvoir considérer comme des cas spéciaux:

(i) La lettre LXXVII (no.3 du *Supplément*) dans laquelle Montesqieu part d'une motivation plus spécifique: il s'agit de la fameuse 'réponse' d'Ibben sur le suicide, dont le texte presque entier paraissait déjà dans A et B, mais incorporé à la fin de la lettre originale d'Usbek (LXXVI) sous forme d'une réserve placée à la fin des arguments qu'il avait avancés en faveur de la tolérance envers ce «remède» *in extremis*.

(ii) La lettre XCI (no.4 du *Supplément*); Usbek y relate à Rustan l'apparition d'un ambassadeur de Perse à Paris. Cette lettre avait déjà paru, en 1745, dans un périodique littéraire rédigé en Hollande, *Le Fantasque* (*cf.* l'édition Starobinski, p. 437, n.2)

Les autres additions, dans l'ordre de classement du *Supplément* , sont:

(i) La lettre XV (qui devait d'abord être la lettre X; voir Laurain-Portemer, p. 54, et Schneider, p. 9, pour des interprétations différentes mais compatibles; *cf.* aussi l'édition Vernière, p. 38, n.1). Il s'agit d'une lettre du premier eunuque à Jaron, dans laquelle il lui exprime les sentiments «paternels» qu'il éprouve à son égard.

(ii) La lettre XXII — de Jaron au premier eunuque, cette fois-ci. Il lui parle, dans des termes très révélateurs, de la jalousie et de l'inquiétude croissantes d'Usbek (neuf mois seulement après son départ). La fin de la lettre comporte surtout une sorte de 'prophétie' qui nous paraît d'une ironie éclatante: «...Je sais comment je dois me conduire avec ce sexe, qui, quand on ne lui permet pas d'être vain, commence à devenir superbe, *et qu'il est moins aisé d'humilier que d'anéantir*» (C'est nous qui soulignons).

Si nous écartons pour l'instant la lettre CXLIV (et le transfert de la lettre CXLV de 1715 à 1720), les autres additions s'inscrivent toutes dans la série très remarquable des quinze dernières lettres:

(iii) Lettres CLVII/CLVIII (nos.9 et 10 du *Supplément*):
Ces protestations outragées de Zachi et Zélis accentuent l'effet dramatique de la lettre CLXI, dont elles préparent l'impact, en nous rendant plus explicites les détails du châtiment reçu de Solim.

(iv) CLX (no.11 du *Supplément*):

Enfin, la très dramatique lettre CLX de Solim, qui crée par son emplacement (entre CLIX et CLXI, et portant la même date) un effet de suspens d'autant plus frappant qu'il naît d'un silence; celui

46

qui suit les derniers mots de la lettre CLIX: «Je ne sais si j'attendrai, sublime Seigneur, tes ordres sévères ...»

Cette lettre présente également, dans ses multiples variantes,[24] le phénomène étonnant d'une sorte d'identification virtuelle, dans le jeu des pronoms personnels, entre Solim (eunuque redevenu 'puissant') et Usbek (maître absolu qui se voit pour ainsi dire 'émasculé').

Edgar Mass, dans son étude du développement textuel des *Lettres persanes,*[25] a analysé avec attention l'effet des trois 'séries' de lettres ajoutées au texte primitif (qui servit de base à l'édition B) pour l'édition *princeps* de 1721; séries qu'il désigne comme la série «Rica» (lettres I, V, X, XV, XXII, XXX), la série «Pharon» (lettres XXXIX à XLI) et la série «Harem» (lettres XLV, LXII, LXVIII, LXIX), et il fait des remarques qui vont dans le même sens que les nôtres: ces séries ajoutées «développent le côté sémantique du roman. Elles renforcent la description du caractère d'Usbek et changent, de façon fondamentale, le début des *Lettres persanes*» (*art. cit.*, p. 195-196). En 1754, en revanche, Montesquieu s'occupe avec plus d'insistance du dénouement du drame du sérail: «il retravaille surtout l'histoire orientale de son roman, en y ajoutant toute une série de lettres. Ce sont, avant tout, ces nouveaux textes qui font voir que le suicide de Roxane est une action de libération et d'émancipation» (*ibid.*, p. 197-198). A quoi nous ajouterons simplement qu'il veille aussi à ce que nous ayons un dernier aperçu de l'état d'esprit d'Usbek après cette «révolution», lorsqu'il change la datation des lettres CXLV et CXLVI, et ... l'attribution de la lettre CXLIV ?

Il nous reste à regarder de près les trois autres cas de changements d'expéditeur et/ou de destinataire. Ce sont:

> (i) Lettre XXXIV : «Comparaison des Françaises et des Persanes; gravité des asiatiques; effets du commerce des Orientaux avec leurs esclaves». Dans A et B, elle portait la suscription: «Rica à Ibben», mais dans C et D, on trouve: «Usbek à Ibben».

Les propos contenus dans cette lettre, une fois mis dans la bouche d'Usbek, semblent bien étayer l'hypothèse déjà proposée d'une 'prise de conscience', sinon du «caractère des femmes», au moins du rôle des eunuques et de la nature du despotisme et du pouvoir absolu.

> (ii) Lettre LXVII: «Portrait du décisionnaire»; critique mordante de la 'fausse autorité'.

A, B et C : «Rica à Usbek»

Cahiers et D : «Rica à Ibben»

Cas difficile que ce changement de destinataire qui, à première vue, ne semble pas coïncider avec notre argument; or il y a peut-être une autre conclusion à en tirer. Si Montesquieu a décidé de ne pas faire parvenir à Usbek cette leçon de morale, c'est peut-être que deux lettres plus loin, et *au même moment dans la chronologie des corrections apportées par les cahiers*, Usbek va devenir lui-même l'auteur d'une lettre qui ressemble, sous bien des aspects, à ce portrait satirique:

> (iii) Lettre LXXIV: «Fausse et vrai dignité des grands»; le seul autre cas d'une véritable interversion des noms. Dans A, B et C elle portait la suscription «Rica à Usbek», mais cet ordre est interverti dans le grand cahier, et dans D c'est donc Usbek qui relate, à l'intention de Rica, *ex-auteur de cette même missive*, comment il a fait la connaissance de ce «petit homme si fier» que l'on connaît.

Cette lettre nous semble revêtir une importance capitale pour notre discussion, non seulement parce qu'elle est la seule autre lettre à avoir subi la même interversion des noms, mais aussi parce que les sentiments qui y sont exprimés sont fort proches de ceux de la lettre CXLIV, «Supériorité de la modestie sur la vanité». Le fait que Montesquieu ait décidé, en 1754, d'attribuer ces sentiments à Usbek plutôt qu'à Rica, semble confirmer une fois encore l'hypothèse selon laquelle l'auteur aurait voulu problématiser davantage le point de vue d'Usbek, en renforçant la possibilité d'une lecture de sa 'mauvaise foi'. La lettre LXXIV comporte, elle aussi, une adresse interne assez frappante (§3): «[...] «Ah! bon Dieu! dis-je en moi-même, si, lorsque j'étais à la cour de Perse, je représentais ainsi, je représentais un grand sot!» [...]» (Cette phrase figure entre guillemets dans le texte).[26]

Montesquieu n'a donc pas été inattentif à la cohérence interne des lettres dont il a changé le nom de l'expéditeur et/ou du destinataire. Le soin avec lequel il revit ses cahiers est d'ailleurs souligné par tous les commentateurs.[27] Il a bien pris garde, dans le cas de la lettre LXXIV, de rectifier l'incohérence qui se serait produite dans le corps de la lettre à la suite de l'inversion de la suscription: pourquoi donc n'en aurait-il pas fait autant pour la lettre CXLIV, si cette incohérence apparente n'était pas, en fait, un effet littéraire entièrement intentionnel ?

Si nous revenons enfin à la matérialité même de la lettre CXLIV, telle que la présente le 'grand cahier', nous y trouverons encore des 'indices concordants'. La lettre en question occupe les folios 55v⁰ et 56 du cahier. L'écriture est celle de Florence Fitzpatrick, le dernier secrétaire (Montes-quieu, dans sa vie et surtout vers la fin, eut affaire à plus d'un irlandais!). Nous avons déja signalé que la correction de la suscription a dû avoir lieu pendant la toute dernière des trois phases identifiées, parce qu'elle se présente comme une rature, dont le petit cahier ne tient pas compte. Mais c'est un rature qui se distingue des autres. L'étude des autres pages du cahier rédigées par Fitzpatrick montre en effet que, lorsqu'il s'agit de rayer un mot, ou même une phrase entière, le secrétaire se contente en général de le faire d'un seul trait bien visible — plus rarement de deux. Or la suscription originelle est aussi annulée par des ratures circulaires, au trace large et appuyé, au point d'oblitérer presque totalement les mots. Faut-il y décéler une insistance particulière, le souci de ne laisser aucun doute quant à la dernière prescription de l'auteur? Autre indice intéressant: Fitzpatrick, comme c'était son habitude, a rédigé les premiers mots des nouveaux paragraphes dans une écriture au moins trois ou quatre fois plus grande que la moyenne, de telle sorte qu'on lit très clairement, à la ligne 14 du même folio, les mots: «Oh! Mon cher Usbeck, [*sic*]». La vraisemblance d'une inattention, même compte tenu de la vue alors très affaiblie de Montesquieu, s'en trouve diminuée davantage encore.

Mais l'examen du grand cahier nous réserve encore un dernier élément de mystère. Nous avons déjà signalé son caractère d'instrument de travail.[28] Or, les deux folios 55 et 56, qui contiennent le texte de la lettre CXLIV, constituent un cas unique. Ils ont été attachés au manuscrit, par des épingles dont on distingue toujours les traces, et ... *postérieurement* à la rédaction initiale du cahier: introduits entre les folios 54 et 57, ils interrompent le texte qui, commencé au bas du folio 54v°:

> « pag.310 otés tout L'article *purgatif plus violent* /qui commence par ces mots *prenés dix A** et finit* »

— ne se poursuit qu'au folio 57:

> « par ceux-cy *avec confiance*. / pag.312 otés tout l'article [etc.] ».

C'est à dire que notre lettre (rédigée peut-être séparément) a été ajoutée après coup à un ensemble matériellement constitué, la foliotation ayant même suivi l'insertion de ces deux derniers feuillets.[29] L'inversion des noms d'Usbek et de Rica (et c'est la *seule* correction: le texte de la lettre ne subit aucune autre modification, sauf une, très mineure, de ponctuation) n'a pu être opérée que dans la toute dernière phase du travail, et l'on s'explique ainsi que le petit cahier n'en tient pas compte.

Mais à quel moment précis, et dans quel état d'esprit, Montesquieu a-t-il pu se décider à l'attribuer à Usbek? Combien de fois a-t-il pu la relire avant de prendre sa décision? Et cette décision a-t-elle été prise dans la pleine conscience des facteurs auxquels nous avons déjà fait allusion? Finalement — avec un peu plus de temps, en serait-il peut-être venu, un jour, à 'faire disparaître' cet *hapax* qui a été le point de départ de notre enquête? Autant d'enigmes, autant de questions qui resteront à jamais ouvertes.

Avant de conclure, nous nous permettrons de citer les observations finales de Mme Laurain-Portemer:

'Si «le mérite principal des *Lettres persanes* est de former une espèce de roman avec un commencement, une progression et une fin», le principal mérite des cahiers de corrections est à nos yeux de nous permettre de surprendre Montesquieu en pleine création littéraire, écrivant ou plus souvent dictant à ses secrétaires, les changements qu'il prépare en vue d'une édition nouvelle [...]. Pour nos esprits modernes, si curieux des problèmes d'histoire des textes, c'est retrouver Montesquieu, allant pas à pas, partagé entre plusieurs soucis pour atteindre la perfection'.[30]

Notre discussion s'achève, donc, dans ce 'lieu de rencontre' privilégié que représentent seuls les cahiers de la Brède, aucun manuscrit des *Lettres persanes* n'étant actuellement connu. Nous avons tenté de démontrer, par une analyse étagée sur différents 'plans', que l'attribution de la lettre CXLIV à Usbek, et non à Rica, pourrait avoir été consciente et calculée. Mais il apparaît que cette résolution ne vint à l'auteur que dans les tous derniers moments de son travail de correction. Quelques mois plus tard, et peut-être quelques semaines seulement, Montesquieu mourait, dans une maison rue Saint-Dominique, pleuré par une génération de philosophes. Les *Lettres persanes*, cette *œuvre de jeunesse* qui continua à l'occuper jusqu'à la fin de son existence, restent aujourd'hui son testament le plus brillant et le plus fêté.[31] Une partie de l'éternelle séduction de ce roman, objet littéraire exemplaire dans l'évolution de son genre, tient sans doute aux mille ambiguïtés qui en travaillent le texte et la lecture. En relevant l'une d'entre elles, vétilleuse et pourtant fascinant, nous espérons modeste-ment avoir éclairé sous un jour nouveau un détail de ce chef-d'œuvre des Lumières.

Author's note : This article originally appeared in *Travaux de Littérature*, VI, 1993, pp 173-92, and was awarded the 1994 Annual Prize of the *Association Internationale des Études Françaises*. I wish to express my gratitude to the publishers for permission to reproduce it here.

Appendice no. 1

TABLEAU DES MANUSCRITS ET DES EDITIONS DES *LETTRES PERSANES*

--------------- A 1721 --------------------(?*)--------------------- B 1721

[pour les lettres CXI,
CXXIV et CXLV]

Cahiers 1754
α β γ --------------------------------- *Supplément* + «Quelques réflexions»　　C 1754

D 1758 Richer *(Œuvres complètes)*

[lettre CXLIV]　　　　　　　　　　　　　　　　　　　　*[lettre CXLIV]*

Barckhausen 1897 (1913)	Usbek		Usbek
Carcassonne 1929	Usbek		
Caillois 1949 *(Œuvres)*	Rica		
		Masson 1950 *(Œuvres)*	Usbek
		Adam 1954	Usbek
		Vernière 1960	Rica
		Starobinski 1973	Usbek
		Versini 1986	Rica

0　　[Pour les *Lettres persanes*,
----------------------------- texte de 1721] ----------------------- Ehrard 1992　　ø
　　　　　　　　　　　　　　　　　　　　　　(Œuvres)

(* Voir MASS, E. *art. cit.*, *cf.* note **23** *infra*.)

Appendice no. 2

SUITE DES *LETTRES PERSANES*

Dates	Série A: lettres 105-146	Série B: lettres 147-161
01.09.1717		lp. **147** : Le Grand Eunuque annonce à Usbek les troubles du sérail.
14.12.1717	lp. **106** : Usbek prend la défense des sciences, des arts, du luxe.	
05.01.1718	lp. **108** : A propos des journaux littéraires, Usbek dit son attachement aux valeurs traditionelles et souligne la susceptibilité des auteurs à propos de leurs ouvrages.	
11.02.1718		lp. **148** : Usbek donne les pleins pouvoirs au Grand Eunuque.
05.07.1718		lp. **149** : Narsit apprend à Usbek la mort du Grand Eunuque ... et attend des instructions.
04.10.1718	lp. **111** : A propos des memoires de Retz, Usbek rappelle le pouvoir des pamphlets.	
08.10.1718 ~ 23.11.1718	lp. **113-122** : Lettres d'Usbek sur la dépopulation.	
01.12.1718	lp. **123** : Sur les défaites de Turcs (Usbek rêve d'une réunification de l'Islam.	
01.12.1718	lp. **124** : A propos des libéralités, Usbek dénonce les faveurs accordées aux inutiles aux dépens des citoyens utiles.	
03.12.1718	lp. **126** : Rica annonce à Usbek qu'il lui fait suivre des lettres d'Ispahan.	
25.12.1718		lp. **150** : Usbek donne «des «ordres sanglants» à Narsit.
06.05.1719		lp. **151** : Solim «dénonce «l'imbécilité» de Narsit.
		lp. **152** : Inconscient de la gravité de la situation, Narsit annonce à Usbek la perte de la lettre 150.
04.08.1719	lp. **129** : Sur les lois et les législateurs. (Usbek rappelle qu'il ne faut changer les lois que d'une «main tremblante», fait l'éloge de la puissance paternelle).	

Dates	Série A: lettres **105-146**	Série B: lettres **147-161**
04.10.1719		lp. **153-154-155** : Usbek donne les pleins pouvoirs à Solim, menace ses femmes, dit sa tristesse à Nessir.
02.03.1720		lp. **156-157-158** : Trois témoignages de femmes humiliées, outragées, indignées (Roxane, Zachi, Zélis).
03.05.1720		lp. **159-160-161** : Sadisme de Solim; mort des eunuques et de Roxane.
22.10.1720	lp. **144** : Usbek condamne l'homme vaniteux et célèbre l'homme modeste.	
26.10.1720	lp. **145** : L'homme d'esprit, auteur de livres, est toujours en butte à l'incompréhension, aux injures, aux persécutions.	
11.11.1720	lp. **146** : Lettre-apocalypse sur la corruption de la France après Law.	

NOTES

[1] Ont été consultées les éditions suivantes des *Lettres persanes* et des œuvres comp-lètes de Montesquieu:
- Edition revue et annotée d'après les manuscrits du château de La Brède avec un avant-propos et un index par Henri Barckhausen. Paris, Imprimerie Nationale, 1897; réédition, Paris, Hachette, 1913; réédition, Genève, Droz, 1932.
- Texte établi et présenté par Elie Carcassonne. Paris, Les Belles Lettres, 1929.
- *Œuvres complètes*, texte présenté et annoté par Roger Caillois. Paris, 1949, 2 vol., 'Bibliothèque de la Pléiade'.
- *Œuvres complètes*, sous la direction d'André Masson. Paris, Nagel, 1950-5, 3 vol.
- Edition critique avec notes par Antoine Adam. Genève-Lille, Droz-Giard, 1954.
- Texte établi, avec introduction, bibliographie, notes et relevé de variantes par Paul Vernière. Paris, Garnier, 1960.
- Edition établie et présentée par Jean Starobinski. Paris, Gallimard, 1973, collection «Folio».

- Texte présenté et commenté par Laurent Versini. Paris, Imprimerie Nationale, 1986, collection «Lettres Françaises».

[2] *Cf.* Vernière, *op. cit.*, pp XXXV-XLI, pour une discussion plus complète. Nous avons également suivi la tradition des éditeurs, et l'exemple de Vernière, en désignant les quatre éditions différentes par les lettres A, B, C et D, et les cahiers de corrections par les sigles α (grand cahier, état primitif), β (petit cahier) et γ (grand cahier, état définitif revu et raturé).

[3] *Cf.* R. Shackleton, *Montesquieu : a critical biography*, Oxford, 1961, pp 392-9.

[4] On a souvent cité la lettre où Montesquieu fait allusion à cette demande: «Huart veut faire une nouvelle édition des *Lettres persanes*, mais il y a quelques juvenilia que je voudrois auparavant retoucher...» (Lettre à l'abbé Guasco, 4 octobre 1752, dans *Œuvres Complètes*, éd. A. Masson, t.III, p. 1441).

[5] *Correspondance*, [éd. Masson], t.II, p. 275, Vernière, *op. cit.*, p. XL.

[6] Il vaut la peine de faire remarquer que les examens des cahiers faits par André Masson et Madeleine Laurain-Portemer (voir nos notes 17 et 18) aboutissent à cons-tater avant tout l'hésitation, voire la répugnance de l'auteur lorsqu'il s'agit d'adoucir les *Lettres persanes*.

[7] Unanime, c'est-à-dire, jusqu'en 1992. L'édition des *Œuvres Complètes* qui doit paraître cette année chez la Voltaire Foundation reproduira, pour les *Lettres persanes*, le texte de l'édition A de 1721.

[8] Si les noms d'Usbek et de Rica sont intervertis dans le *texte* de l'édition Vernière, la table des matières conserve néanmoins la suscription: «Usbek à Rica» (p. 406).

[9] Nous avons pu prendre contact avec M. Versini pendant la rédaction de cet article et nous tenons à lui exprimer ici notre gratitude pour l'intérêt et l'encouragement qu'il nous a témoignés, aussi bien que pour les éclaircissements qu'il nous a proposés et qui ont contribué à notre recherche.

[10] P. Testud, 'Les *Lettres persanes*, roman épistolaire', *Revue d'histoire littéraire de la France*, octobre-décembre 1966, pp 642-56.

[11] J.P. Schneider, 'Les jeux du sens dans les *Lettres persanes*: temps du roman et temps de l'histoire', *Etudes sur le XVIIIe siècle*, publ. de la faculté des Lettres moder-nes de Strasbourg, 1980, pp 5-38.

[12] Ce genre d'analyse, évidemment, n'a été possible qu'après le travail de R. Shackle-ton, 'The Moslem chronology of the *Lettres persanes*', *Lettres Romanes*, 1954, pp 91-113.

[13] Pour Testud, voir surtout les pp 649-53, et pour Schneider, les pp 9-16.

[14] Voir le tableau annexe no 2. de Schneider (*op. cit.*, pp 36-7), que nous reproduisons également en appendice.

[15] L'édition de Vernière est toujours précieuse à consulter, en raison surtout de l'ampleur et de la valeur des renseignements fournis sur la génèse du texte.

[16] Schneider, *art. cit.*, p. 14.

[17] Rappelons qu'entre les lettres CLXI et CLXIV, il ne s'écoule que 167 jours, soit 5 mois et 14 jours. Une fois admises les observations de Schneider sur le délai d'acheminement des lettres entre Ispahan et Paris (pp 11-2 de son étude), force est d'admettre que, si vraiment la lettre CXLIV émane d'Usbek, sa rédaction se situerait au plus tard une dizaine de jours après la réception de la lettre de suicide de Roxane.

[18] M. Laurain-Portemer, 'Le dossier des *Lettres persanes*', dans *Revue historique de Bordeaux et du département de la Gironde*, 1963, pp 41-78.

[19] A. Masson, 'Les dernières ratures des *Lettres persanes*', dans *Actes du Congrès Montesquieu*, Bordeaux, Delmas, 1956, pp 71-82.

[20] *Cf.* Laurain-Portemer, *art. cit.*, pp 52-3 pour l'explication. La copie faite par Fitzpatrick des lettres destinées à ce *Supplément* (folios 130-53 du dossier) est elle aussi postérieure au «grand cahier», car elle tient compte de l'inversion des noms d'Usbek et de Rica dans la lettre CXLIV (*cf.* folios 142v⁰-44).

[21] Schneider, *art. cit., p. 15.*

[22] Est-il besoin de rappeler l'article le plus célèbre qui soit dans la «Table» de l'édition de 1758?: «MONTESQUIEU (M.De). Se peint dans la personne d'Usbek» (*cf.* le commentaire de J. Starobinski, *éd. cit.*, pp 451-2; *cf.* aussi les observations de Louis Desgraves, dans *Montesquieu*, Paris, Mazarine, 1986, pp 401-4).

[23] Il faut tout de même avouer que la phrase 'choque' un peu. Mme Laurain-Portemer relève l'incohérence, sans toutefois proposer de commentaire (*art. cit.*, p. 78, n.105). Nous avons recensé les autres exemples de cette adresse: Usbek dit souvent: «mon cher [Rica/Ibben/Rhédi, etc.]» à ses amis, et *vice versa*, mais jamais à lui-même. Les seuls à s'adresser à «mon cher Usbek» sont ses amis persans; ses femmes, à une exception près (la lettre VII de Fatmé), n'ont pas droit au pronom possessif: elles l'appellent toutes «cher Usbek». Toutes, c'est-à-dire, sauf Roxane – qui s'adresse, dans la lettre CLXI, à «*cruel* Usbek»!

[24] *Cf.* le tableau des variantes établi par Mme Laurain-Portemer, *art. cit.*, p. 76. Voir aussi les observations d'Alan J. Singerman dans 'Réflexions sur une métaphore: le sérail dans les *Lettres persanes*', *Studies on Voltaire and the Eighteenth Century*, 185, 1980, pp 181-98.

[25] E.Mass, «Le développement textuel et les lectures contemporaines des *Lettres persanes*», *Cahiers de l'Association internationale des études françaises*, 1983, pp 186-200.

[26] Tout de suite après, il continue: «Il aurait fallu, Rica, que nous eussions eu un bien mauvais naturel [...etc.]». Or avant 1754, évidemment, le texte donnait à lire: «Il aurait fallu, *Usbek*, [...etc.]». Mais dans le cas de la lettre LXXIV, la deuxième correction (— nécessaire, cette fois-ci) est bien indiquée dans le grand cahier (folio 32v⁰).

[27] *cf.* Laurain-Portemer, *art. cit.*, p. 51 et suiv., et la préface d'E. Carcassone, *éd. cit.*, p. x. Et l'on note aussi, généralement, que la perfection littéraire a été préférée à l'exactitude historique.

[28] *Cf.* Laurain-Portemer, *art. cit.*, p. 47, n.25.

[29] Tout le folio 54 v⁰ et le début du folio 57 sont rayés; les corrections qu'ils contenaient (concernant la lettre CXLIII, « Rica à Nathanaël Lévi, médecin juif, à Livourne ») ont été reprises dans leur majorité au folio 55.

[30] Laurain-Portemer, *art. cit.,* p. 57.

[31] «Rien de plus élégant ne fut écrit. Le changement du goût, l'invention de moyens violents n'ont pas de prise sur ce livre parfait» (Paul Valéry, «Préface aux *Lettres persanes*», *Variété* II, Paris, 1930).

MUSIC

4

THE MUSIC OF GERALD BARRY AS AN INTRODUCTION TO CONTEMPORARY IRISH ART-MUSIC: TWENTIETH-CENTURY MUSIC IN THE NEW LEAVING CERTIFICATE SYLLABUS (1999-2001).

GARETH COX

In 1996 the Department of Education published a new syllabus for music in the Leaving Certificate at both higher and ordinary level and selected Gerald Barry's *Piano Quartet no. 1* (1992) as the prescribed twentieth-century work for the period from 1999-2001 for both levels. As one of the most prominent Irish composers working today, Gerald Barry (b. 1952) has already achieved international recognition with such operas as *The Intelligence Park* (1982-89) and *The Triumph of Beauty and Deceit* (1991-92) and his music remains perhaps the most widely-disseminated of all twentieth-century Irish composers through numerous international performances and a publishing contract with Oxford University Press. This paper reflects firstly on the Department of Education's objective in selecting Barry's quartet as a prescribed work and then examines some aspects of the compositional style of Barry's music, in particular his selection and employment of pitch material, certain structural, linear, dynamic and agogic features of his music, whilst dealing specifically with the *Piano Quartet no. 1*.

Since 1976, the Leaving Certificate syllabus has included pieces by twentieth-century composers amongst its list of prescribed set-works: Igor Stravinsky's *Firebird Suite* (1911) and "*Dumbarton Oaks*" *Concerto* (1938), Manuel de Falla's *The Three-Cornered Hat* (1919), Aaron Copland's *El Salón Mexico* (1936), and Benjamin Britten's *Serenade for Tenor, Horn and Strings* (1943) have all provided a couple of generations of Irish post-primary students with their first taste of art-music from the present century. In 1988 the Department began introducing works by contemporary Irish composers into the syllabus, John Buckley's *Sonata for Unaccompanied Violin*, for the period 1988-1998 (appearing alongside Copland's *El Salón Mexico)*, followed recently by Gerald Barry's *Piano Quartet no. 1* for 1999-2001 and Raymond Deane's *Seachanges* planned for 2002-2004. There is very good musical (not to mention domestic) justification for prescribing a work by an Irish composer in the national syllabus but one could question why major twentieth-century composers such as Berg, Schoenberg, Webern, Hindemith, Ives, Shostakovich, Prokofiev, Sibelius, Boulez, Cage, Glass, Ligeti, Messiaen, Xenakis, Stockhausen, Berio, and Bartòk (to name a few and in no particular order) have never been included. However, since Barry's *Piano Quartet no. 1* is ranked alongside three other representative works of the Baroque and Romantic eras and Popular Music - J. S. Bach's cantata, *Jesu, der du meine Seele* (BWV 78), Tchaikovsky's overture, *Romeo and Juliet,* and Freddie Mercury and Queen's *Bohemian Rhapsody* respectively[1] - it can therefore be assumed that it is considered to be correspondingly representative of the Twentieth-century or "Modern" era, and more specifically, indicative of the pluralist and multicultural nature of contemporary music nationally and internationally. On the question of the implied hierarchy and equality of status inherent in this list of prescribed works, Harry White deplores "the canonic status (the canonization) conferred upon a vulgar, third-rate pastiche of Italian opera intermixed with the desolations of rock music which is *Bohemian Rhapsody*" and the fact that it is "solemnly presented for scrutiny alongside the pitifully reduced presence of the classical repertoire".[2] The new syllabus specifically states that one of the main objectives is "to encourage students to listen purposefully to a wide variety of musical styles and genres, including music from the past and the present".[3] In order to achieve this, it is imperative for teachers to introduce a representative cross-section of music from this century (given the prohibitive cost of many twentieth-century scores and recordings, this could be achieved in an affordable way by purchasing a compilation, for instance Michael Hall's book (with accompanying CDs), *Leaving Home: A Conducted Tour of Twentieth-Century Music with Simon Rattle* based on the successful Channel Four series.[4]) The higher-level students could also study the context of Barry's work by choosing the music of contemporary Irish composers as their elective in listening, as is suggested in a list of suitable study topics from all areas of music in appendix G of the syllabus.[5] Students selecting such a topic would be required to *listen* to (as opposed to read about[6]) available recordings[7] of such diverse post-war and contemporary composers as Frederick May (1911-1985), Brian Boydell (b. 1917), Gerard Victory (1921-1995), Seóirse Bodley (b. 1933), Frank Corcoran (b. 1944), Jane O'Leary (b. 1946), Eric Sweeney (b. 1948), Roger Doyle (b. 1949), John Buckley (b. 1951), Raymond Deane (b. 1953), Eibhlís Farrell (b. 1953), Fergus Johnston (b, 1959), and Marion Ingoldsby (b. 1965) to name just a short selective list. The very active Contemporary Music Centre, Ireland in Dublin can assist in procuring material for any such topic.

Gerald Barry was born in Clarecastle in Co. Clare in 1952. He graduated from University College Dublin with the B.Mus. in 1973 and an M.A two years later and also studied in Amsterdam with Piet Kee (organ) and Peter Schat (composition). From 1975 to 1981 he lived and worked in Cologne and studied composition with Karlheinz Stockhausen and Mauricio Kagel (with a year in between in 1977/78 when he went to Vienna to study with Friedrich Cerha). He returned to Ireland in 1982 to take up a lectureship in music at University College Cork where he stayed for four years. In 1986 he was elected to the Irish state-sponsored academy of creative artists, *Aosdána* which gave him a certain amount of financial independence and he has since worked as a free-lance composer. He now enjoys an enviable reputation and recognition abroad and his music has been critically acclaimed with some major performances in London in the late 1980s. The orchestral piece, *Chevaux-de-frise* was commissioned for the Promenade Concerts in London's Albert Hall in 1988 and his opera *The Intelligence Park* was staged at the Almeida Festival in 1990. Another opera, *The Triumph of Beauty and Deceit* was performed on Channel Four TV in 1995 and is currently being recorded on CD. His recent successful appearance as one of the featured composers at the 1996 Huddersfield Contemporary Music Festival where his *Piano Quartet no. 2* was premièred is an indication of his growing reputation. Also in 1995 a CD of his chamber music earned him much favourable criticism in the press and was nominated by *Classic CD Magazine* as the best CD of music by a living composer issued in 1995.[8]

Barry's output is relatively small and he has withdrawn all his works before 1977.[9] He now composes mostly to commission although he has said that the danger is that "with more and more commissions [...] you lose that sense of direct contact with whatever it is that you do and sometimes a sense of weariness sets in".[10] Perhaps this is why he has drawn so liberally on existing works, as in the case of *Chorales, Water Parted, What the Frog Said, Sweet Cork, Swinging Tripes and Trillibubkins,* and *Of Queen's Gardens,* all of which are derived from *The Intelligence Park.* Perhaps this is also why his style has settled down to being such a recognisably personal one, a style which could be described as being energetic, melodic, heterophonic, multi-sectional, and unpredictable. More on these adjectives later. Vincent Deane describes this style most succinctly when he writes:

> Gerald Barry's music is a music of brittle extremes, which it makes no attempt to bridge or reconcile. It favours stark contrasts above graded transitions; jumping from one section to the next, its discontinuities clearly marked by widely diverging tempi and dynamics. If his titles often suggest comparisons with painting, this is more than a simple analogy. For here sound is a

tangible physical material, to be manipulated like paint or clay. American Abstract Expressionism has been a strong inspiration, and concentrated assaults on the same or similar basic materials over several pieces have resulted in sets of works that illuminate one another collectively, like painterly studies.[11]

He was influenced to a certain extent by his main teacher in Cologne, Mauricio Kagel, particularly in his use of quotation techniques and his preference for the genre of music theatre (quite apart from his operas, many works display elements of theatre and histrionics such as his *Piano Concerto* of 1977, for instance, in which the soloist gesticulates but the sound appears from another pianist.[12]) Baroque influences are featured in his operatic works, *The Intelligence Park* and *The Triumph of Beauty and Deceit*: Here much of his compositional material is derived from 17th and 18th century sources, in particular Bach and Handel. Barry clearly enjoys borrowing material and changing it, by, as he says "shedding light on it in some unexpected way or by showing it in a new light".[13] Barry has also derived his pitch material aleatorically from such abstract sources as the words of the BBC Radio 4 shipping forecast or a chart showing the locations of manuscripts by John Jenkins (as in the graphically entitled (' _____ '), or dissonant harmonies formed by selective use of passing notes in Bach chorales as in *The Intelligence Park*. Barry states that he has:

> always been interested in things formed in the cracks - those pauses, say, which occur in Purcell, where he has symmetrical periods in the music, and at the end of a phrase there's an infinitesimal moment, which has to do with the power of the music and the rhythmic energy it generates.[14]

The *Piano Quartet no. 1*[15] was first performed at the Institute of Contemporary Arts in London in 1992 and was recorded by Nua Nós and Noriko Kawai (piano) on an NMC Recordings label (NMC D022) in 1993.[16] Barry wrote this quartet following on within a long tradition of the genre of piano quartet which includes important works by Mozart, Mendelssohn, Schumann, Dvořák, Fauré and Brahms.[17] He has supplied an excellent and detailed analysis of the piece himself in the "Composer's Notes on the Piano Quartet no. 1" for the Department of Education's Resource Material Pack, and all students and teachers will receive this information. He explains that the piece "does not fit any standard form" but that "the only guide was intuition".[18] He concedes, however, that "it is possible (in retrospect) to trace a clear map of the journey it has taken" and suggests that it "could be regarded as an unusual rondo form".[19] Barry's sequence reads as follows:

A/B1/C1/C2/B2/C3/D1/D2+B3/E1/C4/C5/E2+D3/C6/C7/+C8/C9 /G/H[20].

However, students might be well-advised initially to identify and recognise aurally the following two salient melodic ideas from which so much of the piece's material is derived, namely examples X & Y[21]:

MUSIC EXAMPLE 1:
Gerald Barry, *Piano Quartet no. 1*, bars 53-57: X

MUSIC EXAMPLE 2:
Gerald Barry, *Piano Quartet no. 1*, bars 108-111: Y

Given that the new syllabus states that the prescribed works must be studied in detail in order "to understand, identify and describe the range of musical features used" and to be able to "analyse and describe patterns of repetition and change within the music",[22] students should then have little difficulty in identifying the classical techniques of repetition, transposition, inversion, augmentation, diminution, imitation, use of different registrations and dynamics, which Barry employs to vary (rather than develop) his material X & Y. They can then proceed fruitfully to the more detailed analysis provided by Barry.[23]

The Quartet is a typical example of Barry's multi-sectional structures, each section being clearly defined either by an abrupt agogic, dynamic, or instrumental change or by the use of different material. The rhythmic excitement and energy is generated by syncopation, polymetric techniques (superimposition of time signatures, e.g. bars 502-510, and 330 changes of time signature ranging from 1/8 to 4/2 within its 571 bars[24]), changing tempo indications (20 in all), and the sudden punctuation of unexpected pauses. Episodic sections within the piece shift unpredictably and are accompanied by abrupt dynamic and tempo changes. Barry himself calls these "Moments of Changes": "Where it [his music] cuts, that is what I call the moment of change. As a composer you are safe once you proceed along the same path musically, but when you want to change to another musical world that has nothing to do with what precedes it, that is a moment of truth". [As in a painting, where an object meets another object, or one area of colour meets another], "the moment where an object intersects with another is a moment of great mystery, an intangible moment"[25]. The pitch material of the opening and closing sections is derived from two Irish folk songs, *Sí Bheag, Sí Mhór* and *Lord Mayo's Delight* respectively. For Barry this recourse to his national resource of traditional Irish music for pitch material is not unusual, but as always, his source is obscured by the selective and idiosyncratic treatment it receives: other examples of Irishness in his works include the jig in *Bob* (1989), *Hard D* (1992) named after the drone on an Irish bagpipe, and less obvious allusions such as, in the case of *"Ø"* (1979), the addition and employment of inessential contiguous pitches from the Irish melody "Bonny Kate"[26], and "Irish" features such as the use of instrumental heterophony. Certainly one of the salient features of the Quartet (and in many other works such as the *Sextet* (1992/93) for clarinet (bass clarinet), trumpet, piano, double bass, and two marimbas) is his obsession with linearity and in his own word, the importance of melody.[27] For Barry, the instrumental line is more important than instrumental colour; many of his pieces can be played by any instruments: '_____' for chamber ensemble appears as *Au Milieu* (1981) for piano solo and "Ø" (1979) for two pianos was arranged for piano, harpsichord, organ, and instrumental ensemble as *Sur les Pointes*[28]. His melodic material undergoes much contrapuntal treatment: in the Resource Material, Barry notes the many examples of canons in his quartet, for example, in the opening section (bars 1-52).[29] But perhaps "canon" is not the most suitable term and students might well consider it more apt to describe this contrapuntal feature as being heterophonic or perhaps even as displaced monophony, particularly in this quartet where most canons are simply at the octave.[30]

The N.C.C.A. Music Senior Cycle Course Committee has prepared draft sample questions for distribution by the Curriculum Support Team (Music) at cluster meetings. The extract given from the Barry quartet was the opening eighteen bars of the violin part with questions requiring the student to name the work, the genre, the period, and to identify two musical features that they heard in this extract to justify the period stated. I would suggest the following tasks to augment such questions for relevant class work:

1. Identify and play themes X & Y.

2. Identify examples of repetition, imitation, inversion, transposition, augmentation, diminution, syncopation, and different registrations.

3. Explain and locate the following terms: Tone-clusters, *flautando*, *détaché*, tritones.

4. Play bars 89-106 with piano clusters and treble instruments playing the cello line (written in treble clef).

5. Write out eight bars of crotchets in 8 different time signatures and clap as an example of syncopation generated by changing time-signatures.

6. Listen to a recording of the Chopin *Étude*, op. 25 no.10 for an example of double octaves. Or any suitable Polonaise such as op. 44 or op. 53.

7. Listen to Barry's *Sextet* (1992/93) for many similar features to the *Piano Quartet no 1*.

Finally, it is interesting to examine the excursive nature of his music as exemplified in the quartet and other works.[31] Michael Blake writes that:

> one of the most important aspects of his style is the fact that his music is not necessarily going anywhere; it does not need to: The listener derives satisfaction from what he/she experiences on the way and the composer's treatment of the material, rather than feeling the onward thrust of a goal and the inevitable arrival. Therefore in the musical argument we find an elaboration rather than the conventional development of ideas...[32]

Volans and Bracefield trace this aspect of his style back to the 18th century Hiberno-English literature of Laurence Sterne in which "*A Sentimental Journey Through France and Italy* [...] never gets to Italy and *The Life and Opinions of Tristram Shandy* which tells us little of the life and nothing of the opinions of the hero". They note that "the pleasure lies in the conversation on the way, the artistry in handling the language".[33] A comprehensive study of this feature could draw on the hermeneutical deliberations of Hans-Georg Gadamer in *Truth and Method* in which he discusses the art of experience and the work of art, the *Erlebniskunst*. Gadamer states that "an adventure [...] interrupts the customary course of events, but is positively and significantly related to the context which it interrupts.[It] ventures out into the uncertain [...] but at the same time it knows that, as an adventure, it has an exceptional character and thus remains related to the return of the everyday, into which the adventure cannot be taken. Thus the adventure is "passed through", like a test, from which one emerges enriched and more mature".[34] There is no doubt that, like many twentieth-century pieces, Barry's *Piano Quartet no 1* is not teleological and students must be encouraged to also just *experience* the piece and consider the notion of a musical adventure in sound which could well continue indefinitely. As Barry writes: "Here [...] we have a piece ending with completely new possibilities pointing in different directions".[35]

NOTES

[1] The other prescribed works for 2002-2004 are Mozart's *Piano Concerto no. 23* in A major, K. 488, the second and fourth movements of Berlioz's *Symphonie Fantastique*, and a Beatles selection.

[2] Harry White, "A Book of Manners in the Wilderness": The Model of University Music Education and its Relevance as Enabler in General Education in Ireland", paper read to the Music Education National Debate, Dublin, November 1996. To be published in *College Music Symposium* (U.S.A.) with responses by David Elliott and Bennett Reimer.

[3] *Department of Education, The Leaving Certificate: Music Syllabus*, Dublin, 1996, p. 2.

[4] London, 1996; Cds featuring music from the series: Vols. 1&2, EMI CDM 5-66136/7-2. Another brief and affordable overview of the music of this century is, Paul Griffiths, *Modern Music: A Concise History*, London, 1978.

[5] *The Leaving Certificate: Music Syllabus* , p. 25

[6] A limited amount of published material is however available. Apart from Axel Klein's excellent and comprehensive *Die Musik Irlands im 20. Jahrhundert*, Hildesheim, 1996 for which a translation is in preparation [non-German readers should see review by Gareth Cox in *Music and Letters* 78 (4) pp. 624-5].

[7] Some of the readily available recordings include *Ceathrar, Irish String Quartets* (CHAN 9295), *Brian Boydell: Orchestral Music* (Marco Polo 8.223887), and *Celtic Connections* (CPS 8640). The Contemporary Music Centre in 95 Lower Baggot Street, Dublin 2 publishes a relevant CD Catalogue of Irish art-music.

[8] NMC D022. In the same year *BBC Music Magazine* voted it one of the top 50 Cds of 1995.

[9] The first work that he acknowledges is *Things That Gain By Being Painted* (1977), a piece of music theatre set to *The Pillow Book* of the tenth-century Japanese Sei Shonagon.

[10] In interview with Jocelyn Clarke, *New Music News*, February, 1995, p. 9. Barry further: "The great thing about the early days, when you were first writing music and when commissions didn't play any part in anything, was that there was a great passion and spontaneity, and you never thought about writing something because you were being paid for it. You wrote because you wanted to write."

[11] Vincent Deane, Sleeve Notes for Gerald Barry CD, (NMC D022), 1994, p. 3. For further general information on Barry's music see Adrian Jack, "Introducing Gerald Barry", *Musical Times* (cxxix), August, 1988, 229-237 and Antony Bye, "Gay Days Spent in Gladness", *Musical Times* (cxxiv), September, 1993, 496-500.

[12] Cf. Vincent Deane, 'The Music of Gerald Barry", *Soundpost* (2), 1981, p. 15.

[13] Clarke, *op. cit.*, p. 11: he states further that "you have an absolute duty to produce something which is as vivid in its own way as the original".

[14] Adrian Jack, "Unspeakable Practices", *Music Ireland* (5/7), 1990, p. 8.

[15] The author has submitted some of the following material on the *Piano Quartet no. 1* for inclusion in: *Curriculum Support Team (Music) Resource Materials for Leaving Certificate Music*, Department of Education (Dublin, 1997) (at press).

[16] Other CDs of Barry's music include his orchestral music (Marco Polo 8.225006) and *The Triumph of Beauty and Deceit* (Largo 5136).

[17] Certain piano quartets in the twentieth-century use different instrumentation: Webern's *Quartet op. 22* (1930) and Messiaen's *Quartet for the End of Time* (1941) both substitute the viola with a clarinet, and in Webern's case also substitutes the cello with a tenor saxophone.

[18] *Curriculum Support Team (Music) Resource Materials*, p. 6.

[19] *Ibid.*

[20] *Ibid.*

[21] Students should recognise, for example, that Barry's D1 at bars 318-344 is partly derived from the tritone interval of X but that E1, as Barry states, "is heard as new material" even though bars 357-372 are based on a retrograde of the preceding material. *Ibid.*, p. 9.

[22] *The Leaving Certificate: Music Syllabus*, p. 10.

[23] One could, however, question the appropriateness of the composer himself noting that the opening and closing sections are "structurally satisfying", that a section merges "seamlessly" with another, and describing a further section as "a significant and dramatic moment on the music's journey". Other specific comments refer to "the music's sense of abandon", its "ecstatic and hysterical quality", and its "exhilaration and power". *Curriculum Support Team (Music) Resource Materials*, pp. 6-12.

[24] The *Sextet* (1992/93) has nearly 300 changes of time signature.

[25] John S. Doyle, *Sunday Tribune*. 5th March, 1995.

²⁶ Cf. *inter alia*, Hilary Bracefield & Kevin Volans, "A Constant State of Surprise: Gerald Barry and *The Intelligence Park*", *Contact* (31), 1987, pp 9-19.
²⁷ Cf. Clarke, *op. cit.*, p. 10.
²⁸ In 1986 in an interview with Michael Dervan, Barry stated that "in recent years, one of my aims was to find a music which would be independent of tone colour, which could be played on any instruments with the appropriate registers.[...] I think I achieved a certain purity of sound in pieces like *Sur les Pointes*, which has been played, sung and danced in innumerable versions. I find the temptation of letting people hear these pieces from different angles irresistible". Michael Dervan, "Bowers of Bliss, of Blood...", *An Droichead* (1986) Summer, pp. 4-6, quoted in Klein, *op. cit.*, p. 354.
²⁹ *Curriculum Support Team (Music) Resource Materials*, p. 6. Regarding his *Sextet*, Barry specifically notes that "the main mode of expression is canonic". *Contemporary Music from Ireland* (CMC CD01), Gareth Cox, Sleeve Notes, p. 5.
³⁰ In an article in 1991, Harry White noted that "'canonic texture' is a meaningless phrase unless it applies to tonal counterpoint" and suggests that "when deprived of a tonal context, this intrinsic property of craftsmanship disappears [and that] some other term is therefore necessary to describe literal imitation in non-tonal music". Harry White, "The Holy Commandments of Tonality", *Journal of Musicology*, 1991, p. 256.
³¹ Cf. Gareth Cox, "Journey or Jaunt? Gerald Barry's *Sextet* (1992-93)". Paper read at Royal Musical Association Irish Chapter Meeting, Limerick May 1997.
³² Michael Blake, "Barry", *Contemporary Composers*, ed. Brian Morton and Pamela Collins, Chicago and London, 1992, p. 54.
³³ Bracefield & Volans, *op. cit.*, p. 12.
³⁴ Hans Gadamer, *Truth and Method*, trans. William Glen-Doepel (London, 1975), p. 62.
³⁵ *Curriculum Support Team (Music) Resource Materials*, p. 6.

RELIGIOUS STUDIES

5

APPROACHING THE STRANGER

JO O'DONOVAN

But let me tell you, that to approach the stranger
Is to invite the unexpected, release a new force,
Or let the genie out of the bottle.
It is to start a train of events
Beyond your control.. (T.S.Eliot).[1]

When we examine the history of theology and see how it has developed over the centuries, it becomes apparent that development and growth occurs because of theology's reaching out to strangers of all kinds. In the last fifty years the strangers have been mainly science and atheism. In recent times the strangers at the door have been the poor, whose voice we have heard in Latin American liberation theologies, and women, 'the poorest of the poor', now heard in feminist theologies. While these voices will continue to expand the interpretative framework of theology, I think the time has now come to listen to the voices of other world faiths. Muslims, Hindus, Buddhists and numerous other religious groups, whose cultures include women and the poor, as well as atheists and scientists, are no longer confined to exotic remote countries. They are at our doorstep. To enter into dialogue with these strangers is to 'release a new force', in which Christian theology will find itself once again invited to reshape the form and content of its systematics.[2] In short, the Catholic and Christian churches are called to develop a theology of religions.

In Catholic theology in particular, there has always been in place a framework for dialogue with other religions, although in the past, this framework was used to distinguish Christianity's special truth claim, and did not envisage learning anything from the different other. Over the years, the framework was developed by theologians into a tripartite division of exclusivism, inclusivism, and pluralism. The models run crudely as follows. The exclusivist view, sometimes called the ecclesiocentric approach, is the fruit of a specific theological system which holds that other religions are flawed human attempts at self-salvation, and this because of a mistaken understanding of the phrase, *extra ecclesiam nulla salus* ('outside the Church, there is no salvation'). This view is no longer defended by the Catholic Church, following on the clear statement of Vatican II on the possibility of salvation for those who do not belong visibly to the Church.[3]

Anonymous Christians

However, the Catholic Church's exclusive approach always had an inbuilt moderating qualification. While it taught that belonging to the Church through baptism was necessary for salvation, it also taught, and believed in practice, that people outside the Church were saved through 'baptism of desire'. Karl Rahner was to develop this teaching further with his theory of 'the anonymous christian',[4] by which he skilfully moved beyond exclusivism to an inclusive approach. This approach which is officially espoused by Vatican Council II, and which is christocentric, expands the hermeneutical circle and affirms that the saving God who was revealed in Jesus Christ, is present and at work in *all* religions, at least *implicitly* or *anonymously*. There are some problems with Rahner's theme of 'anonymous christians', the most obvious being: does the Hindu believer like to be called an anonymous christian? Despite this objection, the value of the inclusivism is that it holds together two truths which are professed by the Catholic tradition and most mainline Christian churches. These truths are aptly summed up by the author of the First Letter to Timothy, who in one verse tells us that God 'wants everyone to be saved and reach full knowledge of the truth' and in another says 'there is only one mediator between God and humanity, himself a human being, Christ Jesus, who offered himself as a ransom for all.' (I Tim.4-6) .

The pluralistic model attempts to move beyond inclusivism, and exponents of this model vary in the value they give to Christ. But, in general it may be said that the pluralistic paradigm is mainly theocentric.[5] It focuses on God as the unifying core of all religions. It acknowledges that there are concrete manifestations of God in all religions, but it chooses not to give any of them substantive meaning. The pluralistic model also has many streams. For example, some pluralists move away from purely theological-doctrinal questions and focus on praxis or action for human and ecological liberation between religions as a dialogical priority.[6] The main weakness of pluralism, to which I will again return, is that it deals with religions abstractly, and does not appear to enter into dialogue with them as embodied and particular traditions of truth that are strange and different. Pluralists are also caught in another agenda aptly described by the recent International Theological Commission:

> (The pluralist) position springs, among other reasons, from a certain bad conscience over the way missionary activity in the past was linked with the politics of colonialism, even though sometimes the heroism that accompanied the work of evangelisation is forgotten.[7]

A Priori Paradigm Building?

The three models I have briefly summarised have been mainly used as an ecumenical tool, serving the interests of inter-religious dialogue, but they are now being co-opted into the theology of religions, where at least they are providing a launching pad and framework for discussion for this nascent theology into the future. In recent writings, both the inclusivist and pluralist models have come under fire. The assessment of theologians such as Duffy , Dinoia and D'Costa is that both systems of thought engage in *a*

77

priori paradigm building.[8] Both are typically modern. They are based on the unwarranted *a priori* assumption that religions with aims, doctrines and patterns of life and rituals which do not appear reconcilable are, nonetheless, in their deepest reality the same, and that the Buddhist seeking Nirvana is really seeking life with the Truine God. It is characteristic of modernity however to respect the other simply as an image of oneself. It is also characteristic of modernity to explain, and leave nothing unsaid.

But in favour of exclusivism, however, I think it is fair to say that it has been criticised too harshly in the light of what religion means. Religions are incorrigibly plural in the sense of being particular and to that extent exclusive. Religion is always *this* religion. No one dies or kills for a generic religion. Duffy writes:

> What we label exclusivism and equate with imperialistic adventure and colonialist abuse was in its origins not an expression of arrogance but of the absoluteness of religious commitments[9]

And he also adds:

> Perhaps yesterday's missionaries were more accurate observers of other religions, for even in their hostility or superiority they registered differences unseen by the glossing eye of open-minded, tolerant moderns?[10]

If there is a message to be learnt from the frequently denigrated exclusivist model, it is that an *a posteriori* approach should be the basis for a theology of religions. Differences in truth claims are acknowledged as real and are respected. For a pluralism which holds together an interdependence of differences does not result simply from the limitations of the human mind to 'get it all together.'[11] It is the very stuff of reality, the way things are, the way they function. Reality is essentially pluriform: complex, rich, intricate, mysterious.

Open Inclusivism

True, for the Catholic, the inclusive model with its reassuring explanatory power subtly expresses the uniqueness of Christ as universal Saviour. It is my opinion that a Christian theology of religions has to relate to other faiths from its own Christian truth claim. But the question I ask is does the Christian truth claim have to include so much? There must, says Michael Barnes, be a way of speaking that does not include everything.[12] If there is to be room for the stranger, the different other, there must be something that I can learn in the meeting with him/her. David Tracy reminds us that we do not understand unless we understand differently, unless we pass over in some way.[13] That is, pass over to a new truth. In the same spirit, John Dunne writes:

> Passing over and coming back it seems is the spiritual adventure of our times.[14]

From the inclusivist position, is it possible, then, to 'pass over', to 'understand differently'? Gavin D'Costa is one theologian who attempts precisely to address this question, and I favour his thinking. He distinguishes between a 'closed' and 'open' form of inclusivism. 'Closed' inclusivists can be depicted as saying that in Christ or/and the Christian Church we have the truth of God. We can therefore recognise God in other religions in so much as those others look like us, have our God, believe our doctrines, at least implicitly. From our point of view the self-consciousness of these people is anonymously Christian. An 'open' inclusivism, however, would say that the truth of who Christ is not our possession, but is something that possesses us. D'Costa goes on to say:

> Now this is important, for as we do not possess it we cannot control it or limit it or even claim to have a vantage point somewhere beyond it, by which we know it in its entirety. Furthermore, this truth is not closed in the sense that revelation is eschatologically oriented, so while the Church claims to have encountered God in the self-revelation of the Father in Jesus Christ, through the Spirit, it at the same time confesses an ignorance of this God.[15]

Passing Over to the Greater Mystery

Therefore, it is in this 'place' of the surplus of meaning, a place always there because God ceaselessly surprises us with God's otherness, that we find true communion with the stranger. This is a non-controlling place.

> It allows us to ask the question of God without this being a closed question and without it predefining the other a priori (as in the case with exclusivism, pluralism, and to a lesser extent, closed forms of inclusivism).[16]

It thereby allows for the possibility of the person of another faith becoming a question for us, an invitation to understand differently, to passover in Tracy's sense to a larger mystery. I think that it must also be said that an 'open' inclusivism is more faithful to the theology of Karl Rahner, the originator of inclusivism and the pre-eminent twentieth century father of the Catholic spirit. For Rahner, mystery denotes a reality that, instead of growing smaller as we grow wiser about it, can actually be experienced as growing more mysterious and incomprehensible.

> If God's incomprehensibility does not ... draw us into his superluminous darkness, if it does not call us out of the little house of our homely, close-hugged truths into the strangeness of the night that is our real home, we have misunderstood, or failed to understand the words of Christianity. For they all speak of the unknown God, who only reveals himself to give himself as an abiding mystery. . .[17]

Can we not say, therefore, that as divine mystery, the God of Jesus Christ is the region of the 'Known Unknown' who ceaselessly surprises us, and who we may yet come to discover in the self-revealing of the stranger as different?

Manifesting Our Doctrines

The International Theological Commission commends that a "Christian theology of religions must be able to express theologically the common elements and the differences between its own faith and the conviction of different religious groups".[18] Therefore a Christian theology of religions establishes itself on the basis of its own truth claim, while also respecting the truth claims of other faiths. An 'open' inclusivism, poses the challenge of how to mediate the Christian truth claim in ways other than empirical and metaphysical verification which is purely western. In our post-modern times of the breakdown of synthesis, characterised by a love of the *a posteriori* and a wonder at difference, it may be that while the theological understanding of the substantive truths of religion has not changed, the mode of articulation of them has to change. David Tracy writes:

> The truth of religion is like the truth of its nearest cousin, art, primordially the truth of manifestation.[19]

Truth-as-manifestation is aesthetic in quality, and like all symbolic communications, is paradoxically positive and negative, openly revealing and yet darkly hidden. Therefore, there is a place in religious communication for the self-confident, positive proclamation of the prophet who speaks out, and there is also a place for the mystic who knows the Source of the word the prophet speaks, and who reminds the prophet that there is always more that we do not know. Can we say, therefore, that a Christian theology of religions is committed to manifesting Christ, but the reality of Christ is no longer a truth claim we have to somehow get round in order to relate to the other? Rather, it is a truth claim that frees us to say with confidence that because of the revelation of God in Christ, we are enabled and invited to be truly committed to the ever greater mystery of the God who reveals. I have been haunted by the memory of a text of the great French Jesuit, Henri de Lubac, writing on Buddhism in the early part of this century, in which he says that the authenticity and depth of the encounter of Christian interiority with Buddhism are determined by the degree of one's own insertion into the existentiality of Christ.

It is within the mystery of the Known-Unknown God as witnessed to by Jesus that J.A.Dinoia locates what he calls the providential diversity of religions.[20] Because these religions are *there*, a theology of religions must undertake the task of concrete *a posteriori* exposure to their various traditions. This is a daunting task, and I think that in the initial stages of meeting, it will have to be done selectively. This is what Dinoia has in mind when he warns against a theology of religions at a general level and says that:

> the only valid form of Christian theology of religions in present circumstances is one that moves directly toward the development of doctrines about doctrines of specific religious communities.[21]

I take Buddhism as an example. Being non theistic in the Western sense, the difference of Buddhism is that it is the one religion that eludes our temptation to co-opt. It has been said that there are 'unbridgeable gaps' between Buddhism and Christianity. Yet in the opinion of many authors it is precisely at the point where Buddhism most differs that Christianity has most to learn.[22] Because the recognition of difference is at the heart of inter-religious dialogue, then contact with Buddhism is a valuable experience and training ground. A theology of religions might dwell on Buddhist transience, Buddhist teaching on the no-self, and its illuminating attitude to death and dying. Buddhist 'compassion' might be responded to with a resonance to the challenge it poses for the Christian notion of love. And Buddhist Emptiness (*sunyata*) which stubbornly resists the naming of ultimacy, might sensitize us to the unnecessary verbosity of our religious language.

This challenge to dialogue with the great ways of human kind is daunting. We have barely begun and cannot envision what changes it might bring. But as Christian theology contextualizes its tradition along with the scriptures and doctrines from other religions, it will undergo rewriting, and in the process its doctrines will have taken one more step toward catholicity. But paradoxically, when we allow ourselves to say 'This is different,' or 'I do not understand the stranger,' we are also invited to open up a space to let that other person be, her sacred text, her ritual, her belief. And this is not simply a question of curiosity or a desire to know. There is an ethical element here - the element of love. For at heart, the process of inter-religious dialogue - or the more systematic Christian theology of religions - is fuelled by a love for those strange others, and by a respect for what moves them at a faith level and a sensitivity to the clues to holiness in their traditions.

NOTES

[1] T.S. Eliot, *The Cocktail Party*, Act I, Sc. i.

[2] Gavin D'Costa, 'The End of Systematic Theology' *Theology,* xcv (769),1992, pp 324-34.

[3] *Nostra Aetate* ('In Our Times'),1965, the first positive official statement made by an ecumenical council on the status and value of the religious traditions of the world. *NA* is one of the briefer documents of Vatican II but also one of the most visionary. The aim of the document is to establish the principles of interfaith dialogue. *"The Catholic Church rejects nothing that is true and holy in these religions. She looks with sincere respect upon those ways of conduct and of life, those rules and techniques which, though differing in many particulars from what she holds and sets forth, nevertheless, often reflect a ray of that truth which enlightens all men."(Par.2).*

[4] Karl Rahner, 'Anonymous Christians' *Theological Investigations,* 10, New York, 1973, pp 390-8 in which Rahner defends his theory.

[5] J. Hick,and P. Knitter, (eds.), *The Myth of Christian Uniqueness: Toward a Pluralistic Theology of Religions,* New York, 1987.

[6] Paul Knitter, *One Earth Many Religions: Multi-Faith Dialogue and Global Responsibility* New York, 1995.

[7] 'Christianity and the World Religions', *Origins,* 27(10), no.12.(7), 1996.

[8] Stephen J Duffy, 'Christianity in Dialogue: Jesus at the Circumference or Centre?' *The Living Light* 32(2), 1995 pp 61-72; J.D.Dinoia, *The Diversity of Religions: A Christian Perspective.* (Washington D.C., 1992; Gavin D'Costa. 'Discerning Christ in the World Religions', *The Month,* 1994, pp 486-90.

[9] Duffy, *op.cit.,*p.64.

[10] *Ibid.,* p. 66.

[11] Paul Knitter, *No Other Name?* London, 1986, p.6.

[12] Michael Barnes, 'On Not Including Everything: Christ, the Spirit and the Other' *The Way Supplement,* 78, 1993 pp 3-12. Cf. Barnes, *Religions in Conversation: Christian Identity and Religious Pluralism,* London, 1989.

[13] David Tracy, *Dialogue With the Other: the Inter-Religious Dialogue,* Louvain, 1990, p.44.

[14] J.S. Dunne, *The Way of All the Earth,* New York, 1972, p. ix.

[15] D'Costa, *op. cit.,* p. 489.

[16] *Ibid.*

[17] 'Poetry and the Christian' *Theological Investigations,* 4, London, 1974 p.359; cf. Rahner, 'The Concept of Mystery in Catholic Theology', *ibid.,* pp 36-73.

[18] 'Christianity and the World Religions', *op.cit.,* no.100.

[19] Tracy, *op. cit.,* p.43.

[20] Dinoia, *op.cit.,* chapter 3.

[21] *Ibid.,* p. 159.

[22] Paul Knitter, 'Horizons on Christianity's New Dialogue with Buddhism' *Horizons,* 8 (1), 1981 p. 41.

6

NEWMAN'S INTERPRETATION OF THE CHRISTIAN UNDERSTANDING OF HUMAN SUFFERING

MICHAEL CULHANE

John Henry Newman (1801-90) is now acknowledged as having been the most important theologian of the English-speaking world in the nineteenth century. His thought on the topics of ecclesiology, conscience, soteriology *et. al.* is much more in tune with that of the late twentieth century than of his own time. Equally forward-looking (though less well known) was his interpretation of the Christian understanding of human suffering.

In the Victorian era belief in the efficacy of corporal punishment was seldom questioned - except perhaps by those on whom it was perpetrated! Attitudes were governed, not by objective analysis, but rather by traditional approaches such as that which is expressed in the aphorism "spare the rod and spoil the child." One of the presuppositions underlying the practice of corporal punishment, namely that punishment or pain had some intrinsic value was not alone questioned by Newman, it was flatly rejected by him. He also had reservations about the tendency of many of his contemporaries to speak very glibly of human suffering as God's punishment for sin. This article explores Newman's rejection of the notion that

human suffering had an intrinsic value, his unease with the presentation of human suffering as God's punishment for sin, and his own
interpretation of the Christian understanding of human suffering.

The belief that suffering was intrinsically beneficial prevailed in
the nineteenth century. For instance, the severe beatings which
children received, often indeed for petty misdemeanours, were an
expression of this belief.[1] Newman maintained however that,
instead of sanctifying people, suffering normally caused them to
become selfish. In a sermon delivered at the church of St. Mary the
Virgin, Oxford on Sunday 3rd May 1835 Newman stated:

> The natural effect, then, of pain and fear, is to individualise us in
> our own minds, to fix our thoughts on ourselves, to make us
> selfish.[2]

Newman illustrated this point as follows (in language which would
nowadays be described as non-inclusive):

> Weak health, for instance, instead of opening the heart, often
> makes a man supremely careful of his bodily ease and well-
> being. Men find an excuse in their infirmities for some
> extraordinary attention to their comforts; they consider they may
> fairly consult, on all occasions, their own convenience rather than
> that of another. They indulge their way-ward wishes, allow
> themselves in indolence when they really might exert themselves,
> and think they may be fretful because they are weak. They
> become querulous, self-willed, fastidious, and egotistical.[3]

Newman offered examples, too of men and women behaving badly
as a reaction to fear. He instanced the case of people in crowd
situations, when they think that their lives are at risk, their natural
instinct for survival leads them to act with total disregard for
others.[4] Similarly he asserted that on the battlefield most soldiers in
moments of fear will give priority to their own safety over any
other consideration.[5] He also referred to contemporary accounts of
shipwrecked seamen who in conditions of starvation sometimes
committed gruesome deeds.[6] Thus Newman emphasised that fear
and suffering normally lead to self-absorption. He did maintain,

however, that in certain circumstances suffering can be a gateway to new horizons.

I shall deal with the latter aspect of Newman's thought in the final section of this paper. Now however I will briefly examine his reservations on the presentation of suffering as God's punishment for sin. For Newman suffering was part of the human condition. His reservations on speaking of suffering as God's punishment for sin are expressed in a letter which he wrote to Edward Pusey on the 19th May 1839. Pusey had been a colleague and friend of Newman at Oriel College. He had written to Newman at a time when his wife, Maria, was dying of tuberculosis. Pusey looked upon his wife's impending death as Gods punishment for his sins. Pusey wrote:

> I would ask you when you remember me before God, to ask to forgive me those sins, for which, out of the usual course of His dealings He is taking from me, in the midst of her years, one once so strong.[7]

Newman replied:

> But it seems to me you must not suffer yourself to suppose that any punishment is meant in what is now to be. Why should it? I mean, really it is nothing out of God's usual dealings. The young and strong fall all around us. How many whom we love are taken out of our sight by sudden death, however healthy - Whether slowly or suddenly, it comes on those in whose case we do not expect it. I do not think you must look on it as "some strange thing". Pray do not.[8]

Here Newman pointed out to Pusey that an event which belonged to the realm of the natural order of things ought not to be given an unwarranted theological interpretation. Further, in his sermon, *Bodily Suffering*, to which I have previously referred, Newman argued that since bodily pain affects even young children (who are incapable of sin) as well as animals, birds, reptiles etc. (that do not have the capacity to commit sin), it cannot be equated with punishment for sin.[9]

We have seen that in Newman's view human suffering had no intrinsic value, and that the natural effect of suffering was to make people selfish. I shall now explore Newman's assertion that in certain circumstances suffering can lead men and women beyond selfishness to new horizons. The interpretative key to Newman's thought on human suffering, as expressed in his sermon *Bodily Suffering*, is his own experience of serious illness in Sicily two years earlier.[10] While travelling through Sicily he suffered a serious attack of typhoid fever from which he was fortunate to have recovered considering that the treatment which he received was very basic: camomile tea for instance being his only medicine. He came to Sicily at a time of crisis in his life. Two years before that he had lost his post as tutor in Oriel College due to a difference of opinion between him and the Provost, Edward Hawkins. Much of his time was then spent on his first book, *The Arians of the Fourth Century*, which he had just completed before leaving England. The early eighteen thirties were also perceived by Newman and others as a time of crisis within the Anglican Church.[11] Its relationship with the State was undergoing significant change which many people felt threatened its very survival, while at the same time philosophical liberalism was becoming fashionable at Oxford.

Two years later, reflecting on his illness in Sicily, Newman states that it was an occurrence which inspired him to ponder deeply on the direction that his life was taking. Indeed he viewed it as an occasion of conversion. For Newman conversion was primarily about aligning one's will with the will of God.[12] Because the experience of suffering halts us on our journey (so to speak) it can in Newman's view, be a time for reflection on the fundamental realities of life. Thus periods of serious illness and disappointment can be occasions for re-evaluating one's priorities.

Further, the Cross of Christ can provide inspiration for the Christian, in situations of suffering. For Newman believed that Christ redeemed us, not primarily through his suffering, but rather through his love, and that this love survived the harrowing pain of Calvary. Newman asserted that the love of Jesus on Golgotha was evident in his thoughtfulness, when in spite of being transfixed to a cross, he prayed for those who crucified him, pardoned the repentant thief, and expressed concern for Mary, his Mother.[13] Thus in Newman's view, love is the antidote which can help to humanise suffering, and which enables men and women who are oppressed by sorrow to resist the slide towards selfishness.

In summing up Newman's more significant insights on human suffering, three main points emerge. Firstly, he acknowledged that human suffering had no intrinsic value. Thus suffering in itself is not conducive to either well-being or transformation, and normally leads to egoism. Secondly, he was very much aware that illness, grief and disappointment, through halting us on our journey, could stimulate serious reflection and thus give birth to new endeavours. He was conscious, for instance, that the beginning of the Tractarian Movement, in which he was very much involved, took place very soon after his illness in Sicily. Finally the Cross of Christ can inspire Christians in moments of grief and pain. For Christ redeemed his own suffering (so to speak) through his love. Thus the presence of love in the lives of Christians who are oppressed by suffering can in the words of T.S. Eliot turn "shadow into transient beauty with slow rotation suggesting permanence".

On 13th June 1833 Newman embarked on a sailing ship at Palermo. It was bound for Marseilles with a cargo of oranges. He was still recuperating from typhoid fever. Three days later, while becalmed off Sardinia, he wrote the poem entitled *The Pillar of Cloud*, popularly known as "Lead, Kindly Light". The imagery found here is strongly coloured by the experience of this illness in Sicily. The following lines reflect aspects of his interpretation of the Christian meaning of human suffering:

> Lead, Kindly Light, amid the encircling gloom
> Lead thou me on !
> The night is dark and I am far from home
> Lead thou me on !
> . . . I do not ask to see
> The distant scene - one step enough for me.[14]

NOTES

[1] See David Newsome, *Godliness and Good Learning*, London, 1961, pp 39-49; D.W.F. Forrister, *The Intellectual Development of E.B. Pusey 1800-50,* Unpublished Oxford D. Phil thesis.

[2] J.H. Newman, *Parochial and Plain Sermons*, III, London, 1891 p. 147, (cited hereafter as P.S.).

[3] *Ibid.,* p. 145.

[4] *Ibid.,* pp 146-7.

[5] *Ibid.* p. 146.

[6] *Ibid.* p. 147

[7] *Letter to Newman*, 14th May 1839, B.A.O.P.C. 102, Archives of the Oratory, Birmingham..

[8] *Letter to Pusey*, 19th May 1839, B.A.O.P.C. 102, Archives of the Oratory, Birmingham. I am grateful to Mr. Gerard Gracy, archivist at the Oratory, for bringing this letter to my attention.

[9] *P.S.*, III, pp 142-3.

[10] For a more detailed account of the link between Newman's illness in Sicily and his thought on human suffering see Michael Culhane, "Newman on Suffering: Reflections on his Illness in Sicily", Rosario La Delfa e Allesandro Magno (edi) *Luce nella Solitudine: Viaggio e crisi di Newman in Sicilia 1833,* Palermo, 1989, pp 103-14.

[11] See Owen Chadwick, *The Victorian Church*, I, London, 1971, pp 24ff.

[12] See Michael Culhane, "Conversion in Newman's Theology", *Newman Studien, XII,* Gunter Biemer und Heinrich Fries (Hg.) Singmarindorf, 1988, pp 189-97.

[13] *P.S.* III, p. 149.

[14] *Verses on Various Occasions*, London, 1890, p. 156.

HISTORY

7

THE TWELFTH CENTURY REFORM OF THE IRISH CHURCH: A HISTORIOGRAPHICAL STUDY

LIAM IRWIN

The reform of the Irish church in the twelfth century is a topic which has received considerable attention from historians.[1] The survival of extensive source material and the implications of the subject for many crucial questions in subsequent Irish history, which explain such interest, are also key factors in understanding the poor quality of much of this work. The impenetrable linguistic barrier of Old Irish which denied access to much of the political and social history of the period to all but a few specialists, was eliminated by the availability of readily accessible Latin sources. This apparent advantage led, in practice, to a situation where the material frequently did not receive sufficient critical examination or evaluation. The interaction of the emotive issues of religion and the Anglo-Norman invasion made it almost inevitable that authors of general histories would use the reform as evidence to support their particular overall viewpoint rather than as an important topic in its own right. Such approaches, common to many other areas of Irish history, applied equally to writers hostile or favourable to the actual work of the reformers.

In one major aspect, however, the historiography of the reform is unprecedented. The surviving sources indicate clearly that grave and widespread abuses existed in the Irish church and that a lengthy and difficult reform had to be undertaken. Yet historians, almost without exception, have sought to discredit this evidence and deny that serious irregularities existed. Even more remarkably, this has resulted not from any attempt to present a united front but to support differing and frequently diametrically opposed points of view. This factor, added to the significance of the reform for general interpretations of Irish history, makes a study of its historiography particularly fascinating and rewarding.

Much of the historical argument has centred on the authenticity and reliability of the primary evidence. The main sources are the letters of Lanfranc and Anselm, Archbishops of Canterbury, to various people in Ireland between 1074 and 1109, a treatise on church government by Bishop Gilbert of Limerick,[2] three letters from Pope Alexander III written in 1172,[3] the life of St. Malachy by St. Bernard of Clairvaux, [4] and the decrees of the reforming synods.[5] These various documents indicate that it was in the area of marriage practice that the chief abuses existed. Unions within the forbidden degrees of kinship are condemned by Lanfranc and Anselm in letters to Tairdelbach Ua Briain, to Muirchertach Ua Briain, and to Gothric, King of Dublin.[6] Pope Alexander, in his letter to Henry II in 1172, and the decrees of the Synods of Cashel in 1101 and 1172 provide details of these abuses and indicate that incest was included.[7] These sources also show the prevalence of divorce, while St. Bernard charges that the sacrament of marriage had been abandoned by large sections of the population and one of the decrees of Cashel in 1172 appears to confirm this[8] Marriage among the clergy was legislated against in 1101 at the first Cashel synod. [9]

The other major abuse that existed related to the role of bishops. There were too many of them, they were not consecrated properly and they did not fulfil their proper function. Bishop Gilbert's *De Statu Ecclesiae*, essentially a simple blueprint for a diocesan and parochial organisation, indicates a fundamental lack of understanding about the normal forms of church government. The Irish bishops had largely spiritual functions in a church system organised and administered on a monastic basis which explains how the problem of multiplicity and irregular consecrations had arisen.[10] In addition to the testimony of Lanfranc, Anselm and St. Bernard, the legislation of the Raithbreasail and Kells/Mellifont synods provides full evidence of the reform in this area. [11]

There is a lack of such clear-cut agreement among the sources for the other abuses. Lanfranc detailed irregularities in baptism and second decree of the 1172 Synod of Cashel laid down the correct procedure.[12] St. Bernard asserted that confirmation and confession had been abandoned, but no supporting evidence exists for this claim.[13] His statement that tithes were not paid is confirmed by the second Synod of Cashel and Pope Alexander's letters.[14] Lanfranc accused the Irish bishops of practising simony and the first decree of Cashel in 1101 apparently refers to such an abuse, but due to textual difficulties this is arguable. [15]

Both Lanfranc and Anselm have a central role in any discussion about the reliability of the sources for the twelfth century church. Through their consecration of the bishops of the Ostmen towns both men were in close contact with Ireland and apart from their advice on theological matters help with secular problems was also requested. [16] Lanfranc's statement that the Irish law of marriage was rather *'maritali seu fornicaria lege'*[17] is significant as it shows an awareness of the Brehon Law basis for the Irish practice. Their credibility has occasionally been attacked on the grounds that their ambition to control the Irish church gave them a vested interest in emphasising and exaggerating its defects. The Ostmen bishops who were consecrated at Canterbury swore oaths of obedience to the Archbishop.[18] In the oath of Bishop Patrick in 1074 Dublin is described as *Metropolis Hiberniae*: if this false status accorded to Dublin is taken in conjunction with Lanfranc's claim to be *Britanniarum primas* and the insistence on the oath of obedience even as late as 1138, then a case appears to exist for the view that Canterbury hoped to incorporate the Irish church under its dominion.[19] However, the true motive appears to have been merely pastoral concern, and when the welfare of the church could be shown to be served without such control it was readily abandoned. Anselm simply offered his congratulations and hopes for a successful reform to Gilbert who had been consecrated bishop of Limerick without the knowledge or consent of Canterbury.[20] The fact that a precedent had been created for independent action in this area appears to be of no concern to Anselm. The reliability of the Archbishops as sources cannot be seriously undermined in this manner.

The letters of Pope Alexander III must also be regarded as dependable. Papal information on the state of the Irish church came largely from the reforming Irish bishops.[21] Policy in Rome would also have been influenced by the visit of St. Malachy in 1140 and the journey to Ireland of the special Papal Legate, Cardinal Paparo, in 1152. Paparo met the leading reformers at the Synod of Kells/Mellifont where he presented the pallia for four Archbishoprics. The inclusion of Tuam and Dublin, though pallia had only been requested for Armagh and Cashel, indicates that Rome was aware both of the political and religious tensions in the country. The increased political importance of Connacht under Turlough O'Connor demanded that an Archbishopric be sited there, while the continued assumption of unauthorised power by the Bishop of Dublin could only be solved by acceding to his demands.[22] Such sensitivity, coupled with the personal experience of Paparo, suggests that Papal information on Ireland was both adequate and up to date. St. Bernard's information for his *Life of St. Malachy* derived from his friendship with his subject, and from Congan, abbot of an Irish monastery, who supplied an account of Malachy's early career in Ireland.[23] Despite such impressive informants, Bernard's work has to be treated with extreme caution. He was writing hagiography not history, and his description of the Irish church was primarily to highlight the daunting task which faced St. Malachy. His general condemnations are sweeping and expressed in extreme language, but his specific references to abuses occupy merely two sections from a total of seventy-five. His treatment of marriage provides a guide to his overall reliability. He mentions the subject three times, once in the statement that there was "no entry into lawful marriages" and twice that this had been fully corrected in Malachy's lifetime.[24] If he was aware of the full details regarding marriage irregularities in Ireland it seems inconceivable, given his aim of highlighting the poor state of the church before the advent of Malachy, that he would not put greater stress on the subject. One must assume that neither Malachy nor Congan explained fully to him the exact nature of those abuses. The major criticism that can be levelled against his work, therefore, is not, as many historians suggest, exaggeration but lack of precise information about Irish practices. This interpretation is reinforced by his simplistic belief that the hereditary succession at Armagh was the chief cause of the general laxity throughout the Irish church.[25]

The decrees of the synods are not free from interpretative problems either. The legislation at Cashel in 1101 against marriage abuses, if taken literally, would suggest that the only faults were unions within the forbidden degrees of kinship. It is clear that this decree shows merely the extent to which the reformers considered it politic to legislate for change at that particular time. Similarly the decree on marriage at Cashel in 1172, while indicating that the problem was not totally solved, does not give any firm information on what progress had taken place. The correct translation of some decrees is in doubt, and the absence of direct copies of the decrees from Rathbreasail and Kells-Mellifont further restricts our knowledge about these assemblies.

The source materials for the reform, therefore, while not free from omission and ambiguities are nevertheless more plentiful and accessible than those for most other topics in this period. The consequent ease with which those interested in the subject could pursue their own research and use the authority of primary sources to bolster their arguments has been a major factor in the heated controversy which is the main characteristic of the writing on this topic.

The historiography of the reform begins, in a sense, as early as 1317. In that year the Irish chiefs, under Dónal O'Neill, addressed a remonstrance to Pope John XXII denouncing the evils of English rule in Ireland. In outlining the events leading to the original invasion, the church reform and the part played by Pope Adrian IV is mentioned. He is castigated for issuing the Bull *Laudabiliter* and for supporting Henry II in his expansionist plans. It is stressed that his judgement was affected by his concern for English interests which arose, not so much from his place of birth, as from "feeling and character".[25] This concern to minimise the importance of his English nationality is a reflex of the events which led to the remonstrance. In a petition for recognition of Edward Bruce as the lawful Irish king, a stress on the importance of birthplaces would not have been very politic. The attack on the English Pope is, however, significant as it marks the beginning of a trend which has continued to the present day.

In the seventeenth century Geoffrey Keating's account of the reform shows strong[26] influence of a Counter Reformation mind. The creation of discipline and order within the church is seen as having been paramount. Control by lay princes is ended and the main abuses listed are simony, usury and non payment of tithes. The reforming synods are presented as forerunners of the Council of Trent and the abuses of his own day are transferred to the twelfth century. His main concern is to demonstrate that no justification existed for Henry II to invade Ireland. The reform, far from showing a need for outside intervention, actually proves that the Irish had successfully conducted their own reform. He strongly refutes the notion that Canterbury had jurisdiction over the Irish church and specifically mentions Hanmer's error in this regard.[27] He concedes that the Ostmen did have links with Lanfranc and Anselm, but he sees the racial bond between Normans and Vikings as largely responsible for this. He skilfully uses the examples of the building of abbeys like Mellifont and Holy Cross as proof that the Irish church had completed its reform by the mid-twelfth century. No reference is made to the fact that these monasteries were foreign-inspired and merely part of the attempted reform. To have acknowledged that native impetus had not been paramount at any stage would have weakened his fundamental argument that the state of the church did not justify in any way the involvement of Henry II in Irish affairs.

In the nineteenth century there were two major stumbling blocks for historians dealing with this topic; the explanation of the irregularities in sexual behaviour and the papal authorisation for the Norman invasion. The most common tactic in dealing with the latter embarrassment was to place considerable stress on the nationality of Pope Adrian. The implication that this led him to make an unjust decision is clear, though interestingly it is never explicitly stated. There was no scapegoat readily available for the sexual abuses and various attitudes were adopted. Ignoring them completely was one solution, and Emily Lawless and P.W. Joyce, for example, list the abuses simply as heresy, lack of episcopal jurisdiction and failure to pay tithes or Peter's Pence.[28] M. Haverty, the most widely read popular historian at the turn of the century, asserted that St. Bernard was the only source to mention such irregularities. As the saint had no personal experience of Ireland and was noted for his exaggerated vision of the corruption of the world, he could not be regarded as reliable. Haverty thus implicitly denies their existence by undermining the main source and omitting any mention of other evidence which would sustain the charges.[29] Monsignor E.A. D'Alton on the other hand, confronts this issue squarely with a curious mixture of vivid detail, Victorian moralising and ingenious explanations. In twelfth century Ireland a lengthy waiting period existed between the ceremony and the consummation of a marriage which led, in his view, to these abuses. While they could not be condoned, they were "different from those illicit connections which ignore religion altogether and are founded exclusively on the uncontrolled impulse of the passions".[30]

Such variety in approach is absent when the causes and results of the reform are being dealt with. The impact of what P.W. Joyce terms "the Danish troubles"[31] is used without exception to explain why a reform was needed. The Vikings are presented as savage heathens who came with a missionary zeal to destroy the Irish church.[32] The evocative image of Turgesius and his wife defiling the high altar at Clonmacnoise, which had been dreamed up by the clever propagandist author of *Cogadh Gaedhel re Gaillaibh*,[33] is faithfully recorded by these historians as unassailable fact, and used to highlight dramatically the evil nature of the invaders. The particular attraction of this argument for nationalist historians was the placing of the blame on outsiders and thus preserving their general view of the greatness and nobility of the Irish. A stress on foreign contamination is a common characteristic of all such writing with an emphasis on abuses that existed elsewhere in Europe. It was only to be expected, the argument concludes, that the general decay in moral standards should have affected Ireland and no blame should attach to the Irish church.

The modern historiography of the reform begins with the standard work on medieval Ireland by Edmund Curtis.[34] This eminent historian, whose bias towards Gaelic Ireland was largely a reaction to the pro-Norman approach of G.H. Orpen,[35] devoted generous space to this topic. He was basically unsympathetic to the reformers, seeing them as having created a false picture of the decadence in the Irish church. This exaggeration and distortion had been a crucial factor in the decision of the pope to issue the *Laudabiliter* Bull which had provided the legal basis for Henry II to annex the lordship of Ireland. The main responsibility for the ending of Gaelic independence was placed firmly on the shoulders of the reformers, particularly St. Malachy and the bishops who had direct contact with Rome: "Ireland had to pay dearly for the pious exaggerations of her spiritual chiefs".[36] The probable ignorance in Ireland of the existence of this document[37] is swept aside in his determination to explain the Irish kings' ready acceptance of Henry II. His revealing comment, "it is hard to explain otherwise the general and voluntary surrender both in church and state of native Ireland",[38] highlights his own awareness of the inadequacy of the argument. As he develops his case, it becomes clear that he considers there were two separate groups of reformers: a native-minded party, who opposed involvement with Canterbury, and a Roman party, who ignored every other consideration in their campaign to achieve total conformity with the papacy. This interpretative approach leads him into occasional inconsistency. There was no sense of nationality in Ireland, he suggests in explaining Ua Briain deference to Canterbury, yet the Bishop of Lismore is castigated for allowing zeal for the universal church to overcome his patriotism.[39]

Curtis also places an undue emphasis on the ultimate Viking ancestry of the Normans. The link between Canterbury and the Ostmen is seen as resulting from feelings of common kinship. He fails to sustain this argument, regarding the Ostmen bishops as Irishmen to prove that the reform was a native-inspired one while referring elsewhere to the towns as foreign enclaves, hostile to their Celtic neighbours. In dealing with the actual abuses he makes a distinction between the clergy and laity. Uncanonical marriage, for example, was a vice among the latter while toleration of such unions was a fault of the clergy. His main point, however, is that the state of corruption was exaggerated both through zeal for perfection and through the use of intemperate language. His conclusion involves an acceptance of the total success of the reform effort with the important qualifications that it was neither completely necessary nor desirable and was brought about at a heavy price.[40]

J.F. Kenney, in a foreword to his *Sources*,[41] stresses the importance of seeing the reform in its European context: the situation in Ireland should not be regarded as unique but merely as part of the general laxity prevalent throughout the church. He is concerned to give the credit for reform to the Irish churchmen themselves and to minimise the role of Canterbury. He coined the term 'ecclesiastical imperialist' for Archbishop Lanfranc and links his expansionist ambitions with those of Henry II in the political sphere. The Ostmen bishops are excluded from any complicity in Canterbury's design, being motivated by sound theological considerations alone. They subsequently proved this by readily accepting the reformed Irish diocesan and episcopal system. The main fault in the church was, laicisation, and the significant achievements of the reformers were the correction of abuses, development of proper organisational structures and the improvement of the morality and spirituality of the people.

Eoin MacNeill[42] has an interesting duality in his approach. He praises the reformers for providing a native impetus for change without any prompting from outsiders. However, their part in supplying a pretext for Henry II to obtain papal sanction for his annexation of Ireland makes them deserving of censure. Their reports to Rome in "language of pious reprobation" were, in his view, crucial in this instance. On the abuses he carefully conveys the impression that they were relatively minor, particularly by reference to the fact that all "local customs" were frowned on by the church at this period.

Fr. Aubrey Gwynn wrote a highly acclaimed work on this topic.[43] He expertly set it in the wider context of the Gregorian reform in the European church, and argued that this was the only valid perspective from which to approach the twelfth century Irish changes. He accepted that the Irish practice in marriage was never brought into line with canon law during the medieval period but he rejected the idea that incest was widespread or that it was legislated against at the Synod of Cashel in 1101. He postulated that an error may have been made and transmitted in the various manuscripts that contain the text of the decrees. The lack of evidence in the extant literature for this practice and its non-appearance in the decrees of the second Synod of Cashel are used to support his argument. This latter point ignores the fact that by 1172 there had been seventy years of reform work, and if it had made any progress then incest, at least, should have been remedied. In general, however, Gwynn's treatment of the subject showed sound scholarship and balance.

To his translation of St. Bernard's *Life of Malachy*, Dean Lawlor contributed a lengthy introduction placing the responsibility for the degeneration of the church almost entirely on the Vikings. The revival of learning in the tenth and eleventh century monasteries is seen as preparing the way for the twelfth century reform in the same way that a revival of learning preceded the sixteenth century European reformation. The citizens of Dublin, he wrote, "glorified in their subjection to Canterbury".[44] This is his interpretation of the letter from the inhabitants to Ralph, Archbishop of Canterbury in 1122. Its more likely purpose, however, was to flatter the Archbishop so that he would agree to consecrate their bishop-elect and help them to resist the claims of Armagh to primacy of the Irish church. Politics rather than loyalty or emotion was the key factor. In an appendix[45] he lists the abuses mentioned by Bernard and offers his own comments on them. These remarks are mainly designed to qualify the dogmatic assertions of St. Bernard. Marriage, confession and confirmation had not been abandoned but were not performed according to the Roman rite. The saint, he would concede, had some foundation for his criticisms but his inflamed rhetoric presents a false picture.

Protestant writers have basic similarities in approach which transcend their denominational concerns. There is a pronounced lack of sympathy for the reformers who are shown as agents of the papacy, attempting to extend its influence and power. Emphasis is placed on the freedom from Roman control of the church and parallels are drawn between it and the national churches established by the sixteenth century reformation.[46] This idealised version of the early Irish church, noted for the "primeval purity of her doctrine and teaching",[47] necessitated a rejection of all evidence which pointed to corruption and a need for reform. The reformers, Henry II, the Pope and the Archbishops of Canterbury, all receive severe strictures for their roles in the attack on this pre-reformation national church. The English nationality of Pope Adrian is given prominence and a carefully calculated picture presented of a ruthlessly ambitious man prepared to sacrifice both the Irish church and the country's political independence for his own aggrandisement.[48] The Vikings do not fare much better, being singled out for attack both for their initial assault on Irish Christianity and the impetus which their descendants subsequently gave to the reform.[49] The Culdee movement gets prominent mention due to a belief that it represented an organised opposition to the claim for primacy by Rome. This whole movement is misunderstood and distorted by such writers, one of whom even regarded it as continuing until 1625 as a last remnant of the old independent Irish church.[50]

Church of Ireland writers tend to adopt a subdued approach in expressing these views. The apparent existence of some of the essential features of the Established Church at such an early period is presented with unconcealed pride. There is considerable stress on the point that the twelfth century reform merely marks the introduction of a Roman interlude in the Irish church which was corrected again in the sixteenth century, and that this independence has been maintained through the efforts of the Church of Ireland. There is also a definite suggestion that the golden age of Irish Christianity was linked with its freedom from papal control.[51] The most balanced treatment from an Anglican viewpoint is that of St.

103

John Seymour, a widely respected ecclesiastical historian. He provides a survey of the reformers' work and in contrast to most clerical writers sets the events in their proper historical context. He even delivers a gentle rebuke to those who had argued that the reform placed the free Irish church in the bondage of Rome. He shows that closer communion with Rome was unavoidable if the Irish church was to be brought into line with that of Britain and the rest of Europe. However, he thought it necessary to add a reminder that the Papacy was quite a different, and by implication less objectionable, institution at that period than it became subsequently. He shares the accepted viewpoint of the time that the Vikings were militant heathens intent on the destruction of Christianity and even questions the sincerity of their initial conversion in the tenth century. The selection of Irish bishops by the Ostmen towns, who in turn rejected the Celtic church and looked to Canterbury, is noted as unusual and used to dismiss the statement of Geoffrey Keating that the Ostmen looked to Canterbury initially because they feared the imposition of native Irish bishops on them. The reformers are seen as enthusiastic promoters of the Norman conquest using *Laudabiliter* to full and deadly effect. The decision to reject the involvement of Canterbury but accept English political control is presented as the fatal error. The connection with England not alone failed to improve religious life in Ireland but exacerbated the problems which already existed. On the other hand, had the reformers worked for Papal approval through Canterbury rather than dealing directly with Rome, "the Irish church could have been an independent church in full communion with Rome".[52]

Presbyterian authors take a far more extreme view. The reform is used as an object lesson in the perfidy of Rome and the continual malign designs of the papacy. The need for constant vigilance to prevent such an occurrence is stressed as are aspects of the contemporary situation: "Irish Roman Catholics should bear carefully in mind that it is to the Pope of Rome they owe their subjugation to Britain of which they complain so much". The polemical nature of most of this writing is further underlined, *e.g.* "Being the infallible head of an infallible church, surely he did not err?".[53] Considerable liberties are taken with the facts to further this objective as evidenced by the assertions that the reform resulted in indulgences being openly sold, purgatory preached for the first time, simony becoming widespread and the bible being discarded.[54] An effort is also made to show that an embryonic Presbyterian system existed in the early Irish church. The impotence of the bishops, and the lack of contact with Rome provide the basis of argument through the Culdees are an important plank for other writers.[55] The general lack of success in making such a thesis plausible is underlined by the conclusion of one of its foremost proponents, the Rev. Thomas Hamilton:

> the church was characterised by much of the simplicity and freedom of Presbyterianism .... it was certainly much more essentially Presbyterian than Popish or Prelatic.[56]

A further distinctive aspect of Presbyterian historiography is a stress on the purity of early Irish Christianity. Contact with Rome in the twelfth century led to contamination which was only eliminated four hundred years later with the advent of their church.[57] Hamilton again typifies this attitude as well as the intemperate language frequently employed:

> for centuries the Christianity of Ireland was purer than that of any other nation... but little by little the pure stream became corrupted until it was lost in a foul and foetic quagmire, reeking with filth".[58]

Protestant writers, therefore, had a twofold purpose: they wished to link the early church with their own individual sects and show continuity of belief, practice and organisation, and in addition, to present a justification for the sixteenth century reformation by showing that Rome had imposed its authority a mere four hundred years earlier. In this context it was necessary to present the reformers in the most unfavourable light possible. The Ostmen, Irish and Normans who were involved are censured as the dupes or willing accomplices of the power-hungry papacy. For moderate writers this was sufficient, but the more extreme author felt it necessary to include further interpretative and often highly inflammatory descriptions of the detrimental effects which the twelfth century changes had on religious life in Ireland. This deplorable regression was not to be reversed until "the era of the reformation arrived bringing hope of better things".[59]

The authors of school text-books found this topic generally uncongenial. The lives of Malachy, Bernard and Laurence O'Toole were useful in showing that the twelfth century could produce spiritual giants, but the difficulties of explaining the deterioration from the much emphasised 'Golden Age' outweighed this advantage. The most common approach was to have an introduction detailing the intense anti-Christian activities of the Vikings and then attribute the decline in morality to the Norse attacks. It was, in the circumstances, an understandable approach, and the inevitable distortion and omission of important facts was no greater than in other, supposedly more academic, works.[60] Modern school texts have shown a major improvement in this, as in most other, areas. The emphasis on St. Malachy at the expense of the details of the abuses and their reform is due to modern educational ideas on history teaching rather than to any attempt to deny unpalatable truths.[61]

The most significant modern published works which discuss this topic are by John Watt.[62] Lay control of ecclesiastical affairs is given an undue emphasis in explaining the abuses particularly in regard to marriage where the influence of Irish law was undoubtedly more significant. His use of phrases which describe Ireland as "the admiration of Christendom" suggests that the 'Island of Saints and Scholars' style of writing will not easily be eliminated. The most challenging modern work has come from W. L. Warren, who, in the course of a controversial essay on the century in general, argues that the reform was largely a parchment one. The letters of Pope Alexander III, hailing as the will of God the submission of the country to Henry II, are seen as the real death-knell of Irish independence. Papal motives, he suggests, were distrust of a reform too closely associated with monks, and it is frequently overlooked that Adrian IV was instrumental in transferring power in the church from monastic orders to bishops. The main flaw in this argument is the lack of evidence for such mistrust. Malachy had originally wished to stay at Clairvaux but Pope Innocent II had decreed that he would be "employed to more profitable advantage in Ireland". Malachy went to meet Pope Eugenius in France in 1148, "as he need not fear that he should have any difficulty with him". The sending of Paparo as Papal Legate in 1151 clearly indicated papal approval of the structure and personnel of the reform. Warren's most original suggestion is that King Henry's intervention in Ireland was first suggested by the Archbishop of Canterbury, the loss of primacy over the Ostmen towns having made the Archbishop fearful for the future of the church in Ireland. Henry would rectify this and also recover for Canterbury what they saw as usurped rights.[63]

The historiography of this topic provides an object lesson in the pitfalls of not studying history for its own sake irrespective of its effect on cherished ideas of the past.. The popular idea of Ireland as the 'Island of Saints and Scholars' was threatened by the highlighting of moral and organisational abuses for which correction was sought. This undermining of a basic plank of much nationalist historical writing was aggravated by the evidence presented of papal authorisation and support for the Norman invasion. The impetus given to reform by the Ostmen of Dublin, Limerick and Waterford was an embarrassment as it weakened the generally accepted view of all Vikings as ruthless destroyers of Christianity. The closer relationship with Rome, which was fundamental to the reformers' work, was a special point of controversy for Protestant writers.

As a result the treatment of the reform, depending on the function it was intended to serve, varied in emphasis, distortion or omission. The common factor which transcended these individual concerns was a siege mentality. Particular denominational, sectarian or political viewpoints had to be defended. The degree to which they were vulnerable dictated the extent of the deviation from acceptable standards of historical enquiry. The historiography of the twelfth century church reform in Ireland, therefore, provides some extremely valuable insights into the diverse assumptions, preoccupations and prejudices of historians, both lay and clerical, from the medieval era to the present day.

NOTES

[1] I am grateful to Professor Donnachadh Ó Corráin of the Department of Irish History, University College, Cork. who first suggested to me that this subject might repay investigation.

[2] Printed in *The Whole Works of the Most Rev. James Ussher,* eds. C.R. Elrington and J. H. Todd, Dublin, 1847-64, vol. iv, section 3, 'Veterum epistolarum Hibernicarum sylloge'. The letters of Lanfranc (1070-89) and Anselm (1093-1109) are on pp 490-530 and the 'De Statu Ecciesiae' of Bishop Gilbert pp 500-10.

[3] Printed in E. Curtis and R. B. McDowell, *Irish Historical Documents,* London, 1943, pp 19-22.

[4] *St. Bernard of Clairvaux's Life of St. Malachy of Armagh,* ed. H. J. Lawlor, London, 1920.

[5] S. H. O'Grady ed., *Caithreim Thoirdhealbhaigh,* London, 1929; a list of the eight decrees of Cashel 1101 in an early modern version of the *Senchas Síl Bhriain;* translation *ibid.,* v. ii 185; the decrees of Cashel 1172 from Giraldus Cambrensis *Expurgnatio Hibernica* are printed in *Irish Hist. Doc;* G. Keating, *History of Ireland* Irish Texts Soc. ed.. 1908, pp 296-307, is an extract from the lost Annals of Clonenagh and our only source for legislation of Rathbreasail and Kells-Mellifont.

[6] Ussher, *Sylloge,* pp 490, 492-4, 521.

[7] *Irish Hist. Doc.,* pp 18, 21; K. Hughes, *The Church in Early Irish Society,* London, 1966, p. 246; A. Gwynn and D. F. Gleeson, *A History of the Diocese of Killaloe,* Dublin, 1962, p 112.

[8] Ussher, *Sylloge,* pp 492, 521, 523; Lawlor, *Life of Malachy,* p. 37; *Irish Hist. Doc.,* pp 18, 21.

[9] M. Dolley, *Anglo-Norman Ireland,* Dublin, 1972, p. 7, decree 5 of Cashel 1101.

[10] This question is still the subject of much debate, for a recent discussion of the problem see Colmán Etchingham's comments in Kim McCone and Katherine Simms, ed., *Progress in Medieval Irish Studies, Maynooth, 1996 pp 139-40*

[11] Ussher, *Sylloge,* pp 493, 500-510, 521, 524; Lawlor, *Life of Malachy,* p. 46; John Watt, *The Church and the Two Nations in Medieval Ireland,* Cambridge, 1970, p. 12; Dolley, *Anglo-Norman Ireland,* p. 7.

[12] Ussher, *Sylloge,* p. 493; *Irish Hist. Doc.,* p. 18.

[13] Lawlor, *Life of Malacliy,* pp 18 and 37.

[14] *Ibid.,* p. 37; *Irish Hist. Doc.,* pp 18, 21.

[15] Ussher, *Sylloge,* p. 493. The textual arguments are dealt with by K. Hughes and A. Gwynn; see in particular *Irish Eccles. Rec.,* vol. 66, 1945, pp 83ff.

[16] Ussher, *Svlloge,* pp 495-597.

[17] *Ibid.,* p. 493.

[18] *Ibid.,* pp 564-6.

[19] *Ibid.,* pp. 565-6, oath sworn by Patrick, Bishop of Limerick.

[20] *Ibid.,* p. 513.

[21] Letter from Pope Alexander printed in *Irish Hist. Doc.,* pp 19-20.

[22] Ussher, *Sylloge,* p. 530; letter from Anselm to Samuel, Bishop of Dublin reproving him for using the forms and symbols of an Archbishop.

[23] Lawlor, *Life of Malachy,* pp 4, 131-7; the saints met during Malachy's journeys to Rome in 1140 and 1148.

[24] *Ibid.,* pp 18, 37, 39.

[25] *Ibid.,* p. 46.

[25] This document is printed in *Irish Hist. Doc.,* pp 38-46.

[26] G. Keating, *Foras Feasa ar Éirinn,* ed. P. S. Dineen, London, 1908, vol. iii, pp 299-317.

[27] *Ibid.,* p. 301.

[28] Emily Lawless, *Ireland,* London, 1887; P.W. Joyce, *A Short History of Ireland to 1608* , Dublin, 1924, pp 240-7.

[29] M. Haverty, *The History of Ireland,* Dublin, 1906, pp 163-4.

[30] E. A. D'alton, *A History of Ireland from Earliest Times to the Present Day,* vol. i, Dublin, 1906, p. 187.

[31] P. W. Joyce, *A Short History of Ireland,* Dublin, 1800, p. 238.

[32] For a contrary view of the Viking presence in Ireland see A. T. Lucas, "The Burning and Plundering of Churches in Ireland, 7th to 16th Century", in E. Rynne (ed.), *North Munster Studies, Essays in Commemoration of Monsignor Michael Moloney,* Limerick, 1967, pp 172-229, and "Irish-Norse Relations: Time for a Reappraisal?", *J. Cork Hist. Archaeol. Soc.,* vol. 71, 1966, pp 62-75.

[33] J. H. Todd (ed.), *Cogadh Gaedhel re Gallaibh: The War of the Gaedhil with the Gaill,* London, 1867, p. 226.

[34] E. Curtis, *A History of Medieval Ireland, 1086-1513,* revised ed. London, 1938.

[35] G. H. Orpen, *Ireland Under the Norinans,* 4 vols., Oxford, 1911-20.

[36] Curtis, *Medieval Ireland,* p. 37.

[37] According to Giraldus Cambrensis it was first produced at a Council in Waterford some years after the invasion, Watt, *op. cit.,* (1972), p. 33.

[38] Curtis, *Medieval Ireland,* p. 60.

[39] *Ibid.,* p. 61.

[40] *Ibid.,* pp 13-4 and 59.

[41] J. F. Kenney, *Sources for the Early History of Ireland. Ecclesiastical,* New York, 1929.

[42] Eoin Mac Neill, *Phases of Irish History,* Dublin, 1919 (reprinted 1968), pp 238-87.

[43] A. Gwynn, 'The Twelfth Century Reform, in P. J. Corish ed., *A History of Irish Catholicism,* vol. ii, Dublin, 1968; see also his articles in *Irish Eccles. Rec.,* August 1945 and Feb. 1946.

[44] Lawlor, *Life of Malachy,* intro. p. xxii.

[45] *Ibid.,* appendix, pp 161-3.

[46] R. Mant, *History of the Church of Ireland,* London, 1840; J. Macbeth, *The Story of Ireland and Her Church,* Dublin, 1899; W.A. Philips ed. *The History of the Church of Ireland,* 3 vols., Oxford, 1933-34; C. Pike, *Story of Religion in Ireland,* London, 1895; J. Olden, *The Church of Ireland,* London, 1892.

[47] Macbeth, *op. cit.,* p. 107.

[48] G. Gordon, *History of Ireland,* London, 1806, p. 65; Pike, *op. cit.,* p. 28.

[49] Macbeth, *op. cit., p.* 100; Olden, *op. cit.,* p. 167; Gordon, *op. cit.,* p. 54; R. Murray, *Ireland and Her Church,* London, 1845, p. 112.

[50] Gordon, *op. cit.,* p. 54.

[51] Macbeth, *op. cit.,* p. 107; Gordon, *op. cit.,* p. 52; Olden, *op. cit.,* p. 216.

[52] St. John D. Seymour, *The Twelfth Century Reformation in Ireland,* Dublin, 1932; I am grateful to Prof. Etienne Rynne, Dept. Archaeology, N.U.I., Galway, for bringing this publication to my attention.

[53] T. Hamilton, *History of the Irish Presbyterian Church,* Belfast, 1887, pp 20-1.

[54] D. Stewart, *The History and Principles of the Presbyterian Church in Ireland,* Belfast, 1907, pp 13-4, 17; Hamilton, *op. cit.,* pp 20-1.

[55] Gordon, *op. cit.,* p. 54.

[56] Hamilton, *op. cit.,* p. 36.

[57] Stewart, *op. cit.,* p. 12.

[58] Hamilton, *op. cit.,* p. 19.

[59] *Ibid.,* p. 22.

[60] J. Ryan, *Ireland from A.D. 800 to A.D. 1600,* Dublin n.d. but 1927; J. F. O'Doherty, *A History of the Catholic Church,* Dublin, 1943; M. Hayden and G. A. Moonan, *A Short History of the Irish People,* Dublin, 1925.

[61] G. MacGearailt, *Celts and Normans,* Dublin, 1969; J. Feeny, A *History of Ireland,* Dublin n.d.

[62] J. Watt, *The Church and the Two Nations in Medieval Ireland,* Cambridge, 1970 and *The Church in Medieval Ireland,* Dublin, 1972.

[63] W L. Warren, "The Interpretation of Twelfth Century Irish History", in J. C. Beckett ed., *Historical Studies VII,* Belfast, 1969, pp 1-19.

8

THE ROYAL DUBLIN SOCIETY AND THE ADVANCEMENT OF POPULAR SCIENCE IN IRELAND, 1731-1860

KIERAN R. BYRNE

It was, appropriately enough, at the rooms of the Philosophical Society, Trinity College, that the Dublin Society was formally established on 25th June 1731.[1] Among those present on the occasion were Thomas Prior,[2] Thomas Molyneaux,[3] Arthur Dobs,[4] and William Maple.[5] The expressed purpose of that meeting was to found an institution for improving 'husbandry, manufacture and other useful arts'.[6] Significantly, at a subsequent meeting on 8th July 1731, it was pointedly agreed that 'sciences' be appended to the originally stated objectives.[7] With its emphatic utilitarian philosophy the newly established society marked a new departure in the Irish educational tradition. At a time when a deep-rooted classical education tradition predominated in Ireland, the Royal Dublin Society challenged this conservatism in an attempt to foster a spirit of industrial and economic regeneration. Through its endeavours the economic prosperity was highlighted and confirmed. Scientific research was supported and a national campaign for the advancement of science, art and agriculture was pioneered and popularized.

In pursuit of a historical perspective for this new enterprise a number of contexts must be considered. The establishment of the Royal Dublin Society may not be attributable to any particular causal factor; it was, rather, the outcome of a complex of economic and political conditions which prevailed in Ireland at the beginning of the eighteenth century. The opening decades of that century witnessed a sharp decline in Irish economic fortunes. That decline, it was argued, stemmed directly from restrictive legislation which either prohibited or curtailed the export of Irish produce. A further pronounced obstacle was the backward state of Irish agriculture, with an absentee land-owning class which was wantonly apathetic towards any proposals for renewal, expansion or investment.[8] The decade 1720-1730, for example, was a critically difficult period, with poor harvests, aggravated by falling prices, contributing to outbreaks of famine in 1728.[9]

Ironically, however, it was the bleakness of that reality which provided the spur for the expression of a radical political and economic outlook which in turn spawned a tangibly patriotic movement that has since been described as a brand of 'economic nationalism'.[10] That movement derived pivotal support from second and third-generation settlers who were by commitment reformist and were impelled by a need to secure improved conditions for their adopted country. The publication of William Molyneaux's controversial *The Case of Ireland Stated* (1698) marked the beginning of that campaign. Arguing that the subordination of the Irish legislature was illegal and unprecedented, Molyneaux made a bold claim for Irish legislative independence.[11]

Although his publication was the object of hostility in the House of Commons and was censured by a Committee of Commons, subsequent editions were published[12] and its contentions provided the sinews for further demands for legislative and economic emancipation for Ireland. Consistent with these sentiments and chiming with an emerging instinct for economic expansion, Thomas Prior's *List of Irish Absentees* (1729) indicated those who thrived abroad on rent wrung from the Irish tenantry,[13] and in the same year Arthur Dobs contributed further to the controversial debate with his *Trade and Improvement of Ireland*.[14] Above all, however, it was Dean Swift who best captured this new-found spirit of national enterprise. Laced with generous measures of biting satire and irony, his pamphlets attracted a wider audience and further inflamed the demand that Ireland's economic destiny be left in the hands of a native Parliament.

One other important context must be acknowledged. The Royal Dublin Society was heir to a marginal scientific movement inspired by the Hartlib circle in Ireland during the period of interregnum. Although the precise proportions of that enterprise are not easily established, there remains sufficient evidence to suggest that through the activities of Myles Symner, Archbishop Ussher and Robert Child Ireland was a least alert to the advances of the 'New Learning'.[15] The founding of the Dublin Philosophical Society in 1683 may be attributable, in part, to the endeavours of these forerunners. Designed along structures that were noticeably similar to the Royal Society in London (founded 1660),[16] the Dublin Philosophical Society had a career that was both short-lived and fitful. Nevertheless, a precedent had been established for the founding of formal scientific societies in Ireland which was in keeping with the more general pattern then emerging in Europe and in England.

In 1731 one fundamental difference was evident, however. The Royal Dublin Society, as will be observed from its stated objectives, was overtly utilitarian in aspect and was much less theoretically oriented than its precursors, the Royal Society and the Dublin Philosophical Society. The faith its members had in the possibility of regenerating society through agricultural and industrial production had obvious implications for education, and further evidence of this drift towards utilitarianism is manifest in the educational writings of other eighteenth-century authors. Two examples will serve to illustrate this trend. The Chief Secretary for Ireland, Thomas Orde, in a plea for a reformed educational system (1787) called, in particular, for a syllabus comprising several branches of learning, which included accounts, navigation, mathematics, husbandry, mechanics, geometry and manufacture. The purpose of this revision, he observed, was to educate the most useful members of society, 'the artificer, the farmer, the accountant and the manufacturer'.[17]

Equally innovative in this regard was Robert Burrows' book, *Observations on the Course of Science Taught at Present in Trinity College, Dublin*, published in 1792. His utilitarian arguments were posited on the premise that

> The great Seminaries of public Education should certainly teach that knowledge which is attended with substantial practical utility for the Community at large: and when the quantity of this necessary knowledge is considered, together with the shortness of time in which it is to be acquired, it must be clear there is but little room left for teaching anything else.[18]

It was the intention of the Royal Dublin Society, therefore, to convert the sum of these utilitarian principles into practice and that commitment was clearly set down in its constitution. The 19th rule stated that

> every member of this society at his admission be desired to choose some particular subject either in Natural History, or in Husbandry or agriculture or Gardening or some species of Manufacture of other branch of improvement and make it his business by reading what has been printed on that subject by conversing with them who made it their profession or by making his own experiments, to make himself master thereof and report in writing the best account they can get by experiment or inquiry relating thereunto.[19]

Furthermore, the 20th rule emphasized, in true accord with the tenets of Salomon's House, the importance of the empirical collection and compilation of appropriate data.[20] At a meeting on 7 April 1737 it was agreed that the papers and findings of each scientific meeting be published, once they amounted to a sufficient number, and that these were then to be made available for distribution throughout the country.[21] Aaron Rhames was appointed first printer to the Society, and the first publication was a work entitled *Horse Houghing Husbandry,* by Jethro Tull.[22] The Society also engaged in practical experiments, raising different kinds of trees, plants and roots, and for that purpose a plot of land adjacent to the city was acquired.[23]

In an effort to cultivate and reward Irish inventive genius the introduction of a premium system was a further important aspect of the Society's educational campaign from an early date. A committee was assembled to manage the scheme and the expertise of those qualified in matters of husbandry, trade and manufacture was solicited to adjudicate at premium contests. Subsequently, national prizes were awarded in the categories of hops, flax, malt liquor, earthenware, and lace.[24]

One of the earliest and more direct educational undertakings on the part of the Society was the establishment of a drawing school in 1746. To accommodate this new venture premises were secured at Shaw's Court in Dublin and Mr West from Waterford was appointed drawing mater in 1750. Initially the main emphasis was on ornamental drawing, but gradually the syllabus was expanded to include figure drawing, architectural drawing and modelling in clay.[25]

At the beginning of the nineteenth century, the Royal Dublin Society began to devote more attention to scientific development. Conscious, no doubt, of the many newly founded scientific institutions throughout the United Kingdom, it appointed a committee to report on the progress of the recently established London Institution. That report revealed the Society was well abreast of developments elsewhere but called for a more total approach to the diffusion of scientific knowledge.[26] Motivated by this recommendation, the Society set aside accommodation for professorships in hydraulics, mechanics and allied subjects. Between the years 1800 and 1804 a sum in excess of £17,000 was expended in the renovation of premises at Poolbeg Street to facilitate the new scientific expansion.[27] The noted scientist, Sir Humphry Davy, was invited as guest lecturer in 1810 and again in 1811.[28] Two new appointments were made in 1812; Professor Jameson of Edinburgh as professor of mineralogy and Richard Griffith as mining engineer.

In 1834 a young Robert Kane[29] was appointed lecturer in natural philosophy. Kane's impact, as is well known, was immediate and enduring, and his popularity as a public lecturer at home and abroad was widely acclaimed. Of his course of public lectures at the Society in 1838 the *Freeman's Journal* recorded that

> the learned and deservedly popular gentleman awakened so strong an interest in the public mind that the theatre of the society was found incapable of accommodating the numbers who were anxious to avail themselves of this fascinating mode of instruction.[30]

By the 1830s the Royal Dublin Society had achieved considerable success, support and status. On the scientific front much progress had been made and this was accompanied by consistent growth in its agricultural department. It was against the foil of this success, then, that the controversy to which the Society fell victim in 1835 stands out in sharp contrast because of its sometimes bitter, sometimes petty, nature, but principally for its having tarnished the pedigree of the Society, which until then had insulated itself against the social, religious and political rancour which characterized the opening decades of the nineteenth century in Ireland. Over the period 1825-35 allegations that the Society was quickly developing into a club constituted of Tory supporters and members of the Established Church were becoming more widespread. These suspicions culminated in the rejection of the application of Archbishop Daniel Murray (Roman Catholic Archbishop of Dublin) for membership on 25 November 1835. While Dr Murray preferred that the matter rest and though he sought to court no controversy by it the whole affair was to have more far-reaching effects.[31]

In 1836 William Smith O'Brien moved, in Parliament, for an inquiry into the administration of the Society on the grounds that it was not performing as useful a national service as would justify its parliamentary grant. He held the Society to be inaccessible to the public generally and believed it to be of the character of a club. Moreover, he remarked on the Society's failure to reform itself after the *Select Committee of Inquiry into Irish Miscellaneous Estimates* (1829)[32] had directed that admission by ballot be discontinued along with other practices of the Society, especially the purchase of newspapers for the reading room. Mr Frederick Shaw addressed the House on behalf of the Society detailing its record and pointing up the national loss which would ensue were the Society to be circumscribed in any way. After further debate the House divided, indicating a majority of 49 to 13 in favour of an inquiry.[33]

Under the chairmanship of William Smith O'Brien the inquiry sat for five months and interviewed a total of seven witnesses, all of whom were prominent in the affairs of the Society. The commissioners themselves tended to be drawn from those who sought reform - a clear indication of where the government stood.[34] The Society's admission procedure, and more specifically the Murray case, formed the staple of the debate.[35] In addition, the possibility of extending the Society's facilities to the provinces came under scrutiny and the Society's administrative structures naturally did not escape attention.[36]

When finally presented the report contained a total of fourteen recommendations. Admission procedure was to be less inhibiting. Newspapers and political journals were to be prohibited in the library and reading room. At least one lecture course, free of admission, was to be given annually. By far the most important and far-reaching of the proposals was that which recommended an increased role for the Society on a national scale. It was urged that the Society extend its activities to the provinces on a more permanent basis whereby lecturers were to be despatched to deliver courses at rural centres.[37]

Administration did not, on this occasion at any rate, lag behind suggestion. The reaction to this recommendation was swift and came to remarkable fruition with the introduction of what became known as the 'provincial lecture scheme'.[38] This new enterprise was managed by a specially designated committee and a sum of £500 from the annual grant was set aside to fund the undertaking. In execution of its duty the committee proceeded with an agreed set of criteria. When an application was received from a particular quarter it was reviewed on the basis of population and the facilities available at the centre in question. The applicant party had to guarantee an advance contribution of £10 to cover expenses. When the committee was satisfied on these matters a lecturer was then commissioned and assigned to the specific locality.[39] The provincial lecture scheme met with immediate success. A detail of the expenditure of the £500 allocated for the year 1844 is revealing of its popularity (see Table 1)[40] If in the financial context of the mid-nineteenth century a fee of £40 appears somewhat expensive it should be explained that a course of lectures often involved as many as ten individual lecturers, rarely fewer than four.[41]

Table 1.

Royal Dublin Society, a detail of the expenditure of the sum of £500 granted by Parliament-session 1844, for defraying the expenses of professors giving lectures in provincial towns in Ireland.

Lecture	Subject	Place	Amount	Date
Mr E B Brayley	Geology	Cork	£40.0.0	March 1844
Doctor Meyler		Maryborough	£40.0.0	May 1844
same	same	Nenagh	£40.0.0	June 1844
Doctor Cahill	Astronomy	Carrick-on Stuir	£40.0.0	May 1844
Surgeon Lover	Physiology	Waterford	£40.0.0	May 1844
Doctor Kane	Natural Philosophy	same	£40.0.0	June 1844
same	same	Galway	£40.0.0	June 1844
Professor Davy	Agricultural Chemistry	Killarney	£40.0.0	June 1844
same	same	Coleraine	£40.0.0	June 1844
Mr Tho. Odham	Geology	Clonmel	£40.0.0	June 1844
Doctor Allman	Natural History	same	£40.0.0	June 1844
Professor Nicholl	Astronomy	Cork	£40.0.0	June 1844
Doctor Meyler	Carriage of apparatus		£4.0.0	
Dr Kane	do	do	£2.19.6	
Professor Davy	do	do	£8.0.0	
Advertisments-postage etc			£3.5.0	

Demands upon the provincial lecture committee were ever-increasing. In 1845, for instance, since the total allocation had been utilized, applications received from Newry, Dungannon, Armagh and Parsonstown (Birr), were refused.[42] In the same year the Waterford Mechanics' Institute, along with several other bodies, petitioned Parliament to have the subsidy for provincial lecturers increased, but to no avail.[43] In fact, so numerous were the claims made upon the whole system that it gave rise to a certain degree of tension between regional institutions and the Royal Dublin Society itself. In 1840 the provincial lecture committee found it necessary to insist upon closer adherence to the rules pertaining to the lecture system.

It was noted that applicants had hitherto assumed the right to nominate the lecturer of their choice along with the lecture subject. This practice, it was believed, led to abuse since some of the lecturers selected by applicants gained that nomination through local influence and popularity rather than on professional merit. It was, therefore, perceived that to put the lecture scheme beyond abuse the provincial lecture committee would itself have the authority to nominate the lecturer and, should that not be possible, a prominent lecturer known to the committee was to be appointed. Furthermore, it was directed that the subject of the lecture courses be confined to the stipulated syllabus, which constituted three main areas: natural history, chemistry and natural philosophy.[44]

Dissatisfaction at the introduction of these regulations was expressed by the Dundalk Mechanics' Institute and particularly by the Drogheda Mechanics' Institute.[45] The Drogheda discontent was transmitted in a 'Memorial of the Lords of the Treasury' in 1849, and again in 1851 - this time to the Lord Lieutenant.[46] In the latter memorial it was alleged that the grant was being mis-appropriated sine applicants were no longer afforded the right of selection. The Drogheda Mechanics' Institute believed this to be detrimental to its interests, for, it was said, lecturers popular in the area always succeeded in drawing an attendance, whereas other lecturers no less eminent but lacking in local appeal failed to attract the same attention. The memorial contained a further, more significant objection. Lecturers from the Royal Dublin Society, it was claimed, were 'better adapted for giving instruction to pupils in high Schools of Science than imparting that elementary knowledge necessary for the artizan, and labourer of the provinces'.[47] Stung no doubt by these criticisms the Royal Dublin Society replied:

> The committee are of the opinion that a sound and useful knowledge can best be disseminated by sending down lecturers not locally connected, and who from their practice and experience in metropolitan institutions must necessarily be considered as most competent to inculcate and diffuse such improvements as are progressing in scientific learning.[48]

With this, the Society remained adamant that no change was to be made in the procedure for appointing lecturers. Despite these differences the provincial lecture scheme continued to prosper. The lecturers rarely failed to attract a numerous attendance, usually constituted of small merchants in country towns, members of mechanics' institutes and literary and scientific societies, and senior pupils from the national school system.

With first hand experience of the provincial lecture scheme Robert Kane reflected in 1864:

> I believe them to be extremely useful. I believe they are the means of diffusing through the country at large a taste for the appreciation of scientific studies that is highly valuable, tending to give the young men in the country towns something to think of other than drilling and marching, and tending to turn their attention to employment which would be really productive of benefit to the country and to themselves.[49]

That the provincial lecture scheme brought benefits to many regional scientific institutions, not least the mechanics' institutes, and that the scheme made a significant contribution to the advancement and diffusion of scientific knowledge is lucidly attested to in enthusiastic responses to a circular of the Science and Art Department in 1860 which attempted to measure the value and utility of the provincial lectures. The Bailieborough Literary Society responded: 'That they have been of use, real use, in forming a taste for practical science, and in directing the minds of many young persons to valuable subjects they treat of, I have not the slightest doubt.[50] In Ballymahon the lecturers 'gave the greatest satisfaction and were well attended by all classes and creeds; some having walked long distances to be present'.[51] Grateful, too, was the Clonmel Mechanics' Institute:

> The lectures of such men as Sir Robert Kane...Professor Nicoll, Professor Allman......Davy, Sullivan........and others, which were attended by large audiences, could not fail to make a very useful impression on the minds of our citizens, and to this, in a great measure the Committee attribute the growth, extension and success of the Clonmel Mechanics' Institute.[52]

It was with a sense of bitter disappointment, then, that the abrupt decision to discontinue the provincial lecture scheme was greeted in 1860. By that time the Science and Art Department had been established and on the introduction of the payment by results system science schools and classes had become more numerous in Ireland. The provision of provincial lectures with a state subsidy of £500 was consequently deemed superfluous by a penny-pinching Treasury and the subsidy was withdrawn.[53] That decision, not unexpectedly, did little to enhance the popularity of the South Kensington Institution in Ireland, and over the period of the following decade, 1860-70, a campaign to secure for Ireland a separate and native Science and Art Department was energetically mounted.[54] Although at first conceded in 1869[55] and then brazenly reneged upon at the intrigueful instigation of the bureaucrats of South Kensington,[56] that objective was finally accomplished in 1899 with the passing of the Agriculture and Technical Instruction (Ireland) Act.[57] The outgrowth of that legislation was the establishment of the Department of Agriculture and Technical Instruction, which then undertook, as part of a wider brief, the responsibilities previously discharged from London.[58]

121

NOTES

[1] *Minutes of the Meetings of the (Royal) Dublin Society,* 25 June 1731. The Society was incorporated in 1749, from which time it became the Royal Dublin Society and received an annual state grant of between £7000 and £10,000.

[2] Thomas Prior (1682-1761) is generally regarded as the founder of the Society. He acted as secretary for twenty years. See H. F. Berry, *A History of the Royal Dublin Society,* London, 1915, p. 7.

[3] Thomas Molyneaux (1661-1733) was the brother of William Molyneaux, author of the controversial *The Case of Ireland Stated,* published in 1698.

[4] Arthur Dobs (1689-1765), was Surveyor General in Ireland and had an intimate knowledge of its agricultural and trade problems.

[5] William Maple was keeper of Parliament House and through his good offices the Society was afforded rooms there until more permanent accommodation could be found. See Berry, *A History of the Royal Dublin Society,* p. 10.

[6] *Mins. Dublin Society,* 8 July 1731.

[7] L.M. Cullen, *An Economic History of Ireland since 1660,* London, 1972, pp 34-44.

[8] *Ibid.*

[9] *Ibid.*

[10] J.G. Simms, *Colonial Nationalism, 1698-1776,* Cork, 1976, p. 9.

[11] *Ibid.*

[12] E. Curtis and R., B. MacDowell (eds.), *Irish Historical Documents, 1172-1922,*
London, 1943, p. 183

[13] Desmond Clarke, *Thomas Prior 1681-1751, Founder of the Royal Dublin Society,*
Dublin, 1951, pp 16-17.

[14] Cullen, *An Economic History of Ireland,* p. 51.

[15] K, Theodore Hoppen, *The Common Scientist in the Seventeenth Century,* London, 1970, pp 1-24; also T. C. Barnard. 'Myles Symner and the New Learning', *Royal Society of Antiquities of Ireland Journal,* 102, 1972, pp 129-42; and T. C. Barnard. 'The Hartlib Circle and the origins of the Dublin Philosophical Society' *Irish Historical Studies,* xix, 1974, pp 56-70.

[16] Barnard, 'The Hartlib circle' p. 62.

[17] 'An overlooked system of national and technical education for Ireland', *Irish Builder,* 1 June 1882, p. 157.

[18] Robert Burrows, *Observations on the Course of Science Taught at Present in Trinity College, Dublin ,* Dublin, 1792, pp 6-7.

[19] W. H. Brayden (ed.), *Royal Dublin Society Bi-Centerary Souvenir, 1731-1931,* Dublin, 1931, p. 11.

[20] Terence de Vere White, *The Story of the Royal Dublin Society,* Tralee, 1955, p. 15.

[21] *Mins. Dublin Society,* 7 April 1737.

[22] Berry, *A History of the Royal Dublin Society,* p. 11.

[23] *Mins. Dublin Society,* 12 September 1733.

[24] *The Royal Dublin Society,* Dublin 1965, 3 (no author).

[25] Berry, *A History of the Royal Dublin Society,* pp 111-12.

[26] de Vere White, *The Story of the Royal Dublin Society,* p. 23.

[27] *Ibid.,* p. 58.

[28] *Report of the Select Committee on the Royal Dublin Society* (1836) (445.) XII 355 (q.) 501.

[29] Robert Kane (1809-90 - afterwards Sir Robert) was a keen advocate of industrial education, a founder member of the Dublin Mechanics' Institute (2nd phase 1837) and a prominent lecturer in industrial education in Ireland and England. He was appointed first President of Queen's College Cork (1845) and Director of the Museum of Irish Industry (1847). He is most noted for his publication *The Industrial Resources of Ireland* (1844).

[30] *Feeeman's Journal,* 26 July 1838, 'Dr Kane's lectures - Dublin Society'.

[31] de Vere White, *The Story of the Royal Dublin Society,* p. 92.

[32] *Report from the Select Committee into the Miscellaneous Estimates Relative to the Royal Dublin Society* (1829) (342) IV 127.

[33] *Analysis of the Report and Epitome of the Evidence taken before a Select Committee of the House of Commons in the Session of 1836 on the Royal Dublin Society: together with Notes and Illustrations,* A Member of the Society , Dublin, 1836, p. 31.

[34] The committee of 15 members included William Smith O'Brien, Mr Sharman Crawford, Mr Wyse, Mr More O'Ferall and Mr Villiers Stewart.

[35] *Report of the Select Committee* (1836). See, e.g. 1518-32, 2480-8.

[36] *Ibid.* See, for example, 906-28.

[37] *Report of the Select Committee (1836),* xix-xxi.

[38] *Announcement of Regulations for the Administration of Provincial Lectures* (Royal Dublin Society, 6 May 1844).

[39] *Queries to be Answered by Applicants for Provincial Lecturers, and Returned as Soon as Possible* (Royal Dublin Society, 1851) (Chief Secretary's Office Registered Papers [CSORP] 91913. State Paper Office Ireland [SPOI].

[40] *Royal Dublin Society, a Detail of the Expenditure of the Sum of £500 Granted by Parliament - Session 1844, for Defraying the Expenses of Professors Giving Lectures in Provincial Towns in Ireland,* 14 February 1845 (CSORP 91913, SPOI).

[41] Public Announcement, *Clonmel Mechanics' Institution: Syllabus of a Popular Course of Lectures* (1844).

[42] *Royal Dublin Society to T. F. Freemantle,* 15 February 1845 (CSORP 91913, SPOI).

[43] *Mr Davis, Secretary Waterford Mechanics' Institute to Sir Robert Peel,* 18 February 1846 9CSORP 91913, SPOI).

[44] *Royal Dublin Society, Report of the Committee on Provincial Lectures to the Council and by the Council Ordered to be Transmitted to the Several Bodies Applying for Lectures,* J. M. Neligan, Chairman, 24 April 1849. That report comprised 13 individual resolutions.

[45] *To His Excellency George William Frederick Eark of Clarendon, Lord Lieutenant Geraal Governor of Ireland. The Meorial of the Myor Aldermen and Burgesses of the Borough of Drogheda,* Monday 9 June 1851 (CSORP 91913, SPOL).

[46] *Ibid.*

[47] *Statement Adopted by the Committee on Provincial Lectures and Ordered to be Transmitted by the Hon Secretaries of the Royal Dublin Society of His Excellency the Lord Lieutenant in Reference to a Memorial from the Corporation of Drogheda,* 1853 (CSORP 91913, SPOL).

[48] *Report from the Select Committee on Scientific Institutions (Dublin); with the Proceedings, Minutes of Evidence, Appendix and Index* (1864) (495) XIII.I. (q) 1404.

[49] *Report from the Select Committee on Scientific Institutions (Dublin)* (1864), Appendix III.

[50] *Ibid.*

[51] *Ibid.*

[52] *Ibid.*

[53] *Report of the Commission o the Science and Art Department in Ireland: 1868/69, Vol. II; Minutes of Evidence, Appendix and Index* (1868-9), (4103-1) XXIV.42., (qq) 1321-8.

[54] *Ibid., Appendix I, 650-3*

[55] *Ibid., 4099*

[56] George Butler Bradshaw, *Condemned for their Country: Or 'No Irish Need Apply', an uthentic but Startling Expose of the Delinquencies of South Kensington Museum; and a Plea for the Projected 'Royal Institute'* (Dublin, 1868), 182-201.

[57] *62 and 63 Vict., c. 50, The Agriculture and Technical Instruction (Ireland) Act 1899.*

[58] *Ibid.,* Part I, Section 2, pa.2.

9

POPULAR MEMORY AND IDENTITY: STREET BALLADS IN NORTH MUNSTER IN THE NINETEENTH CENTURY.

MAURA CRONIN

In January 1850 a letter under the pseudonym 'Felon Peasant' appeared in the radical nationalist newspaper, *The Irishman*, describing in romantic terms the influence of the broadside ballads of the time:

> ...The ballads... are to be found in the pockets of every peasant in the country - read and sung by each fireside... they keep alive in the heart of the Irish peasant the sense of bondage - the deep unquenchable hatred of the oppressor..[The ballads] are the literature of the peasantry and a ballad singer is a more powerful missionary of the cause than a thousand pamphlets.[1]

More critical observers described the ballads as 'thousands of yards of nonsense daubed on tea-paper', pointing out their combination of political naiveté and literary awkwardness and attempting to supplant them with more refined patriotic poems more recently described as 'lace curtain ballads'.[2] These latter poems, often themselves of little literary merit but extremely emotive when wedded to appropriate airs, were mainly the production of the Young Ireland movement of the 1840s, though the way had been opened for them by the patriotic compositions of Thomas Moore in the late eighteenth and early nineteenth centuries. Whatever their literary status, these more sophisticated patriotic songs certainly succeeded in their main purpose of rousing nationalistic sentiments and creating and perpetuating a set of historical myths which became part of the stock-in-trade of history textbooks after the creation of the new state in 1922. Until the 1960s (and perhaps later) Moore's 'Let Erin Remember' and 'O, breathe not his name', along with Davis' 'A Nation Once Again' and 'The West's Awake' remained among the most rousing songs of the nationalist tradition. Other patriotic poems of the mid-century, particularly those of Aubrey de Vere, which are very relevant in the Limerick context, never developed beyond the poetry stage to become popular songs. Nonetheless, they remained prominent in the repertoire of patriotic verse-speakers into the mid-twentieth century, while the great depth of feeling accompanying their recitation bore testimony to the sincerity (if not the historical accuracy) which prompted their composition in the first place.

While the Davis-type ballads did, in the latter part of the nineteenth century, become interwoven at times with the more rumbustious and vibrant street-ballads, the two genres remained largely separate and distinct. So what were these less refined street ballads? The descendants of a very ancient genre of popular poetry whose rhythm may have been geared to accompany dancing, ballads were generally built on four to eight line stanzas with alternate lines rhyming. This stylistic simplicity was matched by a thematic simplicity. Usually based on a single incident and underdeveloped characters, the focus was on narrative rather than analysis, so that all was black and white - spotless heroes, base villains - and no attempt was made to progress beyond the majority value system of the community from which the balladeer sprang.[3]

All these elements attach to the ballads sung around north Munster during the nineteenth century, but some surprising features also emerge, relevant less to the style than to the theme of the compositions in question. The patriotic poets of the Young Ireland school had understandably concentrated a great deal of their attention on the events of the late seventeenth century when composing ballads relevant to Limerick and the surrounding areas. The *Nation* newspaper and the repeatedly published songbook, *Spirit of the Nation*, churned up a continual diet of the events of the Williamite wars and their aftermath with such poems as de Vere's 'Ballad of Sarsfield', 'The Last Struggle', and the more famous 'Ballad of Athlone', Davis' 'Death of Sarsfield' and 'Battle of Limerick', and Gavan Duffy's 'Rapparees'.[4] However, the common broadsides sold around the fairs and markets of the area largely ignored the events of the 1690s although passing references were made to the main 'highlights' of the period. A ballad sung at Bruff in October 1843 recalled (with delightful disregard for accuracy) the

> Sage [*sic*] of Aughrim when Sarsfield was betrayed,
> By bribes and villainy they took Athlone and Limerick.[5]

In the same year 'A New Repeal Song' sung at Kilmallock admonished:

> Let the Treaty of Limerick lay [*sic*] fresh in your veins,
> And banish those tyrants as you conquered the Danes.[6]

If such references are evidence of confused historical perspectives, their infrequency also suggests that the Young Ireland recussitation of the events or myths of the 1690s had little immediate impact on the popular mind of the time, even in the very area where one might expect folk memories of a period only 150 years in the past to have survived. Nor had the Young Ireland influence permeated much deeper into the folk mind by the late 1860s, when references to Williamite days were as scarce as ever, though the occasional balladeers did weave the late seventeenth century events into the theme of contemporary sectarian animosity. A singer in Castleconnell fair in 1869, for instance, referred in his ballad 'The Downfall of Heresy' to

> ....what William signed
> When *Shemas* was defeated.[7]

The north Munster folk memory as revealed through the street ballads actually appears quite short-term, certainly not extending back in any meaningful way to the seventeenth century. The only incident from the distant past which was recalled in the popular ballads of this region was the execution of Fr. Nicholas Sheehy in Clonmel in 1766. Charles Kickham's novel, *Knocknagow*, first published in 1873 and based to a certain extent upon his personal observations of south Tipperary life in his youth in the 1830s and '40s, suggested the vibrancy of this popular memory of Fr. Sheehy, and the ballad 'The Shanvanvucht' sung in the country between Borrisokane and Carrick-on-Suir in the summer of 1843 kept the memory alive with promises of future revenge for current ills:

> Remember Fr. Sheehy, says the Shanvanvucht,
> For him our veins are bleeding, says the Shanvanvucht,
> For we're ready at a call and are willing for to fall,
> So we'll thrash the villains all, says the Shanvanvucht.[8]

The Fr. Sheehy reference is, however, the exception which proves the rule that the ballad reflection of folk memory, unlike the artificial historical memory created by Moore, Davis and de Vere, seldom extended back more than half a century. If Davis' poems covered such remote events as the rise and fall of the Fitzgeralds, the death of Eoghan Roe O'Neill and the enactment of the Penal Code, such themes receive next to no mention in the street ballads.[9] Certainly, there were constant references to the 'evil' of the Protestant reformation and to the gory events of the 1798 rebellion, but such references lacked detail and the events were generally used as a backdrop against which to narrate more recent happenings.[10]

The average street ballad in north Munster, as elsewhere, was spawned by contemporary events, chief among which in the 1830s was the anti-tithe agitation which rocked the countryside in Munster and south Leinster until the tithe issue was more or less settled by the Tithe Commutation Act of 1838. Several clashes occurred between the protesting peasantry and the forces of the law during that campaign, several resulting in deaths on both sides. A particularly gruesome incident happened at Carrickshock near

128

Knocktopher in south Kilkenny in 1831 when the peasantry ambushed those going to enforce the collection of tithe - an incident which resulted in several dead on the authorities' side and became the focus for vicious (if understandable) peasant triumphalism for a long time to come and for many miles outside the original scene of the conflict.[11] By August 1832 a ballad called, appropriately, 'The Downfall of Tithes' was being sung in Clonmel and also as far away as Kilmallock, some fifty miles from Knocktopher, to commemorate the incident:

> May Heaven prosper you, sweet Knocktopher,
> No bard but Homer could your praises chant.
> You loyal subjects that fought victorious,
> Fire and smoke could not your courage daunt...
> ... Who could desire to see better sporting,
> To see them groping among the rocks,
> Their skulls all fractured and eyeballs broken,
> Their fine long noses and ears cut off...[12]

Vicious stuff, indeed. Many of Davis' 'lace curtain ballads' were not without their own modicum of violent sentiments:

> .... May God wither up their hearts,
> May their blood cease to flow,
> May they walk in living death -
> They who poisoned Eoghan Roe.[13]

Davis' violent sentiments, however, were not in the verbal technicolour displayed by the street ballads. Was the balladeer's delight in recounting gory deeds partly due to a social difference between him and the Davis-style poets of the Young Ireland revival? The latter were largely lower middle class men and women and 'respectable' artisans with, what can be described as, Victorian sensibilities and an abhorrence of violence. The balladeers, on the other, hand, anonymous though they usually were, seem to have come from the lower classes of both country and town - a sector of society which was in no way sheltered from violence. The nature of agrarian violence in the nineteenth century, perpetrated against

129

humans and animals alike, bore witness to a rural lower class inured to violence through circumstance and necessity, while urban violence during foot riots, elections and trade union disputes was equally frightening in its intensity. To such a society the niceties of middle class refinement and the O'Connellite message of passive resistance can have had little real meaning. The ballads, therefore, with their ultra-gory language, act as a window into what the 'lower orders' perceived (often correctly) as oppression. While the street ballads with their violent language, then, are both comic and deeply upsetting, they are more revealing of folk attitudes in the nineteenth century than Davis' and Young Ireland's poetry could ever aspire to be.

The street ballad, moreover, combined the role of 'Top Ten' and news bulletin, as it transmitted news from faraway places, kept alive the sense of grievance or triumphalism which such events produced, and at the same time was a source of entertainment for the listener and remuneration for the singer. The news transmission aspect was vital. If the Carrickshock incident was commemorated, as noted above, in one ballad sung in Kilmallock in late 1832, it was being publicised a year previously even further away in Killaloe by a separate ballad, 'The Roman Bull of Wollengrange' sung by a ballad singer who had only just arrived from Kilkenny. On this occasion the news spreading function of the ballad was underlined by the fact that the same ballad singer was singing and selling another similar piece. This was an 'Elegy on the Death of Catherine Maher' which detailed a further tithe-related confrontation from the less distant location of Thurles, while at the same time a ballad sung in Fethard, Co. Tipperary, narrated the events of a County Wexford tithe incident.[14] In like manner, news travelled outwards from north Munster to other provinces. In 1852 a broadside prose narrative entitled 'Murderous attack on the people at Six-Mile Bridge' describing the shooting of election rioters in County Clare, was found circulating around Carlow, almost a hundred miles from the scene of the event and being 'eagerly bought up by the people'.[15] Nor did the subject matter of the news-transmitting ballad deal exclusively with violent and popular incidents. It could also act as publiciser of parliamentary debates and decisions. Such was the case with a ballad sung at Carrick-on-Suir in June 1843 which lauded a parliamentary speech given by Mark Blake of Ballinafad, M.P. for Mayo - an unlikely subject for a ballad sung in Munster.[16] In some ways, the ballad could fulfil for the poor the function of the local newspaper whose price and limited distribution network put it outside the reach of the rural lower classes. The broadside bridged this information gap by reporting on significant events and public meetings as in the case of 'A New Song on the Glorious Repeal Meeting at Cashel' sung from Carrick-on-Suir to Roscrea in the summer of 1843.[17] Where ballad composers found their material is a matter of conjecture. Some may have been gleaned from newspaper reports and more may have come from eye-witness accounts, but until further detailed study is carried out on the subject, this question must remain unanswered.

If we look on the ballad as the nineteenth century version of the 'Top Ten', then the relative popularity of different ballads at different times must be considered. The chart-topper for 1843, unconfined by locality, was undoubtedly the seditious ballad entitled 'A Speedy Repeal' sung around Roscrea and Borrisokane in June of that year. In the same month it was also being sung in Carlow; by July was circulating as far south as Waterford and as far west as Galway; in September it was reported from County Cork; and by October it was spreading northwards through counties Louth and Tyrone.[18] Though the anti-Protestant sentiments of this particular ballad were hardly any more virulent than those of the average ballad of the pre-famine period, they were considered, in the highly excited atmosphere of the 'Repeal Year' called by O'Connell for 1843, to be particularly provocative:

> Ever since the reformation our heroes suffered sore,
> The tyrants, thank God, is broke around the Shamrock shore.
> Our clergymen they will attend whilst blood runs in their veins,
> And Granua's sons with pikes and guns will chase them like the Danes.....
> ....We'll have an Irish parliament, fresh laws we'll dictate
> Or we'll have satisfaction for the year of ninety-eight...
> Then Luther's generation must take a speedy flight

131

> And go into Hanover from the land of sweet delight.
> All heretics must cut their sticks and leave this fertile land
> For 'twas decreed that Harry's breed would fall by God's
> command.[19]

It was not surprising that in the years immediately preceding the famine Protestants all over Munster were terrified of a popular catholic uprising aimed at their destruction. The memories of the sectarian confrontations of 1798 were not far in the past, and what the Protestant population feared the catholic lower classes anticipated with a wicked delight - the extirpation of 'heretics' and the seizure of their lands and privileges (perceived as well as real). It was no accident that the favourite villains of the ballads were largely classified on religious grounds, and from the past came a veritable rogues' gallery which included not just the inevitable 'Danes', but Luther, Calvin, Henry VIII, Elizabeth I and Cromwell, while from more recent times came Pitt and Castlereagh who 'stole away the parliament from Erin', the tories, the 'Orange dogs', and Protestants in general - the 'tyrants of Luther's black race'.[20] Though the ballads made occasional gestures towards a more tolerant attitude based on the conciliatory policies of O'Connell, and though everyday relations between Protestants and Catholics were not inevitably hostile, the ballads kept up the sectarian dimension of popular identity.

This sectarianism was at its most virulent in the 1830s and '40s when the anti-tithe agitation, the dissemination of spurious anti-Protestant prophecies like those of Pastorini, and the hopes of great change to accompany O'Connell's political movements combined to produce a highly volatile atmosphere of mass expectancy:

> All heretics must cut their sticks
> And leave this fertile land,
> For 'twas decreed that Harry's breed
> Should fall by God's command.[21]

A modern study of nineteenth century Irish popular politics suggests that the theme and the language of the ballads became less sectarian in the latter half of the nineteenth century:

After the famine, the language of the songs became so laundered as to render them (if not their reciters) almost acceptable in the most bourgeois of surroundings. A kind of indirect neutering had spread from Young Ireland's genteel warblings and from the artificial 'literary' ballads increasingly popular in nineteenth century drawing rooms.[22]

Though this is certainly true in a general sense, there were some exceptions. In the early 1850s, for instance, the Ecclesiastical Titles Bill and the Stockport Riots produced another crop of sectarian ballads - though not in any way as flourishing a crop as in the previous two decades. Again, twenty years later in the wake of church disestablishment, yet another series of triumphalist anti-Protestant ballads appeared. Though only a handful on this occasion, these ballads' sentiments and mode of expression were as violent as anything of the pre-famine period. At Castleconnell, County Limerick, in August 1869, the topical song 'The Fenians' Welcome to Ireland', while largely substituting 'Saxons' for 'heretics' as the villains, still referred in 1830s fashion to 'tyrants of Luther's black race' while a ballad sung in Kilmallock in the following month was even more explicitly sectarian. This latter, appropriately entitled 'A New Song on the Downfall of Heresy' crowed (none too poetically) over the disestablishment of the church and what it gleefully foresaw as the outcome:

> The parson now will lose his fat,
> His cheeks that were rosy is [sic] slacking.
> His coach and four horses and all his stock
> Are terminated nearly out.
> His wife must sell her vail [sic] and hat
> And buy India mail [sic] for herself.
> She must wean herself from bread and tea,
> To potatoes and buttermilk.[23]

The lack of character analysis which had always been a feature of the ballad genre certainly applied, then, to the popular street broadsides of north and mid-Munster in the nineteenth century.

Nothing stirred the vocal chords of the singer or the emotions of the audience quite like a truly hateful villain, and with the wide choice open to the balladeer - from the 'heretics' of the past to those of their own day - there was no dearth of raw material for topical songs. Heroes of varied hues were equally accessible to the popular bard, and as the villains were of deepest black, the heroes were blameless.

Chief hero of the pre-famine ballads was, of course, O'Connell, who was celebrated with a strange mixture of awe and intimacy. Credited with aims and accomplishments which frequently had no basis in reality, he was the messiah, the hope of his people for, as the ballad singer at Kilmallock expressed it in August 1832,

> When all our woes are terminated
> And all those tithes are dead and gone,
> Poor Irish captives liberated
> All by the means of our lovely Dan.[24]

A year later at Fethard, Co. Tipperary, an Irish ballad proclaimed in similar vein:

> Tá Donal 'sa throop i gcúis an daingean chugainn
> Is deimhin gurb eagalach don dream nár ghéill;
> Beidh ministrí galla ar ball 'na sagartaibh
> Agus gurb geall le easpaig iad ag scrudú léinn.
> Beidh *Orangemen* 'na dteannta ar slabhraibh ceangailte
> Is ná leofaidís labhairt ag iarraidh cabhair ar ár n-eaglais,
> Dófaim a leabhair agus mo lom, ní h-eagal dúinn,
> Taimíd 'nár gcodhladh agus ár gcúis dá plé.[25]

Another hope of the pre-famine ballads was Napoleon's son - Young Boney - in whom was seen the continuing possibility of French aid.[26] The revolutionary events in Paris in 1830, when King Charles X was replaced by Louis Philippe, sparked off these groundless hopes again, as John Drew from Patrickswell, singing at Kilmallock in November 1831, proclaimed:

> But now all France is blazing
> With greatest preparation,

I wish they'd wait with patience
To free this country.
To burst their chains asunder
That long have kept them under,
Young Boney and O'Connell
Will set old Ireland free.[27]

Such hopes were short-lived for young Napoleon's death in 1832 put an end to the ballads in his name, while the 1830 revolution in Paris produced a regime which turned out the opposite of revolutionary. Yet even without the 'big names' so popular with the ballad singers, rural and small-town Ireland provided many a 'village Hampden' of its own to stand as hero of the street ballads. Popular priests, along with local businessmen and public officials who took the 'right' side in the political confrontations of the day, found a place in the repertoire of the balladeer. The song 'Fr. Cantwell's Triumph', the singing of which was considered by the authorities as 'calculated to cause a riot' around Thurles in 1853, celebrated the actions of a local priest who roused very understandable Protestant indignation by administering the last sacraments to a dying Protestant woman, while another typical composition sung through the county of Tipperary in 1843 had exhorted its audience to give preference of custom to a Cashel baker who was pro-O'Connell:

Bold Repealers all, both great and small, whenever you are able
You have a loaf from Mr. Nagg's to grace your breakfast table.
Let no man fail with him to deal from the goldsmith to the nailor,
His heart is pure, you may be sure he is a bold Repealer.[28]

The ballads needed martyrs as well as heroes, and those killed in confrontations with the law were given an immortality which they would never have found if their lives had remained untouched by violence. If the newspapers of the time generally took a pro-authority stance, the ballads more than redressed the balance by portraying the popular side not just as victims but as innocent victims. The confrontation between the forces of law and order and the anti-tithe demonstrators at Newtownbarry in County

Wexford in 1831 had been, in reality, the product of provocation on both sides. However, the ballad on the incident, sung around south Tipperary soon afterwards put forth an admittedly trans-parent picture of popular injured innocence:

> A few unfortunate boys some stones they chanced to throw,
> Which gave an opportunity to fill the town with woe,
> The road on all sides those tyrants left streaming with blood,
> Whilst numbers from the carnage slept in the Slaney's flood.[29]

In similar manner, the 'Ellogy [*sic*] on the Death of Catherine Maher' who 'fell a victim to the infernal fury of a nefarious tithe proctor in the parish of Thurles' in 1831, exhorted:

> All you enlightened Christian hearts with me now humbly pray
> That Catherine Maher may find eternal joys on the great Judgement Day

and added a significant postscript in prose reminding the audience that 'this departed heroine hopes her spirit shall not be forgotten.[30] The official press account, needless to say, differed considerably from the ballad's version of events, describing how thirty police protecting a process server were

> furiously assailed by a mob of at least one thousand persons, who commenced pelting the police violently with stones, and using all kinds of threats and gestures at them. Many of the constables were knocked down with stones and several of their carbines were broken in two. The police were in the act of retreating with Fleming [the process server] in order to save his life from the lawless miscreants, when they doubly renewed their attack, by firing on the constables, following it up with a tremendous volley of stones, many of which took effect on the policemen. They at last conceiving of their lives and that of the process server in immediate danger, were obliged to fire on the mob, when one woman was shot dead on the spot and a number of men wounded.[31]

The innocent victim was, thus, a common motif of the ballads of the 1830s and 1840s. From 1848 onwards, however, the motif re-emerged in a new form - i.e. the victim of foreign misrule who had sacrificed himself for his native land. This was the main theme of the ballad entitled 'John Mitchel's Farewell to Ireland' sung in August 1848 at Newcastle West, but through the entire summer of that year reported as popular through the country as far afield as County Longford:

> Farewell fond wife and children dear,
> Your father bids you now farewell,
> Thy piercing words brought forth my tears
> When parting in the felon's cell.
> Yes, dear wife, you to me said:
> 'My hero, yield not to be a slave,
> Bear a patriot's noble name,
> And Heavens bless you when far away.[32]

Two decades later, the tragic martyr-hero had become even more established in broadside literature with the unsuccessful Fenian rising and the imprisonment of many of those involved in the movement. 'Bourke's Dream', a popular ballad sung through out County Limerick in the autumn of 1869, commemorated the imprisonment of Richard O'Sullivan Bourke who had master-minded the abortive attempt to release Fenian prisoners in Manchester in 1867 and whose own unsuccessful prison break attempt occasioned the Clerkenwell explosion and a further penal servitude sentence of fifteen years.[33]

The latter two ballads differ quite obviously from their equivalents of earlier decades, not just in terms of the type of hero-victim they portray, but also in their style of expression and their mastery of English. The ballads of the pre-famine decades, though most of them were written in English, frequently showed a lack of facility with the language, often descending into mere nonsense as they groped for the correct form of expression. The more deliberately nationalistic ballads of the post-1848 period, on the other hand, while cloying and melodramatic in expression, were perfectly at home with the English idiom. They shared the style of the often third-rate patriotic poetry published in the *Nation*, the *United Irishman*, the *Irish People* and similar patriotic periodicals of the time, and were modelled in sentiment on the poems which Young Ireland had produced in the 1840s. The motif of the patriot dreaming of home and of past heroes as he lies languishing in his prison cell (the main theme of 'Bourke's Dream') echoed Kells Ingram's rousing 'Memory of the Dead' and the touching 'Felons of Our Land' as did the theme of the Irish patriot exiled for his country's sake. Rhythm, too, could be borrowed from the 'Davisised' poetry of the 1840s. 'Bourke's Dream', for instance, was exactly modelled on the rhythm of O'Donnell Abu, and presumably sung to the same air:

> On with the Saxon, then,
> Fearing our Fenian men,
> Soon they reeled back from our pike volunteers.
> The cry was loud and shrill -
> 'Wexford and Vinegar Hill,
> New Ross, Fr. Murphy and the Brave Shelmaliers!'[34]

At the same period the 'Fenians' Welcome to Ireland' sung around Castleconnell was to the rhythm and air of the 'Limerick Rake'.[35]

Borrowing from known songs and familiar rhythms was not, however, peculiar to the later ballads. Back in the 1830s and '40s songs from the Gaelic tradition had been used as models, lending not just a rhythm and an air but also familiar refrains and, more importantly, memories of past events which could merge with current happenings to rouse popular excitement. The rhythm and air of the 'Sean Bhean Bhocht' was used for the identically titled ballad 'The Shanvanvucht' sung through County Tipperary in the summer of 1843 and, indeed, for many similar topical doggerels sung outside Munster at this time.[36]

More interesting is the interweaving of an older air and theme in two other topical ballads of the early 1830s. One was 'I dream 'tis asleep though awake I be' sung at Fethard, County Tipperary, in 1831 and obviously based directly on the traditional 'Táim-se im' chodhladh 's ná dhúistear mé'. The Fethard song was much more than the love song which the original Irish version had been. It was typical of the macaronic political songs of its day, the English lines innocuous and those in Irish being quite seditious, ending with the ominous line - 'Táimíd 'nár gcodladh agus ár gcúis dá plé' (We're asleep while our cause is being pleaded) - whose implicit warning was calculated to inspire fear in the hearts of the hated 'heretic'.[37] Equally significant, of course, was the overall format of the song - an *aisling* or vision poem. Work by Ó Madagáin has shown how vibrant the *aisling* form was in County Limerick in the early nineteenth century and this is certainly confirmed from the records of the authorities in Dublin Castle which showed that genre being used on very many occasions by the street ballads - Irish, English and macaronic - to rouse popular political feelings.[38] The second ballad, sung in 1832 throughout the triangle where the counties of Limerick, Cork and Tipperary meet, was alternately entitled 'The Downfall of Tithes' and 'Slievenamon'. It was directly modelled on the Cork poet Micheál Óg Ó Longáin's poignant lament for 'ninety-eight - 'Sliabh na mBan'. Written by a more competent handler of the English language than was 'I dream 'tis asleep though awake I be', this song followed the exact rhythm of Ó Longáin's song, and though its theme was the 1831 tithe affray at Carrickshock, the concluding line of each stanza, like that of the original Irish song, transformed an isolated contemporary event into a link in the chain of historical oppression and a harbinger of the great revenge to come. And so, just as Ó Longáin had promised:

> Go mbeadh claoi ar mhéirleach is an adharc dá shéideadh
> Ar thaobh na gréine de Shliabh na mBan,
> [That the traitors would be defeated and the horn blowing
> On the sunny side of Sliabh na mBan]

so the 1832 song foretold a similar revenge:

> ....Yet all that's past is but a token
> Of what we'll show them on Slievenamon.[39]

Who were the ballad singers who spread these compositions throughout the countryside? In most cases we can only assume that they were poor - though hardly illiterate if they could read the broadsides from which their songs came. It is only in cases in which the law intervened in their activities that we have any information on their identity, and in such instances all we have are names and brief descriptions. John Drew from Loughmore near Patrickswell, County Limerick, for instance, was taken up for singing ballads in Kilmallock in 1831. Michael Waters of Nenagh sang ballads on a circuit between Clonmel and Carrick-on-Suir in 1832, and Mary Anne Maguire of Limerick sang in the environs of the city in 1846.[40] Sometimes, however, the information is more comprehensive and allows one to suggest the background of the balladeers. Women frequently plied the trade, and though the census gives little information on their numerical strength, there was apparently a large number of women singers, many accompanied by their children and apparently supplementing their seasonal begging with ballad singing.[41] Others sang in the company of their husbands, as did Mary Higgins who sang in Bruff in late 1843. Her husband did not sing with her - just as husbands did not actually engage in begging themselves but left it to the womenfolk - but made himself useful by threatening to beat up the policemen who arrested her.[42] Other singers were ex-soldiers or militia men who were supplementing their pensions or had fallen on hard times. In 1843 one John Osborne, discharged from the Seventh Fusiliers, sang at the fair of Roscrea and was apparently still following the career of ballad singer eight years later when (if it's the same John Osborne) he sang at Thurles in the company of one Patrick Fitzpatrick.[43] A similarly circumstanced individual named Delaney, a pensioner of the 88th Foot, sang ballads around Tipperary Town in 1844 while in 1832 one Edmund Barry of Ennis, who described himself as a yeoman, had travelled from Kilrush to Listowel where he was arrested for singing seditious ballads at the fair.[44] Barry had a tale of woe to tell the authorities, a tale which, though hardly without its frills, revealed the marginalised existence of the wandering ballad singer and, surprisingly, his assertiveness in the face of what he considered unfair treatment by the forces of the law:

> Petitioner is a poor man, who in consequence of ill-health is obliged to earn a livelyhood [sic] by singing ballads. That petitioner went to the fair of Listowel in the County of Kerry -

from Kilrush in this county, and was in the act of selling the ballads which he had, when petitioner was arrested by John Redmond, Esq., a Justice of the Peace residing near Listowel. That petitioner was kept three days and three nights confined in a cold bridewell in Listowel by order of Mr. Redmond and was given only potatoes and salt herrings to subsist on, and the cold flags to sleep on...[45]

Other ballad singers were migrant labourers - *spailpíní*- who turned their hands to singing when labouring work was scarce, and who - unlike the female singers and the distressed military pensioners mentioned above - were young, tough and able-bodied.[46]

The main feature of ballad singing was mobility. As we have seen, ballads served in the 1830s as spreaders of news from south Leinster to north Munster and *vice-versa* and even further afield. Ballads sung in Castleconnel and Kilrush recounted events from Kilkenny, while news from Limerick was spread by ballads eastward to Carlow and northward to Longford and the north midlands. The mobility of singer and song alike had the effect of bush telegraph, and if ballad-borne news was never fully accurate with its element of '*dúirt bean liom...*' it was considered all the more detrimental to public order. Both the authorities and respectable citizens alike hated to see ballad singers in town because of their propensity to cause public excitement which frequently led to rioting, but because it was difficult to procure a conviction for ballad singing and because the authorities were genuinely sympathetic towards the miserable singers brought before them, they generally preferred to secure a conviction against the printer of the ballads.

Such an attitude was obvious in the case of Michael Grogan, the Limerick printer brought to trial in 1831 for printing the seditious 'New Song called the Catholic's Advice' - a composition of doubtful literary merit but of a distinctly provocative nature:

> You sons of Milesians, I pray you will cheer up your hearts,
> I hope you'll not blame me for speaking so much of this art,
> For many a brave hero was laid quite flat on his back
> On Aughrim plains or with shame on Limerick trap.[47]

Grogan was netted by the authorities through the use of an approver who went to the printing shop, bought copies of the offending ballad and then testified in court against the printer. Even with this success in tracking down, Grogan, however, a conviction proved difficult to procure. The jury attempted to produce a 'popular' verdict by combining in it the contradictory elements of guilt and exoneration which they ingeniously worded - 'guilty but not with a malicious intent'. Only when the judge refused to accept such a verdict and threatened to summon the court for a second day did the jury bring in a verdict of 'guilty with a recommendation to mercy' - this time in the remarkably short space of two minutes. Grogan got a sentence of either one or three months (different newspaper accounts are in conflict) and was treated to an admonitory speech from the judge who informed him, for the benefit of others, that the sentence would have been much heavier if he had been the author rather than the printer of the ballad.[48] Some printers were, in fact, suspected of being authors of the wares they sold, although most ballads were anonymous compositions. On rare occasions the writer obligingly identified himself, as did the composer of 'Fr. Cantwell's Triumph' in 1852 by concluding his piece with a reference to 'the prayer of the poet, poor Patrick Ryan'.[49] In like manner, the author of the 'Fenians' Welcome to Ireland' in 1869 signed himself the 'Old Poet, J. W.', identified by the Dublin Castle authorities as one Walsh from Limerick who frequently visited O'Sullivan's Hotel in Kilmallock.[50] In most cases, however, the authorship of the ballads remained a matter of conjecture and these elusive bards continued to cause headaches for the enforcers of law and order until the end of the century.

By the 1870s the broadside ballads, though still sold and avidly bought up at fairs and markets, were being gradually replaced by a new headache for the authorities - patriotic songbooks which were sold in shops and railway station stalls in towns like Limerick and Kilkee.[51] These publications were considered less mischievous than the broadside ballads 'because [they were] not disseminated in the same way'.[52] They were much more akin to the parlour ballads of Moore, Davis and de Vere, although they also included a number of rousing numbers from the Fenian tradition - 'The Rising of the

Moon', 'Slievenamon' (Kichham's composition) and 'The Bold Fenian Men'.[53] They were manifestly less sectarian and more nationalistic than the former street ballads, having substituted England for Protestantism as the source of all evils, and while they could hardly be classed as literary, their level of literacy and their facility with the English language (in which they were all written) was far ahead of that of the old broadsides.

Nonetheless, perhaps the function of these more modern popular nationalist songs did not differ fundamentally from that of their predecessors. They promoted a sense of solidarity against the perceived oppressor, a sense of pride in an often imagined past, and an admonition to emulate dead 'heroes' - most of whom had been raised to that status only after their deaths. In many ways, the over-romanticised view of the street ballads which the self-styled 'Felon Peasant' sent to the *Irishman* newspaper back in 1850 still applied to the songs of the later period:

> The same spirit pervades them all - love of country, hatred of the tyrant, and a firm belief in 'a day to come'.[54]

Even if in reality they were, in the words of the earlier cynic, 'nonsense daubed on tea-paper', their role in reflecting - and perhaps forming - popular memory and identity was still significant.

NOTES

[1] *Irishman* 19 January 1850.

[2] Charles Gavan Duffy, *Four Years of Irish History*, Dublin, 1885, p. 66; K. T. Hoppen, *Elections, Politics and Society in Ireland 1832-1885*, Oxford, 1984, p. 428.

[3] I am indebted for this definition of ballads to Fr. Hugh Duffy, Head of the English Department, Mary Immaculate College

[4] Published in many poetry collections of the latter half of the nineteenth century, several of these poems became part of the primary and secondary school English curriculum of the new state after 1922.

[5] Chief Secretary's Officer Registered Papers, Outrage Reports, National Archives of Ireland (cited hereunder as CSORP.OR) 1843, 16/24131.

[6] CSORP.OR 1843 16/22979.

[7] Fenian Papers, National Archives of Ireland (cited hereunder as FP) 1869, 4590R.

[8] CSORP.OR 1843, 27/13, 13337.

[9] Davis' poems on these themes were 'The Geraldines', 'Lament for Eoghan Roe O'Neill', and 'The Penal Days'.

[10] Georges-Denis Zimmermann, *Songs of Irish Rebellion*, Dublin, 1967, pp 35-50.

[11] State of the Country Papers, National Archives of Ireland (cited hereunder as SOC) 1831, L. 1572.

[12] *Ibid.*

[13] 'Lament for Eoghan Roe O'Neill'.

[14] CSORP.OR, 1831, B. 120.

[15] CSORP.OR. 1852/16, filed with 1855/8631.

[16] CSORP.OR. 1843, 27/13343.

[17] CSORP.OR. 1843, 27/12117, 13343.

[18] CSORP.OR. 1843, 5/13187, 3/12391, 11/14217, 6/17767, 28/20575, 20/21769.

[19] CSORP.OR. 1843, 27/12177.

[20] Georges-Denis Zimmermann, *Songs of Irish Rebellion*, p. 135; CSORP.OR. 1832, W/1223, FP 1869, 4681R.

[21] CSORP.OR. 1843, 27/12177.

[22] K. T. Hoppen, *Elections, Politics and Society in Ireland*, p. 427, FP. 1869, 4681R.

[23] FP. 1869, 4681R.

[24] CSORP.OR. 1832, L/1572.

[25] CSORP.OR. 1831, B/101:
   'O'Connell and his forces are holding the fort for us,
   And it will go badly for those who will not yield,
   Foreign ministers [or religion] will soon be made into priests
   And they will study [Catholic] learning as bishops do.
   Orangemen will be with them, bound in chains,
   And they'll have to look for help from our church,
   Their books will be burned and, indeed, there's no fear of us,
   We're asleep as our cause is being pleaded.'

[26] Georges-Denis Zimmermann, *Songs of Irish Rebellion*, pp 32-4.

[27] CSORP.OR. 1831, B/101.

[28] CSORP.OR. 1853/9131, 1843, 27/12117, 13343.

[29] CSORP.OR. 1831, B/101.

[30] CSORP.OR. 1831, B/101.

[31] *Limerick Chronicle* 8, 15 October 1831.

[32] CSORP.OR. 1848, 19/233.

[33] Leon O Broin, *Fenian Fever*, New York, 1971, p. 210, FP 1869, 4681R.

[34] FP 1869, 4681R.

[35] FP, 1869, 4590r.

[36] CSORP.OR 1843, 27/13, 13337; Georges-Denis Zimmermann, *Songs of Irish Rebellion*, pp 133-7.

[37] CSORP.OR 1831, B/101.

[38] Breandán Ó Madagáin, 'Limerick's Heritage of Irish Song' in *North Munster Antiquarian Journal*, vol. xxviii, 1986, pp 84-7.

[39] CSORP.OR. 1832, L/1572, A/1581.

[40] CSORP.OR. 1831, B/101; 1832, C/1431; 1843, 16/8261.

[41] Maura Murphy, 'The Ballad Singer and the Role of the Seditious Ballad in Nineteenth Century Ireland: Dublin Castle's View', *Ulster Folklife* vol. 25, 1979, p. 87.

[42] CSORP.OR. 1843, 17/21651, 24131.

[43] CSORP.OR. 1843, 27/12177; 1851, 27/377.

[44] CSORP.OR . 1844, 17/7641; 1832/2608.

[45] CSOPR.OR. 1844, 17/7641.

[46] Maura Murphy, 'The Ballad Singer and the Role of the Seditious Ballad', pp. 83, 94.

[47] *Limerick Chronicle* 16 March 1831.

[48] *Limerick Chronicle* 12, 16, 23 March 1831.

[49] CSORP.OR. 1841, 6/5191; 1853, 9131.

[50] FP 2869, 4681R.

[51] FP 1870, 6791R, 6314R.

[52] FP 1870, 6314R.

[53] Charles O'Connor, *Ballads and Songs of Ireland*, Dublin, 1869.

[54] *Irishman* 19 January 1950.

10

WORLDS APART - THE GAELIC LEAGUE AND AMERICA, 1906-1914

ÚNA Ní BHROIMÉIL

Tír na nDollar. This was the Gaelic League's perception of the United States when Douglas Hyde embarked on the League's first fund-raising mission in 1906. The League's finances were in poor shape and when an American lawyer and patron of the arts, John Quinn, offered to organise the rubrics of the tour, Hyde agreed to go.[1] And there was every reason to regard the United States in this light. The concept of a mission was not a new one. Parnell had travelled the United States collecting funds as had Michael Davitt and, as recently as 1903, W.B.Yeats.[2] Famous personages were not the only ones embarking on missions. According to Quinn in 1905, Douglas Hyde would be competing with "a travelling Irish band, a travelling Irish Ladie's choir, a priest collecting for the Irish national church at Spiddal and another priest collecting for the O'Connell Memorial Church."[3]

But for those already settled in America, the Gaelic League and the revival of the Irish language meant something other than providing funds for the home organisation. Irish classes and Gaelic societies had been a feature of American immigrant life since 1872. A Gaelic class had been founded by Michael J. Logan in Brooklyn that year.[4] The first society in the United States, the Philo-Celtic

Society of Boston, was founded in April 1873 and was closely followed by the Brooklyn Philo-Celtic Society and others throughout the 1870s and 1880s. The teaching and speaking of the Irish language was an integral part of the work of these societies as were dances, picnics, balls and recitals. Though the numbers attending the society's meetings fluctuated, the average membership of each society was between 60-100 dues-paying members. Joining a Gaelic society provided an opportunity to learn the language and to use it in the company of like-minded others. According to many members the possession of an ancient and civilised tongue would raise the status of the Irish in their own eyes and in those of other immigrants.[5] By 1884 it was claimed that there were over fifty "Irish schools" or societies in the United States.[6] Logan also published a bi-lingual journal, *An Gaodhal,* which provided material for classes, songs, stories and enthusiastic exhortations from Logan to get organised and restore the language as the primary route to patriotism. "Celtic Departments" were published in five other newspapers in 1888.[7] By the time the Gaelic League was founded in Ireland in 1893, there was already an admittedly small, scattered and disunited group of societies focused on the same goal in the United States.

The foundation of the Gaelic League in Dublin initially gave new impetus to the societies in America and *An Gaodhal* published lists of known language enthusiasts who could set up branches in their towns. If the language could be spoken in the United States according to Logan, it would "put the shoneens to shame" in Ireland. But as early as 1895, *An Gaodhal* published an appeal from the Gaelic League in Ireland to "the various and disconnected Irish language societies outside of Ireland". It asked for two types of assistance: to form a link with each other and with the Gaelic League to ensure strong and combined action, and to consider the best means of providing funds to sustain the movement in Ireland.[8]

From the beginning the Gaelic League intended to tap the resources available to the Gaelic societies in America. Appealing always to the "patriotism and generosity of the Irish race in America" for support, the Gaelic League regarded American money as vital to the language movement in Ireland. A decision by the Knights of Columbus to donate money for a chair of American history at the Catholic University of America in Washington stunned and angered *An Claidheamh Soluis*. The writer grudged the money believing that American history was not in danger whereas the Irish language was.[9]

Yet when the *Irish World* organised an Irish language fund drive in 1899 to support the Gaelic League financially, John Devoy noted that the Irish language societies in the United States were not to the forefront of the fund-raising campaign. Subscriptions were acknowledged from private individuals, county associations, branches of the Ancient Order of Hibernians, but no concerted effort from the Gaelic societies.[10]

This same trend was clear during Hyde's mission to the United States 1905-6. All Gaelic societies perceived the visit as a recognition of their work in the States and looked forward to the mission with great anticipation. In the six months prior to the arrival of Douglas Hyde in America, the Gaelic societies in the State of New York reported an increase in membership of about 30% and the foundation of several new branches.[11] Hyde's stated aim was to explain the ideals and achievements of the Gaelic League to Irish America and to appeal to them for money to support and continue the League's work in de-anglicising Ireland. But John Quinn, the instigator and organiser of the mission, made sharp distinctions between missionary work, or morale raising, and the practical work of collecting as much money as possible for the Gaelic League.[12] Although *An Claidheamh Soluis* maintained that the reason for the trip was "to forge a bond with the Irish all over the world as one race and one group so that they may stand forever together," [13] Quinn measured the success of Hyde's mission in terms of dollars rather than in terms of hurrah and applause.

This led to misunderstandings and conflict during the course of the mission. John Quinn was not, and had never been, a member of a Gaelic society. His aim from the beginning was to secure as much money for Hyde's cause as possible and, to this end, wealthy people had to be wooed. The Gaelic societies were not patronised by the very wealthy[14] and when they saw their president hijacked by others who had never before deigned to put in an appearance at a picnic, ball or meeting they were understandably aggrieved. In New York, Hyde was visited by seven men who complained that the "proper" people were not in charge of the welcome and that the "tuxedo" crowd had never done anything positive for Ireland.[15] Martin P. Ward, in Oakland, California, complained to Hyde that:

> sir, your greatest enoyance on this coast is from an army of Bores who until you came had no more love or respect for the Irish language than the balled-na-m-borroge jack-asses has. And as soon as you lave (sic) it will be the same old tale.[16]

For his part, Quinn dismissed the Gaelic societies contemptuously stating again and again in letters to Hyde that "they, as you know, don't give money". A personal antagonism between Quinn and Hyde's advance agent, Tomás Bán Ó Coicheanainn, centred on the work that the latter was doing with the Gaelic societies and local organising committees. Quinn maintained that Ó Coincheanainn was wasting time and rolling up expenses talking and setting up committees rather than starting fundraising. He was therefore "only fit to work among the Gaelic Societies and money doesn't come from them."[17]

The main business of the mission was collecting money in Quinn's view. Lest Hyde be swayed by rapturous but cash-less welcomes, he kept reminding Hyde of business:

> Cross (Hartford) also says that you 'have captured all their hearts'. To hell with their hearts say I, unless they open their pocketbooks and contribute. Cross' letter is full of what we here call "hot air" that is "fulsome gush".[18]

And Hyde essentially agreed:

> I had not come to the States to promote Irish and Irishness alone but to collect money also. As I needed money, I had to go to those who had money to give. This was not clearly understood by all my friends.[19]

Hyde himself measured the success of his tour in dollars. After expenses were deducted, $50,000 [£10,056] was the amount returned to Dublin to further the work of the Gaelic League with a stipulation that no more than £2,000 was to be spent in any given year.[20] It was a successful tour on many levels. It gave the Gaelic League recognition at home and abroad and it swelled the empty treasury of the League. But it also allowed the League in Dublin to believe that America would come to their aid for the asking, and that the Gaelic societies in the United States were engaged in the same struggle as themselves. Hadn't the League's president been received with rapturous welcomes wherever he went ?

Although subscriptions continued to come from America after 1906, they were irregular and inconsistent. The various societies of the New England Gaelic League decided in 1906 to devote the first week in February every year to the raising of funds for the Gaelic League in Ireland. But in 1908, the secretary, Pádraig Ó hEigearta, reported that out of thirteen branches in New England he had only received contributions from three branches.[21] Despite an appeal for funds "to help the good work in the old land" by the Gaelic League of the State of New York and signed by notable New York figures such as Dr. Thomas Addis Emmet and Daniel F. Cohalan, the public was unresponsive. *Resolutions* of support were passed by the Gaelic societies regarding the League's campaign for Irish in the University, but little money was forthcoming.[22]

According to the *Gaelic American* in 1910, this falling off in subscriptions could be remedied by sending envoys to the United States to organise the country on behalf of the League and to convey personally the need in Ireland for financial assistance.[23] Ultimately, this is what the Gaelic League decided to do in 1911. But it was not organisation alone which was lacking. Had the Americans received anything other than a warm glow for all their subscriptions in the past? Letters to Hyde from various sources suggested practical ways of maintaining American interest in the Gaelic League:

> The American is always on the lookout for a quid pro quo . . .a certificate of membership, illuminated in the Irish style and suitable for framing . . . I should think that roughly speaking the

cost of premium and postage need not be more than $1.50 per membership, which would leave $3.50 of the $5.00 contribution net. for the Gaelic league , and I am sure that it would not be difficult to have this special American fund yield $10,000 per annum.[24]

Other proposals included a "Roll of Honour" to be kept in a proper place in Dublin so that when Ireland would be free the names of these patriotic donors would be inscribed in Ireland's "National Temple of Honour."[25] Altogether the suggestions were a clear indication that the Irish-Americans wanted a visible and demonstrable recognition of their contributions. The knowledge that good work was being done in Ireland was not enough to ensure the flow of contributions from the United States.

This was reiterated by the envoys sent to the United States on the second Gaelic League mission 1910-12. Fionán Mac Coluim and Fr. Micheál Ó Flannagáin, veterans of the Gaelic League were not Douglas Hyde. Their brief was to demonstrate to Americans the type of work the Gaelic League was doing at grass roots level to Gaelicise Ireland, and the ultimate aim was to get financial assistance for this project from the American Irish. To this end, they travelled the length and breadth of the United States giving lectures, organising feiseanna and displaying an "Industrial Exhibition" of lace-making, carpet weaving and embossed leather work. This time the Gaelic societies were in charge of proceedings. John Quinn pledged $250 and lent his name to an appeal for funds but was not actively involved in the mission. The envoys were well received with good attendances (1,000-3,000) recorded at public meetings.[26] But the proceeds were poor. When all expenses had been deducted $15,000 (£3,000) was collected in eighteen months.[27]

The envoys themselves were acutely aware of the paltry sum accumulated by them after all the hard work and diverse efforts that they had made while on the mission. Before he left the United States Fr. Ó Flannagáin rounded on the rich Irishmen and millionaires living there, accusing them of being token Irishmen who wore green waistcoats on St. Patrick's Day but who "spend their thousands in collecting wild birds' eggs in the South Sea

Islands or bugs in Madagascar."[28] But they were not the ones to blame. Controversy over Synge's 'Playboy of the Western World' had threatened the League's primary sources of support in the Gaelic societies, and when Hyde dissociated the League from the play it ultimately cost them the support of John Quinn and in his opinion, that of "many cultivated people in this town".[29] Other Irish issues intruded on the message of the Gaelic League, especially the issue of Home Rule.[30]

The Gaelic League was only one of a number of movements with a claim on Irish-American time and money. To stake this claim the League had to maintain a constant presence in the United States. If not, other movements would gain precedence. If the Gaelic League did not maintain a presence in the United States, appeals for funds would be useless. This was the most important message the envoys believed had to be communicated to the Gaelic League in Ireland.

If funds were to be forthcoming the American Irish had to be treated properly. Yet when Mac Coluim returned to the United States in 1913 he found that subscriptions received in Dublin were not even acknowledged by the Gaelic League. In a scathing letter to the League's executive committee in 1914, he castigated the members for failing to recognise the efforts of the Irish Americans. The names and addresses of all American subscribers had been sent to the Gaelic League by the envoys since 1911 with requests that letters of thanks, as well as newspapers or pamphlets containing articles on current affairs in Ireland, be sent to them to keep them in touch. While Douglas Hyde had done a good deal by writing personal letters of thanks to subscribers, the Gaelic League had not instigated any "keeping in touch process":

> The keeping in touch process however [has] not been properly carried out. Many subscribers whom I met on my second trip complained that they had never received anything . . . The weak point is that nobody seems responsible here [Ireland]: nobody seems to care whether [they] get recognition or not once their contributions are received. Apart from other considerations, this is bad financial policy.[31]

Again Mac Coluim reiterated the proposals suggested to Hyde on his return in 1906.

> There are thousands of too busy or too lazy, well-to-do, fairly
> patriotic Irishmen, "good fellows" who would never study Irish
> or attend meetings or do any organising work but who would
> subscribe if approached provided they feel we can give them
> some distinction and adequate recognition of their subscriptions,
> supply them with periodical reports as to what we do with their
> money and give them some quid pro quo in the line of journals
> and literature as free gifts. They would consider it a good ad to
> have their names appear on a distinguished list, international in
> scope, tastefully brought out each year.[32]

Recognition was important to the subscribers. And they were not
getting any from the Gaelic League. If they subscribed to the
building of a church in Ireland (or in America) they had practical
proof that their money was put to use and a plaque was usually
erected to the subscribers in the building. Their financial assistance
was acknowledged in a public manner, they were seen to be
"involved" with the old country without having to make a huge
amount of effort. How was Mac Coluim or any other envoy
supposed to convince the American Irish of the worthwhile cause
of the Gaelic League when the League in Dublin accorded so little
recognition to the subscribers?

But the gulf between the Gaelic League in Ireland and the
movement in the United States was a wider one than that of
recognition alone. On the third and final Gaelic League mission to
America 1913-14, one of the envoys, Tomás Ashe described the
gulf that he perceived to exist between the two groups who were
ostensibly at one as regards culture:

> I often sing the songs I know over here and I must admit the Irish
> Americans enjoy them as well. But it is only in Ireland that there
> is a proper understanding of them . . . I shudder when I know that
> the next song that will follow will be "How did Rip Van
> Winkle's Mother Pay the Rent" or some other such inane tango.[33]

Certainly Ashe was extremely homesick in America and this may
have contributed to his disillusionment. But although other reports

of rousing concerts and entertainments were sent to Dublin by the envoys, the only reports on the American mission recorded in the minutes of the executive committee were those regarding money. When the envoys were recalled to Ireland upon the outbreak of World War I, the sum of $4,500 was sent to the Gaelic League by the Treasurer for the Gaelic League Fund in America, Judge Keogh. Most of this money had been collected through a card system instigated by the second envoy, Diarmuid Lynch in contributions of $5-$25. According to the president of the Gaelic League, State of New York, very little of this money would have been realised had it not been for Diarmuid Lynch's previous connections with the Gaelic League when he lived in America:

> If it were not for Mr. Lynch's personality, and his original connection with the work of the Gaelic League here, the recent mission of the representatives would have been an absolute failure, because, as you are well aware, the evident apathy of the Gaelic League at home, coupled with its unwise and persistent policy of sending delegates to America year after year, has had the effect of lowering the League's prestige, and of alienating a large part of its support.[34]

The Gaelic societies were not the only ones weary of Gaelic League entreaties. John Quinn wrote to Judge Keogh in a rage in 1915 having been approached once again for support:

> Damn Damn Damn the Gaelic Leaguers,
> Damn the Parliamentarians too.
> Damn Damn Damn the Clan na Gaelers
> Damn all the Irish missions through and through.[35]

The Irish-Americans' nostalgia for their lost Gaelic heritage made them one with their Irish counterparts at the turn of the century. But the empathy didn't last. In the eyes of the Gaelic League in Ireland the language movement at home and abroad had the same mission and the same agenda - the revival of the Irish language in Ireland. The League therefore expected the Gaelic societies to function as fund-raisers abroad and to finance the campaigns of the

League "at home". But the American Gaelic societies provided a forum for the expression of ethnic pride and cultural conviction within the confines of the United States. The recognition by the Gaelic League in Ireland of a language movement in the United States gave that movement a role and status. The Irish language was recognised in the United States as an authentic cultural symbol, and it became a common "plank" in the programmes of nationalist organisations. The Gaelic societies did subscribe to the Gaelic League . But as societies, they concentrated on the needs of their members, whether that was a desire to learn the language of Ireland, the history of Ireland, to sing Moore's melodies or to dance the rince fada. The fact that they were affiliated to the Gaelic League in Ireland gave an added impetus to their own endeavours. It did not necessarily mean, however, that their focus was solely on Ireland and on the problems besetting the League there. And if the Gaelic League realised this on their missions to America, they chose to ignore it.

The attention of the Gaelic League in Ireland was firmly centred on Ireland and on how to define itself as a movement in the midst of constant political upheavals and wars between 1916 and 1923. The American Irish were also taken up with politics. Although on a mission to collect funds for the Gaelic League in 1914, Tomás Ashe and Diarmuid Lynch also brought home with them the first instalments of the $50,000 which Clan na Gael had collected for the Irish Volunteers.[36] Although there were numerous missions to America throughout this period, most notably that of Éamon De Valera in 1920, the missions of the Gaelic League were no more.

NOTES

[1] Janet E. Dunleavy and Gareth W. Dunleavy, *Douglas Hyde-A Maker of Modern Ireland*, Berkeley, 1991, p. 244.
[2] F.S.L. Lyons, *Charles Stewart Parnell*, London, 1977, pp. 106-15; T.W. Moody, *Davitt and Irish Revolution 1846-82*, Oxford, 1981; Norman A. Jeffares, *W.B. Yeats--A New Biography*, London, 1988, ch. 8.

[3] B.L. Reid, *The Man from New York: John Quinn and his Friends,* New York, 1968, p. 41.

[4] Fionnuala Uí Fhlannagáin, *Mícheál Ó Lócháin agus An Gaodhal,* Baile Átha Cliath, 1990, p. 22.

[5] *An Gaodhal,* May, 1882.

[6] *Irish World,* April 12, 1884.

[7] *An Gaodhal,* April 1898.

[8] *Ibid.,* April, 1895.

[9] *An Claidheamh Soluis,* April 5, 1899.

[10] *The Gaelic American,* October 24, 1903; December 19, 1903.

[11] *Ibid.,* June 10, 1905; September 16, 1905.

[12] John Quinn to Douglas Hyde, October 27, 1905, Ms. 17,299, National Library of Ireland. [N.L.I.]

[13] *An Claidheamh Soluis,* October 21, 1905.

[14] Proinsias Mac Aonghusa, "An Ghaeilge i Meirceá" in Stiofán Ó hAnnracháin, (eag.), *Go Meirceá Siar: Na Gaeil agus Meirceá: Cnuasach Aistí,* An Clóchomhar, 1979, p. 27.

[15] An Craoibhín Aoibhinn, *Mo Thuras go hAmerice,* Baile Átha Cliath, 1937, p. 7.

[16] Martin P. Ward to Douglas Hyde, February 15, 1906, Ms. 18, 253, N.L.I.

[17] John Quinn to Douglas Hyde, March 30, 1906, Ms. 17,299, N.L.I.; February 11, 1906, Ms. 24,992, N.L.I.

[18] John Quinn to Douglas Hyde, December 6, 1905, Ms. 17,299, N.L.I.

[19] An Craoibhín Aoibhinn, *Mo Thuras,* p. 6.

[20] *Ibid.; An Claidheamh Soluis,* June 30, 1906.

[21] *Ibid.,* May 30, 1908.

[22] *Ibid.,* February 12, 1910.

[23] *The Gaelic American,* May 14, 1910.

[24] Joseph Dunn to Douglas Hyde, undated but post 1906, Ms.18,253, N.L.I.

[25] *An Claidheamh Soluis,* January 25, 1908.

[26] *The Gaelic American,* January and February 1911.

[27] *An Claidheamh Soluis,* August 17, 1912.

[28] Minute Book of the Executive Committee of the Gaelic League, 1912-1917, Ms. 9,770, N.L.I.

[29] Dunleavy and Dunleavy, *Douglas Hyde,* p. 322.

[30] Fr. Ó Flannagáin to the Gaelic League, published in *An Claidheamh Soluis,* November 18, 1911.

[31] Fionán Mac Coluim to the Executive Committee of the Gaelic League, February 11, 1914, Ms. 9,770, N.L.I.

[32] *Ibid.*

[33] An tAthair Seosamh Ó Muirthile, *Tréithe Thomáis Ághas,* Baile Átha Claith, 1967, p. 21.

[34] P. Kavanagh, President, Gaelic League, State of New York to Judge Keogh, December 14, 1914, published in *An Claidheamh Soluis,* January 9, 1915.

[35] Reid, *The Man from New York: John Quinn*, p. 212.
[36] John Devoy, *Recollections of an Irish Rebel - a Personal Narrative,* New York, 1929, p. 393.

11

JOHN CHARLES McQUAID: CHURCH AND STATE - A REASSESSMENT

DEIRDRE McMAHON

In 1965 *Studies* published a tribute to Archbishop John Charles McQuaid, "The Church in Dublin: 1940-1965", on the occasion of the silver jubilee of Dr McQuaid's episcopate. Thirty-three years on, this article remains a major source for his episcopate. In the intervening period a number of important studies have appeared which have shed more light on aspects of his career: John Whyte's seminal *Church and State in Modern Ireland 1923-1979*; Dermot Keogh's work on relations between the Vatican and the Irish hierarchy, and his and Sean Faughnan's research on the drafting of the 1937 constitution. On the Mother and Child scheme, perhaps the most controversial episode of McQuaid's career, our under-standing of the murkier aspects of the controversy has been enhanced by the memoirs of Noel Browne and James Deeny, and by Ruth Barrington's monograph *Health, Medicine and Politics in Ireland 1900-1970*. Other aspects of the post-independence Church have been illuminated in J.J. Lee's analysis of the 1944 Vocational Organisation Report, and the research of Diarmaid Ferriter, Finian O' Driscoll and Eamon Dunne on Catholic social thought and Catholic lay movements. Bernard J. Canning's *Bishops of Ireland 1870-1987* is an invaluable reference source for the hierarchy. The study of church-state relations after independence has been greatly facilitated by the opening of the Irish government's archives since the mid-1970s but this has been one-sided since access to the hierarchy's various archives is extremely limited. There has only been one biography of McQuaid, a short eighty-eight page work by the late John Feeney in 1974. However, the archdiocese of Dublin has just begun to release Dr McQuaid's papers and there are now reported to be four biographies of him in preparation. In a sermon delivered in 1955 on the occasion of the Catholic University centenary, McQuaid referred to his distinguished predecessor Cardinal Paul Cullen with evident empathy: "No writer has done adequate justice to his character or stature..Silent, magnanimous, farseeing, Cardinal Cullen would seem to be as heedless of self-justification after death, as he was intrepid in administration during life. Not his the multitude of letters and scrupulous autobiography that help a later age to reconstruct the picture of the unspeaking dead".

John Whyte, who interviewed Dr McQuaid for his book, described him as the "most-talked about Irish prelate" of his time. In the twenty-five years since his death McQuaid's name has become synonymous with hidebound Catholic reaction and, like the politician whose career was so intertwined with his, Eamon de Valera, both men have been the subjects of crude, not to say lurid, historical caricatures. The reality is far more fascinating and complex. In examining the role of the Church in the period since independence, there has been a tendency to concentrate on such issues as the preoccupation with sexual morality, censorship, opposition to the welfare state, patriarchy in its various forms while ignoring for the most part the political, social, economic, cultural, religious and local contexts in which they operated. We know very little about the institutional side of the post-independence Church and particularly the seminaries and colleges, both in Ireland and abroad, which educated the Irish clergy. With the exception of McQuaid and some other prominent contemporaries such as Bishop Michael Browne of Galway and Bishop Cornelius Lucey of Cork, we know practically nothing about the other members of the hierarchy. McQuaid lived and worked in a period of extraordinary change in

Ireland which coincided with the first five decades of independence. His achievements, and his failures, cannot be understood without reference to this context of change in the life of his Church and his country. Biographers ignore this at their peril.

In retrospect, the timing of the 1965 *Studies* tribute was of great significance for McQuaid himself, for the Irish Catholic Church, and for the country. The Second Vatican Council was nearing the end of its deliberations and the winds of change which the Council had stirred were slowly making their presence felt in Ireland; the fruits of the *First Programme for Economic Expansion* were ushering in a new and more confident prosperity. The following year, 1966, was the fiftieth anniversary of the 1916 Rising. Viewed within the historical context of Irish Catholicism, the conjunction of McQuaid's silver jubilee with these events symbolised a turning point. As Patrick Corish noted in *The Irish Catholic Experience* (1985), from the 1880s the post-Cullenite Catholic Church acquired the characteristics of an establishment which was becoming more interlocked with the state. The problem was that the respective development of the Irish Church and the Irish state was out of historical kilter. McQuaid, who was very much in the Cullenite mould, reflected this. Born in Cootehill, Co. Cavan, in 1895, he was twenty-six when the Anglo-Irish Treaty was signed in 1921, a treaty which created the new Irish Free State but which also partitioned McQuaid's native province of Ulster. He also inherited Cullen's deep distrust of the secularism which had been ushered in by the French Revolution, a theme constantly found in McQuaid's writings.

In his article "Church and State in the Constitution of Ireland", published in the *Irish Theological Quarterly* in 1961, Father Enda McDonagh observed that "the Church did not come into the world with any well-defined set of principles for dealing with the State".
The nature and mission of the Church were essentially unchanged but the nature and mission of the state had changed radically. This produced inevitable tensions which in Ireland were delayed until the period of McQuaid's episcopate. The Cullenite and post-Cullenite Catholic Church had kept its distance from the British authorities at Dublin Castle except where fundamental interests

like education and disestablishment were concerned. But it did develop a considerable suspicion of state bureaucracy, manifested in its reaction to a powerful body like the Congested Districts Board created in 1890, which carried over into the new state after 1922.

The hierarchy welcomed the 1921 Treaty but it led to two major consequences which were to affect the Church and its relations with the new state: partition and the Civil War. With regard to partition, the Catholic Church on the island of Ireland now had to deal with two states, three at a further remove if we take into account the British government's sovereignty over Northern Ireland. The Civil War had particularly profound psychological consequences in the Twenty-Six Counties which have yet to be explored in detail by historians. Its ruthlessness and cruelty appalled churchmen but the Church's support for the new Irish Free State government aroused bitter hostility from a large minority of republicans. The depth of this hostility with its potential for anti-clericalism shocked many in the clergy and the hierarchy. In the years after the Civil War the bishops' pastorals were full of gloomy, doom-laden pronouncements about the inherent sinfulness of the people and the need for constant vigilance against threatening influences which might corrupt them. The picture of a triumphalist Catholic Church in post-independence Ireland has now been set in stone but on closer examination this triumphalism was deceptive. The Church was, in fact, deeply insecure about its role in a new state which had been born out of violence, a violence, moreover, which had revealed how volatile and unstable its flock could be. The political turbulence which was the legacy of the Civil War was to agitate the new state to varying degrees until the late 1930s.

McQuaid's appointment in 1940 to the archdiocese of Dublin, the most important and populous in the country, came at a more stable point in Irish politics. The Emergency had produced a new mood of national consensus and McQuaid's relations with the Taoiseach, Eamon de Valera, were excellent, in contrast to most of the hierarchy who were distinctly cool towards de Valera. From the evidence of recently released Irish government archives, we now know that de Valera had pressed McQuaid's candidacy on the

Vatican although whether the Vatican actually needed much urging is debatable. True, McQuaid was a long-standing friend of the de Valera family from his time as headmaster of Blackrock College (which de Valera's sons attended) and he had advised de Valera on the 1937 constitution; but he also had an outstanding reputation as a Catholic educationalist and had been close to Archbishop Edward Byrne of Dublin, his immediate predecessor. McQuaid's name had already been mentioned in connection with his native diocese of Kilmore.

But de Valera was later to state that he had also been impressed by McQuaid's social concerns at a time when the hardships of the war were particularly affecting the poor. The hierarchy and clergy of the Irish Church reflected the views of the strong and middling farmer class from which they were mostly drawn and were largely uncomprehending of, and unsympathetic to, urban life and poverty. McQuaid, as de Valera knew, was different and this was evident in his first Lenten pastoral in 1941. "The very widespread yearning for social peace is itself proof of the grave need of social reform", McQuaid wrote. But he emphasised that "whatever shape the detailed reform of the social structure ultimately may take, the only lasting basis of reconstruction can be the True Faith that we profess". Within four years of his appointment McQuaid had set up the Catholic Social Service Conference (CSSC) to co-ordinate Catholic charity work, and the Catholic Social Welfare Bureau to look after the thousands of emigrants who were going to Britain for war work. In 1943 the government appointed him chairman of the youth unemployment committee. He gave financial help to the victims of air raids in Dublin, was instrumental in setting up VD clinics, and actively promoted better care for TB patients, the elderly, the physically and mentally handicapped, and sick children. In *Church and State in Modern Ireland 1923-1979*, John Whyte observed that "if Dr McQuaid appeared reluctant to countenance the extension of State services, it must be remembered that the success of the C.S.S.C. had given him a model of what the most fruitful balance of State and voluntary enterprise would be". The problem was that McQuaid's formidable endeavours were taking place at a time when the state was assuming a far more interventionist role in social and economic policies. This was not only due to the exigencies of the Emergency. Since the election of de Valera in 1932, his Fianna Fail administrations pursued more dirigiste social and economic programmes than had their Cumann na nGaedheal predecessors and the Emergency gave these a greater impetus. In 1942, as the official archives reveal, the government embarked on a comprehensive post-war planning exercise. At the end of that year the Beveridge Report was published in Britain and received extensive coverage in Irish newspapers and periodicals. It also provoked considerable discussion among ministers. Two years later, the first Children's Allowances Act was introduced and the government embarked on an expansion and reform of Irish health services, culminating in the 1947 Health Act.

It is easy to forget why the power of the state seemed so threatening to many people in the late 1940s. Its potential for abuse had been amply demonstrated by the dictatorships of the right and the left which had dominated Europe since the First World War. Catholic social thought, which came late to Ireland, reflected the priorities, fears and insecurities of the Irish Catholic middle-class which was more rootless than historians have assumed. Catholic social thinkers were preoccupied with state power and in Ireland this preoccupation focused on the bureaucracy and the dangers of centralisation. The "bureaucrats" had been singled out for attack in the 1944 Report of the Commission on Vocational Organisation which had been chaired by the Bishop of Galway, Dr Michael Browne. The bureaucracy, as government files on the reactions to the Report reveal, retaliated by effectively rubbishing it. James Deeny, a prominent lay Catholic who became Chief Medical Adviser to the new Department of Health in 1947, had some sympathy with the Church's concerns. The Church, he wrote in his memoirs *To Cure and To Care* (1989), wanted a society with plural institutions: "it was not a question of Rome Rule, but of a responsible society, with a maximum amount of decentralisation, local community groups, industries and professions remaining independent and the preservation of the family as the basic social unit".

John Whyte commented on the oddness of the Mother and Child controversy. Expanded medical services and social welfare systems were being introduced in most of western Europe after the Second World War but produced nothing like the convulsions they did in Ireland. It was, he observed, the only instance in which a Catholic hierarchy sought to influence the precise provisions of a country's social services. Why? One can point to the fear of bureaucracy noted above and the anxiety that contraception and abortion would be introduced under the cover of state health services. There was also the Church's control of the voluntary hospitals and its symbiotic relationship with the doctors (McQuaid's father was a doctor and doctors were one of the privileged professions recognised in the 1944 Vocational Organisation Report.). Ironically, James Deeny, was the main architect of the 1947 Health Act with its mother-and-child provisions and on this subject he thought that the Church not only overplayed its hand but chose entirely the wrong issue for a showdown with the government. With Irish tuberculosis and infant mortality statistics among the highest in the world, health was an issue of considerable popular concern. By allying itself with the conservative medical profession in fulminations against socialised medicine, the hierarchy seemed to be out of touch with harsh social realities though in McQuaid's case this was certainly untrue.

The contours of the Mother and Child controversy are now fairly clear. The long gestation of the controversy, going back to 1944, is evident from the government's archives and the 1951 crisis must be placed within this context. The role of a hitherto shadowy but major player, in the form of the Irish Medical Association, has also come under greater scrutiny. Deeny's memoirs and those of Noel Browne flesh out the narrative with more personal perspectives. (Deeny considered Browne to be "..ruthless, calculating....and indeed possibly vindictive" and thought that a sensitive portfolio like Health should never have been given to such an inexperienced minister.) But we know very little about the state of play within the hierarchy itself. McQuaid has attracted most of the lightning hurled at the hierarchy for their rejection of the Mother and Child Scheme but what about Bishop Browne of Galway and Bishop Lucey of

Cork who had made equally forthright pronouncements about the abuse of state power ? When the crisis erupted again in 1953 after Fianna Fail's return to power and the introduction of a new health bill, de Valera was clearly aware of Cardinal D'Alton's discomfort about the subject when he urged him to secure the withdrawal of the hierarchy's press statement objecting to the new health bill.

By 1953 McQuaid's relations with de Valera had soured. His intervention in the 1946 national teachers' strike, when he expressed sympathy with the strikers' cause, had greatly annoyed the government. In reiterating their opposition to the new health bill in 1953, McQuaid and the rest of the hierarchy attempted the same divide-and-rule tactics they had employed so successfully in prising Noel Browne apart from the Inter-Party government but were frustrated by de Valera and James Ryan, who were altogether cannier political operators. McQuaid's failure to get a red hat, as Dermot Keogh revealed in *Ireland and the Vatican* (1995), was due in part to lobbying from Joseph Walshe, the Irish Minister to the Holy See, who warned the Vatican that if McQuaid was made a cardinal "the Nuncio would have endless difficulties, in every sphere of his activities, owing to this deplorable weakness in [McQuaid's] character, already so well known to the Holy See". McQuaid also clashed with other administrations. During the second Inter-Party government 1954-57, James Dillon's plans for a national Agricultural Institute were attacked by McQuaid as an attempt to take over higher education. Dillon was forced to back down. McQuaid also criticised provisions in the 1952 Adoption Act and the 1959 Intoxicating Liquor Act. On some of these issues his criticisms were well-founded. On adoption, for example, he thought that the rights of the natural mother were being over-looked while the Intoxicating Liquor Act showed that Lemass's government seriously underestimated the prevalence of alcoholism.

During McQuaid's episcopate the population of Dublin increased to over 800,000 people. The number of diocesan clergy increased from 370 to 600 and the number of religious from 500 to 800. To meet the needs of the increased population in the new suburbs over 60 new parishes were founded, bringing the total to 131 in 1972. In the 1960s McQuaid's social concerns embraced new problems such as juvenile delinquency, itinerant resettlement, and drug addiction. He was also active in other, more unexpected areas. It was paradoxical that McQuaid, who hardly ever made use of either the radio or the television (one exception was his 1948 radio appeal for funds to help the Christian Democrats in the Italian elections), helped to set up the Catholic Communications Office, and sent a number of priests to the US for television training in preparation for the opening of RTE. In 1965 he established a diocesan press office. But despite all this activity criticism of McQuaid began to escalate. With hindsight, the Patrician Year, 1961, seems like the apotheosis of McQuaid's episcopate and the kind of Catholicism he represented. The following year Pope John XXIII summoned the Second Vatican Council which introduced extensive changes in the liturgy, placed more emphasis on lay participation, and encouraged a greater interest in ecumenism.

McQuaid's deep unhappiness with these changes was apparent. On the question of lay participation, his sporadically thorny relations with groups such as the Legion of Mary, the Society of St Vincent de Paul, and Muintir na Tíre were well known. As for ecumenism, McQuaid was the first Irish bishop to expressly forbid Catholics to study at Trinity College, Dublin without special dispensation, a move followed by the rest of the hierarchy in 1956. His discouragement of the inter-denominational Mercier Society in the early 1940s rankled for many years with people like Erskine Childers and the distinguished civil servant Leon O Broin who had been actively involved in it. O Broin wrote in his memoirs *Just Like Yesterday* (1986) that McQuaid had "carried to Dublin with him the antagonisms of [his] Border area. He certainly displayed them in his approach to anything in which he saw organised Protestant involvement". And yet, O Broin acknowledged, he was progressive in other areas and personally "there was a nice side to the man ... he had a quiet sense of humour which told in his favour". As Lesley Whiteside observed in her biography of Dr George Otto Simms, former Church of Ireland Archbishop of Dublin, there was scarcely any enthusiasm for ecumenism among Dr Simms's own flock although McQuaid was on friendly terms with Dr Simms and especially with his wife.

Serious criticism of McQuaid's personality and policies appeared in July 1965 in the theological journal *Herder Correspondence*, some months before the *Studies* tribute. The article, "Curial Mentality in Dublin Arch-diocese ?", may have contributed to the uneasy mix of adulation and defensiveness which characterised the *Studies* article. *Herder Correspondence* returned to the attack in April 1966 and argued that while the *Studies* essay was "well-informed and charmingly written", it had concentrated only on those aspects of Catholic life in Dublin which had interested McQuaid. While acknowledging McQuaid's charity and excellent administration of the diocese, it criticised his failure to inspire the clergy and the laity and ascribed this to McQuaid's personality with its "unconquered shyness, the martyr complex, the dislike of public occasions, [and] the penchant for the unnecessary harsh or humiliating phrase". The article concluded: "Perhaps it does not matter quite so much to Christians what their bishop is like; but one of the boomerang effects of a century and more of clergy identifying the Church with themselves alone is that it matters very much what the bishop is like - it matters inordinately". This article prompted two correspondents to cancel their subscriptions.

Two years later *The Changing Face of Catholic Ireland* (edited by Desmond Fennell who was also the editor of *Herder Correspondence*) urged that a radical restatement of the Christian message was vital because of the seismic changes talking place in Irish society. Among these were included the increasing access to second and third level education, and increasing affluence and urbanisation. Most serious of all, the weakening of Irish nationalism as a buttress to Catholic belief and practice was creating an ideological vacuum. The Irish Church had "failed to make an adequate creative response to these changes". Chapter 9 of Fennell's book was titled "Dublin's Archbishop". It contested some of the more ill-founded criticisms of McQuaid such as his alleged hatred of Protestants but was particularly critical of McQuaid's Lenten Pastorals which, although "masterly expositions of doctrinal themes", seemed to assume "a devoted audience with earnest theological interests rather than the multifarious laity of a capital city, people involved in rapidly changing living conditions".

McQuaid, it was argued, had singularly failed to give guidance and leadership after the Vatican Council.

This failure was picked up by other commentators. The renewal and reform of the Second Vatican Council, wrote Seán Mac-Réamoinn in 1969, was being stifled within the Irish Church. No one could doubt McQuaid's immense integrity, genuine pastoral concern and commitment but what was in doubt "is his position in a changing Church and a changing Ireland, or, more specifically, his awareness of and attitude to change". Writing in *Christus Rex* in 1969, Declan Costello, who was then Fine Gael T.D. for Dublin North-West, observed that while there was a good deal of evidence to suggest a failure of effective communication between bishops and priests in the Irish Church, "the communication between the laity and the clergy has been almost negligible". But he urged churchmen and politicians not to avoid controversy: "Politicians should [not] be deterred from political action in which they believe merely because it may invoke episcopal wrath. Equally, however, Church men should not be deterred from criticising social conditions merely because they anticipate ministerial anger". In Costello's opinion this had been one of the more pernicious consequences of the Mother and Child crisis because it had given the faint-hearted the excuse to avoid controversy in public affairs. He concluded with a prophetic warning. The Church "still has the active allegiance of the vast majority of the Irish people. It would, however, be a mistake to depend on an unswerving allegiance in the future".

In a radio documentary about McQuaid broadcast by RTE. Shortly after his death in 1973, the late Cardinal Heenan of Westminster predicted that history would vindicate McQuaid. History is still awaiting that task. The quarter century since his death has witnessed passages in church-state relations more turbulent than McQuaid ever experienced. Our understanding of them remains stunted because our knowledge of the post-independence Church is so limited. For an institution of such huge significance in Irish society, this ignorance is much to be deplored but the fault lies as much with the Church as with historians. The opening of Dr McQuaid's archives by the Dublin archdiocese is a most welcome step. Twenty-five years after his death, the career, achievements and failings of one of the most remarkable figures in post-independence Irish history are long overdue for serious assessment.

PHILOSOPHY

12

EMBODYING MORAL BELIEFS IN LAW

JOHN HAYES

Patrick Hannon, the professor of moral theology at St. Patrick's College, Maynooth, has written a timely book[1] with the aim of answering a quite specific question: 'how is a Catholic expected to vote on certain types of issue involving morality and law?'[2] Prof. Hannon has in mind 'issues of family and sexual morality', notably divorce and abortion—about which, as he says, 'in Ireland.. public controversy is still, it seems, most readily aroused'.[3] However, he also wants to discuss the appropriate political and legal response to the plight of the powerless (including the old and the young, the hungry and the homeless, the undocumented immigrant and the unemployed worker) and those inequities in society which give rise to 'dole-queues or emigration'.[4]

Fr. Hannon's answer is that for Catholics the resolution of such issues is 'at its core the same as [it is] for any [other] politician or citizen'. When it comes to the 'embodiment of a belief in law' Catholics are essentially in an autonomous area viz., that of 'civic or political judgement, the province of citizen or politician as such, and about which there may be difference of opinion'.[5]

I intend to consider here how Fr. Hannon defends this view as a Catholic one. This has to be a chief concern since his book is openly and primarily an essay in Catholic theology. There are, however, at least two other relevant viewpoints on the book, which connect it with wider contexts but which I can do no more than signal in this article. Firstly, it would be important to consider how adequate this answer appears from the perspective of the wider Christian tradition with particular regard to a Protestant evaluation. This viewpoint is adverted to rather than explored in the book.[6] For, while Fr. Hannon declares himself to be in the transformationist [Augustinian] tradition[7] of Christian theology shared by many Protestant theologians, he is, at the same time, notably Catholic in his insistence on the autonomy and relative goodness of the secular order. And he acknowledges that there is a deep Lutheran objection to the doctrine of natural law, on which he reposes much of the argument in this book precisely on the grounds that it 'makes too much both of nature and reason, ignoring the radical damage to humanity which is expressed in the notion of the Fall'.[8]

Secondly, a consideration of the relationship of Prof. Hannon's enterprise to recent Anglo-American philosophy would be germane. Again, this dimension is mentioned,[9] but not further elaborated on. He deals extensively with the Devlin-Hart jurisprudential debate in the late 1950s and 1960s about the enforcement of morals by the criminal law but I have in mind the more recent period of reflection in Anglo-American social philosophy inaugurated by John Rawls's *Theory of Justice* (1971). This book focused the liberal tradition on distributive justice and so has much to say about the wider 'social' issues that Fr. Hannon wishes to discuss in addition to the personal and familial ones commonly debated in Ireland. Rawlsian liberalism has lately, in its turn, come under criticism from several quarters. Much of this criticism has been inspired by the communitarian thought of Alasdair MacIntyre's (Thomistically influenced) interpretation of Aristotle to be found in *After Virtue* (1981) and *Whose Justice, Which Rationality* (1988). However, the only social philosopher from this latter period discussed in the book is John Finnis, whose work, superficially at least, connects readily enough with the traditional Catholic natural law approach - but Finnis is hardly representative of recent Anglo-American social or political philosophy.

Separating Church and State

As Prof. Hannon makes clear, the answer he gives to his question seemed to be accepted as a creditable Catholic one in the early sixties when the Catholic presidential candidate John F. Kennedy denied that his religious affiliation would hamper his upholding the religious freedom guaranteed in the first amendment of the US Constitution, as obliged by his oath of office. However, the American version of Church-State separation was not then the preferred Roman Catholic solution - particularly in the Republic of Ireland, which unlike America, had an overwhelming Catholic majority. While religious freedom was legally assured in this State at that time, the intimate informal relationship between the Roman Church and civil society that had long characterised Church/State relations was still widely expected to issue in a strong and detectable influence of the Catholic hierarchy's moral views on the shape of legislation and on ensuing bureaucratic decisions.

Ireland has changed considerably in recent years. As a result, new political and, less clearly, legal initiatives, are being taken towards bringing about an informal as well as formal separation of Church and State. This is the case in the areas of education, health-care, and the related area of morals, which is Prof. Hannon's particular concern. His book seems to echo the pragmatics of Kennedy, intellectually buttressed by John Courtney Murray, and translates them to the newly emerging Irish situation in that it gives a kind of *nihil obstat* to liberal views in our society regarding the correct Church/State relationship when moral issues are at stake.

It is interesting that at a time when the American Catholic Church seems to seek to exert greater influence over its communicants in the exercise of their political powers in moral matters (at least in the case of abortion) than in the sixties, the text under consideration is pointing in a contrary direction for Irish Catholics. In contrast to the supportive attitude of Kennedy's friend, Cardinal Cushing of Boston, Cardinal O'Connor of New York remonstrated publicly with the Democratic candidate for the Vice Presidency,

Geraldine Ferraro, in 1984, for distinguishing between her personal 'religious belief' in the area of abortion and her duty as a public official to uphold the 'right to choose' laws that followed on a 1973 decision by the US Supreme Court.

Geraldine Ferraro's description of her belief as 'religious' meant that the ensuing debate was conducted on the same basis as that invoked by Kennedy - the First Amendment guarantee of freedom of religion. This was more difficult ground for the cardinal than had he fought primarily for a fundamental 'right to life' i.e., a right formally based not on religious belief but on the sacredness of life, which is respected by all civilised persons and societies, whether religious or not. However, because Cardinal O'Connor in fact entered into the question of the scope of the First Amendment guarantee and because the debate was conducted in the heat of a political campaign, it is not as instructive as it might otherwise have been.

It must be said however - and Fr. Hannon says it - that Catholics are commonly understood by both themselves and others, to be guided by the leaders of their Church not only in matters of faith but also of morals. Prof. Hannon goes to considerable lengths to examine this common understanding. An extended analysis of the *Letter to the Romans* shows how it was implemented in the early missionary church. In particular, Prof. Hannon points out the parallels with and borrowings from contemporary ethical teachings (Stoic) in New Testament descriptions of 'Christian' ethics. He goes on to rule out 'divine command' theories of the origins and authority of morals. The author of the rules of morality, he believes, is

> the human mind, reflecting on human experience, discovering what is or is not fit living for a creature with a human nature...The answer to the question, why be moral? is not because society or the Church or even God requires it, but that it is through being moral that we become truly human.[10]

Human creativity, exercised in moral decisions, is one of the ways in which man (as *imago Dei*) mirrors his Creator. Such an approach, giving 'morality its own independent weight', has, he points out, the additional advantage of being 'intelligible to people other than religious believers'.[11] Prof. Hannon then proceeds to argue for a correspondingly different understanding of the scope of the *magisterium* when teaching on morals rather than on matters of faith.

The Freedom and Human Dignity

In developing his case, Prof. Hannon is himself magisterial in his command of the relevant theological sources; the book could profitably be read for his lucid presentation of a vast range of material alone. However, though he trawls the tradition for old riches - notably, the relevant practice of the early Church and Aquinas on the teleology of law - his most important argument is an innovative one applying a principle enunciated in the *Declaration on Religious Freedom* by the Second Vatican Council. He carefully sets this *Declaration* in the context of the ecclesiology of the Council, as developed and systematised by Avery Dulles. He considers as most apposite to his enquiry the models of the Church as herald of salvation and servant of the Word, supplemented by images of the Church as sign of Christ and as people of God and reminds us that 'the entire significance of the institutional elements of the Church resides in their reference to the Church's meaning and mission'.[12] These institutional elements include: hierarchical constitution, apostolic succession, the primacy of Peter and his successors, and the teaching authority of Pope and bishops.

Having set the scene, Fr. Hannon proceeds to focus in on the conciliar declaration that as a corollary of the recognition of the dignity of the human person, nobody should be either coerced into or restrained from following any religious practice - 'within due limits' or, (as a gloss), subject to the 'just requirements of public order'. His next point is that 'coercion is no more at home in the quest for moral than it is for religious value'. Hence, 'in morality as in religion there should be freedom of belief and action, in public and in private, for individuals and for groups, subject only to the requirements of peace, justice, and public morality'.[13]

177

Prof. Hannon says of his argument here that 'fortunately ...[it] is not complicated'[14] but it might have borne fuller elucidation along the following lines: It seems to be the case that the conciliar recognition of a right of non-communicants freely to practise their religion entails a recognition of a right to act on moral convictions freely as well. It also seems to entail support for those political and legal structures which would permit such freedom. If Catholics should vote for those (liberal) political structures which allow due freedom to those of other moral persuasions, it is clear that, willy nilly, they will have created a society which is copious of more moral practices than its own authoritative teaching recognises. Theoretically, the only boundary-maker would be the due limit of 'public order' and this would be the chief permissible consideration in disputed questions - for example, abortion and divorce.

It is not a new thesis, as Prof. Hannon makes quite explicit, that Catholics are free to vote for legislation that allows behaviour offensive to Catholic morals - though it was usually argued for in the past on grounds that he now wishes to add to. From the earliest times, the Christian community tolerated pagan customs, excepting the worship of false gods. Also influential in shaping attitudes towards culture, society and state - but in a more specific way - was St. Paul's insight that law in itself can be a kind of occasion of sin.

The view has often prevailed that it is unwise to legislate the best practice for fear that it may lead (given the human propensity to gibe at authority) to the breakdown of even minimal standards. Brothels have often been tolerated under this rubric. In similar vein, the USA found in the thirties that the prohibition of alcohol (under the influence of fundamentalist Christianity) bred worse vices than drunkenness *viz.*, the strengthening of organised and violent crime. If corruption is likely, the legislator has to be aware that '*corruptio optimi, pessima*'. Laws that enforce ideal behaviour are prone to a breakdown more catastrophic than laws that seek to enforce the minimum.

While Prof. Hannon is sensible of this view, his key argument is one based on the insight that freedom is a constituent of every moral action. Thus Catholics should work for a civil society that allows in its legal system maximum freedom in religious and moral matters because of a desire to respect the dignity of others - and, no doubt, with a hope that others will respect their dignity in the same areas of life. It is clear that the *Declaration on Religious Freedom* did not explicitly address the political or constitutional implications of its invocation of the principle of freedom even in relation to religious matters. *A fortiori*, it did not ask how such an affirmation might impact on the relationship between the leaders of the Church in the exercise of their teaching function in the area of morals nor on its own communicants in the exercise of their political roles as voters and, in some cases, legislators.

What About Irreformable Moral Norms?

Prof. Hannon recognises that the position he is outlining inevitably raises the question of Church authority in morals and gives a clear account of the recognised sources of 'irreformable' doctrine. He observes that the highest degree of authoritativeness, infallibility, has never been attached to any 'concrete [i.e. action-directing] moral doctrine'.[15] He appears to suggest that this may have sprung from a recognition that the character of *magisterium* exercised in morals is different from that obtaining in matters of faith.[16] Whether that is so or not, he also points to the variety of motivations/intentions of moral actors and the circumstantial (time-bound; culture-specific) character of concrete (or material) moral doctrine. The presence of these factors means that it is 'impossible to universalise a negative material norm ...say killing or taking someone else's property without his or her consent'.[17] Many theologians agree that since 'it is impossible to anticipate every possible combination of circumstance and motive/intention....it is not feasible to hold that there are concrete norms which always bind, to which there are no exceptions, which are not open to change'.[18]

This is a controversial view for, as Prof. Hannon acknowledges, 'in the Catholic tradition there are universal prohibitions which at least look like material norms: examples are the prohibition of lying, fornication, adultery, and of the direct killing of the innocent'.[19] However, the 'at least look like' is justified by a reason

179

EMBODYING MORAL BELIEFS IN LAW

which I found so cryptically put as to leave me unenlightened. An example which defined lying as 'deception of someone not entitled to the truth',[20] which presumably from the context has a redundant negative, did not help.

It must be said, however, that although controversial, the thesis that moral norms are not fit candidates for irreformable formulations has a certain tradition behind it in the Aristotelian-based proposition that at least some moral norms hold only for *most* - but not *all* - cases. This is a promising line of approach deserving more than the two sentences (and a footnote) given in the book.

The above considerations are cited to show that since infallibility cannot be exercised in respect of concrete moral truths, a theologian, acting responsibly, is free, according to Vatican norms, to hold a dissenting view on any concrete moral question - at least in private. However, this hardly helps the ordinary Catholic voter or legislator, especially the latter, who cannot function in private.

What looks like a poor example concentrated me on the area where this freedom might be argued against most strongly *viz.*, where, to borrow a phrase from the Irish political arena, 'core values' are at stake. In discussing the changing circumstances that (it is thought) make material norms impossible to state for all times, Prof. Hannon gives the example of the just war prohibition against killing non-combatants - a norm that he says is 'meaningless in the context of all-out nuclear war'. Quite so, and that's why Cardinal Ottavianni, surely correctly, found nuclear warfare morally repugnant - as against the contemporary acceptance by John Courtney Murray and Paul Ramsey of a certain level of non-combatant deaths. I believe that the norm holds, and that it is a most civilising one. Again, and more germane - but invoking the same principle concerning the inviolability of innocent human life - the Catholic position on abortion, for example, is quite clear and has been made so continually by repeated statements.

A Consistent Life Ethic

Papal teaching aside, Fr. Hannon discusses in his book the exercise of authority - as has become quite common - by conferences of bishops, an exercise that clearly is of lesser status than an exercise from the Roman chair. But even here, and in regard to abortion, there is certainly no recognition of a right of dissent: on November 5th, 1992, the Irish Catholic hierarchy stated that 'the intentional destruction of innocent human life, at any stage from conception to natural death, is gravely wrong' and 'admits of no exceptions'. This is, I think, as Prof. Hannon explains it, a material as opposed to a formal or tautologous norm or principle - and it is presented quite explicitly as exceptionless and incidentally, as flowing from a right that in a letter of Pope John Paul II to the Irish bishops of September 25th, 1992 springs from 'the very dignity of every human being', like the freedom on which Prof. Hannon bases his main argument.

Abortion is, of course, a most sensitive issue but one that cannot be avoided since it has implications for a substantial part of the Catholic ethic. Prof. Hannon himself cites Cardinal Bernardin's presentation of Catholic ethics where in respect of such 'life-threatening' actions as abortion, warfare, capital punishment, and the care of the terminally ill the principle that 'it is wrong directly to take innocent life' provides a consistency of approach in all cases.

Fr Hannon still maintains that 'even the most strongly expressed teaching by an episcopal Conference cannot override the prior responsibility of each citizen to make up his own mind'.[21] This is, of course, true - and because it is true, considerable reflection must take place before Church leaders or members begin to enlist the criminal law in defence of a moral position. He does not, however, altogether rule out the invocation of the criminal law to defend such a position (mentioning explicitly the abortion case) but argues that the basis on which it is done is essentially no different for a Catholic voter or legislator than it is for any other citizen; the matter of ecclesiastical authority does not enter into it in any essential way. The limiter, as already noted, is that 'the just requirements of public order' are observed.

The term 'public order' in Catholic social teaching encompasses the ensuring of that measure of peace, justice, and public morality that will enable the members of society to flourish in freedom and so achieve the 'common good'. The most problematic phrase here is 'public morality' and he quotes John Finnis's view that it should refer to 'the regulation of individual rights'. These rights have been stated negatively in the liberal tradition such that they prohibit certain actions rather than assert positively what is to be done. Thus, the right to life means that no one may interfere with another's life so as illegally to take it away.

This century has seen, in contrast, the affirmation of rights which oblige positive action which would create an environment for the enhancement of human life. It is now widely appreciated how meaningless it is to respect a person's right to life in the 'liberal' sense of doing nothing to destroy it, while leaving that person to starve to death.

Is The Hart/Devlin Debate Still Relevant?

The thrust of this section of the book, however, is on 'public morality' as the regulation of individual rights of freedom of action (understood as freedom from coercion). It is in this context that he discusses the Devlin/ Hart debate (about the legal proscription of immorality) that occurred following the publication of Wolfenden report of 1957 (on the regulation of homosexual behaviour). Wolfenden made crucial use of a distinction between private and public behaviour - and argued that the law should only concern itself with the latter. Devlin took the view that the criminal law could reach into so-called 'private' behaviour if that behaviour is understood, after mature reflection by the 'man in the jury box', to be threatening a society's existence. Hart defended the Wolfenden principle and proposed that the relevant consideration governing the proscription of behaviour in the criminal law was the pre-vention of 'harm to others or, in certain circumstances, the protection of peoples from their own destructive impulses'.[22]

Prof. Hannon does not think that either Devlin or Hart found the key to all the problems - though I suspect that he thinks Hart had the better of the argument - but enlightenment can be found in both thinkers. He recommends certain 'elastic principles' espoused by Devlin, finding in him a bias towards freedom and privacy - notwithstanding his view that the law can reach into the 'private' domain. He commends such later developments as the calculus of 'harm' (reminiscent of Bentham's pleasure-calculus but based on Hart) devised by Simon Lee and also some proposals of John Courtney Murray which were developed first in regard to censorship of art and literature but are applicable to the development of a public consensus among divergent social groups.

For Prof. Hannon, 'the key question of everyone in any community is whether a measure which gives or withholds a particular liberty is or is not likely, all things considered, to promote the best social conditions for human flourishing'[23] and that in deciding this 'the standpoint of the legislator - or of the citizen in regard to legislation - is not that of purely personal moral agency'.[24]

He is well aware, however, that within the Catholic tradition (and even in the minds of others about that tradition) there is an understanding that certain behaviour -abortion pre-eminently- is so inimical to the sacredness of human life that its legalisation is contradictory to the foundations of all law - and furthermore (a Devlin point) socially destructive. Thus, in the Irish Episcopal statement of 5th November, when faced with Hobson's choice of what seemed to be *some* direct abortion versus *perhaps much more* direct abortion, the joint episcopal view was that voters, though free to choose, were to have the intention to 'reflect a total abhorrence of abortion and the determination to make that abhorrence clear' in their voting. This is clearly a teaching to enforce a particular moral view in the constitution - and in ensuing legislation, if it is enacted.

Prof. Hannon does not discuss the abortion question in detail but in commenting on Cardinal Bernardin's viewpoint that 'law and public policy can ... be instruments of shaping a public consensus',[25] he does say that some issues are more susceptible of this approach than others: 'One might say that when a measure affects in the first place an *institution* rather than personal life it is more apt for use in the forging of consensus'. The example given of the first kind of measure is capital punishment and of the second, abortion 'which is a matter which reaches directly into the personal life of individual women'.[26] I am not sure that the example given illustrates the distinction; in any case, it was developed for a situation where a consensus against abortion has been lost - and this is not the Irish situation.

While maintaining the distinction between abortion and capital punishment on the basis given above, Fr. Hannon seeks to illuminate the abortion issue by addressing the 'somewhat less controversial'[27] issue of capital punishment. He does this by focusing on the question: what are the options for an office-holder in a State which allows capital punishment? After a discussion of the Catholic moral theology of 'co-operation in the sin of another', he concludes that there is room for compromise within limits set by considerations such as proximity to the evil action and due proportionality. However, he acknowledges that there is the danger of 'a discontinuity between personal moral conviction and public responsibility' and that the emergence of such a chasm was Cardinal O'Connor's concern in his debates with Geraldine Ferraro.

I would have liked, however, to see the abortion question treated explicitly - particularly the issue of public funding for abortion clinics. Application of the sophisticated terms of analysis provided by the tradition on co-operation might indeed be helpful here. Reading this section was a reminder of the wealth of the patrimony of Catholic moral theology - a wealth that has been shared with the wider tradition of English-speaking moral philosophy to my knowledge by only one prominent thinker - Anthony Kenny.

Morals & Law Now

The criminal law does not prescribe the best behaviour; rather, it delineates what will happen to a citizen if he does not comply with set legal standards. But morality, with its concern for human flourishing, as recognised by Christian and Catholic views, has higher aspirations than those enshrined in the criminal law. And, indeed, sensitive consciences nowadays would like to see the law addressing not only life, limb and property-threatening situations (which are so well underpinned by liberal legal theory) but also becoming more active where human flourishing is impeded because of exploitation of the weak and powerless.

Cardinal Bernardin has pointed out not only the internal consistency provided by the principle of respect for the life of the innocent but also how the Catholic 'life ethic', underpinning this principle, yields a consistency of approach to judging actions that tend to diminish the life of those too powerless to resist. His examples are: prostitution, pornography, male domination and sexual discrimination. However, the experience is that legislation to address such injustice is far from easy to frame and may have unintended and unwelcome outcomes.

Furthermore, as already noted, strong moral arguments are often now put to buttress political demands that our legal codes should establish our neighbour as having just positive claims on us rather than simply being protected against our interference (whether life-threatening or life-diminishing). From a Christian point of view simply avoiding evil is no way to treat our brothers and sisters - and the New Testament understanding of the proper relationship among human beings is familial. But again, here the law can be a two-edged sword.

There may be a danger that stressing the freedom of Catholics in their political life on issues regarding the legal control of personal and inter-personal behaviour, such that the role of church teachers is greatly minimised may also create a climate for ignoring in the political and legal fora what the Church has to say on social issues, an influence which Prof. Hannon clearly wishes to maintain. I think that many Catholics would share with me the view that if a measure of the once considerable influence of the church on the interpersonal matters could now be mobilised in favour of the marginalised, great gains could be made. Morals do not stand apart from religious perspectives and motivations; they are, respectively, enlightened and inspired by them.

This is not to say that the Irish Church may not already fairly lay some claim to praise for helping to arouse, foster, and channel the notably generous spirit that manifests itself regularly regarding the needy. And it is of the essence of generosity that it is free and spontaneous - flowing from the heart; it is the fruit of freedom. Prof. Hannon has some very good things to say about the ecclesiastical, particularly hierarchical, teaching-style and manner

185

of contributing to public debate that would be appropriate to a country come of age and still so manifestly generous.

His whole book bespeaks an intelligence at the service of a belief in the glory of his fellow communicants and fellow citizens fully alive to their political freedoms.

NOTES

* This article is an amended version of one that first appeared in *Doctrine & Life,* 43 January 1993, pp 20-30.

[1] Patrick Hannon, *Church, State, Morality & Law,* Dublin, 1992.
[2] *Ibid.,* p. 1.
[3] *Ibid.,* p. 134.
[4] *Ibid.,* p. 17.
[5] *Ibid.,* p. 86.
[6] *Ibid.,* pp 22, 47, 59, 128.
[7] *Ibid.,* p. 128.
[8] *Ibid.,* p. 23.
[9] *Ibid.,* p. 40.
[10] *Ibid.,* p. 23.
[11] *Ibid.,* p. 24.
[12] *Ibid.,* p. 58.
[13] *Ibid.,* p. 94.
[14] *Ibid.*
[15] *Ibid.,* p. 75
[16] By juxtaposition on p. 70.
[17] *Ibid.,* p. 73.
[18] *Ibid.,* p. 74.
[19] *Ibid.*
[20] *Ibid.*
[21] *Ibid.* p. 84.
[22] *Ibid.,* p. 105.
[23] *Ibid.,* p. 110.
[24] *Ibid.,* p. 116.
[25] *Ibid.,* p. 114.
[26] *Ibid.,* p. 115.
[27] *Ibid.,* p. 118.

13

COMMUNICATION AND THE MIND

STEPHEN THORNTON

It is now widely acknowledged that the construction of heuristic models has been, and continues to be, one of the most productive mechanism in scientific investigation. It is also now generally recognised that the media which facilitate and expedite human communication are socially and culturally significant in a manner which is far deeper than that which was hitherto assumed - specifically, that they are not *products* of cultures at given times, but rather *structure* and *determine* the very fabric and nature of the cultures to which they themselves, in no small part, give rise. Further, the new electronic media have made a number of crucial differences, and are themselves crucially different from their predecessors in at least one respect, viz. that while all media prior to the telecommunication/electronic media extended the range and functioning of the senses, the electronic media, for the first time, offer to us data which are carried by means of a 'sense' which we do not possess, the electromagnetic spectrum. The electronic media are thus not so much an *extension* of our senses as a partial *substitution* for them, and this is what gives them their all-pervasive character. In the contemporary world, the media have entered the home, and have became integrated into the routine of daily life; in doing so, they have acquired a social dimension and configuration which outstrips all previous developments in the facilitation of human communication, and with the increasing convergence of telecommunication and computer technology this trend seems certain to become even more pronounced and significant, at the personal, national and global levels.

In view of this, it is scarcely surprising that the human communicative process should itself now be at the object of a wide-ranging, interdisciplinary investigation, and that the construction of models of communication should be central to this investigation. What is *not* widely recognised, however, is the fact that every model of human communication necessarily presupposes an account of the nature of the human mind and of language-usage - for it is the capacity to invest words and other symbols with meaning, and to fashion and utilise such extraordinarily complex sign systems as natural languages, which is perhaps the most characterising feature of the human mind. And it follows from this that any model of communication is as sound only as the account of mind upon which it is based - which in turn entails that any model which is based upon a fallacious account of mind will itself necessarily be defective.

In what follows I will attempt to show that very many models of communication are defective - some to the point of lacking coherence - in *precisely* this sense, and for *precisely* this reason. I will do so by first giving a generalised exposition of the extremely influential account of mind originating from the work of the French philosopher Descartes, which functions as a foundation for, and largely vitiates, models of communication offered by thinkers as diverse as John Locke and his empiricist successors, semiologists such as Saussure, Barth and Eco, and many contemporary 'postmodernist' thinkers, particularly Derrida. I will conclude by sketching an alternative model of communication to these, which is based upon the work of Wittgenstein in the philosophy of language and of mind.

Descartes' ambition was to derive the whole of human knowledge systematically by a rigorous process of deduction from some absolutely certain truth or truths. To this end he undertook the project of systematically doubting everything which *could* be doubted without self-contradiction, in order to determine whether or not there is anything which lies beyond the logical limit of doubt. God, the external world, even the body, may not exist, he argued, in the sense that it is not *logically* self-contradictory to assert their non-existence. But he famously concluded that one cannot, without self-contradiction, doubt that one doubts, and consequently that one exists *as* a conscious, thinking being. Descartes stated this in what is now perhaps the most widely-known philosophical Latinism: *Cogito ergo sum* ('I think, therefore I am'). This is the foundation of the Cartesian account of mind: the *ego* or self which is revealed in the *cogito* is essentially a non-material, spiritual entity, which has no essential link with any material body. Descartes' account of consciousness is closely associated with this conception of the self. On this view each individual has a unique and privileged access to his own mind, which is denied to everyone else - what I know immediately and with greatest certainty are the events which occur in my mind - my thoughts, my emotions, my perceptions, my desires, etc. - and these are not known *in this way* by anyone else. By the same token, it follows from this that I do not know other minds *in the way* in which I know my own; indeed, if I am to be said to know other minds at all, it can only be on the basis of certain inferences which I have made from what *is* directly accessible to me, viz. the behaviour of other human beings, as this presents itself to my consciousness.

This Cartesian account of mind was, in its essentials, accepted by John Locke, the father of modern British empiricism. Locke's thought is of profound historical importance for a number of reasons, not least in that he offers a theory of language-usage which is *explicitly* based upon the account of mind which he derived from Descartes, and which embodies the first model of communication associated with the Cartesian account of mind. For this reason alone, his model of communication merits close attention.

Man, Locke argues, is a social being, and consequently the primary purpose of language is a social one, viz. to make the communication of private thoughts possible. He put this as follows:

> God having designed man for a social creature made him not
> only with an inclination and under a necessity to have fellowship
> with those of his own kind, but furnished him also with language,
> which was to be the great instrument and common tie of society.[1]

A second, subsidiary function of language, he believed, is to
facilitate *memory* by enabling us to record our own thoughts
privately. If we wish to avail of the primary purpose of language,
and communicate our thoughts to others, the symbolic system
which we utilise must be intelligible to them, and for practical
purposes we fulfil this condition by using a common language,
which we have learnt rather than created. Thus in conversation, for
example, we accept and use the language of the society of which
we are members; this is a necessary precondition to being understood.

This immediately brings us to two of the most fundamental
concepts relating to human communication, meaning and understanding. To take speech as illustrative, we can say that experience
teaches us that it is possible for someone to utter words without
meaning anything by them, and to hear words without understanding them; it follows, therefore, that uttering and hearing alone
are not constituent of significant spoken language usage. Meaning
and understanding are also required. What then are meaning and
understanding, and what is it for a system of words to constitute a
language? It is one of Locke's merits that he answers these
questions clearly and unequivocally. Because God wished us to be
able to communicate with one another by means of symbols, he
argues, He equipped us with the capacity 'to frame articulate
sounds, which we call words.' This ability, however, is also
possessed by parrots, and so is clearly not a *sufficient* condition for
the characteristically human use of language. What is required in
addition to this is the capacity to attach meanings to words and
other symbols. As Locke put it:

> Besides articulate sounds, therefore, it was further necessary that
> [we] should be able to use these sounds as signs of internal
> conceptions; and to make them *stand as marks for the ideas*
> within [our] own minds, whereby they might be made known to

others, and the thoughts of men's minds be conveyed from one to another.[2]

For Locke, then, to attach meaning to a word (or any other symbol) is to make it 'stand as a mark' for one or more 'internal conceptions' or 'ideas' in one's mind - what today might be termed a process of 'conceptual encoding' - and this criterion, he believed, applies with equal validity, whether the meaning in question is 'speaker's meaning' (i.e. what an individual means by what he says) or 'hearer's meaning' (i.e. what an individual understands the utterance of another to mean).

His model of communication follows directly from this. Ideas, which in Locke's philosophy are the units of both thought and of knowledge, are, for Locke as for Descartes, *intrinsically private*, and have their origin, directly or indirectly, in the subjective sensory experiences of the individual who possesses them. To communicate such a particular private thought the individual must translate it into the public medium of language; the listener hearing these objective articulate sounds has to translate them back by correlating them with similar ideas in his mind, thus making communication complete. Locke describes this process explicitly in the *Essay*:

> Man, though he have great variety of thoughts, and such from which others as well as himself might receive profit and delight; yet they are all within his own breast, invisible and hidden from others, nor can of themselves be made to appear. The comfort and advantage of society not being to be had without communication of thoughts, it was necessary that man should find some external sensible signs whereof those invisible ideas, which his thoughts are made up of, might be made known to others. Thus we may conceive how words, which were by nature so well adapted to that purpose, came to be made use of by men as the signs of their ideas.[3]

Thus Locke believed that there is an absolute distinction between *thought*, on the one hand which he tended to think of in terms of a direct, 'internal' contemplation of a series of 'private' ideas, and *the use of signs and symbols,* on the other, and the fact that it is possible to express the same thought in a number of different linguistic forms seemed to him to be clear proof of this.

In relation to the spoken word, then, Locke saw that it is possible to make or hear verbal locutions without meaning or understanding anything by them, and that significant discourse demands not just uttering and hearing, but also meaning and understanding. From this he concluded that meaning is something which one *performs* while speaking, and that someone *speaking and meaning something by it* is engaged in two synchronous activities, 'speaking' and 'meaning', the latter of which is also an intrinsically private mental process. In other words, he assumes that because meaningless utterances can be made, or, more accurately, because utterances can be made without the individual concerned *attaching* meaning to them, to confer meaning upon a locution is to engage in a special form of *activity*, an activity which is completely intra-mental and private.

His philosophy of language thus presupposes a form of what is now called 'meaning privacy', i.e. the theory that the conferring of sense upon an expression is a private uncheckable performance which each person must perform for himself. It also presupposes a second, more extensive form of privacy. For on Locke's principles the private process by means of which terms are given meaning is that of making them 'stand for' ideas, which, as I have indicated, are on this view *themselves* intrinsically private. For Locke, therefore, all the words in any given individual's language gain significance exclusively in terms of the supposedly private, subjective experiences of that individual; their primary function is to designate these experiences and by this means to 'facilitate' interpersonal communication.

But if it was true that all experience is indeed private in this way, and that the starting point, so to speak, for each one of us was just this supposedly private realm of our own experiences, so far from *facilitating* communication, this would render it entirely *impossible*. Were two people to somehow invent completely private notations and make them significant by reference to their respective 'private' experiences, then there could be no possibility of a shared vocabulary between them - no words or symbols could possibly bridge the gulf between their irrevocably private worlds.

Thus the thesis that words gain significance by being made to 'stand as marks' for ideas or mental operations, if correct, falsifies the factual premises upon which it is based, and so, by the principle of the *reductio ad absurdum*, it is self-refuting. For if Locke's model accurately represented reality, and all the words and expressions in my vocabulary gain meaning by being correlated with my allegedly private experiences, then it would be impossible for me to *know* that people sometimes do, and sometimes do not, use words and other symbols meaningfully - this model makes any such principle of discrimination totally vacuous.

Locke's model of communication, then, which is overtly based upon the Cartesian account of mind, leads to directly to solipsism. By *asserting*, on the one hand, that the connection between the sign and the idea which is its meaning is entirely private and intramental, and on the other, by *denying* that the public use of a sign is in any way associated with its meaning, Locke places himself in the position of being unable to answer the question as to how anyone can *know* that the ideas which are before his mind, and consequently (on this model) that the meanings which he attaches to his words, *correspond* to the ideas which are in the minds of those with whom he holds discourse, i.e. that they give the *same meaning* to the words which they use. This conclusion, of which he was apparently aware, Locke dismisses with quite staggering complacency. Admitting that his theory allows that two people *might* use a word in an ostensibly similar fashion and yet give it radically different meanings, he refuses to consider in detail the implications of this on the grounds (a) that it is probably not true; (b) that if it were true, we could never establish when it did or did not occur; and (c) that even if it were true it would not be beneficial for us to recognise this!:

> Neither would it [cause any difficulty if] the same object should produce in several men's minds different ideas at the same time; e.g. if the idea that a violet produced in one man's mind by his eyes were the same that a marigold produced in another man's, and vice versa. For, since this could never be known, neither the

ideas hereby, nor the names, would at all be confounded, or any falsehood be in either.... I am nevertheless very apt to think that the sensible ideas produced by any object in different men's minds, are most commonly very near and undiscernibly alike. For which opinion, I think, there might be many reasons offered: but that being besides my present business, I shall not trouble my reader with them; but only mind him that the contrary supposition, if it could be proved, is of little use, either for the improvement of our knowledge, or conveniency of life, and so we need not trouble ourselves to examine it.[4]

Locke's model of communication, then, is fundamentally incoherent - it is, purportedly, an account of the *nature* of communication, but it has the consequence of making communication an ineffable mystery and, as I have said, taken to its logical conclusion it leads to solipsism, the theory that, *in principle*, I can know my own experiences and thoughts, and nothing else - my supposed knowledge of the existence of the external world and of other minds would, on Locke's model, be totally illusory. And by *any* standards this is an *extraordinary* outcome - a fundamental presupposition to the construction of *any* model of communication (including Locke's) is that communication occurs, and that it is a phenomenon the mechanism of which requires explanation. Yet Locke's model, so far from *explaining* communication, would, if it were true, conclusively demonstrate that interpersonal communication is an *impossibility*: my solipsistic world would logically exclude the category of the 'other-than-self', and with it the possibility of communicating with members of this category (i.e. with other human beings).

It might be thought that Locke's model is a historical aberration - that it is the product of philosophical assumptions which no-one could, or would, take seriously today. This is partly true, and partly false. It is true that this model is the product of philosophical assumptions. Specifically, it is, again, determined by Locke's uncritical and wholehearted acceptance of the Cartesian account of the nature of mind and the doctrines which are associated with this latter. It is quite false, however, to think that these assumptions are limited to Locke, or that they are not to be found in the contemporary world. For the Cartesian account of mind has gained very widespread acceptance in Western culture, to the point where it can be fairly described as now being part of what we call 'common sense' - the almost universal belief in the supposed 'privacy' of thought alone bears testimony to this. As such, it has contaminated, and continues to contaminate, models of communication offered by thinkers whose Cartesian presuppositions are less overt and obvious than Locke's. Indeed, its deeply invidious effects extends to models offered by contemporary luminaries who seem to be oblivious to the Cartesian provenance of their most cherished hypotheses. To see that this is so, one merely has to look at the work of contemporary semiologists, many of whom are amongst the most influential and highly-regarded thinkers in the fields of linguistics and media and/or communication studies today.

Modern semiological analysis began, of course, with the work of two men; the Swiss linguist Ferdinand de Saussure (1857-1913), and the American philosopher / logician Charles S. Pierce (1839-1914). The essential rationale underlying semiology is the belief that we can apply linguistic concepts and linguistic analytical techniques to phenomena other than language itself - that is to say, that we can treat all cultural phenomena (clothing, food, automobiles, media texts, etc.) as being in some way akin to language, in that they are not just objects, but *objects with meaning*, which can therefore be dealt with as *signs*.

As a linguist, Saussure's central concern was with the nature of signs, and in particular with the dynamic way in which signs are made to interact with each other in sign-systems to produce meaning. *A sign*, for Saussure, is *any object or phenomenon with a meaning*; and he argued that all signs are made up of two components, the *signifier* and the *signified*. The signifier is the element of the sign which is perceived - in the case of language the images or marks on paper, on a blackboard, or a computer screen, or the spoken word - while the signified is the mental concept to which these marks, images or sounds refer. Now it is obvious that signifiers (in language, words) differ from culture to culture, but Saussure argues that the same is equally true of *signifieds*, and therefore for *signs as units of meaning* - they are quite culture-specific, and meaning is therefore necessarily different from culture to culture. For this reason, it is a fundamental truth for Saussure that the relationship between the signifier and the signified is a *totally arbitrary, non-necessary one*; there is no necessary connection between word and concept, signifier and signified.

For Saussure, then, it follows that the connections which actually do exist between signifier and signified in any sign-system are entirely contingent or non-necessary, and subject to constant change and revision as the sign-system evolves: they are, in a word, determined by the culturally-relative *codes or conventions* which govern *all* sign-systems. And since mental concepts or signifieds are culture-specific in this way, it follows that the manner in which one cultural grouping conceptualises reality will be different (perhaps radically so) to that of other cultural groupings - signifieds or concepts, as one commentator puts it, are 'man-made, determined by the culture or sub-culture to which we belong. They are part of the linguistic or semiotic system that members of that culture use to communicate with each other.'[5] For Saussure and his followers then, it is the *internal system of relationships* between signs in any given sign-system, and particularly the relationship between signifier and signified, that we must look to if we are to understand the meanings of the signs in that system.

Now in certain respects this marks a distinct advance in our understanding of the manner in which language and other sign-systems operate in human life - in particular, the emphasis placed by Saussure and his followers on the critical importance of the internal relationships between signs *within* sign-systems is of considerable historical and scientific significance. However, what I want to emphasise here are the functional affinities between this account of the nature of meaning and communication and that offered by Locke. For it should be evident that the role assigned here by Saussure and his followers to the 'signified' or mental concept is, in effect, functionally identical to that assigned by Locke to 'ideas' - in both cases identity of meaning and therefore communication itself - is contingent upon the mental ideas (for Locke) or mental signifieds (for Saussure) being the same for all parties concerned. Thus, for example, just as Locke sought to explicate the difference between the manner in which human beings and parrots use language in terms of the presence or absence of mental ideas in the minds of the users, so too the semiologists seek to explain linguistic divergence across cultural groupings *not only* in terms of the differences between the signifiers (such as words) used by each cultural grouping, but *also* in term of variation of the relevant (mental) signifieds across the groupings. This can be seen clearly in the manner in which Fiske, for example, defines, after Saussure, the distinction between signifier and signified: 'The signifier is the sign's image as we perceive it - the marks on the paper or the sounds in the air, the signified is the mental concept to which it refers. *This mental concept is broadly common to all members of the same culture who share the same language.*'[6]. It can also be seen in the manner in which Silverman expounds one of the central elements of Saussure's theory, to which I have already alluded, the arbitrary nature of the link between signifier and signified:

> The point upon which Saussure ... insists is that no natural bond links a given signifier to its signified; their relationship is entirely conventional, and will only obtain within a certain linguistic system. *The signifier "sister" produces a more or less equivalent concept in the minds of all English speakers, but not in the minds of German or French speakers... what enables us to communicate conceptually are certain shared features at the level of the signified.*[7]

Two points need to be noted here. Firstly, the grounds upon which the semiologists base the key role assigned by them to the mental signified in their account of meaning and communication are *identical* to that which convinced Locke of the importance of ideas in the attaching of meaning to words and expressions - an implicit acceptance of the Cartesian account of the mind as a substance in which mental phenomena and operations occur and are situated. Secondly (and for this reason), the semiologists' theory runs into precisely the same insuperable difficulties which Locke confronted. For if the signified is a mental concept, something which resides in the mind of the person who possesses it, as the semiologists insist, then the question arises as to how we can *know*, for example, that such a concept is 'broadly common' to all the members of the same culture, as Fiske asserts, or that an English word like 'sister' produces, as Silverman claims, a 'more or less equivalent concept' in the minds of all English speakers, but not in the minds of German or French ones.

We do of course encounter linguistic diversity, and the semiologists are quite right in their insistence upon language and associated sign-systems as the central characteristics of any human cultural grouping. They are also correct in their assertion that the use of a given language brings with it a unique manner of conceptualising reality - that our language gives us, so to speak, a set of 'conceptual boxes' into which we fit reality in order to comprehend it at all. But these extremely perspicuous and valuable insights are vitiated by the semiologists' entirely Cartesian construction of signifieds / concepts as mental entities. As a result, the models of communication which derive from them are remarkably similar to Locke's - because of their insistence on the allegedly *mental* nature of the signifieds to which signifiers relate, and in conjunction with which they become signs and gain meaning, the semiologists put themselves in the paradoxical position of being unable to specify *when*, and *under what conditions*, communication within a culture or across cultures does or does not take place. It is their acceptance of considerations such as these, in my view, which has led Derrida and other 'post-modernists' to assert the so-called 'indeterminacy' of meaning, and to adopt a position of extreme scepticism about the very possibility of inter-personal communication through language. It is something of an embarrassment that in some quarters today this is counted as the last word in philosophical sophistication - what it is, in fact, is quite simply the ultimate revelation of the incoherence of Descartes' account of mind, and the vacuity of various models of communication, from Locke through Saussure to Derrida, which are based upon that account of mind.

My first conclusion, then, is that models of communication which invoke Cartesianism as part of their critical presuppositions, pose what is sometimes termed 'the problem of the egocentric predic-ament', i.e. the problem of my inferring that other persons have mental lives, and that their mental lives are similar to mine, on the exclusive basis of my allegedly direct knowledge of my own mental life. As it stands the problem is in fact insoluble, and it is of fundamental importance that this is recognised. For it shows quite clearly that our point of departure cannot, as so many post-Cartesians have thought, be our supposedly private mental worlds, and that it is a fallacy to treat meaning and understanding as mental activities.

What is required, then, is a radically different approach, and the one which I propose to take has its origins in the work of Wittgenstein. In the first place, it must be remarked that there is a fundamental methodological difference between Wittgenstein and most of his predecessors (and, indeed, successors) in the treatment of the role which the use of language and other sign-systems play in human life. Locke, for example, approaches this whole, very complex area by attempting to give a philosophical account of meaning, understanding, and communication, each considered individually, the results of which he then tries to weave into a general theory. The approach suggested by Wittgenstein's work, by contrast, is decidedly Kantian. Given that communication *does* take place, and that we know that it takes place, what are the grounds for its possibility? We do not and cannot *privately* correlate our supposedly 'private' ideas with words when we mean or understand them, as Locke thought; rather we first come to learn a public language, which is shared and used by others, and in this way we learn how words and expressions may or may not be used, and to what, if anything, they refer. It is only in this public context too that we come to learn how, and in what circumstances, psychological predicates ('is thinking', 'is seeing', 'loves', 'fears', 'is angry', etc.) relating to our own mental lives and to those of others are applied.

Wittgenstein's most well-known philosophical slogan is that 'meaning is use'; i.e. that the meaning of a word or an expression is its *use* in a public language, and we know whether or not someone understands the meaning of a word or an expression by observing his use of it, in the context of his general (verbal and non-verbal) behaviour. Wittgenstein was fond of bringing out the public nature of language, and of explaining his 'use' theory of meaning, by analogical reference to the game of chess (Saussure too was fond of this analogy, although he used it for very different purposes).

Learning a language, Wittgenstein asserts, is somewhat like learning to play chess. What is important in learning and playing the game is not knowing the material from which the various chess pieces are made (be it wood, ivory, or plastic), but rather the *public rules* which determine what kind of moves can be made with the pieces, and how the rules governing the movement of each piece correlate with one another. The point here is that language is like an infinitely complicated chess game: there are innumerable different kinds of 'pieces', i.e. words, sentences, and expressions, and what is important for an understanding of the language is, once again, not the objects or processes which they denote (*if* indeed they do denote objects or processes), but rather the *implicit rules* which determine the use to which they can be put. The indefinitely large number of kinds of words and kinds of expression which constitute a language-system have a multiplicity of different kinds of use; it is a mistake to think that the only, or even the primary, function of words is to *name* objects or activities.

And here again we can deconstruct one of the classical mistakes made by Locke and the other Cartesians: the word 'meaning', they see, does not name a physical or a neural activity, and since it is assumed that it must name *something*, it is inferred that it has to name a mental activity. But in fact this inference is invalid - the word 'meaning' does not function referentially *at all*, and so long as we keep asking the question 'what does the word 'meaning' name/denote/designate/stand for?' we shall merely become more and more confused. This is because the question itself is based upon a mistake; as Russell once put it in a different context, we tend to automatically assume that if a word or symbol means something, that there must be some *thing* (in the case of 'meaning', a mental act or process) for it to *mean*. To free ourselves of the tendency to look for an object corresponding to every noun, and process corresponding to every verb, it is helpful to keep words like 'there' in mind - in such cases we are not tempted to look for some *thing* which we can call 'the meaning of "there"'

Wittgenstein's account of meaning and understanding can best be grasped by reference to his technical concept of a 'language-game': every language-system, he shows, is composed of an indefinitely large number of language-games, examples of which are questioning, ordering, asking, praying, describing, guessing, etc. This number is not fixed or constant, as new language-games come into existence on a regular basis, while existing ones fall into disuse. Wittgenstein's point is that there is an *intrinsic and necessary link* between the way words are used in the performance of each game and the kind of nonverbal behaviour which is relevant to the game; e.g. the kind of behaviour which is relevant to praying is totally inappropriate in a situation where one is trying to win an argument, and vice-versa. Thus to learn a language-system we must learn how to enter into the language-games - this indicates once again that the rules which we must grasp and follow if we are to speak with meaning or to hear with understanding are *public* rather than private. The view-which is unquestionably of Cartesian provenance - that a private language is a possibility does not withstand critical scrutiny - for what could count as the *misuse* or *misunderstanding* of a word in a completely private language? Nothing! And when the possibility of *misunderstanding* disappears, so too does the possibility of *understanding*. As Wittgenstein puts it, in a putative private language 'Whatever is going to seem right to me is right. And that only means that here we can't talk about "right".[8]

In the past it has very frequently been taken for granted - and Locke and the semiologists once more are very clear cases in point - that the stating and communicating of factual information is the central 'game' in every language-system; that language is designed *primarily* to enable us to communicate our supposedly 'private' thoughts to each other. This, however, is both to misconstrue the nature of thought itself and to fail to comprehend the inherent complexity and multi-dimensionality of language.

In some language-games (e.g. ethical or aesthetic evaluation) knowledge of facts is peripheral to the game; in others, such as praying, it is irrelevant. Further, most uses of language have nothing whatever to do with conveying 'ideas' or states of mind. If I inform a motorist that the road ahead is flooded and extremely dangerous, I am not trying to bring specific 'ideas' or concepts to his mind: I am rather trying to influence his behaviour.

To understand communication itself, then, we have to see it in the overall context of our employment of the language-system in which it finds a place, and, above all, to see that meaning and understanding are determined, not by mental acts, but by the *public use* of words or other symbols which is involved in the mastery of the language-games constituting the language-system. Put very simply, a person knows the meaning of a word or expression if he has mastered the technique of applying the rules which govern it correctly, in a variety of different contexts. And it should be clear by now that the 'use' of words which determines meaning and understanding is not *restricted* to the verbal behaviour of the person involved, but extends to the broad complex of his nonverbal behaviour as well.

This is why Wittgenstein introduces the concept of a 'language-game' in the first instance; his point is that words and expressions are never used in a vacuum, so to speak, but rather always pre-suppose a context, in which the dispositions, behaviour, and capab-ilities of the person involved are *logically* related to the words utilised. That is to say, our *criteria* for ascribing such predicates as meaning and understanding to a person relate directly to his behaviour, to his capabilities, and to his dispositions. This explains how *I* can know that another person understands what *I* say, and how *he* can know that *I* understand what *he* says - in short, how we communicate - for behaviour is *publicly observable*, and capabilities and dispositions are *publicly testable*. Communication occurs within the framework of a language-game or an assemblage of language-games; in the case of speech, for example, insofar as each participant in the game follows the rules which govern it, what he says will be meaningful and comprehensible to the other participants. When a participant transgresses the rules, when his use of a word or an expression fails to match or cohere with the contextual circumstances and/or behaviour-patterns which form the backdrop against which the verbal locution is made, it will become immediately evident to others that something is amiss, and on this public basis, and on this basis *alone*, the question will arise for them as to the meaningfulness of that particular locution.

It might be objected here that this theory enables us to explain the difference between someone who uses a symbol or a set of symbols meaningfully and someone who does not, and that it gives us a general criterion for distinguishing between the two cases, but that it does not explain how we can know that a person who understands what a word/expression *means* nevertheless uses it *without meaning it*, as in the case of a false promise. In answer to this, it must again be pointed out that if meaning was a private mental act, then we could *never* know that someone said something without meaning it, and statements such as 'He said X, but he didn't really mean it', and simple questions such as 'Do you really mean that?' would have no place in our language. But in fact we do make such statements, and ask such questions, and they are, in principle, justifiable. We say of someone that he means, or does not mean, what he says, not (obviously) on the basis of an examination of his brain or mind when he speaks, but rather by virtue of the way in which he behaves, verbally and non verbally, before and/or after he speaks (there are some cases where a person's behaviour, in the general sense, is incompatible with what he says *while* he is saying it, but these are relatively rare). As Wittgenstein points out, 'The process which we might call "speaking and meaning what you speak" is not necessarily distinguished from that of speaking thoughtlessly by what happens *at the time when you speak*. What distinguishes the two may very well be what happens before or after you speak.[9] What is of importance here again is that it is the possibility of a *public check* which makes the distinction intelligible - without the possibility of such a public check the distinction between 'saying X and meaning it', and 'saying X without meaning it' collapses.

At this point I wish to direct attention, almost as an aside, as it were, to the implications which all of this has for the body -mind problem. For Wittgenstein, in his account of our use of language and the nature of communication, demonstrates conclusively that Descartes' picture of the mind-body relation - upon which Locke's and the semiologists' models of communication are based - is radically misconceived. For, again, if it was true, as both Descartes and Locke thought, that in consciousness I am aware only of my own supposedly 'private' mental life, then the reality is that inferences to an external world inhabited by other people, and inferences to the existence and nature of other minds, would always be *invalid* inferences, and solipsism would indeed be inevitable - the egocentric predicament would be one which I could never, even in principle, overcome.

Before I conclude, I want to anticipate, and answer, a possible objection. One is tempted to protest: 'But meaning *is* an experience or a mental act; I mean what I say now, and furthermore, I *know* that I mean it - meaning is something that I *do*!'. To which it can be replied: if this was true, then the link between 'saying X' and 'meaning X' would be an entirely contingent one, and if *this* in turn was true, then not only should it be possible to utter words without meaning them, but one should be able to 'mean' words without saying them (i.e. it should be possible to perform an 'act of meaning' without saying *anything*). Let us perform an experiment then: try meaning some words *without* saying them. Or, as Wittgenstein suggests, 'Say "It's cold here" and mean "It's warm here." Can you do it? And what are you doing as you do it?'[10] The impossibility of performing a mental 'act of meaning' here shows that it is not the performance of such an act which gives meaning to a word or to an expression in *any* circumstances.

In conclusion, then, I will briefly summarise the central points of my argument. The Cartesian account of mind, with its egocentric orientation, its stress on the supposedly private nature of experience and thought, and the associated doctrines of the incorrigibility of my knowledge of my own mind and my indirect and fallible knowledge of the minds of others, creates a view of the human communicative process in which it is seen essentially as a necessary mechanism whereby *points of contact* can be forged between intrinsically private mental worlds. In contemporary times this latter is usually expressed in the language of 'encoding' and 'decoding', where these are seen very much as Locke represents them, as mental acts of meaning and understanding. But the reality is that there are, and can be, *no such mental acts* - if experience and thought are intrinsically private in the Cartesian sense, then strict solipsism is unavoidable. The conferring of meaning is indeed something which *I do*, but I do it in the context of my social immersion in language as a public form of life, and by means of my participation in the public language games which constitute the framework within which human communication occurs. An adequate model of communication must take the inter-subjective, social world which we inhabit, and the public language which we share with others, as its basic points of reference, and this can be accomplished only by a firm and conscious repudiation of Cartesianism. Insofar as thinkers as diverse as Locke, Saussure, Barth and Derrida succumb to the Cartesian temptation to treat the mind as an object, and mental acts as mysterious, private processes, they fallaciously assimilate physical-object words with psychological ones. They are thus led to assume that *all* words are functionally similar to names, and that psychological words work by *naming* mental processes - that the term 'meaning', for example, designates a private mental act. In succumbing to this temptation, and in making these assumptions, they are 'bewitched by language'. The therapeutic function of philosophy, as Wittgenstein conceived it, is to free us from this kind of bewitchment, by exploding conceptual models (in this case, of communication) which, so far from *facilitating* our understanding of the process in question, come to act as insuperable *impediments* to it.

NOTES

[1] A.C. Fraser, (ed.), John Locke, *An Essay Concerning Human Understanding,* Dover, 1959, III. i. i.

[2] *Ibid.,* III.ix.2; my italics.

[3] *Ibid.,* III. ii. i.

[4] *Ibid.,* II.xxxii.15.

[5] J. Fiske, *Introduction to Communication Studies,* London, 1983 p. 49.

[6] *Ibid.,* p. 47.

[7] K. Silverman, *The Subject of Semiotics,* Oxford, 1982 pp 5-7; my italics.

[8] L. Wittgenstein, *Philosophical Investigations* (trans. G. E. M. Anscombe). Oxford, 1953, I, § 258.

[9] L. Wittgenstein, *The Blue and Brown Books,* Oxford, 1958, p. 43.

[10] Wittgenstein, *Investigations,* I, § 510.

14

PHILOSOPHERS ON ABORTION AND INFANTICIDE

FRANK BOUCHIER-HAYES

> Abortion raises subtle problems for private conscience, public
> policy, and constitutional law. Most of these problems are essent-
> ially philosophical, requiring a degree of clarity about basic
> concepts that is seldom achieved in legislative debates and letters
> to newspapers.[1]

The above quote is taken from *The Problem of Abortion*, an
important anthology of articles for anyone with an interest in this
particular moral issue. In this paper, I intend to examine the views
of two leading philosophical figures in the abortion debate. The
emergence of abortion as an ethical issue went hand in hand with
the introduction of practical ethics in the 1960s. Indeed, as L.W.
Sumner pointed out in his book, *Abortion and Moral Theory*:

> As late as two decades ago abortion was nowhere a prominent
> public issue. In virtually every nation of the world, performing
> an abortion was, under all but the rarest of circumstances, a
> criminal act...An organised women's movement was non-existent
> in the fifties. Although the control of reproduction had been an
> issue for decades, the energies of reform groups were largely
> directed to securing legal access to contraceptives. Most such

groups, whether out of principle or pragmatism, took pains to distinguish the availability of contraception from that of abortion. The consensus in all sides was that abortion was a further and much more troubled question, one that it was premature to place on the public agenda. [2]

As soon as abortion was placed on the public agenda, changes in government policy towards, and changes in public opinion on, abortion stimulated philosophers to turn their attention towards this issue in an effort to resolve it. Public issues, then, became matters of philosophical concern. Philosophy appeared to be uniquely suited to resolving issues of public debate. It could analyse these matters in a highly rational, as opposed to a highly emotional, manner. Philosophers began to take a keen interest in abortion in the 1960s, and they have continued to do so ever since.

Joel Feinberg points out that questions about the morality of abortion can be divided in two groups; those concerned with problems about the moral status of the unborn and those concerned with the resolution of conflicting claims - in particular, the claims of the mother and those of the fetus.[3]

As far as the moral status of the unborn is concerned, we find that certain philosophers accord them no moral status whereas other philosophers accord them full moral status. If philosophers view the problem of abortion as a problem of conflicting claims, then they either argue that the claims of the mother supersede those of the foetus or vice versa. All of the above points will be discussed in the course of this paper.

It is important to note, however, that our ideas about abortion do not exist in a moral vacuum. In other words, what I believe in relation to abortion will, whether I like it or not, influence what I believe in relation to other public issues such as infanticide, euthanasia, and eugenics. Arguments that those who favour even limited access to abortion will unwittingly usher in other 'moral ills' such as infanticide, euthanasia, and eugenics are known as 'slippery slope arguments'. These arguments are, not surprisingly, hotly disputed by those philosophers who seek to limit themselves to the abortion issue. However, certain philosophers do not appear to have any problem with certain of the consequences of a positive stance on abortion implied by the 'slippery slope argument'. Michael Tooley, as we shall see, argues in favour of abortion and infanticide.

It is easy to see why 'slippery slope arguments' have become popular among opponents of abortion. These arguments essentially comprise the claim that a lack of respect for any form of human life will result in a gradual eroding of respect for all forms of human life. The common thread running through the arguments of those who support the slippery slope argument is that we must protect the most vulnerable members of our society. Otherwise, we will end up with what is known as eugenics or 'survival of the genetically fittest'. Opinion, needless to say, is divided in the merits and demerits of eugenics. Do we have the right to create a genetically perfect society by any means necessary? If the answer is yes, then abortion, albeit of a limited form, would appear to be permissible. Critics can, of course, argue that the richness of our human culture is as much due to genetic imperfection as it is to genetic perfection, and that, consequently, the creation of a genetically perfect society is not a morally appropriate goal for man.

As far as the structure of the paper is concerned, part one will briefly examine some of the points which Judith Jarvis Thomson raises in her highly influential article,'A Defense Of Abortion.' Indeed, William Parent, the editor of one of Thomson's books, tells us that this article is now " the most widely reprinted essay in all of contemporary philosophy."[4] Judith Jarvis Thomson bases her argument on the assumption that foetuses are persons from the moment of conception. Despite the latter assumption, Thomson argues that this does not necessarily mean that foetuses have a right to life. She is not, however, in favour of infanticide. She is also not in favour of abortion on demand, but argues instead, as Susan Sherwin points out, that:

> if the costs to the mother are not too severe, then it seems it would be proper of her to provide such care (and, in some cases, it would be 'positively indecent' of her not to) but that, even so, it seems she does not have an actual moral duty to do so.[5]

208

Part two will examine some of the points raised by Michael Tooley in an article entitled 'In Defense of Abortion and Infanticide,' which is published in Feinberg's excellent aforementioned anthology, as well as offering a brief summary of Tooley's book, *Abortion and Infanticide*. Michael Tooley accords foetuses and certain infants no moral status. Tooley, unlike Thomson, argues that not only abortion but also infanticide should be seen to be morally permissible on the grounds that both involve the killing of non-persons. Part three will examine some criticisms of Thomson's article. Such criticisms are invariably associated with the thought experiments which she uses to support her position. Indeed, her imaginative thought experiments undoubtedly serve to partly explain the article's continued popularity. Part four will consider Tooley's approach to the issues of abortion and infanticide. I should mention that Tooley also uses thought experiments, but that the spatial constraints of this paper prevented me from either presenting them or criticising them. In any case, a basic understanding of Tooley's central argument does not, in my view, necessarily involve an awareness of his thought experiments. Part five will explore an alternative and, to my mind, more realistic approach to the issues of abortion and infanticide. This approach will indicate new ways in which personhood can be understood in the context of these issues.

My conclusion will be that although Thomson and Tooley have raised some important points which richly deserve our closest attention, they fail to properly relate their arguments to the issues of abortion and infanticide for several reasons. Firstly, Thomson's thought experiment involving an ailing violinist bears no resemblance to the abortion situation. Secondly, Thomson and Tooley have failed to grasp the uniqueness of the abortion dilemma in their arguments. They both place too much emphasis on the woman and too little emphasis on the foetus. They fail to realise that the needs of both beings must be taken into account.

Part One

Thomson begins her article by tackling the premiss which she believes much of the opposition to abortion relies upon, *viz.* that the foetus is a human being or person from the time it is conceived. To claim this, she argues, would be like claiming that an acorn is an oak tree. She does, however, concede that choosing a point in the development of the foetus where we can definitely say that a human being exists, which didn't exist before this point, is highly problematic. Indeed, she tells us that, in her view:

> we shall probably have to agree that the foetus has already become human person well before birth.[6]

She does not, however, believe that a human being or person is present at conception. Despite the latter statement, Thomson is prepared to allow, for the purposes of her argument, the premiss that the foetus is a person from the time of conception.

Thomson proceeds by outlining what she believes to be the argument which certain opponents of abortion would derive from the premiss above-mentioned. The crux of this argument, as Thomson sees it, is that the right to life of the foetus outweighs the right to life of the mother "to decide what happens in and to her body."[7] The subsequent thought experiment which Thomson places before us is an attempt to expose the flaws which she believes exist in the latter statement. The thought experiment involves you imagining a situation in which you wake up in a hospital bed to discover that your circulatory has been connected up to the circulatory system of an unconscious famous violinist. The reason given for this gross abuse of your privacy is that the violinist has a serious kidney infection. Unfortunately, for you, the appropriate treatment consists of connecting him up to you, since both you and the violinist have been found to possess the same rare blood type by the Society of Music Lovers. The hospital director informs you that even though the Society of Music Lovers was wrong to kidnap you and place you in this difficult position, you are morally compelled to remain as you are until such time as the violinist can function independently of you. To do otherwise, he points out, would result in the death of the violinist and to allow this, at least in the eyes of the hospital director, is patently impermissible. Given that the time frame involved is nine months, Thomson asks you whether you would feel morally obliged to defer to the wishes and beliefs of the hospital director. Apparently worried that you will fail to see what she sees as a ludicrous situation which you are under no obligation to tolerate, Thomson stretches the time frame indefinitely. In short, she wants us to accept that the right to life of one person does not override the right of another person to choose what happens in and to his or her body, when the connection between such people resembles that expressed in the thought experiment outlined above.

Thomson acknowledges the fact that opponents of abortion can point to the involuntary nature of the relationship between the violinist and donor, and can liken such a relationship to that between the mother and foetus in a rape-induced pregnancy. She goes on to say that they can then make an exception for such pregnancies and:

> can say that persons have a right to life only if they didn't come into existence because of rape; or they can say that all persons have a right to life, but that some have less of a right than others, in particular, that those who came into existence because of rape have less.[8]

As it happens, Thomson tells us, most opponents of abortion do not make allowances for cases of rape. Thomson is concerned with the phenomenon of unwanted pregnancies in general, and not just with the phenomenon of unwanted pregnancies arising as a result of rape. In order to explain her position on this matter, she claims that it is necessary to "distinguish between two kinds of Samaritan: the Good Samaritan and what we might call the Minimally Decent Samaritan."[9] Thomson uses the famous biblical story to assist her in explaining the distinction. The Good Samaritan in the story, Thomson reminds us, was the person who seriously inconvenienced himself in assisting the person in need. The Minimally Decent Samaritan, had he or she been present in the story, would have been the person who would have helped the person in need by doing less for him than the Good Samaritan did. Hence, it turns out that, according to Thomson, the people in the story who did nothing to help the person in need were not even Minimally Decent

Samaritans " not because they were not Samaritans, but because they were not even minimally decent."[10]

Even if the story of the Good Samaritan was meant to serve as an example of what we should do in similar circumstances, we are not required, according to Thomson, to do more than the Good Samaritan would do in similar circumstances. Society at present, however, Thomson points out, requires women "to be not merely Minimally Decent Samaritans, but Good Samaritans to unborn persons inside them."[11]

Thomson acknowledges the fact that some people might claim that all of her analogies fail to take into account the special relationship which exists between mother and foetus. She, however, contends that no such relationship exists unless one assumes responsibility for the foetus either implicitly or explicitly. Once the parents have assumed responsibility for the foetus, "they have given it rights, and they cannot now withdraw support from it at the cost of its life because they now find it difficult to go on providing for it."[12] Hence, unprotected sex, with foreknowledge of the possible consequences, resulting in pregnancy and carried to term involves, according to Thomson, the implicit assumption of certain responsibilities which cannot be withdrawn if to do so would result in the death of the foetus.

On the other hand, if the parents have "taken all reasonable precautions against having a child, they do not simply by virtue of their biological relationship to the child who comes into existence have a special responsibility for it."[13] What this means for Thomson is that if protected sexual intercourse results in an unwanted pregnancy, then the parents have the choice of either accepting or rejecting responsibility for the foetus but that "if assuming responsibility for it would require large sacrifices, then they may refuse."[14] Thomson tells us that a Splendid Samaritan would assume responsibility for the foetus in the previous situation, regardless of the consequences which such a decision might have for him or her. Thomson points out, however, that a Splendid Samaritan would also assume responsibility for the famous violinist.

Thomson concludes her article with an explanation as to why many proponents of the right to choose will find her argument concerning abortion somewhat lacking in terms of what it can do to assist their argument. Firstly, she points out that she has been arguing that abortion is sometimes, though not always, permissible. She has, in particular, been arguing that cases involving 'Minimally Decent Samaritanism' should be endured, whereas cases of pregnancy involving 'Good or Splendid Samaritanism' needn't necessarily be endured. Secondly, she tells us that she has not been "arguing for the right to secure the death of the unborn child."[15] She acknowledges the fact that, given current medical capabilities, it is easy to make the mistake of taking abortion to mean the fully intended destruction of the foetus rather than the termination of a pregnancy. In other words, because most abortions are carried out when the foetus has no chance of surviving outside the womb under present medical conditions, people often tend to equate abortion with the death of the foetus instead of seeing it as the termination of a pregnancy. According to Thomson, "the desire for the child's death is not one which anybody may gratify, should it turn out to be possible to detach the child alive."[16]

Thomson ends her article by saying that if we accept, as she does, that no person exists at conception or for a period after conception, bearing in mind that "we have only been pretending throughout that the foetus is a human being from the moment of conception," then very early abortions do not comprise the subject matter for moral debate.[17] In other words, only when the requisite physiological development has occurred, in Thomson's view, can we justifiably couch a discussion of the abortion of such an entity in moral terms.

Part Two

In his article, Michael Tooley introduces Feinberg's 'interest principle' in an effort to better explain his position. He tells us that, according to the 'interest principle', only that which has or is capable of having interests can have rights. In addition, interests are in some way related to desires. Tooley finds the interest principle somewhat lacking for his purposes because although it

213

talks of things possibly having rights, it does not talk of things actually having "rights - including, in particular, a right not to be destroyed."[18] He goes on to define a 'particular interest principle' which, he tells us, asserts "that an entity cannot have a particular right, R, unless it is at least capable of having some interest, I, which is furthered by its having right R."[19] This, he tells us, will help to explain why new-born kittens have a right not to be tortured but do not have a serious right to life.

Kittens have a right not to be tortured, according to Tooley, because they can be said to have an interest in not experiencing pain. Kittens do not, however, according to Tooley, have a serious right to life because they cannot be said to have an interest in their own continued existence. Tooley contends that kittens cannot have an interest in their own continued existence because they lack self-consciousness. Moreover, he argues that since not only foetuses but also new-born babies lack self-consciousness and, consequently, cannot have an interest in their own continued existence, they also do not have a serious right to life.

Tooley applies the 'particular interest principle' to the concept of a right to life . Before doing this, however, he replaces the term 'right to life' with the term 'right of a subject of experiences and other mental states to continue to exist'. He makes the point that interests presuppose desires and that desires "existing at different times can belong to a single continuing subject of consciousness only if that subject of consciousness possesses, at some time, the concept of a continuing self or mental substance."[20] The latter point, together with the 'particular interest principle', are used to argue for the necessary condition, viz. that the entity have, at least once, "the concept of a continuing self or mental substance," which something must fulfil in order that it possess a right to life.[21]

Tooley then explores the implications which the latter statement has for the morality of abortion and infanticide. He points out that if, as most philosophers do, one sees the mind and brain as being closely related, then "when human development, both behavioural and neurophysiological, is closely examined, it is seen to be most unlikely that human fetuses, or even newborn babies, possess any concept of a continuing self."[22] What this means, according to

Tooley, is that neither new-born babies nor foetuses have a right to life.

If, however, one chooses to hold that the mind is distinct from the brain, then, according to Tooley, this commits one either to the belief "that it is possible to establish, by means of a purely metaphysical argument, that a human mind, with its mature capacities, is present in a human from conception onward" or to the belief "that it is a divinely revealed truth that human beings have minds from conception onward."[23] He denies the validity of the former belief and points out that doubts about the existence of God create uncertainty about the validity of the latter belief. In addition, Tooley points out that the latter belief does not enjoy widespread acceptance either among religions or within the religion to which it belongs.

Interestingly, Tooley argues that adult members of certain nonhuman species have a right to life because he believes "that some nonhuman animals are capable of envisaging a future for themselves, and of having desires about future states of themselves .. that anything which exercises these capacities has an interest in its own continued existence. And .. that having an interest in one's own continued existence is not merely a necessary, but also a sufficient, condition for having a right to life."[24]

As far as infanticide is concerned, he makes the point that certain philosophers base their moral objections to infanticide on common moral intuitions since common moral intuitions deem infanticide to be morally wrong. Tooley himself argues that "even if [one] grants, at least for the sake of argument, that moral intuitions are the final court of appeal regarding the acceptability of moral principles, the question of the morality of infanticide is not one that can be settled by an appeal to our intuitions concerning it."[25] Any proper rejection of infanticide must, according to Tooley, be based on an impregnable argument. Tooley strongly denies the possibility of such an argument.

Tooley's book, *Abortion and Infanticide*, presents a sustained defence of the position on abortion and infanticide which he presented in his articles on these issues. It also deals with some of the criticisms made of his position on these issues. He offers us reasons why the standard objections to infanticide should be rejected and concludes, among other things, that in order for the issues to be satisfactorily resolved, there must be "much closer co-operation between, on the one hand, philosophers working in this area of ethics, and, on the other, scientists working in areas such as psychology and neurophysiology."[26]

Part Three

Francis Beckwith finds four ethical problems with Thomson's analogy. Firstly, he tells us that in "using the violinist as a paradigm for all relationships, which implies that moral obligations must be voluntarily accepted in order to have moral force, Thomson mistakenly infers that all true moral obligations to one's offspring are voluntary."[27] Beckwith contends that in an unwanted pregnancy the reluctant father has involuntary obligations to his offspring because of "the fact that he engaged in an act, sexual intercourse, which he fully realised could result in the creation of another human being, although he took every precaution to avoid such a result."[28]

Secondly, he tells us that Thomson's volunteerism, discussed above, opposes family morality, "which has as one of its central beliefs that an individual has special personal obligations to his offspring and family which he does not have to other persons."[29] He goes on to say that even if Thomson sees the concept of family as being oppressive towards women, "a great number of ordinary men and women, who have found joy, happiness and love in family life, find Thomson's volunteerism to be counter-intuitive."[30]

Thirdly, he argues that one can establish that the foetus has a prima facie right to the mother's body on the following grounds: the foetus is something which is dependent on its mother; this stage of a human being's natural development takes place in the womb; the foetus, when born, has a natural claim upon its parents that they care for it, even if it is the case that they never actually wanted it; and, finally, there is no reason to deny the foetus a natural prima facie right to its mother's body if, as Thomson allows, it is fully human prior to birth.

Fourthly, he argues that abortion is not simply the withholding if treatment for the foetus, but is in fact the killing of the foetus. He makes the point that "calling abortion the 'withholding of support or treatment' makes about as much sense as calling suffocating someone with a pillow the withdrawing of oxygen."[31]

Quite apart from all of the above criticisms, Beckwith is fundamentally opposed to Thomson's use of the violinist analogy as is clear from the following passage:

> It is evident that Thomson's violinist illustration undermines the deep natural bond between other and child by making it seem no different than two strangers artificially hooked-up to each other so that one can steal the service of the other's kidneys. Never has something so human, so natural, so beautiful, and so wonderfully demanding of our human creativity and love been reduced to such a brutal caricature.[32]

Part Four

Kenneth R. Pahel, in an article argues that as far as the right to life or, to use Tooley's term, the right to continued existence is concerned, foetuses and new-born infants "are beings that will, unless prevented, develop the particular interests, desires, and supporting concepts protected by this right in a normal healthy process of maturation," and that, consequently, "it is not actually having desires at some time that is essential, but the potentiality for naturally acquiring these desires and concepts that constitutes the necessary condition for being a holder of certain rights."[33]

In my view, Tooley must be complimented for investigating what it is that separates human beings from other animals. Our capacity for self-consciousness does indeed serve to separate us from other animals. However, our capacity for morality also serves to distinguish us from other animals. In other words, we can behave morally towards animals by becoming vegetarian or by becoming more humane in our treatment of animals, and towards nature in general by becoming more environmentally aware. Morality, in my view, seeks to include rather than exclude.

217

I do not agree with Tooley's assertion that self-consciousness alone ensures that something has a serious right to life. Tooley argues that only those things which can have an interest in continuing to exist can have a right to continue to exist. Interests, however, Tolley tells us, presuppose desires. In other words, it cannot be in a thing's interest to continue to exist if it is incapable of desiring to continue to exist. It is my belief, however, that even though plants cannot have desires, it is morally objectionable for someone to argue that because of the latter inadequacy they have no right to continue to exist. I am not denying that Tooley has made some important points about what it means to be a rights holder. I am, however, saying that Tooley has not exclusively defined what a rights holder is.

Part Five

Shannon M. Jordan, in article entitled 'The Moral Community and Persons,' suggests that rather than trying to define what person is and thereby establishing which human beings are members of the moral community, we should "invert the order of reasoning to first determine the meaning of moral community, for then we will already understand who is a person."[34] The following passage outlines Jordan's essential characteristics of human life:

> Human life is not and cannot be solitary; it is always lived in community; it is a life in which persons are bound together by rational intentions and actions which constitute their relationships with each other and thus form their moral commitments. The bond formed thereby is a fundamental moral bond which sets persons in moral relationships with each other, constituting them as moral persons. This bond is forged in those circumstances which are fundamentally constitutive of the moral life; birth, nurture, and the community in which one, normally by choice, lives shared lives. In two of these, i.e. birth and nurture, the self is constituted as a moral person through no choice of one's own; only in the third circumstance are some capable of choosing in an autonomous or self-constituting way.[35]

Jordan criticises moral theories which focus on the rational autonomous individual and which hold that as far as the foetus, the neonate, the infant, the retarded, the insane, the comatose, and the senile are concerned, we should act in such a way as to "respect the person one has been or might become, but that failure to do so cannot be as serious an offense as failure to respect the autonomy of a fully competent or rational person."[36] Jordan argues that such theories fail to recognise that it is the moral community which creates persons rather than vice versa. In other words, human beings do not exist in a relational vacuum; they exist through relationships with others. In short, it can be said that the morality of nurturance governs our relationships with foetuses, infants, children and adults. Furthermore, a study of phenomenology coupled with cultural anthropology leads Jordan to conclude that "human survival, both individually and as a species, necessarily requires prescribed patterns of belief, behaviour and relationships - which is to say that human being is always being in a moral community."[37]

Jordan goes on to make the point that infant survival depends on human action which itself reflects rational intentions. In particular, Jordan tells us that the infant is a person not because of his future ability to exhibit rational intentionality, but because "in his infant incompetency the very contingency of his existence is based on membership in a community of rationally intending persons."[38] In other words, Jordan is saying that because the infant only possesses a non-rational self which cannot act with rational intention, it depends upon the 'other' self, *viz.* the moral community, to act with rational intention on his or her behalf. What this means is that the term 'person' does not refer to some grouping within the human species but that any human being "is necessarily being person in-relation, member-of-moral-community, self-in-the-life-world-of-other selves." [39]

I find Jordan's article highly persuasive because it seems to square strongly with our moral intuitions about the vulnerable in society. It also allows us to get around Tooley's principle which excludes foetuses and new-borns from the realm of persons due to their inability to act rationally by arguing that foetuses and new-borns are persons because we, the moral community, are their rational selves until such time as they acquire their rational selves. Moreover, if they can never be said to have acquired their rational selves, then we continue to be their rational or 'other' selves.

Another definition of personhood is provided by Marjorie Reiley Maguire who tells us that the point at which personhood begins is the point when the mother accepts the pregnancy. She argues that when the mother accepts the pregnancy, the foetus' "potentiality for relationality and sociality is activated, because it is brought into a personal relationship with a human person, with the only human person who can actuate this potentiality while the fetus is still in the mother's body and in a previable state."[40] Reiley Maguire echoes the remarks of Shannon M. Jordan in the following extract:

> The fetus cannot become related to the human social community except through the mediation of the mother. It is the mother who makes the fetus a social being by accepting its relatedness to her. Thus, it is the mother who makes the fetus a person.[41]

She goes on to tell us that she would demand that the brain and central nervous system were developed to the extent that the foetus was almost viable before she "would say that a biological reality existed which presumed consent of the mother to the pregnancy."[42] Reiley Maguire opts for viability as the cut-off point while, at the same time, recognising that viability is itself "a shifting area and, in fact, is not even purely biological but is itself dependent on society's standards as technology allows society to take over biology."[43] She points out that when the foetus becomes viable, it no longer needs the mother to establish a relationship for it with the human social community.

Paul Gomberg takes up the notion of nurturance discussed by Jordan, and argues that instead of being a dispute about when a foetus becomes a person, the abortion controversy is a dispute about the morality of nurturance. Gomberg suggests that:

> the abortion controversy derives less from disagreement about how to apply the principle prohibiting the killing of another person and more from the part of our morality that concerns

parental duties of nurturance of the young: what are our duties to our offspring? when do those duties take hold?[44]

Gomberg claims that the suggestion that the abortion controversy concerns the morality of nurturance highlights the following issues:

> It gives a better articulation of the objection to abortion than the claim that abortion is murder; it allows us to understand why many believe that later abortions are morally more problematic than earlier ones; it puts the issue of abortion in the context of the morality that governs family life; and, most important, it allows us to understand why there is, on the one hand, a connection between conservatism on abortion and traditional women's roles and, on the other, a connection between liberalism and affirmation of equality between men and women. [45]

According to Gomberg, it is more appropriate to describe abortion as a failure to nurture than to describe it as an act of murder, because the issue of abortion involves duties towards offspring rather than duties towards adults. In other words, moral relations between adults are characterised by a principle forbidding one person from killing another person whereas moral relations between parents and their offspring are characterised by a principle entailing that parents nurture their offspring until they become self-sufficient. Gomberg also makes the point that because abortion as an issue involves moral relations between adults and their off-spring, philosophers such as Michael Tooley are misguided in their approach to, and solution of, the problems of abortion and infant-icide. Gomberg himself expresses the latter point as follows:

> I doubt that the morality of nurturance is derivable from principles governing moral relations between adults, the principle prohibiting killing of another person being paradigmatic of morality between adults. Hence I doubt the significance of both the attempts to derive a prohibition on abortion from potential to become an adult like ourselves, and the vindications of abortion which rely on criticisms of such arguments. Since the purpose of the present paper is only to understand the abortion debate, I

221

adopt, methodically, a moral intuitionism which articulates the moral imperatives commonly accepted in our culture.[46]

Gomberg echoes the remarks of Marjorie Reiley Maguire when he says that the morality of nurturance takes over when a woman accepts her pregnancy. Gomberg argues that if we accept that a woman's chief role is to bear and nurture children, then the woman is morally required to accept her pregnancy from the moment of conception. He also argues, however, that if we accept that a woman's chief role is not to bear and nurture children, then the woman can choose either to accept or to reject her pregnancy. On the other hand, Gomberg points out that while most of us believe that early abortions appear to be in line with the morality of nurturance, most of us "believe that later abortions are morally and emotionally more problematic" because although "there is no precise point at which it is clear that the morality of nurturance must apply to the fetus, it is clear that the longer we wait to abort, the more like a baby is the thing we destroy."[47]

Gomberg is highly critical of conservatives who see women as being more biologically suited to being mothers and childbearers than to being members of a world of recognised employment. This emphasis on the servile status of women is, as he points out, highly demeaning for women. Keeping the latter point in mind, Gomberg concludes his article by offering a twofold solution to the problem of abortion:

> First, instead of allowing the communism of the family to be undermined by the competitiveness of the capitalist order, the egalitarianism and commitment to others that characterise family relations at their best should be spread to the larger world. Second, nurturing attitudes can represent morality rather than servility in a world where they are cultivated equally among adults; the duties of nurturance must fall equally on men. But where much of our social life is governed by market imperatives, it becomes impossible to share nurturing equally among men and women. This suggests that a satisfactory solution to the problems surrounding the abortion issue will require changing the

> economic structures of our society. The moral problems of
> abortion are really social problems of capitalist society.[48]

Jordan, Reiley Maguire, and Gomberg analyse the issues of
abortion and infanticide as they are experienced by women. They
do not parade elaborate hypothetical examples before our eyes to
support their argument because, unlike Thomson, they do not need
to do so. They adopt a pragmatic approach to the question of
personhood which allows for variation in terms of defining the
term 'person'. In other words, they accept that personhood of the
foetus occurs for different people at different stages of foetal
development. All are agreed, however, that as the foetus
approaches viability, it becomes less and less morally permissible
for it to be aborted. Consequently, then, they are prepared to
accept early abortions, they are strongly disinclined to accept abortions which occur close to the point at which the foetus becomes
viable, and they are not prepared to accept abortions which occur
from the moment that the foetus becomes viable.

Although Jordan, Reiley Maguire, and Gomberg adopt a
moderate or developmental approach to the issue of abortion, they
acknowledge that the mother can choose to recognise the foetus as
a person prior to viability. From that point on, then, we, the moral
community, must also recognise this foetus as a person. In other
words, we must recognise this foetus as something which is as
deserving of our respect as is any other human being with which
we might come in contact.

In conclusion, then, it is my belief that philosophers can make
significant contributions to the abortion debate, but only if they are
prepared to approach the issue of abortion in terms of how it is
actually experienced by the people involved. If philosophers
choose to follow the approaches made by Judith Jarvis Thomson
and Michael Tooley, then I think that no significant advances will
or can be made towards resolving this issue of abortion.

Resolving the issue of abortion involves, in my view, trying to
look at the issue from the perspective of the beings involved, *viz.*
the mother and foetus. When we do this, we will, I think, see that
the abortion issue is not about the rights which we as adults have
against each other or about the capacities which we as persons

have to make rational decisions, but that it is about the duties which we as adults have towards our offspring. Abortion, Paul Gomberg argues, can only morally occur if it occurs in accordance with the morality of nurturance.

According to the morality of nurturance, we have, Gomberg tells us, a duty to take care of our offspring until they become self sufficient. When do these duties of nurturance take hold? This is a difficult question to answer as they appear to take hold at different times for different people. It is not my intention here to attempt to answer this question except to say that an ethic of nurturance allows for a plurality of answers as opposed to one single answer to this question.

Notwithstanding the latter statement, however, an ethic of nurturance such as we have encountered morally prohibits infanticide on the grounds that at viability and, consequently, at birth a person unquestionably exists which has as much a right to life as any other person whereas prior to viability an organism exists which one is not morally required to recognise as a person, even though one may wish to do so.

It will of course be noted that my brief survey of philosophical approaches to the issue of abortion has yielded no definitive answer, but this is, I think, a measure of the philosophical complexity of the issue, and, at any rate, with a paper of this size I can only hope to give a selective outline of the issues of abortion and infanticide as seen through the eyes of certain philosophers.

NOTES

[1] Joel Feinberg, (ed.), *The Problem of Abortion*, California, 1984, p. 1.

[2] L.W. Sumner, *Abortion and Moral Theory*, Princeton, 1981, p. 3.

[3] Feinberg, *The Problem of Abortion*, p. 1.

[4] J.J. Thomson, *Rights, Restitution and Risk*, Harvard, 1986, vii.

[5] S. Sherwin, 'The Concept of a Person in the Context of Abortion' in *Bioethics Quarterly*, vol. 3, 1981. p. 31.

[6] J.J. Thomson, 'A Defense of Abortion' in *Philosophy and Public Affairs*, vol.1, no.1, 1971, p. 48.

[7] *Ibid.*

[8] *Ibid.*, p. 49.

[9] *Ibid.*, p. 62

[10] *Ibid.*

[11] Ibid., p. 63.

[12] *Ibid.*, p. 65.

[13] *Ibid.*

[14] *Ibid.*

[15] *Ibid.*, p. 66.

[16] *Ibid.*

[17] *Ibid.*

[18] Michael Tooley, 'In Defense Of Abortion and Infanticide' in Joel Feinberg, (ed.), *The Problem of Abortion,* California, 1984, p. 124.

[19] *Ibid.*, p. 125.

[20] *Ibid.*, p. 129.

[21] *Ibid.*, p. 130.

[22] *Ibid.*, pp 130-1.

[23] *Ibid.*, p. 131.

[24] *Ibid.*, p. 133.

[25] *Ibid.*, p. 122.

[26] Michael Tooley, *Abortion and Infanticide,* Oxford, 1983, p. 425.

[27] F.J. Beckwith, 'Personal Bodily Rights, Abortion and Unplugging the Violinist' in *International Philosophical Quarterly*, vol.32, no.1, 1992, p. 111.

[28] *Ibid.*

[29] *Ibid.*, p. 112.

[30] *Ibid.*

[31] *Ibid.*, p. 116.

[32] *Ibid.*, p. 114.

[33] K.R. Pahel, 'Michael Tooley on Abortion and Potentiality' in *The Southern Journal of Philosophy*, vol.25, 1987, p. 94.

[34] S.M. Jordan, 'The Moral Community and Persons' in *Philosophy Today.* vol.30, no.2, 1986, p. 109.

[35] *Ibid.*

[36] *Ibid.*, p. 110.

[37] *Ibid.*, p. 113.

[38] *Ibid.*, p. 114.

[39] *Ibid.*, p. 116.

[40] Marjorie Reiley Maguire, 'Personhood, Covenant, and Abortion' in *American Journal of Theology and Philosophy*, vol.6, no.1, 1985, p. 38.

[41] *Ibid.*

[42] *Ibid.*, p. 41.

[43] *Ibid.*

[44] Paul Gomberg, 'Abortion and the Morality of Nurturance' in *Canadian Journal of Philosophy*, vol.21, no.4, 1990, p. 514.

[45] *Ibid.*
[46] *Ibid.,* p. 515.
[47] *Ibid.,* p. 519.
[48] *Ibid.,* p. 524.

GEOGRAPHY

15

POOR PEOPLE OR POOR PLACE? URBAN DEPRIVATION IN SOUTHILL EAST, LIMERICK CITY[1]

DES McCAFFERTY

INTRODUCTION

In its overview statement on *Poverty, Social Exclusion and Inequality in Ireland*, the Inter-Departmental Policy Committee on the National Anti-Poverty Strategy identifies concentrations of socio-economic disadvantage in two general types of urban setting.[2] These are: (1) inner-city areas that have experienced economic and physical decline and restructuring; and (2) large local authority housing estates on the outskirts of urban centres. While the distinction between these two types may be overstated, in particular in terms of the causal factors and processes involved, both types of area are found in Limerick, the third largest urban centre in the country. Research based on the 1991 census of population has demonstrated the existence of a large number of areas characterised by relative deprivation within the County Borough of Limerick. Using a composite index of deprivation derived from thirteen surrogate measures of poverty, sixteen of the 37 wards of Limerick CB have been classified into the most disadvantaged decile (10%) of census districts in the country as a whole.[3] These sixteen wards account for some 48% of the population of the County Borough. At the other end of the spectrum, six wards, containing 20% of the population, rank in the least disadvantaged decile in national terms. Limerick is clearly a highly polarised city in socio-economic terms. Moreover this polarisation has a strong geographical dimension, with wards in the most deprived quintile (i.e., with decile scores of 9 or 10 - see Fig. 1) located in a classical sectoral pattern running north-west to south-east through the city centre. Despite recent strong growth in investment in the local economy, disparities in levels of socio-economic well-being have not diminished; indeed they may have increased.[4]

This paper focuses on social, economic and physical (environmental) aspects of poverty in part of the Southill area of Limerick, an area of public housing located on the southern edge of the city. Southill falls within the most disadvantaged decile referred to above, and was one of the four communities in Limerick city targeted under the EU Poverty 3 programme which ran from 1989 until 1994. The area was developed at a time of major housing shortage in the late 1960s and early 1970s in what was then the largest housing development ever undertaken by Limerick Corporation. While most of the initial tenants were established residents of older areas of the city, who were either living in overcrowded accommodation or displaced by redevelopment, a significant proportion consisted of recent migrants from rural areas who were drawn to the city by the expansion of job opportunities in the manufacturing sector especially. Southill, which is usually defined at parish level, comprises the four housing estates of Carew Park, Keyes Park, Kincora Park and O'Malley Park which together contain approximately 1150 households.

Because the Southill estates are all broadly similar in socio-economic character and were built at about the same time[5], the area has a strong identity within the city. This identity is reinforced by the fact that Southill is delimited by clearly defined boundaries on all sides: to the south and west by undeveloped land or land

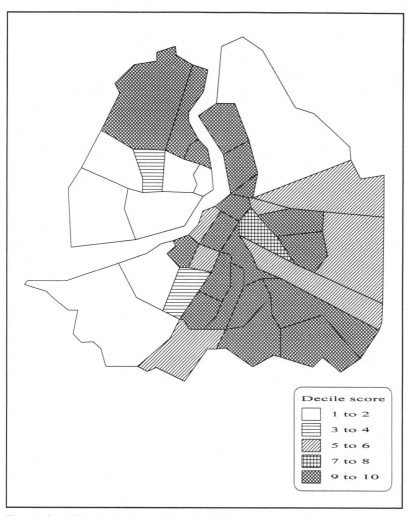

Figure 1: Overall Deprivation Score, 1991, Limerick County Borough (Based on data in ADM 1995)

zoned for recreational use, and to the north and east by industrial land uses and major regional roads. For the purposes of this paper attention is confined to the eastern part of Southill comprising O'Malley Park and Keyes Park which together constitute the Galvone B census ward (Fig. 2). These two areas, and in particular O'Malley Park which is by far the largest of the four estates, constitute the core of the Southill area, containing roughly 66% of its total population. While the sub-area accounts for just 5% of the population of the County Borough as a whole, it exemplifies many of the social, economic and environmental problems that are common to deprived communities in Limerick and other Irish towns and cities, in particular those in large peripheral public housing estates. The sub-area will be referred to throughout the paper as Southill East.

The remainder of the paper is divided into three sections as follows. The first section looks at a number of aspects of the demographic, social and economic structure of the area, focusing in particular on those attributes which have been shown in national studies to characterise households which are at a high risk of poverty. The next section switches the focus to what Smith refers to as "place poverty".[6] It examines key aspects of environmental quality in the area (including housing), and argues that deficiencies in respect of the physical environment have played a central role in the social and economic deterioration of the area. The final section concludes the paper with a brief discussion of the need for policy initiatives, under the rubric of area-based initiatives in particular, to address the problems of deprived peripheral housing estates.

ASPECTS OF THE DEMOGRAPHIC, SOCIAL AND ECONOMIC STRUCTURE OF SOUTHILL EAST

This section of the paper provides a profile of the population of Southill East based on the small area population statistics from the 1991 census of population, which furnishes information on a wide range of demographic, social and economic variables[7]. The focus is on characteristics which are specially relevant to an understanding of the nature of disadvantage in the area, in particular on those

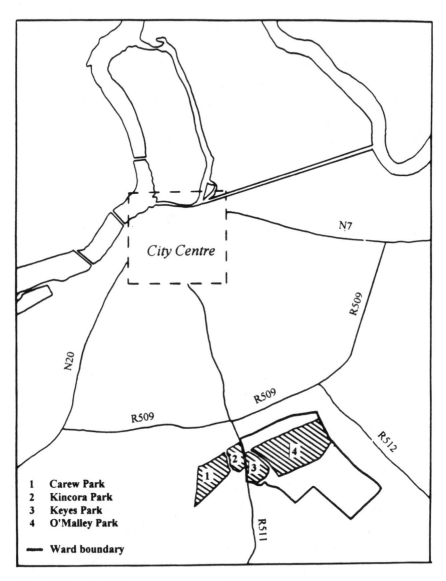

Figure 2: Location Map

attributes which have been shown in national studies based on the 1987 ESRI survey of income distribution to be associated with income poverty, or with income poverty and material deprivation.[8] While the significance of particular attributes depends to some extent on the measure of poverty used, certain household types have been consistently identified as being at a high risk of poverty in the sense that relatively high proportions of such types fall below the various threshold income levels used to establish poverty lines. Among the subset of these for which small area enumerations are available from the census of population are: households with more than four children; households with young female heads; single adult households with children; and households headed by an unemployed person. By looking at the rate of occurrence of these household types in the area, and more generally at the attributes on which they are based (large family sizes, lone parenthood, unemployment), it is possible to get a preliminary picture of the extent of poverty in Southill East.

Population, Household and Family Structures

In 1991 the population of Southill East stood at 2,748 persons. The age structure of the population is illustrated in Table 1, which shows that, relative to the city as a whole[9], the area has a youthful population profile with a preponderance of those aged under 25 years of age, and relatively few aged over 55 years. The cohort aged under 15 years accounted for over one thousand persons - more than one-third of the entire population - and this is reflected in a young dependency ratio[10] of 61.6, over one and a half times that for the city as a whole (38.8). While some maturing of the age profile has occurred in the 25 years since the development of the area - the young dependency ratio in 1971 stood at 106.7 - this has been less marked than might have been expected, especially in view of the general decrease in fertility rates. The persistence of the youthful population profile is related to the pattern of population movements from the area. These movements are central to the problems of the Southill East area and are explored in more detail in section 3.

Table 1: Population Distribution By Age Group

Age Group	Southill East Number	%	Limerick City %
0 - 14 years	1,030	37.5	25.4
15 - 24 years	647	23.5	20.7
25 - 39 years	509	18.5	21.4
40 - 54 years	416	15.1	15.9
55 years and over	146	5.3	16.6

The average household size and average family size in Southill East are above the respective city averages, and 21% of families have four or more children as compared to 14% in Limerick city. In keeping with the relatively youthful population structure, families tend to be at the earlier stages in the family cycle (Table 2). One-third of all families are at the pre-school or early school stages of the cycle, while in over half of all families with children the eldest child is aged under 15 years of age.

Table 2: Stage in Family Cycle

Stage in Family Cycle	Percentage of Families Southill East	Limerick City
Pre-family	3.6	6.3
Pre-school	17.4	11.3
Early school	15.9	12.0
Pre-adolescent	15.4	13.3
Adolescent	19.8	18.6
Adult	24.4	26.9
Empty nest or retired	3.4	11.7

A further aspect of the youthful demographic character of the area is the fact that a large proportion of households are headed by young people. Some 29% of heads of households are aged under 30 years of age as compared to 16% in the city as a whole.

Significantly, 66% of young heads of household, so defined, are female, and households with female heads aged under 35 years constitute 19% of all households in Southill East, as compared to 8% in Limerick city as a whole. The age and sex profile of heads of households suggests a high rate of household formation in the area, driven by a relatively high rate of lone parent families. In fact, lone parent families account for 33% of all families, and for 36% of families with children in Southill East, levels which are roughly twice the respective rates for the city as a whole (16% and 20%). More significantly, lone parent young families, defined as those with all children aged under 15 years, constitute 45% of all young families in the area, roughly three times the city rate (15%)[11]. Overwhelmingly, these families have female heads (Table 3).

Table 3: Lone Parent Young Families
(all children under 15 years)

| | Percentage of all Young Families | |
	Southill East	Limerick City
Lone father	3.03	1.40
Lone mother	41.75	13.18
Total	44.78	14.58

Labour Force Characteristics

The socio-demographic patterns noted above have implications for the functioning of the labour market in Southill East, most obviously through their effects on the labour supply. Recent research has shown a link between family structures and educational achievement,[12] while educational achievement in turn is widely recognised as a key factor in determining the individual's labour market prospects.[13] Both the male and female labour force participation rates are above the respective city norms, but this is largely a function of the age structure of the labour force, which is heavily weighted towards the younger age groups. When the age-specific rates are examined it is clear that below average participation rates obtain in all age groups other than the cohort

236

aged 15 to 24 years (Table 4). Lower than average rates amongst the population aged 25 years and over are due mainly to relatively high proportions of females engaged in home duties, especially in the 25 to 34 age group. This results in a female participation rate for that age group which is just 57% of the city average. The relatively high activity rates in the 15 to 24 years age group are related to a low level of participation in education: 24% of 15 to 24 year olds locally are engaged in full-time study, as compared to a city rate of 50%. This is consistent with generally low levels of educational attainment in the area, as reflected in the fact that 57% of the population aged over 15 years ceased education aged 15 or younger, a rate of early school leaving that is almost twice that of the city (30%).

Table 4: Age- and Sex-Specific Rates of Labour Force Participation

	Southill East		Limerick City	
Age group	Males	Females	Males	Females
15 - 24	73.3	55.8	46.2	45.5
25 - 34	92.9	36.3	94.3	63.7
35 - 44	87.2	28.0	93.5	43.2
45 - 54	78.4	31.2	86.1	36.1
55 - 64	48.9	16.7	57.9	19.7
65 +	5.0	0.0	8.3	2.6
Total	77.5	39.2	67.2	38.7

Given the low levels of educational attainment in the area, it is not surprising that unemployment is particularly acute in Southill East. In fact, unemployment levels are significantly above city-wide levels for all age groups, and the aggregate unemployment rate is almost two and a half times the overall city rate (Table 5). In general, the highest unemployment rates are found amongst the younger age groups, and this together with the higher participation rates of these age groups results in a concentration of un-employment among the younger population: 71% of the un-employed in the area are aged under 35 years. Of these, 35% have never been in employment. In line with the overall trend, the rate of unemployment among heads of household (31%) is close to two and a half times the corresponding city rate.

Table 5: Age-Specific Unemployment Rates

| | Unemployment Rate | |
Age group	Southill East	Limerick City
15 - 24	53.3	30.9
25 - 34	53.7	17.3
35 - 44	49.4	18.2
45 - 54	30.2	16.3
55 - 64	34.4	16.5
65 +	0.0	9.7
Total	48.8	20.5

Limitations of Surrogate Measures of Poverty

The above discussion has highlighted a number of characteristics of households and individuals in Southill East which are relevant to any attempt to assess the level of poverty in the area. In summary, the area has a very youthful population structure, larger and younger families than average, a significant proportion of households with young female heads, a high rate of single parent families, low levels of post-primary educational attainment, and high levels of unemployment, especially youth unemployment. All of these are characteristics known to be associated with higher than average risks of poverty, so that the data presented can be interpreted as evidence that poverty is more concentrated in the area than in the city as a whole. Among the household / family categories considered here, those which are known to have the highest relative risks of poverty are households / families headed by single parents, and those with an unemployed head. Significantly, these are also the categories which show the highest levels of relative concentration in Southill East. The general thrust of these findings is supported by other indicators of poverty such as measures of consumption. For example, car ownership is considerably below the city average with 23.8 persons per car in Southill East as compared to a level of 4.7 in the city (based on 1991 census data). Similarly, 85% of households in the area are without a car, almost twice the corresponding city rate (44%).

However, a number of caveats need also to be borne in mind. First, given that the 1996 census small area statistics are not yet available, the data presented are obviously somewhat dated, which is quite a serious problem in the light of the high level of population turnover in the area (see section 3). Second, there is the problem of the ecological fallacy: it must be remembered that the co-incidence of socio-economic problems at the census ward level tells us nothing about their possible co-incidence at household level, and it is the latter factor which affects both the intensity and pervasiveness of poverty within the area. Third, the approach adopted so far has essentially been a probabilistic rather than a deterministic one: it indicates the *likelihood* of a higher than average proportion of the population living in poverty but does not constitute proof that this is the case. Finally, and perhaps most importantly, a number of those interviewed as part of the present research, including local community representatives and activists, were strongly of the opinion that income poverty and material deprivation were *not* widespread throughout the area, due in large part to the operation of such factors as the black economy in augmenting both income and consumption opportunities for households.

In the light of these considerations it is necessary to adopt an alternative perspective in order to explore the nature and extent of poverty in Southill East. This involves an examination of the characteristics of the physical environment such as housing and estate design. In other words, we can look at characteristics of the place rather than characteristics of the people.

Housing and Environment in Southill East

While not everyone in Southill East is affected by problems such as unemployment, the bundle of externalities which together cons- titute the quality of the environment impinges on all residents. For groups such as the unemployed and single parents, whose activity patterns are less likely to include extended periods outside the neighbourhood, the quality of the residential environment is particularly important. However, environmental quality is notoriously difficult to measure as there are many different aspects to it, and those which are considered important by outsiders may not be so regarded by residents.[14] Even among residents, views on the relative importance of various components of environmental quality are likely to differ according to such personal factors as age, family circumstances and employment status.

Poor access to services has been widely identified as central to the problems of peripheral housing estates in Irish cities,[15] and in Southill East groups such as the elderly and single parents face considerable constraints on activity patterns as a result of the relative peripherality of the estate. Elsewhere, Robertson[16] has suggested that such constraints may be especially severe for lone parents in employment. However, accessibility does not appear to be a critical problem in the area in general, and services such as shops (including a sub-post office), health services, a crèche and pre-schools, primary schools, a community college, a community centre and recreational facilities are located either in, or within walking distance of, the estates. Moreover, while levels of car ownership are low, a reasonably frequent bus service operates between the estates and the city centre. Some indication of residents' priorities in relation to environmental issues is provided by a recent study commissioned by an estate management group in the area which was designed to elicit residents' views on various aspects of the local environment.[17] When asked to indicate which issue (from a pre-determined list) they felt should receive priority in an action programme for their estate, the majority (60%) of respondents said that the condition of housing was the most important issue, with the second highest proportion (21%) prioritising the design and layout of the estate itself. This section begins with an examination of these two aspects of environmental quality, based in part on the results of the 1994 survey, and on the action plan subsequently prepared by Limerick Corporation.[18]

Housing Design and Maintenance

The estates in Southill East were built by the National Building Agency to a standard design. The housing consists predominantly of two-bedroom dwellings in terraces, with a small number of one-bedroom bungalows. While the small size of housing together with the larger than average household size gives rise to a relatively high level of persons per room - 0.88 as compared to 0.63 in the CB - this does not appear from the 1994 survey to be a critical issue for most householders.[19] In contrast however, the situation with regard to the heating of houses was considered to be unsatisfactory or very unsatisfactory by 68% of respondents. In the case of Southill East these problems arise not so much from poor housing design, but from inadequate maintenance. Indeed, general maintenance appears to be the least satisfactory aspect of housing conditions, with 81% of tenants describing the situation as very unsatisfactory. Increasingly too there have been complaints about the condition of houses at the point of re-letting, with some houses reportedly lacking basic fixtures and fittings. A city-wide maintenance survey conducted by Limerick Corporation in 1994 showed that in a large part of the area scores on such items as windows and external doors, fireplaces and roof insulation were significantly below the overall CB average for rented public housing.[20] While some households have been able to compensate for the inadequacies of the maintenance system by undertaking repairs themselves, this is obviously more difficult for groups such as the elderly and single parents.

Estate Design

The design of the estates in Southill East suffers from a number of flaws, in functional as well as in aesthetic terms. Both O'Malley Park and Keyes Park are based on the Radburn layout whereby the traditional relationship between houses and access roads is inverted: houses face onto open green areas, and vehicular access is via cul-de-sacs or "back courts" at the rear of houses. The central principle of the Radburn design is the separation of vehicular and pedestrian traffic, but while this may have been an important consideration in cities where the growing level of vehicular traffic was a major problem,[21] the advantages have been less significant in Southill East given that levels of car ownership are relatively low.

The inversion of the usual relationship between houses and the street has had a number of negative consequences. The provision of vehicular access at the rear of houses creates problems of access for visitors to houses, for taxis and for emergency services. Secure parking is also a problem as there is no provision for this within the curtilage of houses. From the outset, the back courts created problems of security and privacy, but the replacement of the original wooden fences which demarcated the back yards of houses with six foot high walls means that the courts cannot be supervised from the houses. This has led to the marked deterioration of the condition of the back courts in a number of areas. Along much of the boundary of O'Malley Park the houses face away from the rest of the estate, a design feature which from the outset was not conducive to community development in an area newly settled by families drawn from diverse areas within and beyond the city. The large size of the latter estate - 601 houses were constructed initially - has had a similar effect, and efforts subsequently to develop individual housing areas and neighbourhood identities have been compromised by the fact that both the houses and housing areas have few distinguishing features, as well as by the retention of the original 1 - 601 numbering system.

Apart from these basic design problems, the area suffers from too much large-scale open space which is poorly landscaped. The streetscape quality is poor along the loop road which provides the only access to O'Malley Park. The latter is abutted by gable ends of terraces which are not overlooked and lack protection in the form of side gardens or walls. These and other spaces throughout the estate which are deficient in defensible space terms have been subjected to littering, graffiti and vandalism.[22] The poor condition of the back courts, a lack of planting on the green areas and the poor streetscape all combine to present a rather bleak landscape.

These weaknesses in the estate design were exacerbated from the outset by the imbalanced demography of the area and in particular the extremely high concentration of children noted earlier.

Blackwell[23] notes that high child densities especially under conditions of relative poverty cause the local environment to "wear out" more quickly. Page[24] suggests that high child densities are central not just to problems of environmental deterioration in residential areas, but also to problems of vandalism and minor incivilities, which in turn can serve as catalytic factors in the spiral of neighbourhood decline.

Population Flows and Estate Management

The result, and in many respects the most telling indication, of the problems noted above has been manifested in a high level of out-migration from Southill East which has led to a marked decline of population. After the initial growth of the 1970s, which produced a population peak of 3,704 persons in 1981, the population decreased by some 26% up to 1991. This decrease, which in proportionate terms considerably exceeded that pertaining both to the CB and the city, accelerated in the latter part of the decade (Table 6).

Table 6: Annual Percentage Rates of Population Change, 1971-1991

	Southill East	Limerick CB	Limerick city
1971-81	2.43	0.61	1.83
1981-86	-2.08	-1.51	0.27
1986-91	-3.80	-1.54	-0.29

A large part of the movement out of the area was due to the very high levels of emigration which were endemic throughout Ireland in the mid- to late-1980s, as well as the trend towards decentralisation of population experienced by all the major cities in this period.[25] Some of the movement could also have been expected as a result of the maturing of the area in the 1980s. However, while these national and local processes would suggest an out-flow concentrated among the young adult population, migration from the area was in fact more widely spread across the age groups. This is revealed by projecting the 1981 population - disaggregated by age and sex - forward to 1991 and then comparing this with the actual 1991 population. The projected 1991 population is found by allowing for (1) the number of deaths in each age-sex group that would be expected over the period if national age- and sex-specific mortality rates applied, and (2) the amount of net migration that would be expected if the age- and sex-specific net migration rates of the CB as a whole over the same period had applied[26]. The difference between the projected and actual population of each age group reflects what can be termed differential migration i.e., population movements beyond those in line with city wide trends (by focusing on the population aged 10 years and over we can ignore changes due to births during the period).

The results of this exercise (Figure 3 and Table 7) indicate that the 1991 population of the ward aged 10 years and over was some 858 below what would have been expected on the basis of the 1981 population, if the migration rates of the CB as a whole had applied. While the population aged 30 to 39 years in 1991 was slightly higher than expected, the group aged 40 to 54 experienced a differential out-flow of some 245 persons, and those aged 10 to 19 years contributed 422 persons to the differential out-flow. What this suggests is that there was a considerable movement out of the ward of those in early middle-age - the age group which contains many of the original householders of the area (i.e., those aged 20 to 34 in 1971).

Table 7: Age-and Sex-Specific Levels of Differential Migration, 1981-91

Age Group, 1991	Males	Females	Total
10 to 19 years	-213.30	-209.17	-422.47
20 to 29 years	-93.36	-46.74	-140.11
30 to 39 years	16.09	-0.81	15.28
40 to 54 years	-129.86	-114.89	-244.75
55 + years	-29.92	-36.47	-66.40
Total	-450.36	-408.09	-858.45

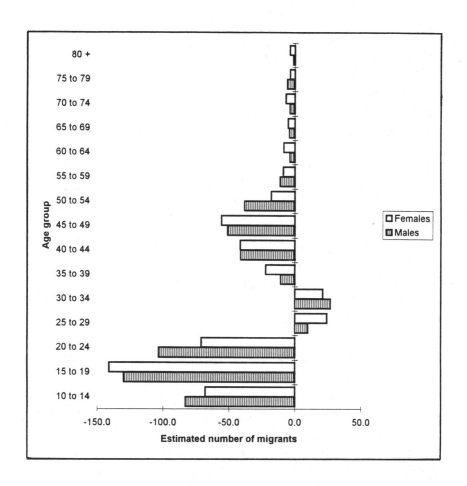

Figure 3: Differential Migration, 1981-91

This out-migration of householders was facilitated by a number of factors. Among these is the low level of uptake of the tenant purchase scheme in the area, a facility which has been recognised as "a key factor in the stabilisation of housing estates, in the up-keep of the houses and in promoting community development."[27] Twenty-five years after the building of the estates in Southill East, 63% of the housing stock is still on rent, as compared to just 42% in Limerick CB as a whole[28]. A more important factor however was the surrender grant scheme in operation between 1984 and 1987 which encouraged local authority tenants to purchase private sector housing. The scheme is generally regarded as having had detrimental social consequences for poorer estates where the differential out-flow of higher income households and households in employment served to depress income levels further and increase area unemployment rates.[29] The impact of the scheme in Southill East was particularly severe. In addition to the economic effects noted by Blackwell, the scheme decimated voluntary activity in the area, creating a major crisis for such activities as the local scouts group, the local community games association and the youth club, all of which barely survived[30].

The differential migration pattern from the area has had a number of adverse consequences. It has served to arrest the normal maturing of the age profile by maintaining relatively high child densities / young dependency ratios. More generally, the exodus of householders has created major difficulties for housing manage-ment, by creating a high level of turnover of tenancies and, more seriously, delays between lettings which result in houses remaining vacant for some time. Between 1990 and 1993 inclusive there were 560 official re-lettings in a part of the area which contains 418 houses on rent.[31] In addition to this there was a considerable (but unknown) number of informal re-lettings not notified to the Corp-oration. Vacant houses have created major problems for residents as they are subjected to extensive vandalism and are often used for anti-social activities. The fact that these vacancies exist at a time when there are over 600 on the Corporation waiting list for housing is indicative of the low level of demand for housing in the

246

area. In this situation, housing in the area tends to be allocated to those who have relatively low priority on the housing list (single parents living at home are often so classified) or who are most desperate for housing. The result is the increasing concentration in the area of those who are most marginalised in the local society.

In conclusion, there is some evidence to suggest that parts of Southill East are caught in a downward spiral, where movement out of the area has either exacerbated existing problems or created a range of new problems that together have the effect of further undermining demand for housing in the area, and increasing the out-flow of residents. While there are many components of this spiral, there seems little doubt but that environmental quality is a central factor. This conclusion is supported, for example, by Pacione's research, in a markedly similar context in Glasgow, which showed that the poor general environment was the most important single reason for movement from a deprived local authority estate.[32]

Conclusions: Peripheral Poverty and Public Policy

This paper has examined a number of aspects of urban deprivation in the Southill East area of Limerick city. While it is obvious that the difficulties of the area cannot be solved simply by pouring concrete or indeed planting trees, it should also be clear that action on the environmental front is essential if the problems of the area are to be tackled successfully. McGregor and McConn-achie[33] identify some of the potential benefits from exploiting the complementarities between the physical and economic regeneration of socially excluded neighbourhoods, especially where physical regeneration is based on housing refurbishment and environmental upgrading. These include the provision of highly visible local jobs for which local residents are likely to possess the requisite skills. The limitation of using physical regeneration as a means of economic revival is, as always, that there can be no guarantee that jobs created will go to local residents. It is for this reason that the benefits of environmental improvement should be seen not so much in terms of economic spin-offs but as a means of breaking the

247

vicious cycle of out-migration and deprivation described in section 2 above. Moreover, while the economic aspects of deprivation require actions (at least those on the demand side) to be taken at the level of the local labour market area, or at regional or national level, solutions to the environmental problems of the area are most appropriately sought at local level. In fact, the case for an area-based local action programme in Southill East has, arguably, a stronger basis in environmental considerations than in consider-ations such as the local incidence of the city's unemployment problem.

Issues of estate design and layout (including landscaping) as well as estate and housing management are central to any such prog-ramme. On the question of estate management there is some cause for optimism, in particular following the publication of the 1991 Plan for Social Housing[34] and the subsequent Housing (Miscell-aneous Provisions) Act of 1992 which introduced measures to improve the management of local authority housing. An active estate management group in O'Malley Park has successfully spon-sored a number of environmental initiatives, and while realistically it will be some time before the group is able to assume the degree of responsibility for estate management which is envisaged in the 1991 plan, a start has been made.

On the question of estate design, the picture is more mixed at present. Following an extensive round of consultations with residents, a comprehensive redesign plan for O'Malley Park costed at £4.65m (net of VAT and professional fees) was drawn up by Limerick Corporation in 1995. However, the plan failed to gain the approval of the Department of the Environment, apparently because it did not include housing measures. A renewed applicat-ion to the Department in November 1996, which placed the emphasis on housing refurbishment, was more successful, and a sum of £680,000 has been allocated for this purpose in 1997, with the possibility of further funding in future years[35]. Limerick Corp-oration has applied these funds to refurbishment in targeted areas of O'Malley Park, where there would appear to have been a drop in the turnover of tenancies.

Notwithstanding these developments, it remains the case that there is a low priority accorded to general environmental improvements in residential areas at central government level, and a lack of discretionary funding for same at local government level. In this context it is worth noting that the total budget for the original O'Malley Park redesign plan is comparable to that which has been allocated to Limerick Corporation for environmental improvement in the city centre under the Urban and Village Renewal sub-programme of the Local Urban and Rural Development Programme. The latter sub-programme (and indeed the earlier urban renewal initiative introduced in 1986) was introduced in large part because of the perceived need to refurbish highly visible city centre areas in order to generate tourism and economic investment. The danger is that peripheral and therefore less-visible housing estates like those in Southill East, which were built as part of the process of inner-city re-development, might now be neglected as the emphasis in development policy swings back towards the city centres.

NOTES

[1] An earlier version of this paper was presented at the 1996 annual conference of the Geographical Society of Ireland on the theme *Poor People - Poor Places. Poverty Patterns, Processes and Policies*, National University of Ireland, Maynooth. A revised version will appear in the book *Poor People, Poor Places* currently being prepared for publication by Oak Tree Press, Dublin.

[2] Government of Ireland, *Poverty, Social Exclusion and Inequality in Ireland. An Overview Statement.* Dublin, 1995.

[3] GAMMA, *Limerick City APC Report.* Dublin, 1995.

[4] PAUL, *The Implementation of the Third EU Poverty Programme by the PAUL Partnership Limerick.* Limerick, 1994.

[5] Keyes Park which was begun in 1966 is the oldest, and O'Malley Park which was begun in 1969 is the most recent development.

[6] D.M. Smith, *Human Geography, a Welfare Approach.* London, 1977.

[7] Small area statistics from the 1996 census were still not available at the time of writing.

[8] See for example T. Callan, and B. Nolan, 'Family Poverty in Ireland. A Survey Based Analysis' in B. Reynolds and S.J. Healy, (eds.) *Poverty and*

Family Income Policy, Dublin, 1988; T. Callan, B. Nolan, B.J. Whelan, D.F. Hannon, and S. Creighton, *Poverty, Income and Welfare in Ireland*. Dublin, 1989; T. Callan, B. Nolan, B.J. Whelan, 'Resources, Deprivation and the Measurement of Poverty' in *Journal of Social Policy*, 22 (2), 1993, pp 141-72.

[9] Throughout the paper comparisons are made with either the County Borough, or the city as a whole (i.e., County Borough plus environs as defined by the census authorities).

[10] The young dependency ratio is defined as the number of persons aged under 15 years per hundred population aged between 15 and 65.

[11] Limerick city itself has a significantly higher rate of occurrence of such families than the national average - 10.7%.

[12] I.Gordon, 'Family Structure, Educational Achievement and the Inner City' in *Urban Studies*, 33, 1996, pp 407-23.

[13] See, for example, R. Breen, *Education, Employment and Training in the Youth Labour Market*. Dublin, 1991; B. Nolan, C. Callan, C.T. Whelan, and J. Williams, *Poverty and Time: Perspectives on the Dynamics of Poverty*. Dublin, 1994.

[14] P. Knox, *Urban Social Geography. An Introduction*, 3rd edition. Harlow, 1995. pp 30-6.

[15] e.g. Department of the Environment, *Ireland. Habitat II National Report*, Dublin, 1996.

[16] I. M. L. Robertson, 'Single Parent Lifestyle and Peripheral Estate Residence' in *Town Planning Review*, 55(2), 1984, pp 197-213.

[17] D. McCafferty, *Redesign Study for O'Malley Park*. Limerick, 1994.

[18] Limerick Corporation *O'Malley Park Redesign Report*. Limerick, 1995.

[19] McCafferty, *op. cit.*

[20] Limerick Corporation, *op. cit.*

[21] E. Relph, *The Modern Urban Landscape*. Beckenham, 1987, p. 65.

[22] Limerick Corporation, *op. cit.*

[23] J. Blackwell, *A Review of Housing Policy*. Dublin, 1988, p. 157.

[24] D. Page, 'Building for Communities - The Key Factors in Ensuring Long Term Viability' *Paper presented to National Housing Conference* (Royal Institute of Architects of Ireland / Department of the Environment), Waterford, April, 1996.

[25] M. Cawley, 'Town Population Change in the Republic of Ireland: The Need for an Urban Policy' in *Regional Studies*, 30 (1), 1996, pp 85-9.

[26] Five-year survivorship and net migration rates were used to project first from 1981 to 1986 and then from 1986 to 1991.

[27] Department of the Environment, *op. cit,*, 1996, p.102.

[28] It should be noted however that there are marked contrasts within the area in the level of tenant purchase, which in Keyes Park is over 62%.

[29] Blackwell, *op. cit.*, pp. 188-9).

[30] Ironically, the recent increase in the level of public housing construction is having similar negative consequences, inducing those on the housing waiting list to "hold out" for the prospect of being allocated a newly built house rather than accept an older house in areas such as Southill East.

[31] Limerick Corporation, *op. cit.*

[32] M. Pacione, 'Evaluating the Quality of the Residential Environment in a Deprived Council Estate' in *Geoforum*, 13 (1), 1982, pp 45-55.

[33] A. McGregor, and M. McConnachie, 'Social Exclusion, Urban Regeneration and Economic Reintegration' in *Urban Studies*, 32 (10), 1995, pp 1587-1600.

[34] Department of the Environment, *A Plan for Social Housing*, Dublin, 1991.

[35] The Corporation's 1996 submission included as supporting documentation an earlier draft of this paper.

GAEILGE

16

SAOIRSE AGUS CULTÚR, CÁS NA hÉIREANN

ÁINÉAD Ní MHUIRTHILE

I dtús an chéid seo in Éirinn, aimsir na hAthbheochana,[1] bhí an dá fhocal sin Saoirse agus Cultúr geall le bheith do-scartha óna chéile. Dhá ghné éagsúil ab ea iad den mhórghluaiseacht um ath-shealbhú ár bhféiniúlachta ag an am san. Tráchtann tuairiscí comhaimseartha go ginearálta ar:

> An increasing taste on the part of all classes of our people for things national, and a juster appreciation of the value of such things as we can still call our own,[2]

ina measc an teanga dhúchais, ar ndóigh, arbh í bunchloch na gluaiseachta í. Go deimhin, ba mhinic gurb iad na daoine céanna a bhí sáite i ngach aon ghné den ghluaiseacht seo, mar a mheabhraíonn Máire Colum ina dírbheathaisnéis dúinn:

> Everybody I knew was working in one or several causes, some people were working in all of them. Any public meeting by any organisation for any movement would very likely be addressed by a selection of people prominent in all of the movements.[3]

Duine acu siúd ab ea an Piarsach a ghlac páirt ceannasach sa réabh-lóid mhíleata agus sa réabhlóid chultúrtha as ar fáisceadh í, fé mar adúirt sé sa bhliain 1913:

> "Our Gaelic League time was to be our tutelage: we had first to learn to know Ireland, to read the lineaments of her face, to understand the accents of her voice; to repossess ourselves, disinherited as we were, of her spirit and mind.... To every generation its deed. The deed of the generation that has reached middle life was the Gaelic League: the beginning of the Irish Revolution. Let our generation not shirk its deed, which is to accomplish the revolution.[4]

Agus na blianta ina dhiaidh sin déarfadh daoine eile ar nós Mícheál Ó Coileáin freisin gurb é Conradh na Gaeilge thar aon rud eile ba mhó fé ndear do ghluaiseacht na saoirse a theacht chun cinn in Éirinn ag an am sin.[5]

As an mborradh seo go léir, chruthaíodar eatarthu, idir scríbh-neoirí is shaighdiúirí, Éire nua. Bunaíodh Saorstát Éireann sa bhliain 1992 is bhí an náisiúnachas i réim anseo ó dheas. Bhí an bóthar réitithe ag gluaiseacht na Gaeilge don Saorstát ar go leor slite agus i dtaca le polasaí saoithiúlachta agus teangan de go speisialta. Thug an Saorstát aitheantas don Ghaeilge mar theanga náisiúnta sa Bhunreacht i 1922: 'Sí an Ghaedhilg teanga Náisiúnta Shaorstáit Éireann ach co-aithneofar an Béarla mar theanga oifig-iúil.' Agus tógadh air sin i mBunreacht na bliana 1937 in Airteagal 8, a théann mar seo:

> 1. 'Ós í an Ghaeilge an teanga náisiúnta is í an phríomhtheanga oifigiúil í.
>
> 2. Glactar leis an Sacs-Bhéarla mar theanga oifigiúil eile.
>
> 3. Ach féadfar socrú a dhéanamh le dlí d'fhonn ceachtar den dá theanga sin a bheith ina haon-teanga le haghaidh aon ghnó nó gnóthaí oifigiúla ar fud an Stáit ar fad nó in aon chuid de.'[6]

Glacadh le hathbheochan na Gaeilge féin mar aidhm náisiúnta. Ar ndóigh, bhí constaicí móra praiticiúla rompu. Tóg an teanga scríofa mar shampla. Ba mhór an crá croí ag scríbhneoirí na Gaeilge an teanga scríofa a bheith gan chaighdeán. Fé mar adúirt Máirtín Ó Cadhain:

> Arae má mhaireann an Ghaeilge, is cinnte nach i ngeall ar hocht gcineál di a bheith ann a mhaireas sí: ná faoi rá is chúig leagan, deich litriú agus dhá chló a bheith ar gach focal.[7]

Bhí na ceisteanna go léir maidir le caighdeánú na Gaeilge fós gan réiteach ag an am - ceisteanna ortgrafaíochta, foclóra is graiméir. Agus ceisteanna conspóideacha ab ea iad a tharraing easaontas is achrann go minic. Dúradh san Claidheamh Soluis:

> Má scríobhann Connachtach leabhar, ní túisce thiocfaidh sé amach ná go mbeidh Muimhnigh is Ultaigh anuas air, ag fáil locht air.[8]

agus arís:

> They hurl scorn, contempt, rage and unbridled vituperation on the head of some brother Gael because he happens to spell sg whereas they spell sc, or sc if they favour sg.[9]

Agus insítear scéal cáiliúil faoin am go raibh 'An Claidheamh Soluis', á chur ar bun sa bhliain 1900, gur chuir an Dochtúir de Hindeberg 'teachtaireacht teintreach' abhaile ó Washington á rá:

> For God's sake spell it with a "b"!(i. Claedib).[10]

Bhí tús curtha ag Conradh na Gaeilge leis an obair ba ghá a dhéanamh ar theanga na Gaeilge féin. Bhí coiste ortografaíochta (nó Coiste an Litrithe) a raibh baint ag Seosamh Laoide leis bunaithe acu ón mbliain 1903, mar shampla. Agus bhunaíodar Coiste na dTéarmaí a raibh Pádraig Mac Piarais agus Eoin Mac Néill ag obair air, sa bhliain 1907. Ach thit cúram an chaighdeánaithe ar an Saorstát tar éis a bhunaithe. Bhí ról nach beag sa ghnó so ag Rannóg an Aistriúcháin a bunaíodh i 1922 le haistriú a dhéanamh ar dhlithe an Stáit do thithe an Oireachtais. D'úsáideadar san an Cló Rómhanach ón tús, mar shampla. Is bunaíodh Coiste Téarmaíochta i Roinn an Oideachais i 1928 chun leabhráin téarmaíochta a chur le chéile agus dheineadar amhlaidh: tuairim is trí leabhrán déag idir 1928 agus 1959.

Níor mhiste foclóir an Duinnínigh a lua sa chomhthéacs seo freisin - "arbh í buidéal diúil riachtanach í ag scríbhneoireacht i dtús fáis."[11] Foilsíodh an chéad eagrán de i 1904 agus an dara heagrán i 1927. Ar impí an Taoisigh, De Valera[12] i 1945 'sea a thosnaigh de Bhaldraithe ar a fhoclóir Béarla-Gaeilge[13] a chur le chéile. Agus is é a spreag Rannóg an Aistriúcháin le Litriú na Gaeilge: Láimh-leabhar an Chaighdeáin Oifigiúil amach sa bhliain chéanna. Níor chuireadar láimhleabhar na gramadaí (i. Gramadach na Gaeilge agus Litriú na Gaeilge: An Caighdeán Oifigiúil) amach go dtí 1958.

Bhí an-ghá leis na rudaí sin. Is thárla siad. Agus dhein an Stát iarracht ar fhoilsitheoireacht sa Ghaeilge a chur chun cinn go díreach is go hindíreach. Bunaíodh an Gúm a raibh mar aidhm aige idir phobal agus ábhar léitheoireachta a chothú. Tá cuimhne go háirithe ar an bpolasaí a bhí acu leabhair a aistriú go Gaeilge agus ar na deacrachtaí la ghaibh leis sin maidir le fiúntas nó easpa fiúntais na leabhar a roghnaíodh le haistriú. Ba dhóigh leat go mbeadh buntáiste san obair aistriúcháin seo do scríbhneoirí na Gaeilge ar aon nós, tráth nach raibh fáil ar sparántachtaí acu, ní hionann is an lá atá inniu ann. Níorbh ann don gComhairle Ealaíon ag an am san, ar ndóigh.[14] Ach, dar le Máirtín Ó Cadhain gurb amhlaidh a spreagadh daoine chun scríobh "arbh fhearr, b'fhéidir, díomhaoin ná drochghnóthach iad".[15] Agus ní raibh scribhneoirí cruthaitheacha ar nós Seosamh Mac Grianna ró-bhuíoch den gcór-as seo ach an oiread. Ar seisean:

> Bhí mé ag obair le litríocht mar bheadh an té a bheadh ag cruinniú min shábha ag obair le hadhmad ....Dá mairfinn ag cur Gaeilge ar leabhair don Ghúm i bhfad eile níorbh fhéidir don drithleog fanacht beo ionam. Bheadh gléas beatha agam ach bheinn mar bheadh duine nach mbainfeadh agus nach gcaill-feadh.[16]

Rud amháin nár chabhraigh puinn le scríbhneoirí na linne, pé teanga ina rabhadar ag scríobh ná an reachtaíocht chinsireachta a tugadh isteach sa bhliain 1929, agus a cuireadh i bhfeidhm go docht is go minic go ceann 30 bliain ina dhiaidh sin. Mar adúirt Benedict Kiely:

> It just went from bad to worse. They were banning everything. In fact, by the time I got around to the distinction, you'd be dammed nearly ashamed if you weren't banned.[17]

Ach b'í an chinsireacht neamh-oifigiúil ba mhó a ghoill ar scribhneoirí na Gaeilge. Chuir Pádraic Ó Conaire síos air mar seo:

> Dá ndéanfaí trácht ar an olc agus ar an mailís, ar an gcaime agus ar an suarachas bhíos i gcroidhe an duine, thógfaidís a súile agus a lámha le huathbhás agus déarfaidís go mba mheasa an sgéalaidhe sin ná an Sasanach féin agus go raibh sé ag tabhairt masla dá thír agus dá bhunadh agus ag caitheamh droch-mheasa ar Oileán na Naomh is na Sgoláirí.[18]

Is amhlaidh a bhí an náisiúnachas agus an Caitliceachas i réim go buacach sa tír is bhíothas ag iarraidh Éire a chosaint trén doras a dhúnadh ar 'thionchar salaithe' an domhain mhóir. Deir Dónal Ó Corcora:

> After the intensity of our struggle for Nationalistic ideals in the years following 1916, a period of Imperialism, of reaction, of provincialism was in store for us. In the collapse we are still groundling.[19]

Chuir Liam Ó Flatharta níos gonta é:

> Alas! Our little island has been stricken with a triple mange of friars, gombeenmen and poverty.[20]

Bhí an meon aigne seo in uachtar go rábach sa tír go dtí teacht na seascaidí.

Maidir leis na Gaeltachtaí, 16% den daonra a bhí ina gcónaí iontu i 1926. Ceanntracha iargúlta neamhfhorbartha a bhí iontu agus iad á mbánú ag an imirce. Ranna difriúla Stáit a bhí ag plé leis an nGaeltacht ar feadh i bhfad. Níor bunaíodh Roinn na Gaeltachta go dtí 1956. Ar chúrsaí eacnamaíochta don chuid is mó a dhírigh polasaí Gaeltachta an Rialtais. Luaitear ráiteas Tom O'Donnell (a bhí mar Aire Gaeltachta sna 70aidí) mar léiriú ar an bpolasaí sin nuair adúirt sé:

> No jobs, no people: no people no Gaeltacht; no Gaeltacht, no language.

Is i 1957 a cuireadh Gaeltarra Éireann ar bun ar deineadh Údarás na Gaeltachta de ar an gcéad lá de mhí Eanáir, 1980. Níl aon amhras ach gur éirigh leo fostaíocht a chruthú sna Gaeltachtaí. An baol ba mhó leis an gcúram ó thaobh na Gaeilge de ag an am ná gur milieu an Bhéarla a fhéadfadh a bheith ag baint le cuid mhaith de na postanna sin a cruthaíodh. Tuigtear dom gur mó an bhéim atá á cur ag an Údarás na laethanta seo ar an tábhacht a ghabhann le polasaí láidir teangan.

Ar ndóigh, bhí an Ghaeltacht chun tosaigh maidir leis an turasóireacht chultúrtha, ós é sin a thugtar ar a leithéid sa lá atá inniu ann. Spreag Conradh na Gaeilge lucht foghlamtha na teangan (nó na 'Laethanta Breátha', mar a tugadh orthu) chun dul chun na Gaeltachta ón tús. Seo mar a mhol an tAth. Pádraig de Brún i 1926, mar shampla:

> Is fiú dul san Ghaeltacht chun an saol Gaelach do thuisgint agus an sprid Ghaolach d'fhágháil - rud ná faighfeá go deo san Ghalltacht. Is fiú dul ann chun an Ghaedhilge d'fhoghluim: is tré chainnt le daoine gur féidir leo í labhairt go fíor-nádúrtha a deintear san.[21]

Is fiú na mílte milliún punt in aghaidh na bliana é tionscal na gColáistí Samhraidh sna Gaeltachtaí sa lá atá inniu ann.

Ach is baolach go bhfuil an Ghaeltacht ag cúngú léi i gcónaí. Níl amhras ach go gcuireann an fás atá tagtha ar nithe ar nós an turasóireacht agus ar thógáil thithe saoire, brú áirithe ar an teanga. Is tá sí fé bhrú láidir ón mBéarla sna meáin chumarsáide, cé go bhfuil T. na G. ag teacht agus go bhfuil Raidió na Gaeltachta ar fáil ó 1972 - a bhuíochas san cuid mhaith le Gluaiseacht Chearta Sibhialta na Gaeltachta a tháinig chun cinn sna seascaidí is a léirigh féinmhuinín nua ag an bpobal áitiúil is é ag feidhmiú ar a shon féin.

Agus, is dóigh liom go bhfuil an-chreidiúint ag dul do na Comharchumainn a bunaíodh sna ceantair Ghaeltachta i lár na seachtóidí chomh maith.

Ach cad mar gheall ar an teanga a chur chun cinn lasmuigh den Ghaeltacht? Níl aon amhras ach gur ar an gcóras oideachais, ar na scoileanna agus ar na bunscoileanna go háirithe a bhí an Rialtas ag brath leis an gcuspóir náisiúnta a bhaint amach ar fuaid na tíre. Arís bhí an bóthar réitithe ag Conradh na Gaeilge dhóibh, maidir le háit na Gaeilge sa chóras oideachais, fiú roimh bhunú an Stáit.[22] Lean an Saorstát ar aghaigh leis na polasaithe úd. Bhí leanúnachas áirithe pearsanra i gceist freisin, gan amhras. B'é Eoin Mac Néill, duine de cheannairí Chonradh na Gaeilge, a bhí ina chéad Aire Oideachais, fear adúirt:

> For my own part, if Irish nationality were not to mean a disinctive Irish civilisation, I would attach no very great value to Irish national independence.[23]

Mar thoradh ar spreagadh ón gConradh, bhí Ard-Choiste na Múinteoirí Náisiúnta tar éis Comhdháil a chur ar bun i 1921 chun clár bunscoile a leagan amach "a d'oirfeadh forsamhla agus saol na hÉireann". Bunchlár éigeantach a bhí ann le Gaeilge, Béarla, Mata, Stair, Tíreolas, Amhránaíocht, Corpoiliúint agus Obair Shnáthaide. Ghlac an Rialtas leis an gclár sin in Aibreán na bliana 1922. Bhí sé i gceist (i) an Ghaeilge a bheith mar ábhar scoile (ii) ábhair eile a mhúineadh tré mheán na Gaeilge agus (iii) scoilíocht lán-Ghaeilge a chur ar fáil. Agus tógadh an cinneadh gur tré Ghaeilge amháin a mhúinfí ranganna na naíonán agus rang a haon.

Ach cé mhúinfeadh? Ní raibh teastas dhátheangach ach ag 9% de na múinteoirí ag an am sin. Ach chuireadar chuige - tré'n Ghaeilge a fhoghlaim sna Gaeltachtaí go háirithe - agus fén mbliain 1937, dob' fhéidir a rá go raibh formhór mór mhúinteoirí náisiúnta na tíre oilte ar an nGaeilge a mhúineadh. Ar ndóigh, ba chuid den gcóras iad na Coláistí Ullmhúcháin freisin ag an am (a d'imigh as an saol sna seascaidí déanacha).

Ní dóigh liom go bhfuil aitheantas cóir faighte ag an nglúin a bhí ag múineadh bunscoile i rith an ama seo -i. ó 1922-1960, abair - as a gcuid saothair ar son na Gaeilge, ná baol air. Dá mbeadh an dua céanna caite leis an dteanga dhúchais i réimsí eile de shaol na tíre ag an am, ní bréag a rá go mbeifí i bhfad níos cóngaraí don sprioc náisiúnta a bhaint amach.

Ag an dara leibhéal, bhí pas sa Ghaeilge éigeantach chun pas a ghnothú sna scrúdaithe teastais. Cuireadh deireadh leis sin i 1973. Maidir le Coláistí 3iú leibhéal, bhí an Ghaeilge éigeantach sa scrú-dú máithreánach go gairid taréis bunú na hOllscoile Náisiúnta i 1908, agus leagadh cúram ar leith ar Ollscoil na Gaillimhe faoin Acht i 1929 cúrsaí a chur ar fáil tré mheán na Gaeilge.

Ar an iomlán, is dócha gurbh fhéidir a rá gur sroicheadh buaic-phointe na Gaeilge sa chóras oideachais fé luath-pholasaí an Stáit ins na daicheadaí. I 1940, m.sh., bhí roinnt ábhair á múineadh tré Ghaeilge i 43% de scoileanna na tíre agus scoileanna lán-Ghaeilge ab ea 12% eile acu. Is ag titim a bhí na figiúirí sin i gcónaí as san amach - go dtí gur bhain gluaiseacht na nGaelscoileanna casadh eile as an roth áirithe sin le deireanas.

Thárla athraithe móra sa tír seo sna seascaidí. Tháinig polasaithe nua eacnamaíochta, tionscalaíochta agus sóisialta chun cinn le linn do Lemass a bheith ina Thaoiseach idir 1958 agus 1964. Aithníodh an t-oideachas a bheith ina chuid riachtanach den infrastruchtúr ba ghá le cur i bhfeidhm na bpolasaithe úd agus infheistíodh mórchuid airgid ann. Tógadh go leor scoileanna nua agus ceapadh siollabais nua. Is ag an am seo a tugadh an Buntús isteach, m.sh., a bhain úsáid as na háiseanna nua closamharc. Agus b'fhacthas d'an-chuid daoine gur tháinig athrú ar pholasaí an Rialtais maidir le Gaeilge sa chóras oideachais is go raibh cúlú ón bpolasaí luath i gceist.

Bhí ré nua an idirnáisiúnachais ag breacadh - i gcúrsaí géilleagair, i gcúrsaí taistil, i gcúrsaí cumarsáide. Is bhí gaoth an idirnáisiún-achais seo ag séideadh trén oideachas chomh maith. I ndiaidh ball-raíocht na Éireann sa Chomhargadh i 1972, ba mhinicí a bhíothas ag caint faoin 'ngné Eorpach' is fé thábhacht nua-theangacha na hEorpa. Ar cheart athbhreithniú a dhéanamh ar áit na Gaeilge sa chóras scoile dá réir? - "The thing is totally useless, anaesthetically dull and aesthetically repugnant"[24] - leathanach tosaigh an *Sunday Independent*. Ionsaí an-láidir ar an nGaeilge agus ar staidéar na Gaeilge ag leibhéal na hÁrdteiste, go háirithe, a mhaíonn go bunúsach gur bac é ar staidéar níos tábhachtaí na mórtheangacha Eorpacha. An-chosúil leis an tuairim a nochtadh san ráiteas seo:

> What use is it to us here in this busy part of the Empire to teach our children the Irish language? What use would it be to them? Is it not leading them along a road which has no practical value?

ach gur 60 bliain ó shin adúradh an méid sin agus gurb é Viscount Craigavon, a bhí ina Phríomh-Aire i dTuaisceart Éireann an té adúirt[25] - Ar ndóigh, tá dul chun cinn áirithe déanta maidir le háit na teangan sa Tuaisceart ó shin. Ag labhairt dó i dtús na seachtóidí, dúirt an Cáirdinéal Tomás Ó Fiaich:

> While the days when a government spokesman would refer to it as as archaic tribal tongue were probably over, it is tolerated rather than encouraged by the state.[26]

Tá straitéis nua, dála an scéil, ag Gael-linn i mbliana i leith cur chun cinn na Gaeilge agus a hoidhreachta i measc an dá phobal ó thuaidh, straitéis a bhfuil ag éiri go han-mhaith léi, de réir dealraimh.

Tá an ráiteas is tábhachtaí dar dhein an Rialtas na hÉireann le fada an lá, dar liom, ar a pholasaí i leith na Gaeilge sa chóras oideachais, le fáil sa Pháipéar Bán, Charting Our Education Future, a foilsíodh níos luaithe i mbliana. Níl agam ach an leagan Béarla; níl an leagan Gaeilge de ar fáil go fóill.[27] Athdhearbhaítear ann stádas agus tábhacht náisiúnta na Gaeilge:

> In the Constitution, the Irish language as the national language is the first official language. The promotion and preservation of the language has been an important aim of every Irish Government since the foundation of the state. The language occupies a central place in the culture and heritage of the Irish people. Learning Irish also helps to develop linguistic skills and so encourages students' facility in acquiring other languages.

Leagtar síos dualgas an chórais oideachais i leith na Gaeilge:

It is the function of the educational system to provide the means for students to learn the Irish language and to make them aware of its inherent value.

Agus i ndeireadh na dála, faightear soiléiriú ar an tionchar atá ag úsáid agus seasamh na teangan lasmuigh den seomra ranga chomh maith le dearcadh na ndaoine ina leith ar thoradh iarrachtaí an chórais oideachais:

> Students' proficiency in the language is crucially related to their motivation and the opportunities for them to use the language outside the classroom. These, in turn, depend on the attitudes of parents and the community, the extent to which the home encourages the learning and use of Irish, and how far Irish is used or its use encouraged and appreciated in the community. Without significant support from both home and community, even the best language programmes and pedagogical methods will have limited success.[28]

Agus cad é dearcadh mhuintir na hÉireann i gcoitinne ar an nGaeilge inniu? Léiríonn na suirbhéanna i 1975 agus arís i 1983 nach ionann é agus dearcadh chomhfhreagraí an *Independent*:

> The average person would seem to place considerable value on the symbolic role of the Irish language in ethnic identification and as a cultural value in and of itself.[29]

Leathnóimís amach an cheist,áfach. 'Sé mo thuairim nach mór dúinn ceist na Gaeilge, ar cheist náisiúnta í i dtús an chéid, a shuíomh go hidirnáisiúnta anois i ndeireadh an chéid. Féachfaimís uirthi i gcomhthéacs na hEorpa i dtosach. Cén dearcadh atá acu sin ar an scéal? Ach ná stadfaimis ansin. Mar ceist dhomhanda í, dáiríre, ceist seo cosaint na féiniúlachta agus ní miste dhúinn breathnú uirthi sa chomhthéacs san chomh maith. B'é Cearbhall Ó Dálaigh, a chaith seal mar Uachtarán na tíre, adúirt an méid seo chomh fada siar le 1961:

> Tugagaí fé ndeara, fiú i ré seo an idirnáisiúnachais, nach bhfeic-fidh sibh aon chine ag caitheamh a theanga agus a shinsireacht

264

uaidh; a mhalairt sin, is amhlaidh atá siad á gcosaint agus á gcaomhnú agus á gcur chun cinn. In ionad an t-idirnáisiáunachas do bheith ag caolú líon na gcultúr dúchais agus do laghdú uimhir na dteangacha iasachta, is amhlaidh dáiríre atá sé á láidriú agus á n-iolrú.[30]

Tá breis is 35 teanga namhfhorleathan san Aontas Eorpach agus tá pobal labhartha de bhreis is 60 milliún duine ag na teangacha úd. Sin duine as gach seisear de phobal an Aontais Eorpaigh san iomláine. Agus tá sé mar aidhm ag Aontas na hEorpa cúram a dhéanamh de na teangacha so go léir. Is chuige sin a bhunaíodar dhá bhliain déag ó shin an Biúró um Theangacha Neamhfhorleathana, a bhfuil a cheanncheathrú i mBaile Átha Cliath. Mar go n-aithnítear san Aontas Eorpach gur ceannródaithe sinne in Éirinn sa tuiscint seo ar thábhacht na dteangacha neamhfhorleathana. Teastaíonn ón Aontas Eorpach go gcothófaí sna córais oideachais ar fuaid na hEorpa meas ar chultúir agus ar theangacha eile, go mbeadh glacadh leo is go mairfidís; 'sé sin go n-aithneofar cearta na gcultúr sin agus cearta na dteangacha sin.

Ar ndóigh, an chéad rún a ritheadh i bPairlimint na hEorpa (i 1979) a bhain le cearta na dteangacha neamhfhorleathana i gcúrsaí oideachais, is Éireannach a dhein é a mholadh. Ceannródaí ar go leor bealaí eile freisin é an feisire Eorpach a bhí i gceist i. John Hume, duine a thuigeann an tábhacht a ghabhann le hiolrachas cultúir. Ag caint dó ag Comhdháil IBEC i mBaile Átha Cliath le déanaí, dúirt sé: "You have got to respect difference. Difference is not a threat, difference is natural, difference is the essence of humanity".[31] Rud a thugann focail W.H.Auden chun cuimhne:

All real unity commences
In consciousness of differences.[32]

Ach tá domhan ann níos fairsinge ná Aontas na hEorpa agus tá na prionsabail thábhachtacha seo, cearta cultúrtha dearbhaithe ag an leibhéal domhanda freisin. Leagadh síos agus aontaíodh prionsabail faoin gcomhoibriú cultúrtha idirnáisiúnta i 1966 ag Comhdháil Ghinearálta de chuid UNESCO. Deir Airteagal 1:

Each culture has a dignity and value which must be respected and preserved. Each people has the right and the duty to develop its culture.[33]

Ar an 26 Samhain, 1976, ghlac UNESCO le moladh a ritheadh faoi rannpháirtíocht an phobail i gcoitinne sa saol cultúrtha. Ceistíodh an smacht a bheith ag dream beag ar tháirgiú agus ar scaipeadh an chultúir. Tá an méid seo le rá fé na meáin chumarsáide, a bhaineann leis an ábhar a bhí idir chomáin ag Bob Collins[34]:

They should not threaten the authenticity of cultures or impair their quality;....Member states should encourage media to pay special attention to the protection of national cultures from the potentially harmful influence of some types of mass production.[35]

Agus labhair an MacBride Commission amach i 1980 i gcoinne báthadh na mionchultúr:

Cultural identity is endangered by the overpowering influence on and assimilation of some national cultures, though these nations may well be heirs to more ancient and richer cultures. Since diversity is the most precious quality of culture, the whole work is poorer.[36]

Mholfadh an Coimisiún sin go mbunófaí polasaithe náisiúnta a chothódh is a neartódh an tsainiúlacht chultúrtha:

Such policies should also contain guidelines for safeguarding national cultural development while promoting knowledge of other cultures.[37]

Bhain tuairisc an South Commission deich mbliain ina dhiaidh sin le sainiúlacht chultúrtha. Is déanann sé pointe an-tábhachtach nuair adeir sé nach ionann cúram a dhéanamh den bhféiniúlacht chultúrtha agus diúltú glan don saol mór lasmuigh:

The concern with cultural identity does not imply rejection of outside influences. Rather, it should be a part of efforts to strengthen the capacity for autonomous decision making, blending indigenous and universal elements in the service of a people-centred policy.[38]

Leagadh béim ar ról an stáit i gcaomhnú agus i saibhriú oidhreacht chultúrtha na sochaí agus mhol an Coimisiún do Rialtaisí glacadh le cairt speisialta don bhforbairt chultúrtha a leagfadh amach bunchearta na ndaoine i dtaca le cultúr de.[39] Nach bhfuil sé in am againne in Éirinn 'Cairt na Gaeilge' a bheith againn ?

Táim imithe sa chaint seo[40] ó ré an náisiúnachais seachtó éigin bliain ó shin go dtí ré an idirnáisiúnachais inniu. Cruthaíodh Éire nua i dtús an chéid seo. Tá Éire nua eile ar tí a cruthaithe i ndeireadh an chéid seo. Tá de cheart againn is de dhualgas orainn féachaint chuige go mbeidh ár sainiúlacht is ár dteanga dhúchais beo agus ar fáil don uile dhuine san Éire Nua sin atá le teacht. Is bíodh 'fhios againn go bhfuil an Eoraip is an domhan mór taobh thiar dínn san aidhm sin. Ní beag san.

NÓTAÍ

[1] "We use the word Renaissance for the Gaelic revival, springing from the rediscovery of the ancient language and literature" T. Mac Donagh, *Literature in Ireland: Studies Irish and Anglo-Irish*, London, 1918.

[2] *Irisleabhar na Gaeilge*, iml.1, uimh. 3, lch. 95.

[3] M. Colum, *Life and the Dream*, *(Autobiography)*, Dublin, 1966.

[4] 'The Coming Revolution', (Nov., 1913),P. H. Pearse, *Political Writings and Speeches*, Dublin, 1952, lch.92-5.

[5] D. Greene, *Scríbhneoireacht Ghaeilge an Lae Inniu*, Cork, 1972.

[6] *Bunreacht na hÉireann*.

[7] *Ar Aghaidh*, Iúil, 1948.

[8] *An Claidheamh Soluis*, Meitheamh 17, 1905.

[9] *Ibid,*, Feabhra 3, 1906.

[10] É. Ó Néill, 'Cuimhneacha Fánacha an Ard-Chraoibh, 1894 - 1944' *Ireland To-Day*, iml.1, uimh.1, 1936.

[11] *An Claidheamh Soluis*, Mí na Nollag 31, 1904.

[12] S. Ó Riain, *An Phleanáil Teanga in Éirinn agus i Quebec*, 1985 (tráchtas, Coláiste na Tríonóide)

[13] T. De Bhaldraithe, *English-Irish Dictionary*, B. Á. C., 1959.

[14] Ón mbliain 1969 tá teacht isteach na n-údar aitheanta ar shaothar foilsithe saor ó cháin.

[15] M. Ó Cadhain, 'Conradh na Gaeilge agus an Litríocht' S. Ó Tuama, (eag.) *The Gaelic League Idea*, Cork, 1972, lch.60.

[16] S. Mac Grianna, *Mo Bhealach Féin*, B. Á. C., 1940, lch.8-10.

[17] J. Carson, (ed.), *Banned in Ireland*, London, 1990, p.23.

[18] *Old Ireland*, Feabhra 21, 1920: 'Lucht Leabhar agus Lucht Peann: Cén donas atá orthu?'.

[19] D. Corkery, 'How She Stands': *Guth na nGael*, Márta, 1928:

[20] L. O'Flaherty, 'The Irish Censorship': *The American Spectator* 1, November, 1932

[21] *Irisleabhar Maighe Nuadat*, 1926.

[22] Féach: cuntas ag T. Ó Fiaich, 'The Great Controversy' S. Ó Tuama, (eag.) *op.cit.*, lch. 63-75.

[23] *Irish Statesman*, October, 1925.

[24] Alt le Johanathan Philbin Bowman, *Sunday Independent*, 20 August, 1995.

[25] Northern Ireland Parliamentary Debates, 24 March, 1936.

[26] Ó Fiaich, *op. cit.*, lch.74.

[27] Tá fáil air ó shin: *Cairt do Oideachas san Blianta Romhainn*, Páipéar Bán ar Oideachas, Rialtas na hÉireann, 1995.

[28] *Charting Our Education Future*, White Paper on Education, Government of Ireland, 1995, lch.23..

[29] P. Ó Riagáin, 'Language Planning in Ireland' M. de Gruyter, *International Journal of Sociology of Language*, New York, 1983.

[30] *Athbheochan*, B.Á.C., 1961.

[31] N. Whoriskey, 'Spill Your Sweat': *Business and Exporting*, August, 1995, p.14.

[32] W.H.Auden, *Collected Poems*, London, 1968.

[33] *Cultural Rights as Human Rights*, UNESCO, Paris, 1970.

[34] Léacht a thug Bob Collins ag an Daonscoil faoin teideal 'Saoirse Náisiúnta agus Idirnáisiúnta'.

[35] C. Wells, *The UN, UNESCO and the Politics of Knowledge*, London, 1987.

[36] International Commision for the Study of Communication Problems: *Many Voices, One World*, UNESCO, Paris, 1980.

[37] *Ibid.*, lch. 259.

[38] South Commission, *The Challenge to the South*, Oxford, 1990.

[39] *Ibid.*, lch.113

[40] Caint a tugadh ag Daonscoil na Mumhan, 19-26 Lúnasa, 1995, a raibh 'Arbh Fhiú an Braon Fola?' mar théama scoile aici an bhliain sin.

17

AN GEARRSCÉALAÍ IS A GHEARRSCÉALTA

PÁDRAIC BREATHNACH

Is í an scal an chéad ghin i mbeatha gearrscéil. Seo í an dreancaid a lingeann san aigne as a bhfásann an crann. Is éard is 'scal' solas a lastar. A lastar de phreab. Mianach tréan; mianach díograiseach. Ach gan inti ach lasair bhídeach. Fad trí shoicinid as réimse chuig nóiméad déag, nó leath uair a chloig, b'fhéidir.

Siúlann file síos sráid chathrach. Feiceann sé seanbhean i siopa ag cuardach a sparáin súil rud éigin a cheannach; feiceann sé seanfhear ag faire cácaí milse i bhfuinneog; cuimhníonn sé ar an uair a raibh sé mall chun na scoile, ar bhronn sé máimím bláthanna ar an máistréas is gur chaith sí i mbosca bruascair iad; cloiseann sé mná i gcomhluadar ag cúlchaint go gránna ar charabhean a d'fhág an dáil; siúlann ógbhean thairis, a bróga triopallacha ag baint cheoil as na leacracha; siúlann ógbhean eile ina threo, tá péint ar a béal, tá húla húpanna ina cluasa.

Scalanna iad seo. Tá a fhios aige go hinstinneach scéal iontu. Níl amhras ar bith air faoi sin. Táid ag tíocht aige go rialta. Gan sos. Lá i ndiaidh lae, tá scalanna dhá bhualadh.

Tógann sé nótaí orthu. Arae níl deis aige a múnlú fós. Triaileann sé stop a chur leo, arae níl an t-aga aige. Is brón leis nach féidir leis a n-aithris uaidh ach caithfear chuile cheann acu a ghor. A chion ceart ama a thabhairt do chuile ceann acu, agus murab ionann is ál uibheacha caithfear chuile ghearrcach acu seo a ghor leis féin, ina nead féin. Sicín cuaiche chuile cheann acu seo agus ní hé an modh céanna goir, an cíneál céanna nide, an t-achar céanna aimsire atá ó chuile scéal acu, ní hea, ach nead difriuil, cúram difriúil, tógáil difriúil.

Is é an mionlach scalanna dhá bhrí sin a thagann chun foirfeachta. Roghnaíonn an file ceann le dul ag obair uirthi. B'fhéidir gur scal nua é nó ceann a raibh sé ag togáil nótaí go fánach le píosa air.

A leathnú amach atá uaidh anois; ligean don scal í féin a mhéadú. Ligean do ghaetha na scaile dul síos sna féitheacha beaga, sna bóithríní a bhí ag casadh sileadh uaithi an chéad uair, lena n-at. Ligean dhá bachlóga bláthú.

Go hiondúil snaidhmeann féitheacha na scaile go tapaidh le míreanna as saol an fhile; le míreanna as a shaol féin nó le míreanna as saolta daoine a bhfuil nó a raibh aithne aige orthu. Láidríonn a matáin. Leathnú aimhréidh neamheagraithe atá anseo. Ach is éard atá ann, an t-amhábhar.

I mo chás féin nuair a thugaim faoi scéal a scríobh is iondúil liom an scal a thógáil go beo i m'intinn amach faoin tír. Gabhaim ag siúl faoin tuath nó faoin gcathair san oiche agus ligim do dhraíocht síorathnuachana an tsaoil dul i bhfeidhm orm.

Sin anois an t-ábhar aige.

Is ina dhiaidh seo ámh a thagann an chuid is deacra, an file ag iarraidh a theacht ar fhoirm nó ar struchtúr feiliúnach. Is í an fhoirm a thugann an ceol don ábhar.

Beidh ar an bhfile an-chuid ceisteanna a chur air féin. Cén cineál carachtair go díreach atá uaidh? An gcuirfidh sé ag comhrá é, nó an leor go nochtóidh sé a intinn trí shruth smaointe? Cé mhéid cainte a dhéanfas an reacaire uilechumhachtach, nó an abróidh sé tada ar bith? Go hiondúil tá eithne an charachtair sa scal agus níl ag an bhfile a dhéanamh ach faire go dílis uirthi, éisteacht léi agus fanacht go humhal; an eithne a fhorbairt chomh dílis don scal is a fhéadas sé; déanamh cinnte nach gcasfaidh sé suas culbhóithríní a thabharfas cor cam don scéal, cúlbhóithríní mealltacha gur deacair a theacht slán as a gcrúba. Tá comhairle amháin práinneach aige, íonbhlas na scaile a chaomhnú.

Ceisteanna eile aige: cá dtosóidh sé? An bhfuil gá le réamhrá le cúlra is suíomh a réiteach? An mbeidh an scéal leantach ó thaobh ama de? Nó a bpreabfaidh sé siar soir ag athrú aimsirí? An féidir an t-aontas a choinneáil leis an bpreabadh seo? Cé mhéid breathnaithe siar a bhfuil gá leis?

An cheist mhór: an bhfuil an t-ábhar agus an chaoi a bhfuil tú lena láimhseáil spéisiúil an dóigh leat? Spéisiúil don léitheoir agus spéisiúil duitse? Mura spreagann sé thú féin is beag seans go spreagfaidh sé an léitheoir.

Is é tús an scéil is deacra a aimsiú. Bíonn an-deacracht agam féin le tús scéil. Bíonn orm a scriobh arís is arís eile. Ní hé go mbím ag iarraidh tús 'pleascach'. An áit cheart sa scéal a bhíonn uaim. Brathfaidh an 'phleasc' ar an scéal féin i ndeireadh báire, ní ar an abairt tosaigh. Ach bíodh an abairt tosaigh tarraingteach más í a fheileann. Bíodh sí scafánta le aird a dhíriú uirthi, más í atá ceart. Ach i ndeireadh na dála, abairt ar bith mórán - 'Lá breá samhraidh a bhí ann', 'Bhí fear ann fadó' - tabharfar áilleacht agus éifeacht di, agus má deirim é 'pléasc' más san ionad ceart í.

Is é deireadh an scéil is éasca i bhfad. Is iondúil é seo agat an-luath. Chun tosaigh ar an tús. Ar bhealach tá sé faighte sa scal agat.

Seo í an chontúirt, arae is í an chríoch is tábhachtaí uilig. Brathann éifeacht uilig an scéil ar a chríoch, agus má tá sí sin fabhtach nó easnamhach tá thiar ort. Caithfidh brí is spreacadh a bheith sa chríoch, arae níl tada is anacraí ná scéal ag críochnú go lag. Lagbhrí uilig é. Ach tugann críoch a bhfuil speach inti speach don chuid eile. Ach is rómhinic, faraoir, críochanna laga ar scéalta arae ní dhéantar a saothrú mar a shaothraítear túsanna. Tugann siad ró-éasca.

Ceann de na tréithe is éasca i gceird na scríbhneoireachta is ea 'stíl'. Uait féin ar fad í. Amach asat féin a chuireann sí. Ag cur go nádúrtha. Ní chuireann scríbhneoir roimhe a chuid scéalta a bheith fada nó gearr, brathann sé go nádúrtha ar ábhar an scéil. Ní chuireann sé roimhe ach oiread a chuid altanna a bheith ar aon fhad áirid. Nó a chuid abairtí. Bíonn abairtí fada nó gearra aige de réir mar a instear go hinstinneach dó a bheith ceart. Tá luas agus rithim cheart ina chloigeann. Tá sé ag éisteacht le ceol an ghiota. Is é an

271

ceol sin a rialaíonn fad na n-abairtí. Is é a shocraíonn an abairtí fada a bheas aige nó abairtí aonfhoclacha. Is é a bheartaíonn abairtí ar cónasc a dtús, go bhfágtar briathar ar lár, etc.

Tá stíl údair ag síorathrú, go ceann i bhfad ar aon nós. Comhartha fáis é seo. Stíl 'ala na huaire' a bheas go minic aige. Is é sin stíl ghiúmair. Ach is féidir leis fanacht níos rialta, níos caighdeánaí i stíl más maith leis sin. Féadfaidh sé 'práta' a thabhairt ar 'fhata' nuair a imíonn ghiúmar an fhata uaidh. Féadfaidh sé fanacht rialta i litriú, i ndeilbhíocht, i gcomhréir agus mar sin de. Is é sin is féidir leis srian a chur lena fhás; buairín a chur uirthi, agus seans gur ceart dó sin ma mheasann sé gur fás ritheach atá sé a chur.

Airím go raibh Máirtin Ó Cadhain an-tugtha do stíl 'ala na huaire', go háirid ó thaobh litrithe agus deilbhíochta de: "Ba sheanchathair í. Cho haosta sin is go raibh aimhreas faoina tús "[1] Ta 'shamhlaigh', 'shamhalaigh', 'shamhala', srl., aige. É ag athrú, agus gan é in ann a bheith cinnte ciocu ba chirte agus ba chóra, ach é ag claoi leis an gceann a d'airigh sé ceart ó thaobh crutha, rithime is fuaime ag am áirid.

Le sampla de mo chuid féin a thabhairt daoibh. Tá na habairtí seo agamsa i 'Bosca': "Ar chúl. An fhoirgnimh mhóir. Aird." Ceist rithime, luais, is alltachta a bhi uaimse anseo. Bheadh difríocht ann dhá n-abróinn mar seo é: "Ar chúl an fhoirgnimh mhóir aird." Nó: "Ar chúl an fhoirgnimh mhóir. Ard." B'fhéidir go mba dheise le duine an bealach gnách caighdeánach: "Ar chúl an fhoirgnimh mhóir aird." B'fhéidir go mba dhe-ise leis a chruth. Ach ní hé an léamh céanna nó an chiall chéanna a bheadh leis. Tá mothú agus paisean difriúil i gceist.

Tagann dóigh scribhneoireachta go minic agat gan a hiarraidh. Ar nós na scaile roimhe seo labhraíonn guth ionat. Tabharfad sampla den rud as "Uaig-neas" liom féin. Ach is mó de cheist teicníce ná de cheist stíle í seo is dóigh:

> Na lusanna cromchinn ar na fuinneoga bhíodar dreoite. Dhá mhám gasanna i searróga. Na lusanna cromchinn a bhi chomh hur, (Chomh hÓg), chomh bui. A ndearna a mbuíochas tadhall, a láidre, léire, a ghléine is a bhí...

Ach bhíodar múchta anois. Feoite. (Dreoite). Buaicis dóite,
(Chrinnte) ba dh'ea na bláthanna . . .

Guth a dúirt liom lúibíní a chur isteach agus cinnlitreacha sna
lúibíní. Bhí orm an chomhairle seo a scrúdú féachaint ar fheil sí.
D'fheil. Leis na lúibíní d'fhéadfaí níos mó focal a chur ag obair
agus rogha a thabhairt don léitheoir. Bhain na lúibíní de thábhacht
na bhfocal iontu, ach chuir gradam ceannlitre an tábhacht sin ar ais
arís. D'fhéadfaí na focail idir lúibíní a fhágáil ar lár ar fad dhá
dtógrófaí air sin, nó d'fhéadfaí a bhfeidhmiú in ionad na gceanna
rompu dhá mb'é sin an cinneadh ab áine.

Ach is teicníc nó nós é seo nár cheart a úsáid rómhinic. Chuirfí
fearg ar léitheoir. Thuirseofaí é. Is deise leis rudaí rialta, ach ní
haon dochar feancadh agus obair a bhaint as uaireanta. Gnóthaíonn
an feancadh brabach. Breathnaigh an modh oibre geiteach atá i
'Glantachán Earraigh' le Máirtín Ó Cadhain.

Mar a dúras is stíl ghiúmair go minic í stíl 'ala na huaire' agus is
minic an scríbhneoir féin dhá hathrú, dhá caighdeánú, dhá srianú ar
ball, th'éis don ghiúmar sin a bheith ídithe ann agus ghiúmar eile in
uachtar - ghiúmar is ciotianta. Tá contúirtí agus buntáistí sa mhéid
sin. Thiocfadh le stíl nó le toradh ghiúmair a bheith ró-ritheach
agus go mb'fhearr a bhearradh. Ach ar an taobh eile má tá sí ceart
is cóir a coinneáil. Bíodh dóchas ag an scríbhneoir go ndéanfar í a
léamh sách grinn, agus bíodh sé féin sásta a léamh sách grinn. Is
cóir ghiúmar a chaomhnú, arae sí an fhilíocht go minic í.

Airím féin má éiríonn liom an chéad alt i scéal a scríobh réasúnta
sásúil go bhfuilim píosa fada ar m'aistear faoi sin. Go dtí go mbím
réasúnta sásta leis an gcéad alt ní thig liom dul ar aghaidh. (Mar a
chéile leis an teideal. Ach bíonn an teideal agam chun tosaigh ar
chuile shórt eile, cés moite den scal.) Ach is gnás liom an chuid sin,
abairt ar abairt, a thógáil i mo chloigeann, agus go deimhin leagan
amach an scéil ar fad shula suím síos lena scríobh.

Th'éis dom an leagan garbh a chur díom tá an conaire déanta. Is
iondúil an struchtúr ceaptha sa chéad leagan nó ar a laghad ar bith
sa dara dréacht. Teara a chur ar an mbóthar atá le déanamh anois.

Faoi thrí go hiondúil a scríobhaimse scéal. Is é sin an t-iomlán de,
dhá eagrú is dhá dheisiú, ach is saothar stíle uilig sa leagan deiridh
é. Tá cúrsaí friotail chun tosaigh anois, cúrsaí deilbhíochta is

comhréire. Tá marcanna curtha agam ar fhocla nach ró-shásta atáim leo. Bead sa tóir anois ar an bhfocal ceart. Bead ag faire amach don phoncaíocht cheart, don rithim, don cheol. Bead ag iarraidh an chothromaíocht fheiliúnach a aimsiú. Seo í an uair is an áit a ndéantar an marú. Tá gá le faobhar ar an scian d'fhonn an gheir is na gríscíní a ghearradh. In am seo na cinniúna caithfidh tú a bheith sách crua le do leannán féin, do ghrá geal, a dhíothú más gá, beart is deacair. Ach cuir uait í, nó beidh thiar ort: strillíní fánacha ag sileadh ó do chuid déantúis. Tá sin fíor fúmsa i 'Móire Mheirtneach', scéal ar cuireadh comhairle orm siosúr a thabhairt dhá dheireadh. Ní dhearnas sin ach tá's agam anois go raibh an chomhairle sin ceart. An iomarca faoi smacht mo natha álainn, "poll pise ar bheagán fiuntais", a bhí mé!

Stíl simplí éasca an stíl is meallacaí. Stíl éasca, is stíl chrua í. Criostalach. Sí is sofaisticiúla ar fad. Ní hionann stíl simplí is abairtí gearra. Féadfaidh na habairtí a bheith fad ar bith is mian le duine, ach is féidir a dtuiscint réasúnta réidh. Féach abairtí deiridh, 'An Eochair': "Ba í breith an dochtúr neamhspleách, ar chuir Teachta an Allais, Tomás 'ac Broma, Cáisc ó Sé agus Seán ó Saothraí faoi deara cead isteach a thabhairt dó, gur thrombóis chorónach ba chiontsiocair, ar luathaigh ocras agus tart go háirid léi, i dteannta fuadach croí as imní agus scáfaireacht. Níor aontaigh dochtúr Stáitsheirbhíse leis sin ach ghabh sé de chead a fhianaise féin a fhorchoimeád go dtí coiste an chróinéara. Thug Bord na nOibreacha Poiblí leo a gcion fein den chreach, an dá chuid den Eochair Bhriste."[2]

Scríbhneoireacht den scoth í sin. Tá an abairt fhada sa phíosa sin pulctha lán. Tá abairtí/clasáil laistigh den phríomhabairt (ba í breith an dochtúr neamhspleách gur thrombóis chorónach ba chiont-siocair) agus breathnaigh a chumasaí is ar déanadh a n-oibriú le forainmneacha. Go fiú's tá an phríomhabairt bearrtha. Níor déanadh a críochnú ach fágtar fúinne a líonadh isteach, beart is éasca. Abairt an-sofaisticiúil í sin frí chéile ach féach a shimplí is atá sí curtha. Níl smaoineamh ar bith nach féidir a rá go soiléir ach an smaoineamh sin a ghor sa chloigeannghorlann chóir. Is bradach an mhaise dúinn, mar a deirtear go minic, doimhneacht a iomrall ar dhoiléireacht. Stíl chumasach scríbhneoireachta is féidir a léamh ar a son féin. Is ríméad a léamh. Ar son a háilleachta féin; ar son íonthréanáilleacht a friotail, a siombailí, a próis.

> What one searches for and what one enjoys in a short story is a special distillation of personality, a unique sensibility which has recognised and selected at once a subject that above all other subjects, is of value to the writer's temperament and to his alone....[3]

Seo í an eochair, an tobar, an t-uarán as a bhfásann chuile chineál. An Phearsantacht. Seo é an "artistic temperament", an chumhacht nó an tréith speisialta a dhealaíonn duine ó dhuine eile; a fhágann gur file é.

Duine goilliúnach é an file. Duine áirid. Éan cuideáin a fhágann go corrach míshocair é; na múrtha grá don saol aige.

Is í an tsaoirse an bheatha is mó atá uaidh. Is í an tsaoirse a olldhuais, a mhórbhronntanas. Gan saoirse tá sé gan aer gan anáil. Níl rud ar bith is contúirtí don scríbhneoir ná rialacha. Srathair anuas air is ea iad. Úmacha, geimhleacha. Saoirse len é féin a chur in iúl. A luaithe is atá bagairt rialacha air tosaíonn an réabadh, tosaíonn réabhlóid istigh ann, tosaíonn sé ag cur a chos uaidh. Agus is cineál réabhlóidí é chuile scríbhneoir. Caithfidh sé a bheith dána, caithfidh sé a bheith beagán chun tosaigh, go nádúrtha. Ní haon dea-theist ar a scríbhneoireacht go ndéanfadh a mháthair a moladh. Caithfidh sé a bheith fionnachtach thar a chomhdhuine. Níos docheansaithe ná é. Dúirt duine éigin:

> An artist imposes his madness on an audience less mad, or at least unaware of its madness.

Dúirt an Piarsach

> We would have every young writer remember that his first duty is to be unafraid. If he has a message to deliver to the world, let him speak out: and the fact that his message is one that has not hitherto been delivered in Irish should not deter him, but rather urge him on.[4]

275

Tuigeann an scríbhneoir an tréith seo ann agus caithfidh sé a bheith sásta a 'spáint. Ach gan a dhul thar cailc uilig le nach ndéanfar a chur i bpríosún, a scriosadh ar fad. Tuigeadh sé gurb iad diabhail an lae inniu naoimh an lae amáraigh, agus más naomh inniu thú nach bhfuil amárach ionat ach amadán. Tuigeadh sé leis, an rud is pornagrafaíocht do dhuine amháin gur léamh spioradálta do dhuine eile é.

Léirmheasanna a fuair mise ar 'Na Déithe Luachmhara Deiridh' ar an *Sunday Tribune* agus ar an *Irish Press* chuireadar an-ríméad orm, arae thugadar an-mhisneach dom. Dúirt Redmond O'Hanlon ar an *Irish Press* : "...these are earthy, wickedly observed facets of life, at times startingly outspoken". [5] Agus b'é dúirt Risteard Ó Glaisne, *inter alia*: "his work has a raw force. It's frank. Things like sex don't frighten him".[6]

Scríobh léirmheastóir Oireachtais, Tomás Ó Floinn, faoin gcnuasach scéalta liom, "Lilí agus Fraoch", a ghnóthaigh Duais Chuimhneacháin Sheáin Uí Éigeartaigh ag Oireachtas na bliana 1979 (ach nár cuireadh go dtí foilsitheoir fós), go raibh na téarmaí 'tóin', 'pis/pit', 'slat', 'bod', 'mún', srl., chomh flúirseach trí mo scéalta le cuiríní i mbáirín breac. B'fhéidir gur fíor sin, ach bheadh na cuiríní sách gann más fíor. Lena chruthú níor mhór báirín breac áirid a lua, a scrúdú, agus breithiúnas cóir a thabhairt. Ní chuirimse romham téarmaí gnéis a bheith dhá scríobh agam, ach tuigim go bhfuil pis ar chuile bhean agus is deas le fir go bhfuil sin amhlaidh.

Daoine a léigh 'Buicéad Poitín' agus 'An Lánúin' liom bhí iontas orthu a fhoghlaim go rabhas pósta. Caithfidh go mba bhean an-aisteach a bhí pósta orm, a dúradar. Dúradar freisin go mbeadh náire orm fós, nuair a d'fhásfadh mo ghasúir suas.

Léirmheas géar is iondúil go gcruthaíonn sé go bhfuil tú go maith. Is éard atá ann an léirmheastóir ag léiriú a chuid imní gur fearr thusa na é féin. Ach is garúla go mór fada léirmheas géar ná ceann peata, uch!

Tá spéis mhór ag an bhfile sa saol. Comhluadar an tsaoil atá uaidh. A chomhluadar socair, aduain, an-ghrách. Is tábhachtaí go mór aige daoine ná leabhra. Ag taisteal ar thraein dó tá na fuinneoga an-tábhachtach dó - na crainnte is na páirceanna amach uaidh, na beithígh is na héin, na heanacha is na heascaí; comhrá is gáire a chomhphaisinéirí; pictiúir; fógra i bpáipéar. Is tábhachtaí dó na rudaí fánacha seo uilig ná a chloigeann a bheith tumtha i leabhar.

Is éard atá ón bhfile, cluichí peile, rástaí capall is con, géabha, gabhair, scaitheanna glogair, glasóg ar chlaí, bachlóga ar chrann, caochphoill, luachair, seileastram. Corrach. Is leis chuile threallán, chuile thincéara, chuile fhear trochailte ar an tsráid.

Tá aige a bheith in óstáin ag faire. I chuile phrochóigín dorcha. Is leis chuile ógbhean a bhfuil ór ina gruaig, a bhfuil ribín ar a ceann, a bhfuil *lipstick* ar a béal, a bhfuil veilbhit ina ceathrúintí. Is den *hoi polloi* é. Is leis na réalta, (*les étoiles*). Mura leis ní scríbhneoir é. Níl namhaid ar bith is géire, is scriosmhaire, ag an scríbhneoir ná coistí. Fear coistí, ní scribhneoir ar bith é.

Bhíos i Quinnsworth i Luimneach inné. Chonaiceas fear ansin. Bhí sé éagsúil le chuile dhuine eile. Thuigeas go mb'as an tuath é. Fear as Cill Eaguala a chuir sé i gcuimhneamh dom. A raibh muid an-mhór le chéile ag dul ag an scoil. Bhíos lán de ghrá dó láithreach. D'airíos chuile fhéith díom ag líonadh le lacht an ghrá. Ar ala na huaire chuir sé go mór le mo shaol. B'é an fear ba tábhachtaí i Quinnsworth uilig é. Sa chathair. Sa tír ar fad. Ní raibh duine ar bith eile tábhachtach. Arae ba dhaoine maide, nó máirle, chuile dhuine eile. B'ionann iad uilig.

Ach ba ionadaí pobail é seo. Ionadaí thar ceann paróiste. Ionadaí cultúir. Ar a ghuaillí seisean bhí traidisiún iomlán ag brath. Cultúr eile. Cultúr nach raibh scaradh aige uaidh. Dhá bhuíochas. Bhí sí ann ina éadan, ina bhaithis, ina shrón, ina lámha móra, ina chulaith éadaí, ina chaipín ar a cheann, ina sheasamh, ina shiúl, ina shúil, ina iompar, ina chluasa ar spadchluasa iad.

Bhí éad orm leis, a fhoirfe, a iomláine i gcultúr, ina chultúr féin, is a bhí sé. Ba dóigh liom ag breathnú air nach raibh truailliú ar bith tagtha airsean, murab ionann is ormsa. Bhíos-sa smálta, idir dhá mheá, idir dhá stól, ach bhí seisean bunaithe lonnaithe go cloch-dhaingean sa chultúr inar, as ar, fhás sé.

Ach smaoiníos nár mhó ná sásta a bheadh sé leis seo. Dhá dtuigfeadh sé é. Ach níor thuig. (Caithfear a bheith taobh amuigh díot féin le thú féin a thuiscint, mar a dúirt duine éigin). Ach thuigfeadh sé nár bhaineamar le chéile mar a bhain fadó. Ní fhéadfadh an dlúthchairdeas céanna a bheith eadrainn, an dáimh shocair chéanna, arís go brách.

Ach ba ealaín é an fear sin. Arae is éard is ealaín "an intensification of life". Is ealaín í an nead cailíní atá ina gcónaí síos an tsráid uaimse, a sceitheann a gcuid áilleachta chuile mhaidin go hóg nuair a fhágaid an nead sin, soir siar, dul i mbun a ndualgaisí oibre. Tugaid ardáilleacht gheiteach don dúiche sin, a thugann ar a lucht féachana gairdeas a thabhairt, glóire sna harda a ghairm le Dia.

Is ealaín agamsa Sliabh an Aonaigh arae is dúiche m'anama í. Is tábhachtaí dom lá i mbun iascaigh ansin ná duais dhá méid. Ealaín agam sléibhte agus machairí Mhaigh Cuilinn óir is iad a bheathaigh mé. Is iad a garranta, a bóithríní is a pobal a choinníonn teannas álainn grá ag sníomhrith trí mo shaol.

Caithfidh duine a bheith bainteach le pobal. Caithfidh a shuíomh beag féin a bheith aige. Sa chaoi sin tá aithne aige ar chuile pháircín ann. Tá chuile chúilín, shúilín ar eolas aige. Is uathu sin a eascraíonn a scéalta. Neart scéalta i chuile chúinne. Sna driseacha atá an draíocht. Sna sabhaircíní úra faoina scáth. Na plúiríní sneachta cúthaile. Na coim an ime. An mhismín dearg teolaí. An tathfhéithleann chumhra. Uathu seo a eascraíonn an grá agus is éard tá i chuile ealaín, grá.

Don ealaíontóir is í a ealaín atá tábhachtach. Is di agus dhá dul chun cinn atá chuile shórt eile dírithe. Dise agus dise amháin i ndáiríre a leagann sé amach a shaol. Tá aon mhórchríoch amháin aige, a ealaín a fheabhsú, a leathnú, a fhorbairt. Gabhann sé amach ag siúl faoi aer glan na tíre, buaileann sé scuais, gabhann sé ar laethanta saoire, gabhann sé ag damhsa, go dtí roller-discó, ar phicnic i ngort eornan, ag iascaireacht - ar son a ealaíne. Aon chuspóir mór ollthábhachtach amháin atá ina shaol, craobhú is bláthú a ealaíne. Ní bheadh sé beo gan í. Níorbh fhiú dó a bheith beo.

Tá áthas air nuair a thuigeann se a dhul chun cinn, nuair is léir dó fás. Tugann sé seo misneach dó. Is deas leis a chumas cor nua a chur i bhfocal nó i nath. Tá muinín aige focal nua a chumadh. Feiceann sé a stíl ag athrú. Is fearr anois ag peannphictiúirí é. Is géire a mhothaíonn sé an áilleacht ann. An t-iontas, draíocht an tsaoil, diamhair na beatha, is tréine a chráid anois é. Is aoibhne leis an t-eanach ná riamh cheana. Is breátha í an easca. Níl cur síos ar dhathanna an mhada rua sa luachair, na druide sa chorrach; nó ar íonsheimhaille an léana Mhuire sa mhóinéar. Chuile fhear, chuile bhean, cráid an scríbhneoir . . . .

De réir mar atá sé ag dul ar aghaidh déanann an scríbhneoir scagadh ar a shaol. Baineann sé as na codanna is neamhthábhachtaí: coistí, cruinnithe, léachtanna. Arae ní dóigh leis am dóibh sin aige feasta. Arae ta a thréimhse ar an saol seo róghearr. 'Gus ní fheabhsaíonn siad seo a ealaín. Ní hé ábhar na léachta is spéis leis feasta ach dóigh na léachta.

Tá sé lán d'aiteas. Lán de dhóchas. Seo atá uaidh mar luach saothair: é i dtiún leis féin, é i ngrá le héigse an tsaoil. É i ngrá leis an saol idir mhaith is olc, idir dhonáin is dhea-dhaoine, idir gheanmnaíocht is dhamantacht, idir ábhaillí is dhea-ghníomhartha.

Tá aitheantas uaidh agus oibreoidh sé sa tóir air sin. Is é sin oibreoidh sé ar a dhícheall leis an bharrchéim ina ealaín a bhaint amach. Ní hionann aitheantas agus poiblíocht. Is maith leis poiblíocht ach tuigfidh sé go luath gur rud contúirteach í féin. Rud an-fholamh is ea poiblíocht. Níl am ar bith a fhaighimse poiblíocht nach n-airím nochtaithe ina diaidh. Bíonn cathú uafásach orm imeacht i bhfolach, daoine a sheachaint, dul amach ar an uaigneas, go bhfásfaidh mé culaith nua éadaí; lomra eile olna a chur a chlúdós mo loime. Baineann an phoiblíocht an draíocht aisti féin in achar ar bith; níl draíocht ar bith inti. Goideann sí uait barraíocht is a thugann sí duit. Níl am ar bith a mbím ar chlár nach n-abraím liom fein ina dhiaidh, ab shin é anois é, ab shin a bhfuil ann, tuilleadh den tseafóid chéanna?

San ealaín amháin atá an bhrí. Agus faigheadh sé aithentas socair uirthi. Ar an gcaoi sin mairfidh sé. Go brách.

Ceist a chuirtear go minic orm, tuige gur i nGaeilge a scríobhaim. Bhuel, is í is feiliúnaí dom. Is í is fearr a réitíonn le mo mheon. Tá oiread sin grá i mo chroí agamsa don Ghaeilge nach mbeinn beo gan í. Tá mé breá sásta dul sa chré léi más sa chré atá sí a dhul.

Aisteach an rud é an grá, pósann duine an té atá uaidh, í saibhir daibhir, agus sin mar is ceart. Ach ní teanga bhocht í an Ghaeilge. Teanga uasal bhródúil í, chomh huasal le teanga ar bith, agus tá traidisiún fada ag gabháil léi. Údar misnigh 'gus údar meanmnan don scríbhneoir Gaeilge é sin. Tuigeann sé freisin go bhfuil gá leis sa Ghaeilge agus is binn leis fóidín a iompú.

Tá draíocht sa Ghaeilge domsa. Tá mé faoi gheasa aici. Níl fhios agam baileach céard é féin, an t-iliomad rudaí is dóigh, ach tá sé ann. Sna focla is dóigh; i bhfuaimeanna na bhfocal. Arae táim faoi gheasa ag ceol na Fraincise freisin cé gur beag di atá agam. (Nuair a fheicim fógra i bhFraincis ar pháipéar bím ar bís chuici: *Une Semaine de Vacances, Son et Lumiere, Nous rions tout le temps,* srl. Nuair a fheicim ainm os cionn dorais: *Poisson, La Femme, La Plus Belle,* srl., corraítear go mór mé. 'Gus bím síoraí ag cumadh teideal i bhFraincis ar scéalta liom féin: *Chez Marcel, Pour Toi, La Joyeuse, A l'Ombre,* srl.)

Ach tá rud éigin eile freisin ann seachas fuaim na bhfocal is na ceangailtí a ghabhann leo. I gcás na Gaeilge ar aon nós tá an guth nó an uaill ársa seanda; a ghlaonn amach go taibhsiúil le contráth na hoíche as na garranta is as na bóithríní, as na cosáin, as na fothraigh tithe; as na maighin, as na liosanna, as na heaguail. As scáilí na bhfear láí, as scáilí na bhfear céachta. Tá a macallaí i gcónaí ag tíocht go dtí mé. Cloisim a nglórtha. Feicim ina seasamh ar aird na gcnoc iad: báiníní orthu, brístí ceannasna. Táid ag dul ar an bportach, taid ag dul ag baint arbhair le speala, táid ag dul Gaillimh, táid ag dul stiléireacht poitín.

San áit ina rugadh mise ba bhreacGhaeltacht (má ba bhreac-Ghaeltacht lag féin) san am é, agus is cineál breacGhaeltachta cuid mhór de Mhaigh Cuilinn fós tá áthas orm a rá. Ach bhí an Béarla, má ba Bhéarla briste féin é, go mór in uachtar. An Ghaeilge ag dul le fán, b'iad na seandaoine amháin a labhair í go nádúrtha. Chloisinn iad dhá labhairt ar ócáidí meithle - baint fhataí, bualadh arbhair, tórraimh, srl. 'Gus b'í an Ghaeilge a bhí i bpaidreacha is i mbeannachtaí an-chuid daoine: "Bail ó Dhia ar an obair", "Go ngnóthaí Dia dhuit!", "Lá /tráthnóna maith agat!", etc. 'Gus bhí sí dhá húsáid ar bhealaí beaga magúla: "scaoil amach an pocaide", "ó bhó go deo", "tabhair dhom póigín", srl. Ach bhain si leis an seansaol 'gus ní raibh meas ar bith uirthi. Ba údar fonóide dháiríre í.

Ach chuaigh sí i gcionn go mór ormsa ó bhí mé an-óg. Bhí roinnt Gaeilge, cuid mhaith, dhá labhairt sa teach againn féin i gcoinne an deontais £5, ach níor bhreathnaigh mé riamh uirthi mar theanga cheart. B'í Gaeilge cheart na seandaoine a spreag mise. Bhíos an-tógtha, an-tóiriúil ar a gcomhluadar. Bhínn dhá gceistiú faoi chuile chineál ruda, ainmneacha plandaí is luibheanna ach go háirid. Luibh, bláth nó lus ar bith a d'fheicinn chuirinn ceist fúithi. Níor shuim liom na hainmneacha Béarla chor ar bith, ní bhacainn lena gcoinneáil i mo chloigeann. Chloisinn daoine áiride ag baint úsáide as focal Béarla ar nós 'fen' agus 'dell', a fuaireadar i leabhra nó ó dhaoine isteach, agus chuirtí le bainí mé. Ba ghráin liom ainmneacha chomh Gallda - ba leatrom ceart é, facthas dom - ar cheantar chomh tíriúil Gaelach le *eanach* nó *gleann*.

Tá gradam sa seanrud, airím. Tá cúlra, taca, aige. Moing aoise air! Tá tuiscint aige. Dínit.

Bhíos istigh Tigh Bholuisce i mbaile an Spidéil le gairid; ar mo bhealach aniar as ceantar an Phoill ansin. Suite i mbialann áirgiúil in airde staighre is ann a bhí mé. Mé liom féin ann. Sócúlacht bhrónach i mo thimpeall a chuir uaigneas orm. Béarla galánta a raibh snas Gallda uirthi a bhí ag an bhfreastalaí. Ní raibh smid Ghaeilge aige. Ba cheol Gallda an ceol a bhí ar an raidió, é dhá phúscadh amach. Bhí an-chumha orm ag cuimhniú ar Spidéal m'óige nuair a bhínn ar na haontaí le m'athair ansin. Nárbh é an Spidéal a bhí athraithe! Ba mhó ná sin an díomá a chuir ainm an tí orm, ámh: Tigh Bholuisce. Ba leatrom ceart ar an dúiche sin an t-ainm seo. Ba ghadaíocht ghránna uilig é. Bhí baile Bhuaile Uisce faoi ionsaí; Leitir Meas, An Poll, Leitir Péic, Seana-Garráin, Tulach na nUan, Doire Thoirc, Sliabh an Aonaigh - bhíodar uilig dhá gcreachadh, dhá gcriogadh. Chriogfaí iad. Bhí na putóga sceanta astu cheana.

De sciotán, ámh, bhí duine éigin ag gabháil fhoinn ar an bhfeadóg stáin. Ar an raidió a bhí sé. Ar an raidió céanna. Ceol caointeach. Ceol a bhain le farraige is le sléibhte. Ceol a bhain le ceannabháin is le dumhcháin móna.

Bhíog mé. B'í seo mise, a thuigeas. Ba léi a d'fhanfainn fad is a mhairfinn. Ní raibh cinneadh ar bith le déanamh agam, bhí an cinneadh déanta dom. Sea, a mhaisce, b'í seo mise agus b'í amháin a bhí uaim; ní raibh tada eile uaim.

Sea, i nDomhnach, is iad bóithríní agus garranta Mhaigh Cuilinn, Chill Ainnín, Uachtair Aird agus Chonamara frí chéile atá uaimse, arae is iad a choinníonn an t-anam ionam; is iad a eascraíonn is a bhorrann mo ghrá. Níl tada fiuntach sa saol seo ach an grá. Tá an scríbhneoireacht bunaithe ar an ngrá. Is grá uilig í.

Aigne an linbh í, is minic sin ráite. Neach corr é an leanbh. Neach contráilte. I sprochtanna a thagann chuile shórt go dtí é. I ríoganna ábhalmhóra corra corracha. Má iarrtar air pictiúr de sheomra ranga a léiriú, ní hiad na gasúir ina gcuid suíochán nó an mháistréas ag ceann an tseomra a léireos sé. Ní hiad ach an gasúr ábhailleach ina sheasamh sa chúinne; an gasúr ag tíocht isteach an doras agus é mall; a gcótaí ar crochadh. Má iarrtar air pictiúr de bhus a tharraingt, is é is dóichí gurb í áit an pheitril ar thaobh an bhus an chuid is suntasaí a bheas aige.

Seo í aigne an fhile freisin. An rud suntasach, an rud neamhghnách. Aigne an duine fhásta an chuid eile.

Tá bunáite céad scéal scríofa agamsa anois. Tá áthas orm a rá go bhfuil oiread eile ag cur i mo chloigeann. Bím ag tógáil nótaí orthu. Cuimhním ar Sheán Ó Conaill, seanchaí, a raibh sé ráite faoi go raibh breis is trí chéad scéal ina chloigeann aige. Chuirtí iontas mór orm faoi sin gur fhéad aon duine oiread sin scéalta a choinneáil dealaithe ina cheann. Ach feicim go bhfuilim féin in ann os cionn céad scéal a choimeád ag cur. Sa bhfo-chomhfhios atá a mbunáite ach a luaithe is a thagann smaoineamh úr chugam bíonn a fhios agam ar an bpointe boise an bachlóg de scéal nua e nó géigín de sheancheann atá ag síneadh.

Cuireann an fios seo aoibhneas agus áthas orm. Tuigim ar a laghad ar bith bua amháin a bheith agam, bíodh is mé ag meas go minic nach dtig liom tada a dhéanamh. Agus deirim: go bhfana an bua seo agam!

Seo í freisin an freagra ar an gceist, tuige nach dtugaim faoi úrscéal a bhreacadh? Tá an iomarca gearrscéalta ag borradh ionam. Ní fhiafraítear d'fhile, tuige nach scríobhann sé úrscéal.

Is minic ráite é gur dó féin a scríobhann an scríbhneoir. Is fíor sin ar ndóigh, ach is fire amanta ná a chéile é. Amanta is beag a bhionn ar siul ach é dha chur fein in iúl. Thiocfadh leis beonna níos toirtiula as a chnuasach uibheacha a roghnu ach ismaith leis spóirt, achuid aistíle sainiúla féin a fhoilsiú. Seo faoi deara agamsa leith-éidí, 'Cíorthuathail', 'Leathcheann', 'Céimí O', is eile a bhreacadh. Caitheamh glogar ar chaoi é seo nó beathú ealaí i leaba géabha ach tugann sé faoiseamh. Saoirse é.

NÓTAÍ

[1] Máirtín Ó Cadhain, An tSraith ar Lár, B.Á.C., 1967, p. 9

[2] *Ibid.*, p. 260.

[3] Seán Ó Faoláin, *The Short Story*, London, 1948, p. 44.

[4] P.H. Pearse, "About Literature", *An Chlaidheamh Solais,* 26 Bealtaine 1906, lgh. 6-7

[5] *Irish Press,* 15 January, 1981.

[6] *Sunday Tribune.* 11 January,1981.

18

MANUSCRIPT MEN

EILÍS Ní DHEÁ

Already amongst the Celtic, and exclusively Irish-speaking population, there existed a class called Manuscript men, whose pride it was to read, to study, to transcribe, and to preserve any writings they could find in their native tongue. These were generally old legends, bits of Irish history, or sometimes fragments of the classics .[1]

Iníon mhinistir a scríobh an méid sin sa bhliain 1887 agus í ag trácht ar bheatha a hathar, Rev. John Alcock agus ar an saol a bhí ann ag tús na haoise sin. Is ar an aicme áirithe sin, .i. na *manuscript men* a bhí ag saothrú i gContae an Chláir san ochtú agus san naoú céad déag a dhíreoimid ár n-aire san alt seo. Deir an t-Athair Pádraig Ó Fiannachta linn nach féidir labhairt le héifeacht ar litríocht na Gaeilge gan eolas éigin a bheith ag duine ar ár n-oidhreacht lámhscríbhinní:

> Ciallaíonn *litríocht* fós i measc scoláirí áirithe Gaeilge, litríocht na lámhscríbhinní. Nuair a deirtear, tá sé "le fáil sa litríocht" sé bhíonn i gceist . . . . ná go bhfuil sé le fáil sna lámhscríbhinní, luath nó déanach. Leid is ea an méid sin de thábhacht na lámhscríbhinní . . . . Tar éis an tsaoil, is orthu sin atáimid ag brath go hiomlán, geall leis, le heolas a chur ar ar scríobhadh sa

teanga go dtí bunú Chonradh na Gaeilge . . . . . Is iad ár
lámhscríbhinní ár bhfoinse dár litríocht agus dár dteanga.[2]

Más tábhachtach linn ár noidhreacht lámhscríbhinní, is ríthábhach-
tacht linn lucht a scríofa. Nuair a thugann duine aghaidh orthu sin a
bhí ag saothrú an traidisiúin i gContae an Chláir san ochtú agus sa
naoú céad déag, ní miste ar dtús, b'fhéidir, súil ghairid a
chaitheamh siar ar an oidhreacht a tháinig anuas ag na scríobhaithe
sin. Ba sna seanmhainistreacha dúchais a scríobhadh formhór na
lámhscríbhinní atá tagtha anuas chugainn ón 9ú go dtí an 12ú
haois. On 13ú haois anuas go dtí an 17ú haois, ní sna mainistreacha
a bhí príomhchuisle an léinn ag borradh a thuilleadh ach sna
teaghlaigh mhóra liteartha a d'fhorbair is a d'eascair sa ré úd.
Níorbh aon eisceacht é Contae an Chláir maidir le saothrú an
traidisiúin dhúchais; bhí a chion féin de scoileanna léinn ann. Ar na
teaghlaigh liteartha ba mhó cáil sa chontae, bhí muintir Dhúbh-
dábhoirinn a raibh scoil thábhachtach dlí acu i gcathair Mhic
Neachtain sa Bhoireann. Ó lámh Dhómhnaill Uí Dhubhábhoirinn a
thagann ls. Egerton 88, i Leabharlann na Breataine [B.L.],
lámhscríbhinn 23 Q 6 (d) in Acadamh Ríoga na hÉireann [R.I.A.,]
agus blúire lámhscríbhinne atá ar caomhnú sa *Kongelige Bibliotek*
in Copenhagen agus dátaí ó 1564-1569 leo. Ó dheas, bhí scoil Uí
Mhaolchonaire san Ardchoill. Ón gclann sin agus ó na dear-
tháracha Seán agus Iollann ina measc, tagann lámhscríbhinn i Má
Nuad [M.N.], C.I, cóip de cheann de na leaganacha is sine dá
bhfuil againn de *Táin Bó Cuailnge*. Ina theannta sin, is ó pheann
Iollain a tháinig R.I.A. 23 D 2 agus R.I.A. 23 0 19 ina bhfuil cóip
de *Foras Feasa ar Éirinn* a scríobhadh sa bhliain 1643. Taobh leo
siúd, bhí Clann Mhic Fhlanncadha i Ros Muineachair lena
mbaineann B.L. Egerton 98, 99. Bhí lámhscríbhinní leighis á
ngraifneadh chomh maith, mar shampla R.I.A. 24 P 26 ó láimh
Dhonnchaidh Óig Uí Iceadha sa bhliain 1469 agus B.L. Egerton 89
a scríobh Domhnall Albanach Ó Troithigh in 1482. Le cois orthu
siúd, bhí clann Mhic Cruitín agus clann Mhic Bhruaideadha a bhí
mar ollúna do mhuintir Bhriain, do mhuintir Dheá agus do chlann
Mhic Chonmara, agus muintir Dhálaigh a raibh scoil bhairdne acu
ag Fiodhnach Bhearna sa Bhoireann. Níor bheag an oidhreacht,

más ea, a bhí á seachadadh ag lucht an léinn nuair a scuabadh na cosa uatha leis an scrios a deineadh ar na huaisle Gael a bhí mar phátrúin orthu sa 16ú agus sa 17ú haois. Le maidneachan an 18ú haois, is beag oidhre ar na seanteaghlaigh léannta nach raibh imithe le faill. Ní raibh aon Ó Dubhdábhoireann ó Chathair Mhic Neachtain ná Ó Maolchonaire ón Ardchoill, ní raibh aon Dálach ná Mac Fhlanncadha ó Ros Muineachair. Níor sheas an fód go dtí an dé deiridh ach clann Mhic Cruitín ó Mhoghlas. Ní hamhlaidh go ndeachaigh an léann in éag d'aon bhuille tubaisteach amháin; i ndáirire, níor imigh an dé as riamh. Fiú murar leor ceird na litríochta a thuilleadh chun snáth a choimeád faoin bhfiacal, tháinig glúnta daoine ar an bhfód a bhí lán-sásta a bheith ag gabháil de shaothrú an dúchais ar bhonn pairtaimseartha. An féidir sampla níos fearr a fháil ná an té a dúirt,

> is fearr ceirde mé agus is m'aimsir dhiomhaoin doroine me an cnuasacht so. Dá bhrí sin ní féidir é a bheith chomh slachtmhar le scríbhinn do dhéanfadh fíor chléireach.[3]

Bhí ré na scríobhaithe seo nárbh 'fhíorchléirigh' iad faoi bhlath sna 18ú agus sa 19ú haois, iad ag scríobh mar chaitheamh aimsire nó ar íocaíocht fhánach ach iad ag baint amach slí bheatha dóibh féin mar mhaistrí scoile sna scoileanna scairte, agus cuid eile fós ina bhfeirmeoirí nó ina bhfir cheirde. Corr dhuine anseo is ansiúd a d'aimsigh patrún buan dó féin. Bhí lear maith daoine ag scríobh i gContae an Chláir i gcaitheamh an dá aois seo, - tá lámhscríbhinní tagaithe anuas againn ó isteach is amach le céad scríobhaí a bhí i mbun pinn am éigin i rith na tréimhse seo. Tá suas le leath-mhíle lámhscríbhinn a bhaineann leis an gClár ar caomhnú inár leabharlanna in Éirinn agus thar lear a scríobhadh sa dá aois seo, a bhformhór i mBaile Átha Cliath, cuid eile i leabharlanna ár gColáistí Ollscoile, sa Bhreatain i Meiriceá agus an beagán fós i seilbh phríobháideach. Ar éigean is gá a lua nach bhfuil sa leathmhíle seo ach fuílleach scáinte an áir. Go deimhin, níl aon scanradh ach a bhfuil de chuntais ar lámhscríbhinní a dóadh nó a cailleadh nó a chuaigh le faill bealach amháin nó bealach eile. Fiú ón líon lámhscríbhinní atá ar marthain, is léir dúinn go raibh saibhreas maith scríobhaithe sa Chlár san dá aois atá i gceist. Cad ina thaobh an dlús seo scríobhaithe i gContae an Chláir, i gContae Chorcaí agus i gCúige Mumhan i gcoitinne thairis ceantair eile? Ní hamháin gur tábhachtach linn an cheist sin ach laistigh den chontae féin, ba í Corca Bhaiscín lárionad an léinn ó Inis Díomáin go Ceann Léime agus soir go Cill Ruis. Níor mhór cúinsí staire, toisí tíreolaíochta agus antraipeolaíochta a mheá go cruinn chun léamh sásúil a dhéanamh ar dháileadh na n-ionad léinn san dá aois inspéise seo.

Chun tuiscint níos fearr a fháil ar an ré seo, díreoimis ar chúpla scríobhaí ar leith. Tosnaímis in iarthar an Chláir i Magh Ghlas lámh le Mullach, mar is ann a shaothraigh scríobhaí mór agus file chomh maith, Aindrias Mac Cruitín. Seo a leanas an colafan atá ar ls. 23 0 10 atá ar caomhnú in Acadamh Ríoga na hÉireann: 'Foras Feasa ar Eirind, an dara leabhar, mar a nochtar príomhdhála Eiríond ... do sgríobhadh le hAindrias Mhic Cruitín ... A.D. 1703 a cClochan Mhaoil na Tine a n-Aoibh Breacáin a cContae an Chláir.' Tá cúig ls. eile againn ó lámh Aindréis Mhic Cruitín ina bhfuil cóip de 'Foras Feasa ar Eirinn'; tá trí cinn díobh sin san Acadamh,[4] tá ceann amháin sa Leabharlann Náisiúnta[5] agus an ceann deireanach i Leabharlann na Breataine.[6] Ní fios cé mhéid cóipeanna eile de *Foras Feasa* a dhein sé nach bhfuil ar fáil againne inniu. Maireann trí chóip dá chuid de 'Trí Bhiorghaoithe an Bháis'.[7] Luaitear an log Dún Ogáin le ceann de na cóipeanna sin, ls. 3 C 18 san Acadamh, '.. Aindrias Mac Cruitín de Dunogane in Comitatu Clare AD MDCCIX,'[8] agus tugtar ainm sealbhóra 'Padhraig Leithleas (Pat Lillis) 1804' agus nóta le B(rian) O' L(ooney). Tugann an t-Ollamh Brian Ó Luana blúire eolais i dtaobh na lámhscríbhinne sin in *Proceedings of the Royal Irish Academy:*[9]

The ms. was discovered at a place called Inch in the parish of Ballyea about three miles west of Ennis by .. labouring men who were engaged in removing an old foss and clearing out an old drain ... It was written AD 1709 and possibly from Keating's original by Andrew Mac Curtin one of the best Irish writers in succession to Dr. Keating himself of whom we have any knowledge. He was a native of West Clare and Ollamh and historian to the O'Briens of Thomond, and author of a history of the Dalcassians and their country, known as Mac Curtin's "Book of Munster".[10]

Cóip eile de Trí Bhiorghaoithe an Bháis is ea ls. Renehan [R.] 66 atá ar caomhnú i gColáiste Phádraig, Má Nuad. Is léir gur cheannaigh agus gur athdhíol comhscríobhaí an ls. áirithe seo breis is céad bliain tar éis bhliain a scríofa agus tugadh praghas maith uirthi de réir an nóta atá léi; 'Do cenna mise an leabhair seo air seacht scillinge(?) $_7$ .. Is liomsa Micheál Ó Raghalliodh an leabhar seo, óir do cheannaigh mé é ó Dhomhnall Ó hUiginn'.[11] Meán Fomhair 1828 agus Deireadh Fomhair 1825 na dátaí atá le nóta an Raghallaigh, agus maidir le Domhnall Ó hUiginn - b'shin Domhnall Ó hUiginn ó pharóiste Dhroma Chléibh, Inis, a bhí ag scríobh sa 19ú céad. Tá go leor scríofa ar shaol Aindréis agus ina theannta sin, d'fhoilsigh Liam Ó Luaighnigh bailiúchain dá chuid dánta, Dánta Aindréis Mhic Cruitín - níl an bailiúchán iomlán ar ndóigh, agus deireann Ó Luaighnigh linn sa réamhrá:

> not only was he a poet but a genealogist and antiquarian as well. He made several excursions thro' the country in search of genealogical and literary materials, but was not a wandering bard, like so many of his profession at the time. The narrow limits of his income compelled him to become a schoolmaster of his native place.. His chief benefactors were Edward O'Brien of Ennistymon, Sorley Mac Donnell of Kilkee and his wife, Isabel O'Brien, daughter of Christopher O'Brien of Ennistymon.[12]

Chítear, más ea, go raibh fós ar an saol, clanna ar nós Shomhairle Mhic Dhomhnaill agus a bhean a dhein patrúntacht ar scríobhaithe, agus, dála na laethanta a bhí, dhein an scríobhaí an cúnamh seo a chúiteamh i bhfoirm véarsaíochta. Féach 'Aiste agus duain a n-onór do Shamhairle Mac Domhnaill agus dá bhean, Isibéal, inghean Chríostóra Uí Bhriain, Innis-Tigh-Meadhon' - mar atá in *Dánta Aindréis Mhic Cruitín*, agus ina dhiaidh sin arís, tá dán eile i ls. eile de chuid an Chruitínigh, C41 i Má Nuad:

> dhon uasal fhíor cráibhthigh darb pearsa an leabhar so ... i. Seabhán, inghean tSeamúis Mhic Con Mara Aindrias Mac Cruitín cct. Tos.: "A bhile gan bhéim is gléire suidheas gach lá".[13]

Bhí Seabhán Nic Conmara pósta ar Eamon Ó Maolruanaigh. Is léir, go raibh Aindrias ag bogadh ó phátrún amháin go pátrún eile - níor éirigh leis pátrún buan a bhaint amach dó féin riamh. Castar Aindrias orainn arís agus é ag athscríobh Leabhar Uí Lochlainn i gcóir mhuintir Lochlainn de chuid an 18ú céad - tá an ls. sin san Acadamh, E iv 3. Sa bhliain 1721, dhein Aindrias cóip de Chaithréim Thoirdhealbhaigh, i. stair mhuintir Bhriain, agus tá an ls. sin ar caomhnú i gColáiste na Tríonóide inniu, ls. H. 1. 18. Ba í eiseamláir Aindréis ná bunchóip an údair féin, más fior - .i. Sean Mac Ruairí Mhic Craith, ollamh le stair do mhuintir Dhál gCais sa 15ú céad. Tá stair an-suimiúil leis an ls. seo de chuid Mhic Cruitín. Tháinig sí i seilbh an Easpaig Seán Ó Briain i gCorcaigh uair éigin roimh 1762 agus deireann Breandán Ó Conchúir linn[14] gur dhein Micheál Ó Longain cóip di agus gur shíolraigh ó chóip seo an Longánaigh, go díreach nó go hindíreach formhór dá bhfuil anois againn de chóipeanna. An mó ls. dá chuid atá tagaithe anuas againn, más ea? Tá trí cinn is fiche áirithe agamsa atá ar caomhnú sna leabharlanna éagsúla. Scríobh sé i bhfad Éireann níos mó ná sin, - agus mar fhianaise air sin, níl le déanamh againn ach féachaint a mhinicí is a luaitear ls. leis mar eiseamláir lss. eile, agus an chosúlacht ar an scéal go bhfuil cuid mhór dos na heiseamláirí sin imithe le faill. Cad eile ar chuir Aindrias suim ann seachas saothar Chéitinn? Dála morán da chomhscríobhaithe, bhí sé an-tugtha do Bheathaí na Naomh - maireann trí ls. uaidh ina bhfuil cóip de *Bheatha Phádraig*.[15] Maireann cóip dá chuid de *Chath Maighe Mucroimhe*[16] agus d'athscríobh sé go leor cóipeanna *d'Eachtraí*. N'fheadar sinn cathain go díreach a cailleadh Aindrias. Táim sásta glacadh le dearbhú Mhichíl Uí Raghallaigh a deir: 'Déanadh é a adhlacan a gCill na bhFear Buidhe a nIbh Briceán ... AD 1749'[17] Dob é Aodh Buí Mac Cruitín, colseisir le hAindrias, a scríobh marbhna dó: 'Ní buan brón go bás ollamh Truagh an cás a dtuadh 'úin'.[18]

Tá ls. ar caomhnú in Acadamh Ríoga na hÉireann faoin uimhir 23 H 22 agus seo a leanas nóta an scríobhaí:

Pettar Ua Conaill san cCeathramhain Dhoithte (?) a cContaoi an Chláir 1803.[19]

Deir D. F. Gleeson:

> The name "Carne" is not now to be found on the Ordnance
> Survey map in that form but is still used locally. The original
> Irish form was either "Ceathrú Dóite" or "Carn Dóite" now
> shown on the map as "Carrowdotia".[20]

Má bhí an cháil amuigh ar Aindrias Mac Cruitín go raibh sé ar 'one
of the best, if not the very best scholars of his day[21] ní comórtas
aonair a bhí ann, mar seo a leanas an cur síos a dhein James
Hardiman ar Pheadar Ó Conaill thuasluaite,

> the compiler was the best scholar of latter times. He was 40
> years occupied on his Dictionary to which he was continually
> adding to until his death, which happened near Kilrush ... 1826.[22]

Níl aon amhras ná gur scoláire é Peadar Ó Conaill agus nuair a
luann Hardiman "compiler" ansin, is ag tagairt dá fhoclóir Gaeilge
- Béarla a bhí sé, gan dabht, a bhfuil an bhunchóip shínithe i
Leabharlann na Breataine inniu, Egerton 83. Máistir scoile dob ea
Peadar agus tugann Eoghan Ó Comhraidhe cuntas air:

> About the year 1812, Dr. O'Reardon of Limerick took him into
> his house ... he remained with Dr. Reardon 'til about 1819 when
> they disagreed upon the mode of publishing the Dictionary; upon
> which O'Connell went down to his brother's Patrick O'Connell
> of Carne, taking all his manuscripts with him and remained there,
> unheeded, until his death in 1824.[23]

Tá go leor tuairiscí ar cad a d'imigh ar an bhfoclóir tar éis bhás
Pheadair .i. gur thug Dónall Ó Conaill droim laimhe d'Anthony
O'Connell (mac dearthár Pheadair) nuair a d'iarr sé ar Dhónall an
ls. a thógaint uaidh an lá úd i dTrá Lí. D'éirigh le James Hardiman
greim d'fháil uirthi agus ba é a deireadh ná gur díoladh í le
Músaem na Breataine - .i. mar a luadh ó chiannaibh Egerton 83.
Dhein Seán Ó Donnabháin cóip di agus sin iad Egerton 84 agus
Eg. 85 sa leabharlann chéanna. Tá cóip eile di i gColáiste na
Tríonóide 4. 5. 27 móide ceann eile fós san Acadamh, 25 B 34. Is

léir go raibh suim thar na bearta ag Peadar i bhfoclóireacht agus i gcúrsaí gramadaí. Foclóireacht agus sanasáin atá i seacht gcinn dá lsí. a mhaireann. D'oibrigh Peadar Ó Conaill do Charles O'Connor, Belanagare, tá a fhios againn é sin ó ls. san Acadamh 23 L 21 arbh é Peadar a scríobh cuid (b) di, mar bhí sé ag scríobh ó bhunchóip le Charles O'Connor a bhí ina phatrún ag an am. Luaitear na blianta 1787, 1785, 1791 leis na leathanaigh seo, agus an áit scríofa 'Coláiste na Tríonóide láimh re Seandún Duibhlinne', luaite an log 'Tullowbrack' chomh maith. Scríobh sé ls. eile - Addendum 4707 i gCambridge, scríobh sé í 'a gcoláiste Bhaile A/C a mí November 1791'. Dhein Peadar roinnt mhaith scríbhneoireachta do Theophilus O'Flanagan m.sh. RIA 23 H 39 a scríobhadh sa bhliain 1787. Ní amháin sin, ach is léir go raibh an bheirt áirithe sin ag obair i bpáirt ag cur lsí. le chéile - m.sh. RIA 24 G 20; 23 F 12; 24 D 7; 24 D 2; chomh maith le trí ls. eile i Leabharlann na Breataine agus C99 i Má Nuad. Patrún eile a bhí ag Peadar Ó Conaill ná an Chevalier Ó Gormáin. Bhreac sé RIA 24 D 2 'for the use of the Chevalier O'Gorman' móide 24 D 7 ina bhfuil ginealaigh mhuintir Ghormáin. Do scríobh an Chevalier teastas molta do Pheadar sa bhliain 1797; is féidir linn teacht air sin i ls. Má Nuad, C 74 (g) 8. Seo a leanas an téacs de:

> I hereby certify that I have known Mr. Peter O'Connell these several years, and more particularly, these last five months that he has lived with me. I have frequently employed him in translating some obsolete Irish books which he has done to my satisfaction. He always behaved himself honestly and soberly which I attest at Dublin this 19 April 1797. Chev. O'Gorman.[24]

Tá go leor eolais bheatháisnéise againn ar Pheadar Ó Conaill. Is fiú tagairt do chuntas suimiúil a foilsíodh in *The Irish Monthly* sa bhliain 1886 ag Mrs. Morgan John O'Connell.[25] Cuntas ar an seanchaí Teige Mac Mahon atá ann ach is mó d'eolas a thugtar ar Pheadar Ó Conaill. Mhúin an Conallach Tadhg agus insíonn Tadhg scéal faoi Murtagh McMahon ó Chluain Fhiodhna, fear ar theastaigh uaidh go rianfaí a ghinealach dó.

Murtagh then appealed to a certain learned Irish scholar name Considine, who had not the courage to avow his incompetence, but asked for time and visited the hedge-school where Peter (Ó Conaill) held sway. Peter knew where to come at the required information, but had no notion of telling it to his brother scholar.[26]

Gheall sé do Mhac Consaidín go bhfaigheadh sé an t-eolas dó dá bhfanfadh Mac Consaidín i bhfeidhil na scoile. Tharla amhlaidh agus bhí Ó Conaill in ainm a bheith ag taisteal na tíre ag bailiú an ghinealaigh:

I suspect however (a deir Mrs. O'Connell) he simply got at the papers of Hugh Mac Curtin ... and he presented himself not to his brother pedagogue, (Mac Consaidín), but (rather) to Murtagh Mac Mahon of Cluain Fhíodhna armed with a voluminous document.[27]

Ní gá a rá gurbh é Peadar a thuill an luach saothair dá bharr fad a bhí an t-ionadaí ag déanamh chúram na scoile dó saor in aisce. Séamas Mac Consaidín an file a bhí i gceist, ní foláir, a thaithíodh tigh Eoghain Mhóir Uí Chomhraí i dteannta Pheadair Uí Chonaill agus daoine eile. Maireann breis is dhá scór ls. ó lámh Pheadair Uí Chonaill, agus níl ansin ach an méid gur féidir linn lámh a leagadh orthu anois. Chomh maith le suim a chur i bhfoclóireacht agus i nginealaigh, tá a chuid lsí. lomlán de dhánta de gach saghas. Tá cóip againn uaidh de *Chaithréim Thoirdhealbhaigh,*[28] de *Bheatha Chríost*[29] agus *d'Aiste Chearbhaill.*[30] I dteannta na lsí. a tháinig óna láimh féin, tá fianaise ann go mbíodh sé ag ceartú agus ag bailiú lss. a tháinig óna láimh féin, le scríobhaithe eile. Níor nós leis na scríobhaithe oiread sin eolais a scaoileadh linn fúthu féin ach ó am go chéile, tagaimid trasna ar cholofan deas. Tá a leithéid sin ag Peadar Ó Conaill i ls. C99 i Má Nuad:

'83 - Father died. '84 - Mother died.
'85 Began trade in May at Tull (low)
'91 In the College
'96 On the ramble

'98 In the County of Clare etc ..[31]

Sa ls. seo chomh maith, tá litir a scríobh Tadhg Ua Flannagáin chuig Peadar Ó Conaill ina ndeireann Tadhg le Peadar go m'bhféidir go gceannódh 'the Gaelic Society' i Luimneach a chuid leabhar uaidh. 'Limerick 21st May 1812' is ea dáta a scríofa. Agus ar deireadh, léimis nóta beag a bhreac Eoghan Ó Comhraidhe ar ls. eile de chuid Pheadair .i., C 38 (k) i Má Nuad, ls. a scríobh Peadar 'sa Tulaig Bric' sa bhliain 1796. Seo a leanas a scríobh Ó Comhraidhe:

> Agus atá an Tulach Breac sin beagán slíghe allaniartuaidh do Chill Irois i fáil Inse Chathaigh. Agus mise Eoghan Og Mac Eoghain Mhóir Uí Chomhraidhe ó Dhún atha Thiar, seacht míle allaniarr don Chill Irois cheadna. Agus ba mhaith agus ba muinnteardha m'aithne ar an bPeadar léigheannta Ó Connaill tuas noch do éag ag an gCarn, .i. ionad a bheatha, allanoir de Chill Rois san mbliadhan 1824, Eugene Curry, 19 Portland Street North, 8th January 1848. [32]

Nóta beag deas ó scríobhaí amháin chuig scríobhaí eile. Ba scríobhaithe móra san 18ú haois Aindrias agus Aodh Buí Mac Cruitín agus Peadar Ó Conaill, ach ba scoláirí iad chomh maith. Ní mór cuimhneamh i gcónaí ar na mionscríobhaithe. Bhí na scórtha daoine nach bhfuil oiread sin aithne orthu ag saothrú leo i ngan fhios don saol, iad ag caomhnú agus ag seachadadh an traidisiúin do na glúnta a bhí le teacht. Duine díobh sin ab ea Seaghan Ó Fionnúcáin a bhí ag scríobh i gCora Fine sa cheathrú deireanach den 18ú haois. Tá ls. cláraithe i Maigh Nuad, SF 1,

> scr. Seagn Ua Fionnughcainn (John Finucane) 1782 an leabhar Muimhneach, Cath Maighe Mucraimhe. Bhí an ls. i seilbh "James Mac Curtin" ar feadh tamaill agus bhreac sé lch. 104, 111-12 (?) "1836". [33]

Tá colafan ar an ls. a deir:

> Finit air na scríobh le Seagn Ua Fionnughcainn cum a úghsaide féin amhail do fuair sgríobhadh roimhe le hAindrias Mac Cruitín an aois an Tigearna 1726 ...

agus

> A leiththeoir ionmhuin, ní bhfuilim ach a pioca gach miondán, duain et gach réad oile na fuairios go forleathan anseo [34]

B'amhlaidh go raibh ls. Aindrias Mhic Cruitín ar iasacht ag Seán, mar deir sé:

> na dhéag so, badh cheart do Dhuain Uí Duinín do bheith sgriobhadh ach ní raibh fhios agam an bhfagfaoi an leabhair agam is fada agus do fagbha.[35]

Fuair an tAthair Pádraig Ó Fiannachta an ls. seo SF 1 móide 4 cinn eile (SF 2, 3, 4, 5) ar buaniasacht i gcóir leabharlann Mhaigh Nuad. Tháinig siad ó thigh John Clancy, Oilean Bán, Inis Diomáin, Oíche Shamhna 1970. Deir an t-Ath. Pádraig in alt a scríobh se i 1974:

> They were particularly attached to one handsome volume, 'Cath Maighe Macroimhe'[36]

seo í SF 1 gan dabht, agus do chuir sé nóta beag leis an gclár i Má Nuad a deir:

> Tá SF 1 ar ais aige fein anois ... Bhí a lán lsí. tigh Uí Fhlanncadha fadó; tugadh leath an bhailiúcháin go Meiriceá.[37]

Agus is mar sin atá an scéal go fóill. Tá SF 1 thar nais in Inis Diomáin. Tugadh an ls. sin SF 1 ó Chora Fine go hInis Díomáin an chéad lá nuair a tharla sí i seibh "James Mac Curtin" a chuir lch. 104, lch. 111 agus 112 léi sa bhliain 1836. Is beag ls. eile de chuid Sheáin Uí Fhionnúcáin a mhair. Ní raibh aon cheann eile leis siúd sa bhailiúchán a tháinig ó thigh Mhic Fhlanncadha, Oileán Bán. Tá ls. amháin leis sa Leabharlann Náisiúnta,[38] agus ceithre cinn eile[39] a tháinig go Maigh Nuad ó fhoinse eile. (Tá ls. eile le Seán Ó Fionn-úcain san Acadamh Ríoga, 23 H 23 ach níl fágtha di ach aon leathanach dúbailte amháin; is é bhí ann ná marbhna Mhurach Uí

Bhriain aistrithe go Béarla ag Micheál Coimín. Dar le hEoghan Ó Comhraí go raibh an chuid seo di imithe ar strae chomh fada siar le 1886, ach sé an tuairim atá agam ná gurb é seo go díreach atá cláraithe i Maigh Nuad fén uimhir C 113 (j) 24. Dá bhrí sin, sin, seans nár cailleadh í in aon chor.)

Fágfaimid an t-ochtú céad déag go fóillín agus raghaimid go hInis Díomáin mar a raibh scríobhaí dúthrachtach i mbun pinn i lár an naoú céad déag. Is é duine atá i gceist agam ná Micheál Ó Raghallaidh. Tá suas le scór lámhscríbhinn áirithe agam ó lámh Mhichíl Uí Raghallaigh. Ní fhéadfá gan gean do chroí a thabhairt don scríobhaí seo mar ba mhionmhinic a chuir sé forrán orainn-ne, na léitheoirí. Tá an colafan is cáiliúla dár scríobh sé le fáil i lámhscribhinn Renehan 69 atá anois ar caomhnú i leabharlann Ollscoil Mhaigh Nuad. Bailiúchán filíochta, filíocht an Chláir ach go háirithe, móide laoithe fiannaíochta atá sa ls. seo a scríobhadh "i bparóiste Chill Mhainithinn a Corcomruadh" sa bhliain 1848 i "mbliadhainn an áir agus an ocrais ionnar éag na mílte duine le uireasbadh bigh". Scríobhadh í "chum usáide Mhichíl i Mhaoldomhna na Baichille". Nuair a bhí deireadh déanta ag Micheál, chuaigh sé siar agus chuir sé an brollach seo leis an iomlán:

Cnuasaíodh na duanta so as iliomad de sheanleabhraibh do tharla liom sa tír seo, go sonraitheach, a bhfuil de laoithe na Féinne ann sa leabhar a scríobhadh i mBaile Áth Cliath tuilleadh agus dhá chéad bliain ó shoin. Mórán den chuid eile is iad filí na Mumhan ro chan iad. Atá beagán diobh do canadh le fir atá ina mbeatha fós, agus do mhair mórán díobh san ochtú céad déag, agus cuid eile roimhe sin. A léitheoir ionúin, ná tabhair aithis ná milleán orm trí olcas an scríbhinn atá sa leabhar seo, óir is fear ceirde mé agus is i m'aimsir dhiomhaoin do rinne mé an chnuasacht seo. Dá bhrí sin ní féidir é a bheith chomh slachtmhar le scríbhinn do dhéanfeadh fiorchléireach. Ach thairis sin, an tan do chonarcas dom nach raibh aoinneach do lucht mo chomhaimsire ag cnuasacht a bheag de shaothar ár bhfillí, do mheas mé gan iad uile do léigean ar fán. Ach is beag an tairbhe iad do chosaint óir is naireach lenár n-aos óg teanga a sinsear a fhoghlaim. Dá bhrí sin ní bhia focal Gaeilge sa ríocht seo i gceann céad bliain, má leanaid an nós atá acu le mo chuimhne féin.[40]

Sa cholafan seo, chítear dom go mbraithimid éirim agus *raison d'etre* scríobhaithe na linne sin:

[1] an tuiscint a bhí acu don sean agus iad ag bailiú leo as na seanleabhair d'fhonn an léann a chaomhnú

[2] an meas a chuaigh do na filí comhaimseartha

[3] an srian a bhain leis an scríbhneoir páirtaimseartha

[4] agus an nóta dobrónach sin faoin aos óg a bheith ag tabhairt droim láimhe dá n-oidhreacht.

Críochnaíonn sé an colafan:

Do bhí mé aimsir imchian ag cruinniú gach saothar dá bhfuil sa leabhar seo. Aitim gach léitheoir do léifeas a bheag den leabhar seo, guí a chuir i láthair Dé re hanam an scríbhneora .i. Mícheál Ó Raghallaigh.

Tá cuid de ls. bhreá eile leis i Maigh Nuad, i R97. Cnuasach de scéalta agus d'eachtraí atá anseo. Thóg sé tamall de bhlianta air an cnuasach seo a chur i dtoll a chéille, Márta 1827 an dáta is luaithe aige agus an 10ú de Dheireadh Fómhair 1846 an dáta is déanaí, mar sin, ní haon ionadh nár mhaith leis go ndéanfaí scríos ar a shaothar. Deir sé:

A léightheóir ionmhuinn dhéarsnuídhe, ag so tionsúghadh, ilchiomasgaighthe do rinne mé ar fabhaillsgéalta do réir mar thárladh a bhfághail a seanleabharaibh eile agus beagán do shaothar ar bhfilidh léighiondadh san aois dhéanach . . . is cearduídhe mé an aimsir díobhainn do sgríobh mé an saothar so. Oir bhí mé morán blíaghanta dá chnuasacht. Atáim dá iaraidh gan leigint d'aos óg nó d'aos ainmbhios dul do sgríobh ar an leabhar so. Má nídhid(h) beith mo mhallacht aca: . . guídheadh ar anam an sgríobhnóir.[41]

Mícheal Ó Raghallaigh.

Arís is arís eile, gabhann an scríobhaí dúthrachtach seo ar bpardún le heagla go mbeadh aon lúb ar lár ina chuid oibre. Dhein sé cóip den Leabhar Mhuimhneach le hAindrias Mac Cruitín - sin í ls. R.70

i Maigh Nuad. Dhá ls. eile leis an Raghallach atá i Má Nuad, C7 agus blúire beag de C71 móide lss. eile a leasaigh sé. Tá ar a laghad ceithre chnuasach ó lámh Uí Raghallaigh ar caomhnú in Acadamh Ríoga na hÉireann.[42] Bhí scríobhaithe áirithe tugtha go maith do bheatha na Naomh. Sampla maith de seo ó lámh Mhichíl is ea 3 B 2 san Acadamh, a chóipeáil sé idir na blianta 1842 agus 1846 in Inis Díomáin. Tá cóip de bheatha Naomh Maighréad agus de bheatha Naomh Seanán le fáil inti seo. Ba í eiseamláir a d'usáid sé do bheatha Sheanáin ná lámhscríbhinn a bhí ar iasacht aige óna chara agus a chomhscríobhaí a bhí ag scríobh thíos i gCill Ruis, i. Micheál Ó hAnnracháin. Rud inspéise i gcónaí is ea féachaint ar na sínithe a bhíonn ar lámhscríbhinní. Seo cúpla ainm ó lámhscríbhinn eile le Micheál san Acadamh, 24 I 9: "John O'Shea of Tullig (1846) . . . Professor of Mathematics etc. "Patrick Austin Taylor, Anniscaul in the County of Kerry" . . . (i bpeannaireacht Uí Shé) Donchadh Mac Mathghamhna" (athair an scríobhaí, Tomás Mac Mathghamhna)..."Patrick O'Connor, Kilrush", sin í lámh Phádraig í Chonchubhair ó Chill Ruis agus tá siniú an scríobhaí Muiris Ó Conchubhair uirthi chomh maith. Luaigh Pádraig Ó Fiannachta cheana go raibh an-bhá ag muintir an Chláir - Tuaisceart an Chláir go háirithe - le Cúige Uladh agus go raibh sé de nós ag clanna a nginealach a rianadh siar go dtí Feargus Mac Róich. I lámhscríbhinn 3 B 31 san Acadamh - tá fianaise bhreá againn go raibh scéalta Uladh beo i gCo. an Chláir ag an am sin, mar tá againn ansin cóip de "Oiliomhuint Conguillionn" tógtha síos ag Micheál ó aithris béil, de réir dealraimh:

> Gabh mo leisgéal, a léitheor ionmhuinn ansná lochtuidh do casfar ort san sgéal so do bhrígh nach raibh éagsompláir againn ach é a chur síos ó fhocail béil duine eile agus is é an fáth fár scríbh mé é do bhrigh nár casadh orainn ar pápaor riamh é.[43]

Tá dhá chnuasach ollmhóra eile ó pheann Mhichíl Uí Raghallaigh i measc na lámhscríbhinní breise a tháinig chuig leabharlann na hOllscoile, Gaillimh. Áirítear iad mar lámhscríbhinn bhreise 2 agus lámhscríbhinn bhreise 9. Filíocht Mhuimhneach, go háirithe filíocht Thuadhmhumhan, laoithe Fiannaíochta agus prós fiannaíochta atá iontu seo. Ar deireadh thiar, b'éigean don scríobhaí dúthrachtach seo snáth a choimeád faoin bhfiacail agus ar ndóigh, ní raibh slí níos fearr ná cúiteamh d'fháil ar a chuid scríobhneoireachta, dá mb'fhéidir é. Faighimid léargas an-mhaith de seo i dtéacs na litreach seo a scríobh Micheál chuig Sir Lucius O'Brien i gCaisleán Dhroim Ólainn:

Ennistymon, July 31st 1841

Hon[rd] Sir. The bearer Patrick McMahon has informed me that your Hon[r] wanted to buy some Irish Manuscripts. He called on me thinking I might have some for sale. I have at present only one manuscript to dispose of as I sold the two only valuable manuscripts I had to Mr. O'Donovan of Dublin and his colleagues of which I have retained a copy and if y[r] hon[r] is anxious to have said copies transcribed or any other worth (sic) in my possession I'm at y[r] Hon[rs] service . . . . I have many fragments of ancient history in prose and verse, also genealogies of the ancient families of the Kingdom. Andrew Finucane Esq[r] of Ennistymon house told me when I wrote a genealogy of that Illustrious Family of that house for his use that he would represent me to you[r] Hon[rs] notice knowing you to be a lover of the language. I take the liberty of subscribing myself y[r] Honours humble and most obedient servant.

Michl O'Reilly.[44]

Ag sin, más ea, éachtaint bheag ar na *manuscript men* (agus fir dob ea iad ar fad geall leis) a bhí i mbun pinn i gContae an Chláir san ochtú agus sa naoú céad déag. Leanadh den traidisiún sin amach sa naoú céad déag le scoláirí móra dála Bhriain Uí Luana agus an scoláire ba mhó dár shíolraigh ó mhuintir an Chláir, an t-Ollamh Eoghan Ó Comhraí. Leanadh den traidisiún chomh maith céanna ag na scríobhaithe beaga, na daoine dílse sin nach eol dúinn go minic fúthu ach a n-ainm nó a lámh.

Noda

Aberystwyth: Leabharlann Náisiúnta na Breataine Bige,
Clár: P. Ó Riain, *Clár na Lámhscríbhinní Gaeilge sa Bhreatain Bhig,* 1968.

Brit. Lib., [B.L.], Cat.: S. H. O'Grady, R. Flower, *Catalogue of Irish Manuscripts in the British Museum,* i, ii, Athchló, B.A.C., 1992, iii, London, 1953.

Leabh. Náis., [L.N.], Cat.: N. Ní Shéaghdha, P. Ó Macháin, *Catalogue of Irish Manuscripts in the National Library,* i-xiii, 1961-96.

Má Nuad, [M.N.], *Clár:* P. Walsh, *Catalogue of Irish Manuscripts in Maynooth College Library,* i, 1943; P. Ó Fiannachta agus P. Ó Maoileachlainn, *Lámhscríbhinní Gaeilge Choláiste Phádraig, Má Nuad,* Clár ii-viii, 1965-73.

R.I.A., Cat.: Catalogue of Irish Manuscripts in the Royal Irish Academy, i-xxviii, 1926-70.

NÓTAÍ

[1] Athinsint air seo ag P. de Brún in *Comhar,* Samhain, 1972, p.15.
[2] Pádraig Ó Fiannachta, 'Lámhscríbhinní Gaeilge Mhaigh Nuad' in *Léachtaí Cholm Cille,* xxiii, 1973 pp 177 ff.
[3] Michéal Ó Raghallaigh a scríobh i *Má Nuad,* R. 66, (i).
[4] R.I.A., 13 0 10; 23 G 9; 23 E 10.
[5] L.N., G 599.
[6] B.L., Add., 91,027.
[7] Aberystwyth, A 21; R.I.A., 3 C 18; Má Nuad, R 66.
[8] R.I.A., 3 C 18, p. 203.
[9] *Proc. R.I.A.,* iml. 3, sraith iii, pp 218-22.
[10] *Ibid.,* pp 218-9.
[11] Má Nuad, R 66, 103-4.
[12] Liam Ó Luaighnigh, *Dánta Aindréis Mhic Cruitín,* Ennis, 1935, pp 31-3.
[13] Má Nuad, C 41, p. 1.
[14] Breandán Ó Conchúir, *Scríobhaithe Chorcaí,* B.A.C., 1982, p. 239.

[15] Má Nuad, C 93; C 58; R.I.A., 23 M 52.

[16] Má Nuad, C 37.

[17] Má Nuad, R 69.

[18] Ó Luaighaigh, *op. cit.*, p. 60.

[19] R.I.A., 23 H 22, p. 47.

[20] D. F. Gleeson, 'Peter O'Connell: Scholar and Scribe', *Studies*, Meán Fómhair, 1944, p. 343.

[21] Ó Luaighnigh, *op. cit.*, réamhrá.

[22] B.L. *Cat.*, 1, p. 161.

[23] *Ibid.*, p. 162.

[24] Má Nuad, C 74 (g) p. 8.

[25] Mrs. M. J. O'Connell, 'The Last of the Shanachies', *The Irish Monthly*, xiv,1886, pp 27ff.

[26] *Ibid.*

[27] *Ibid.*

[28] B.L. Addendum., 20, 718.

[29] R.I.A. 23 C 29.

[30] Maigh Nuad, C 68.

[31] Maigh Nuad, C 99, p. 107.

[32] Maigh Nuad, C 38 (k).

[33] Maigh Nuad, *Clár* vii, p. 7.

[34] *Ibid.*, pp 7-8.

[35] *Ibid.*, p. 9.

[36] P. Ó Fiannachta, 'The Irish Traditions of Clare', *Mount St. Joseph, Ennistymon, 1824-1974*, Ennistymon, 1974, p. 49.

[37] Maigh Nuad, *Clár* vii, p. 7.

[38] L.N., G 1132.

[39] Maigh Nuad, M 111; C 70 (g); C 72 (3); C 113 (j).

[40] Maigh Nuad, R.69, i.

[41] Maigh Nuad, R97, i.

[42] R.I.A., 23 0 40; 24 1 9; 3 B 30; 3 B 2; tharlodh gur leis chomh maith 3 B 31.

[43] R.I.A., 3 B 31, p. 17.

[44] Téacs na litreach seo le fáil i dteannta Ls. G990 sa Leabharlann Náisiúnta ar leath-anach gan uimhir.

19

AN CHLOCH BA MHÓ AR A PHAIDRÍN TADHG GAELACH AR THADHG MAC CÁRTHAIGH RÁBACH

ÚNA NIC ÉINRÍ

A Thaidhg a Chárthaigh chaileannaigh chaoin chliaraigh
mhéidhricc mharthainicc meanaimnicc bhinn bhriaithricc
le déigshearc taithnimh dod theasdas a shaoi thriallas
a bhfeill do thaitithe a shagairt ghil shímhfhialta (v. 1)

Mar sin a labhair Tadhg Gaelach Ó Súilleabháin le Tadhg Mac Cárthaigh, i ndán a scríobh Micheál Mac Peadair Uí Longáin ar lch. 257 den Ls. 23 N 15 (Ac. R É).[1] Is iad na dátaí a fheictear sa lámhscríbhinn sin ná 1740, 1761, 1766, agus 1781. Ba mhaith liom a áiteamh gur cumadh an dán thuas tamall sular céadbhreacadh an lámhscríbhinn.

Coisriceadh Tadhg Rábach ina easpag Chorcaí, Chluana is Rois idir Iúil agus Lúnasa, sa bhliain 1727[2]. "Tugadh moladh foirmeálta na filíochta do gach easpag, nach mór, a riar i ndeoisí Chorcaí go dtí go mall san 18ú céad", a mhaíonn Anna Heussaff[3]. Ar an gcéad léamh gheofá dán molta a ghlaoch ar dhán seo Thaidhg chomh maith. Molann sé an tEaspag leis an aidiacht "caileannach" - (go raibh trácht ar a shinsir sna hAnnála), agus taispeánann sé go raibh baint aige leis an gcléir, nó leis na baird, leis an bhfocal molta "cliarach". Ina theannta sin, is de bharr a ainm a bheith in airde (*"le deighshearc taitnimh dod theasdas"*) a bhí triall Thaidhg Ghaelaigh air ag an am seo. Ba fhada fairsing iad tailte na gCárthach i gCúige Mumhan sa sean ré[4]. "Na flatha fá raibh mo shean roimh éag do Chríost" a mhaígh Aodhagán Ó Raithile fúthu. Níor lig Tadhg Gaelach a mhaidí le sruth á moladh sa dán seo ach chomh beag:

> Cois aidhlean, eatharla, mhainge et bhaoi an iarla
> fáidhsion fleasga is gach amhain an innse fhiacha (v. 5)

Aibhneacha i gCorcaigh, i dTiobraid Árann is i gCiarraí is ea na haibhneacha thuasluaite[5], a mbíodh smacht ag na Cártaigh orthu in anallód, agus a bheadh i ndeoise Thaidhg ón uair a coisriceadh é ina easpag. Carachtrú réalaíoch atá againn anseo, más ea, bíodh go n-áitíonn Breandán Ó Buachalla, agus é ag trácht ar an véarsaíocht molta i gcoitinne, gur léiriú idéalach a dhéantaí go minic ar phearsa an rí chóir[6].

Ar feadh an chuid ba mhó den ochtú haois déag bhí comhacht ag na ríthe Stiobhartacha chun easpaig na hÉireann a ainmniú. Bheadh Tadhg Mac Cárthaigh Rábach ina dtuilleamaí, más ea. Ina theannta sin, bhí Tadhg Gaelach ina "sentimentally fierce Jacobite", dar le léirmheastóirí áirithe[7]; níor leis ba fhaillí, dá bhrí sin, Séarlas Edward a mholadh sa dán seo:

> Éist le Caralus caithmhileadh cloidhm sgiathach
> féidhmnirt fearagach gaisgeamhuil gnímhghliaghach
> ráidhig a sealbh na bhfearannso bhí air iasacht
> ta an fhoighne caite aguin glacfamna chíos bliaghanach (v. 3)

Déantar dia beag de Shéarlas anseo, lena chlaoímh a raibh cosaint ann don lámh - an "cloidhm sgiathach" a tháinig i bhfaisean ón Renaissance i leith. Saolaíodh Séarlas sa bhliain 1720, ach, nuair nach raibh ann ach óganach ceithre bliana déag d'aois, "he had seen war with the Spanish army at Gaeta"[8]. Dó sin a thagraínn an aidiacht "gnímhghliaghach", ní foláir - toisc é a bheith gníomhach i gcath. Níl Éire ach "air iasacht" ag an Rí Seoirse, dar le Tadhg, agus is mithid don Rí cóir teacht agus an cíos bliana a bhailiú uaidh. Roinnfidh Séarlas bailte na Banban "air ghréidhin tsliocht chalama chailce na nGaoidhiol ngrianda" a mhaíonn Tadhg Gaelach i véarsa eile den dán. Ní hé sin amháin, ach, deir sé go gcuirfidh an fear claímh seo i.e. "an lannaire", an Eaglais Chaitliceach i.e. "cealladh na naoimh ndiaga", ina ceart:

> léighisfidh an lannaíre cealladh na naoimh ndiaga
> cidh créidhmthe creachtaithe tachtaithe a ndlíghe ag diabhalaibh
> (v. 5)

Agus é ag trácht ar Éirinn i gcáipéisí na Stiobhartach, ba é a scríobh Patrick Fagan:

> While Gaelic Poets fantasised for most of the century about a Jacobite invasion of Ireland, and there were people like Sylvester Lloyd, the catholic bishop, who from time to time advocated such a course, the truth is that Ireland figured hardly at all in the plans of the Jacobite plotters. Given that their primary aim was the restoration of James to the throne of England, there was little point in mounting an attack on Ireland, which, even if it were successful, would leave them as far away as ever from a foothold on the island of Britain.[9]

Aontaíonn Liam Irwin leis an tuairim sin sa léirmheas a rinne sé ar leabhar Fagan. Easpa suime sin na Stiobhartach sa tír seo, béimníonn sí, dar leis:

> the extent to which eighteenth-century Gaelic poetry, with its obsession about the Stuarts as saviours of Ireland, was divorced from reality[10].

Níl aon amhras ná go léiríonn an file sa dán seo dóchas as an Rí Stiobhartach nár comhlíonadh. Ach má bhí na Stiobhartaigh ar nós cuma liom i leith na hÉireann, ní hionann sin is a rá nach raibh na Gaeil dáiríre ina gcreideamh iontu, agus nár fhulaing siad ar son an chreidimh sin. Sin í tuairim Bhreandáin Uí Bhuachalla, sa ráiteas seo:

> Bíodh gur deacair aon bheachtú cruinn a dhéanamh air, is cinnte
> gur crocadh na céadta in Éirinn sa chéad leath den aois as
> "inlisting for the Pretender"[11]

Ba mhaith liom a áiteamh, áfach, nach mbaineann an dán seo le
seintimintí seánra na haislinge go huile is go hiomlán. Go deimhin
féin, is dóigh liom go bpléitear go réadach le himeachtaí staire a
tharla i gCorcaigh le linn do Thadhg Gaelach a bheith ag bualadh
bóthar na filíochta don chéad uair ina shaol.

Cúpla bliain i ndiaidh choisriceadh Thaidhg Rábaigh ba éigean dó
déileáil leis an Ath. John Hennessy a bhí ina shagart paróiste ar
Dhún ar Aill. Ní dea-cháil, ach a mhalairt, a bhí ar an sagart seo,
agus sa bhliain 1730 ghearáin trí dhuine dhéag dá chomh-shagairt é
leis an Easpag, á chur ina leith "if Lucifer came out of Hell he
could not carry more pride"[12]. Bhí fadhb óil ag Hennessy chomh
maith, dar leo, agus bhí sé cairdiúil leis na Protastúnaigh. Tar éis
dó a dhícheall a dhéanamh, ba éigean don Easpag é a chur ar
fionraí. Ní mó ná sásta a bhí Hennessy agus thug sé fianaise do na
hÚdaráis go raibh an tEaspag ag bailiú airgid chun an Pretender a
chur i gcoróinn arís. Cúig phunt sa bhliain a bhailigh sé ó gach
sagart paróiste ina dheoise, dar le Hennessy. Cuardaíodh teach an
Easpaig, ach níor cuireadh aon choir ina leith, agus chuaigh an
chúis i gcoinne John Hennessy. Mar sin féin, d'fhág an tEaspag a
áit chónaithe agus chuir sé faoi i dTigh Molaige. Luann Anna
Heussaff an eachtra seo, ach is dóigh léi nár cumadh aon dán ag an
am a bhain go réadach, láithreach lenar tharla[13]. Ní réitím leis an
tuairim sin, mar dealraíonn sé gur don eachtra sin a bhí Tadhg
Gaelach ag tagairt i véarsa a dó dá dhán:

> Fághaim na braitear a dadamh ort bí ad bhiatach
> ságaill air baillichrith beathuisge is fion riaraicc
> an oighreacht bharraghil chatharach laoi fiadhtair
> gan mhoill go cabharthach ceanasach suíghe ad tiagarna (v.2)

Áitíonn sé nach bhfuil faic, "a dadamh", le cur i leith an Easpaig,
agus spreagann sé é chun filleadh ar a oidhreacht, i gcathair na
Laoi, a raibh Fionnbharra ina éarlamh aici.

Ghoill eachtraí frith-chléireacha mar an ceann thuas go mór ar easpaig na hÉireann san ochtú haois déag. Scríobh Ambrose O'Callaghan, Easpag Fearna, chuig James Edgar, ar an fichiú lá de mhí na Márta 1734:

> Our post is so uncertain that I'm forced to give new trouble by writing in brief what I writ already somewhat more at large viz. that we are in great fear of the storms lasting.[14]

I litir ó Pharas a scríobh an tAth. John Bourke chuig an Rí Séamas, ar an seachtú lá fichead de mhí an Mheithimh, 1735, léitear:

> The ignorance and the scandalous behaviour of a great number of priests, straggling about without place or employ, are the cause of the decay of religion . . . . . as much as the severity of the Acts of Parliament ..... who being reprimanded, as they have been here, for the irregularity of their lives, turned against those whose duty it was to correct and suspend them. They were priests of this kind that denounced to the Government the Bishop of Cork and some estated gentlemen as collectors for your Majesty, upon which they were pursued so that the bishop could not appear in his diocese almost these three years past.[15]

Tugann an chaint sin le tuiscint go raibh Tadhg Rábach ar teitheadh fós faoin mbliain 1735, agus ní fios cé chomh fada ina dhiaidh sin a d'fhág sé a atharacht gan tiarna; sin é an fáth gur áitigh mé i dtús an ailt seo gur chum Tadhg Gaelach a dhán dó roimh, nó timpeall 1740. Admhaím nár thug an file mionchuntas ar ar tharla; níorbh shin é nós na haimsire, áfach. Sna litreacha a scríobhtaí chuig an Stiobhartach ba ghnách cód a úsáid. Ghlaoití "feirm" ar dheoise, "bainisteoir", nó "feirmeoir" ar easpag, agus "tionóntaithe" ar chléir is tuath.[16]

Bíodh gur ag moladh "Caralus" a bhí an file i dtrí véarsa den dán, ní dheachaidh sé ar strae ar fad, ná níor leis ba fhaillí na comharsana in aice láimhe a lua:

> A mádhma an mhachaire bainfid na trí traithe
> meidheam na ceathanaibh a clanna na cclaoin striapach
> beidh soilse is phsalamaibh aifrinn is buídhion rialta
> na sadhair dhligh aguinne ar halla gach crín spriata (v. 6)

Cairde Thaidhg ba ea "na trí triaithe" a luaitear thuas. Mar seo a chuirtear síos orthu ar lch. 36 den Ls. 23 A 16 (Ac. R.É):[17]

> Freagra Táidhg Gáodhalach ar na ttrí ttriaihi Uilliam Englis an brahair binn briahrach, Seaghain O Cuinigán an snádh sarr shnuite, Eadmhard Do Nógla an taluir tonnach teagarrha

Pé scéal é, is lena gcabhair siúd, dar leis an bhfile, a bhuafar ar "chlanna na cclaoin striapach", agus is de bharr a n-iarrachtaí a bheidh an tAifreann á léamh athuair, agus na hOird Rialta ag cur fúthu arís i hallaí na n-ainniseoirí. Ní ag brath ar an Chevalier atá an file anseo. Agus an toradh a bheidh ar shaothar na gcomharsana?:

> Aghnaibh dearbhphuince sgaipe go fír siansach
> Sydear saxanach cartfaidh a croidhe an chiarso
> gach cládhaire ceachartha cealagach craoismhianach
> sin fághartha gramaruisg mhaillighthe an fhill dhiacharaicc (v. 7).

Níor chuir Pádraig Ua Duinnín fiacail ann agus é ag trácht ar an dán seo:

> This is a poem demanding hospitality from Fr. Tadhg Mac Carthy, called Tadhg Rabach, who subsequently became Bishop of Cork.[18]

Ní féidir a shéanadh ná go bhfuil an-bhéim ar bhia agus deoch sa dán. "Bí flaithiúil ag soláthar bia" a ordaíonn an file don Easpag i véarsa 2 thuas. "Bíodh feoil mhéith agus iasc leasaithe againn" a deir sé, gan trácht ar "uisce beatha is fíon le n-ól". Agus nuair a bheidh lá eile ag an bPaorach, nó ag na trí triatha, beidh fíorphuins ina sruthanna, mar a dúirt an file i véarsa 7, agus glanfar amach ó chroí-lár an bhairille (ciarso/tiarsa) an cheirtlis Sasanach (sydear saxanach).

Nós ba ea é pátrún a mholadh as a chuid féile is flaithiúlachta. Tar éis an tsaoil, is ó mholadh dá leithéid a tháinig an seanfhocal "fáilte Uí Cheallaigh" isteach sa chaint. Ach ní i leith na nósmhaireachta amháin a bhí Tadhg Gaelach anseo, dar liom. Níorbh aon stróinséir é don ghorta. Tharla ceann sa bhliain 1720, de bharr na droch-aimsire. Ach um Nollaig na bliana 1739 thosaigh sé ag cur seaca go trom, agus níor tháinig stad air go ceann seacht seachtaine ina dhiaidh sin. Lean Earrach fuar gan bháisteach é sin, agus mar bharr ar an donas, bhí Fómhar na bliana sin ar an gceann ba fhuaire le dhá chéad bliain. D'imigh dhá bhliain eile thart sular thit fearthainn ar fónamh. Bhí na prátaí sa talamh i bpoill nuair a thosaigh sé ag cur seaca, agus reodh iad go léir. Cailleadh na hainmhithe leis an bhfuacht, agus toisc gurbh éigeandáil Eorpach í, ní raibh fáil ar ghrán ó thíortha eile. Ba é daonra na hÉireann roimh an nGorta seo ná 2.4M. daoine. Cailleadh an cúigiú cuid de dhaonra na Mumhan de bharr an Ghorta. Lean fiabhras agus flosc fola é, agus b'éigean do a lán na bóithre a thabhairt orthu féin.

> Within a ten-mile radius of Dublin, there are at least two prominent monuments ... the obelisk on the top of Killiney Hill, and the extraordinary 140-foot high structure known as Connolly's folly, between Celbridge and Maynooth. These landmarks were erected during the great crisis of 1740-41.[19]

De bharr an Ghorta seo theith muintir an deiscirt go dtí na bailte, ar thóir bia agus oibre. Cá hionadh, más ea, go ndéanfadh Tadhg Gaelach teanntás ar an Easpag. Ní heol dúinn aon tslí bheatha eile a bheith aige seachas a bheith ag díol is ag reic a dhánta, agus ba é an gad ba ghaire don scornach, i.e. an t-ocras, nárbh fholáir dó a scaoileadh ar dtús. Níorbh aon mhaith dó, áfach, Easpag nach raibh i bhfeighil a oidhreachta. Ba é ba lú ba ghann dó dán molta, spreagtha a chumadh ina onóir, le súil go meallfaí ar ais é óna "dheoraíocht" i dTigh Molaga.

Bhuail mé leis an dán seo trí huaire eile i lámhscríbhinní a scríobhadh san ochtú haois déag. Bhreac Risteard Ó Murrian é faoi dhó, uair amháin i Ls. 23 L 38 (Ac. R.É), ar lch. 65, sa bhliain 1765[20] agus uair eile i Ls. C102 (j) (M.N.)[21], lch. 1m. Bhuail mé leis arís eile i Ls. 23 B 38 (Ac. R.É.), ar lch. 200. Séamus Ó Murchúghadh a scríobh é idir na blianta 1778 agus 1779. Ba as Port Láirge don Mhurrianach, agus ba as Loch Garman don Mhurchúghach, rud a léiríonn go raibh glacadh leis an dán i bhfad ó Chorcaigh, tar éis bhás an Easpaig féin, a cailleadh sa bhliain 1747. Bíodh gur cailleadh an file sa bhliain 1795, leanadh de ghrafnadh an dáin, mar ag tús an naoú haois déag faightear ar ais i gCorcaigh é. Bhreac Pól Ó Longáin é i ls. M12 (M.N.), sa bhliain 1818, don Easpag Ó Murchú, agus dhá bhliain ina dhiaidh sin chuir Mícheál Óg Ó Longáin ar phár é i Ls. 23 G 24 (Ac. R.É.). Ba i Ls. 23 0 77 (Ac. R.É.) a bhuail mé leis don uair dheiridh. Seán Ó Dálaigh a bhreac é, sa bhliain 1848. Ba é, freisin a chéadchuir i gcló é sa *Pious Miscellany*, sa bhliain 1868. Lean an Duinníneach (1903), agus an Foghludhach (1929) a shampla siúd. Glacaim leis gur le traidisiún na lámhscríbhinní, seachas leis an traidisiún béil, a bhain sé ó thús, mar gur bheag athrú a tháinig air ó chéadfheictear scríofa é, seachas an focal *chaileannaigh,* a d'athraigh Risteard Ó Murrian go *charthanaigh* sa bhliain 1765 (23L38). Ba mar *charthanaigh* a scríobhadh ina dhiaidh sin é sna lsí. Braithimse slacht agus tíos sa stíl ann, nach ró-fhada ó stíl fhilíocht na Scol í, bíodh gur i meadaracht an Chaointe atá sé scríofa.[22] Níorbh iad na cúinsí staire céanna a ghoill ar Thadhg Gaelach is ar na Baird, ach níl aon agó ná go raibh siad go léir ag tochras ar a gceirtlín féin. Ba ar thóir na pátrúnachta a bhí Tadhg, leis, dála na mBard a chuaigh roimhe.

Bunfhoinsí.

Ac. Ríoga Éireann

23 A 16, lch. 257
23 B 38, lch. 200
23 G 24, lch. 416m
23 L 38, lch. 65.
23 N 15, lch. 257.
23 0 77, lch. 100

Col. Phádraig, Maigh Nuad.

C 102 (j), lch. 1m
M 12, lch. 255.

NÓTAÍ

[1] *Catalogue of Irish Manuscripts in the Royal Irish Academy, (Cat. Ac. Ríoga)*, 1354. Tá tuairisc ar an scríobhaí in Breandán Ó Conchúir, *Scríobhaithe Chorcaí 1700-1850*, B.Á.C., 1982, pp 88-91.

[2] Evelyn Bolster, *A History of the Diocese of Cork, from the Penal Era to the Famine*, Cork, 1989, pp 44-63.

[3] Anna Heussaff, *Filí agus Cléir san Ochtú hAois Déag*, B.Á.C., 1992, p.118.

[4] Diarmuid Ó Murchadha, *Family Names of County Cork*, Dún Laoghaire, 1995, pp 49-65.

[5] Risteárd Ó Foghludha, *Tadhg Gaedhlach*, B.Á.C.,1929, p.149.

[6] Breandán Ó Buachalla, Aisling Ghéar, B.Á.C., 1996 p.502.

[7] Anne M. Brady, & Brian Cleeve, *A Biographical Dictionary of Irish Writers*, B.Á.C., 1985, p. 373.

[8] J. D. Mackie, A History of Scotland, Middlesex, 1978, p. 275.

[9] Patrick Fagan, (eag.), *Ireland in the Stuart Papers*, 2 *Iml.*, B.Á.C., 1995, *Iml.* i, p. 2.

[10] Liam Irwin, "Fagan (ed.) Ireland in the Stuart Papers", *Irish Historical Studies*, iml. xxx, uimh. *119*, 1997, lch. 477.

[11] Ó Buachalla *op. cit.*, p. 338.

[12] Bolster, *op. cit.*, p. 47.

[13] Heussaff *op. cit.*, p. 119.

[14] Fagan *op. cit.*, iml. *l*, p. 195.

[15] ibid., p. 217.

[16] ibid., p. 100.

[17] Cat. Ac. Ríoga, p. 82.

[18] Pádraig Ua Duinnín, *Amhráin Thaidhg Ghaedhealaigh Uí Shúilleabháin*, B.Á.C., 1903, p. 129. Is dóigh liom go raibh dul amú ar an bhFoghludhach agus ar an Duinníneach faoi dháta cumtha an dáin. Mheas siad gur ag tagairt do choisriceadh an Easpaig a bhí sé, i.e., timpeall 1727. Ba é a bhí ag déanamh scime don Fhoghludhach ná gurbh ar éigean a bheadh Corcaigh sroichte ag Tadhg Gaelach faoin am ar tharla eachtra Hennessy. Níorbh eol dó, go bhfios dom gur fhan an tEaspag ar a theitheadh chomh fada sin.

[19] David Dickson, "The Other Great Irish Famine", (eag.) Cathal Póirtéir, *The Great Irish Famine*, Cork, 1985, p. 50.

[20] *Cat., Ac. Ríoga*, p. 855. Tá tuairisc ar an scríobhaí in Eoghan Ó Súilleabháin, "Scríobhaithe Phort Láirge", (eag.). William Nolan & Thomas P. Power, *Waterford History & Society*, Dublin, 1992, p. 292.

[21] *Lámhscríbhinní Gaeilge Choláiste. Phádraig, Má Nuad - Clár vi*, p. 64.

[22] Tadhg Ó Donnchadha, *Prosóid Gaedhilge*, B.Á.C., 1925, pp 48-51.

20

AODH MAC DOMHNAILL - AN CHÉAD FHEALSAMH A SHAOTHRAIGH TRÍ GHAEILGE?

JOHN EUSTACE

I mbliain 1853 chríochnaigh Aodh Mac Domhnaill a leabhar *Fealsúnacht Aodh Mhic Dhomhnaill* agus chuir sé féin an teideal "fealsúnacht" air. D'fhan an leabhar gan foilsiú go dtí ár linn féin nuair a chuir Colm Beckett in eagar agus i gcló é.[1] Ar thug an t-údar féin an teideal "fealsúnacht" ar a leabhar mar shaghas leide dúinn faoin aidhm a bhí aige agus é i mbun pinn? Ar aon chuma bhí sé sásta an mana ardnósach "fealsúnacht" a ghlacadh agus dul sa seans, in ainneoin lucht an dí-chreidimh nár leasc leo a dtuairim faoina fhilíocht a chur in iúl[2]. Tá smut den dúshlán le sonrú san fhocal mór-is-fiú "fealsúnacht" mar sin, ach ní gan chúis atá an focal ann, dar liom.

Is é Colm Beckett, eagarthóir a shaothair, is mó a chuir de stró air féin Aodh Mac Domhnaill a thuiscint agus a mheas i gceart, agus níl aon amhras air sin ná gur saothar fealsúnachta atá ann. Tá an méid sin le rá aige:

> this is a study of nature, based on the teachings of Ancient Greece and of the Bible, on folk tradition and on his own observations. He discourses on the composition of matter, on plants,

caves, insects, fish, birds, animals, and on man and his place in creation.[3]

Más fíor an breithiúnas seo, agus glacaimse leis gurb ea, níl aon dabht ná go bhfuil saothar fealsúnachta ann. Dá mbeadh a theoiric bunaithe ar an mBíobla amháin, bheinn in amhras faoina stádas mar shaothar fealsúnachta, ach tá sé soiléir go bhfuil sintéis faoi leith déanta aige de eilimintí difriúla chun dearcadh indibhidiúil a shaothrú dúinn; tá scáth a phearsantachta le sonrú ar gach líne.

Chríochnaigh sé an saothar sa bhliain 1853. Sé bliana níos déanaí foilsíodh *The Origin of the Species* le Darwin,[4] leabhar eile faoin dúlra ach is mór eatarthu; tá an domhan eatarthu. Cheapfá agus "Fealsúnacht Aodha Mhic Dhomhnaill" á léamh agat nár mhair Linnaeus, Newton, Lavoisier agus a léithéidí riamh. Is féidir le fear na Meán-Aoiseanna *Fealsúnacht Aodha Mhic Dhomhnaill* a thuiscint gan dua. Cheapfá agus tú á léamh, nach raibh an nádúr ina shaineolas, ach go raibh cead cainte ag éinne faoi. Cén saghas duine a scríobh é, agus cad tá taobh thiar de?

Tá sé suimiúl domsa go mbaineann mórshaothar eile na naoú haoise déag - *Cín Lae Amhlaoibh Uí Shúilleabháin* leis an ábhar céanna - an nádúr.[5] B'fhéidir nár mhiste comparáid a dhéanamh idir an dá shaothar mar sin. Ar ámharaí an tsaoil, tá aiste an-bhreá scríofa ag an Ollamh Breandán Ó Madagáin faoi *Cinn Lae Amhlaoibh Uí Shúill-eabháin*.[6] Is é breithiúnas Uí Mhadagáin go ndeachaigh tionchar na scríbhneoirí Béarla i bhfeidhm ar Amhlaoibh. Baineann *Cinn Lae Uí Shúilleabháin* agus *The Natural History of Selborne* le Gilbert White, mar shampla, leis an genre céanna - an dialann ina bhfuil tuairisc laethúil faoin aimsir, radharcanna, ainmhíthe etc. Mar a deir Ó Madagáin:

> An té a bhfuil cur amach aige ar *Chin Lae Amhlaoibh* tuigfidh sé gurb é an t-ábhar ginearálta céanna atá idir lámha aige agus a bhíodh ar bun ag na scríbhneoirí Sasanacha seo: an dúlra, áilleacht na tíre, na barraí, an saol timpeall air.[7]

Más fíor an breithiúnas seo, is léir nárbh fhealsamh Amhlaoibh Ó Súilleabháin. Níor ghlac éinne le Gilbert White agus Thomas Gray mar fheallsaimh go bhfios dom. Is léir go raibh Amhlaoibh Ó

Súilleabháin ag scríobh dialann phearsanta faoin dúlra agus nach raibh ach tagairtí fánacha d'aon saghas fealsúnachta ann.

Ní luaitear Mac Domhnaill i leabhar Uí Mhadagáin agus is trua sin. Bheadh sé suimúil, domsa ar aon nós, a bhreithiúnas a fháil. Gan ach sracfhéachaint a bheith tugtha agam ar *Cín Lae Uí Shúilleabháin,* tig liom a rá nach bhfuil aon léargas faoi leith ann ar chúiseanna na dúlra; ní dhéantar iarracht an nádúr ina iomláine a thuiscint, ná ní mó a lorgaítear prionsabail an nádúir mar chóras. Ní saothar fealsúnachta atá ann, mar sin.

Cé go bhfuil a lán mioneolais faoi luibheanna agus ainmhithe le fáil in *Fealsúnacht Aodha Mhic Dhomhnaill,* tá córas teoiriciúil ann freisin. Cad tá ann? Chun an cheist a fhreagairt tá sé tábhach-tach an fear féin a thuiscint. Bhí baint aige le "The Home Mission", eagraíocht cosúil leis an "Irish Society" a bhí ag iarraidh an Bíobla a mhúineadh do Ghaeilgeoirí.[8] Chaith sé dhá thréimhse ina shaol leis na Bíoblóirí agus is é mo thuairim féin go bhfuil rian de le fáil ina mhórshaothar. Níor mhiste, mar sin, scrúdú a dhéanamh ar an saothar seo. Táimse faoi chomaoin ag Colm Beckett toisc an leagan caighdeánaithe a chuir sé ar fáil dúinne. Mar seo a thosaigh sé a leabhar:

> An té ar mhian leis fios údar agus cáilíocht corp talmhaí agus corp neamhaí a chuardach nó a scrúdú amach, is éigean dó an dá chineál duar a chur i gcompar, ionas gurbh fhearrde ba léir dá chéadfaí na nithe dorcha seo a bhreathnú; agus go mór mór gach claontacht dá leanann dóibh i ré a mbeatha nó a marthana.[9]

Tá sé le tuiscint go bhfuil gach éinne ar a chonlán féin ag scrúdú an domhain ina aonar amhail is nach raibh aon eolas le fáil ón saothar a chuir lucht léinn ar fáil leis na cianta. Tá muidinne arís i ré roimh Socrates in aimsir Tháles nó Heraclítus. Tá sé le tuiscint go bhfuil "an dá chineál duar" ann: "corp talmhaí agus corp neamhaí". Níos déanaí sa leathanach céanna scríobh sé:

> Tá an uile ní arna chumadh de thrí chorp, mar atá, tine, uisce agus gaoth.[10]

312

Táimid arís in aimsir Tháles. Is léir gur rud buan é in intinn an duine an teoiric seo agus níl sé gan dealramh. Lean sé ar aghaidh:

> "Tuig, a léitheoir, gur fearga agus banda a rinne Dia gach ní ar dtús" agus "is í an talamh is máthair mhór do gach ní talmhaí."[11]

Is fíor é ar shlí, mar chaint mheafarach; agus b'fhile é Aodh Mac Domhnaill. Ach an rud is suntasaí ná nach bhfuil aon fhianaise ann sa leabhar gurbh eol d'Aodh Mac Domhnaill go raibh saineolaithe ann a raibh saineolas faoi leith acu faoin nádúr. Scríobh sé mar fhear a mhair i ndomhan béaloideasúil chomh fada agus a bhain sé leis an nádúr.

Tá sé soiléir áfach, ón fhianaise faoina shaol agus ón fhianaise sa leabhar go raibh eolas aige ar an Bhíobla. Níor scríobh sé mar Chaitliceach agus, dá bhrí sin, níl aon tagairt ann don Eaglais. Níorbh fhéidir d'aon Chaitliceach san naoú haois déag gan an Eaglais a chur san áireamh. Sa leabhar seo tá tagairtí ann don "údar" agus "seo a chreideas formhór an domhain" agus é ag caint faoi chruthú an domhain. Is léir nach raibh sé gan taithí ar an chonspóid i gcúrsaí creidimh, e.g.:

> Is é barúil drong eile nach mar sin atá, ach gur aon phearsa agus aon spiorad agus aon dia é, agus nárbh fhéidir an Diagacht a bheith roinnte i dtrí phearsa.[12]

Barúil agus barúlacha! Ní bheadh béim ar bharúil ag an té a ghlac údarás na hEaglaise. Fear neamhspleách a bhí ann a raibh a lán barúlacha cloiste aige. Tá sé suntasach freisin gur chuir sé béim faoi leith ar rúndiamhair.

> Ach ag seo na rúndiamhra nach dtuigeann céadfaí agus nach eol do intleacht duine ó ghlice a bhreathnú.[13]

agus níos déanaí:

> cad é mar tharla seo a bheith, ní féidir do intleacht fealsúna ná filí a thuiscint.[14]

Tá sé suntasach gur chuir Aodh Mac Domhnaill béim faoi leith ar theileolaíocht nó cuspóireacht sa nádúr. Dar leis an teoiric seo ní tharlaíonn aon rud sa nádúr go timpisteach gan chúis ná gan aidhm; a mhalairt glan, tá gach aon rud dírithe ar chuspóir éigin, cé nach bhfuil sé soiléir dúinne i gcónaí. Is é an duine daonna buaicphointe agus críoch agus aidhm an nádúir go léir de réir na toirice seo. Teileolaíocht den saghas sin a bhí mar shaintréith fhealsúnacht Mhic Dhomhnaill:- teileolaíocht shoineanta a bhí bunaithe ar an gcoincheap gur saghas gáirdín í an nádúr ina bhfuil gach rud úsáideach don duine - "tá sé follas go leor go bhfuil gach ní, ó laghad, úsáideach i slí éigin." agus "nach bhfuil aicíd ná galar dá leanann do lucht tíre ar bith nach bhfuil a leigheas le fáil san áit chéanna."[15] Dar liom, gur mhó a bhain teileolaíocht shoineanta den saghas sin leis an gcreideamh Protastúnach ná leis an gCaitliceachas.[16] Tháinig an meon sin i mbláth tar éis na gluaiseachta Rómánsaíochta i dTuaisceart na hEorpa. Ba dheacair é sin a chruthú áfach.

Is iomaí tagairt ann don fhealsúnacht, ach is léir nach í an fhealsúnacht acadúil atá i gceist. Mar seo a labhair sé:

> Ach cad é mar fuair an sclábhaí gruama an t-eolas nádúrtha seo gan oide ná teagascóir? Fuair ó theagascóir is fearr, mar atá - fealsúnacht.[17]

Ní olc "an t-eolas nádúrtha" mar dheifníd ar fhealsúnacht. Níl sé i gceist anseo Mac Domhnaill a mheas mar eolaí ar luibheolaíocht agus a léithéidí. Is fiú breithiúnas Colm Beckett a lua, áfach:

> Léiríonn an "Fhealsúnacht" de ghnáth gur bhreathnaigh Aodh Mac Domhnaill go géar, cruinn ar an nádúr [18]

Cad mar gheall ar Aodha Mac Domhnaill mar fhealsamh? Is é an breithiúnas a thug Breandán Ó Buachalla faoin leabhar ná:

> eolas ar an nádúr is mó atá aige ann agus é bunaithe, cuid mhaith, ar an mbéaloideas agus ar a chuid léitheoireachta, agus bíodh gur beag is fiú mar fhealsúnacht é is breá an cuntas ar

éanlaithe is ar éisc, ar ainmhithe is ar fheithidí; ar luibheanna, ar leigheasanna, ar thalamh agus ar Ghaeilge a cheanntair féin é.[19]

Is fiú breithiúnas eile a lua:

> A poor unlettered peasant, before whose eyes knowledge in the accepted sense of the word did ne'er unroll her ample page; nevertheless, guided, in his own pathetic phrase, by the understanding he received from God and Nature, he showed himself no unworthy scion of the race that gave to the world the greatest philosopher of the middle ages - Johannes Scotus Eriugena.[20]

Ba dheacair domsa, áfach, aontú leis sin. Tá sé ag dul thar fóir a rá gur "poor unlettered peasant" a bhí ann. Múinteoir a bhí in Aodh agus d'oibrigh sé mar chúntóir do Mhac Adhaimh ag bailiú ábhair a bhain leis an nGaeilge. Fear dhátheangach a bhí ann freisin a raibh eolas domhain aige ar léann traidisiúnta. Ina theannta sin chaith sé a shaol i measc daoine a raibh léann acadúil acu; Bíoblóirí Protastúnacha, lucht na hAthbheochana Gaeilge i mBéal Feirste agus filí Gaeilge. Ní raibh oideachas ollscoile faighte aige, áfach, agus níl aon eolas ar fhealsúnacht acadúil le sonrú ina leabhar, ach tá bua faoi leith aige: an bua céanna a bhí ag Tomás Ó Criomhthain. Mar a dúirt Colm Beckett:

> Bhí ar a chumas trácht ar choincheapanna fealsúnachta go simplí soiléir, gan stró, gan saothar.[21]

Rinne sé cur síos ar an nádúr mar fhile, mar aonarán neamhspleách a chaith a shaol ag machnamh faoi mhíorúilt na beatha agus mar dhuine a bhí beag beann ar thuairimí daoine eile. Bhí a leabhar mar shaghas uachta aige don saol mór agus chríochnaigh sé é go dúshlánach:

> Críochnaíodh an leabhar seo i mBéal Feirste, an t-ochtú lá den bhliain úr, bliain d'aois an Tiarna, míle ocht gcéad caoga agus trí bliana, le hAodh Mhac Domhnaill, eadhon, file Ultach, mac Shéamais Mhic aodha chríostaigh, Mhic Phádraig Mhic Alasdrainn, Mhic Raghnaill na gcapall, Mhic Shéamais Mhóir

Lughbhaidh, Mhic sheáin Bháin Lughbhaidh, tá an tséin, á ríomh de réir na tuisceanna a fuair sé ó Dhia agus ó nádúr.[22]

NÓTAÍ

[1] Colm Beckett, (eag.) *Fealsúnacht Aodha Mhic Domhnaill*, B.Á.C., 1967.

[2] *Ibid.* p.2. "Níl a chuid filíochta chomh dona agus a shílfeá dá gcreidfeá Ó Cearnaigh agus MacBionaid."

[3] Colm Beckett, *Aodh Mac Domhnaill: Poet and Philosopher*, B.Á.C.,1987, p.13.

[4] Charles Darwin, *The Origin of the Species*, London, 1859.

[5] Tomás De Bhaldraithe, (eag.) *Cinn Lae Amhlaoibh Uí Shúilleabháin*, B.Á.C., 1973.

[6] Breandán Ó Madagáin, *An Dialann Dúlra : Cinn Lae Amhlaoibh Uí Shúilleabháin agus scríbhinní dúlra an Bhéarla*, B.Á.C., 1978.

[7] *Ibid. p.* 26.

[8] Beckett, *op,cit.,* 1987, pp 6-7.

[9] Beckett, *op, cit.,* 1967, pp 95.

[10] *Ibid., p.* 95.

[11] *Ibid.,* p. 101.

[12] *Ibid.,* p. 95.

[13] *Ibid.,* p. 103.

[14] *Ibid.*

[15] *Ibid.,* p. 115.

[16] Ní raibh an tAthair Seán Ó Duinn sásta, áfach leis an tuairim sin agus an t-ábhar á phlé aige liom.

[17] Beckett, *op. cit.,* 1967, p. 109.

[18] *Ibid.,* p. 20.

[19] Breandán Ó Buachalla, *I mBéal Feirste Cois Cuain*, B.Á.C., 1968.

[20] F. W. O'Connell, "The Philosophy of Aodh Mac Domhnaill", in *County Louth Archaeological Society Journal, vol.iii, no. 4. 1915,* lch. 311-7.

[21] Beckett *op. cit.,* 1967, p. 21.

[22] *Ibid.,* p. 225.

21

SEOIRSE MAC TOMÁIS AGUS OLLSCOIL NA nDAOINE

STIOFÁN NEWMAN

San alt seo tá sé i geist agam cuntas a thabhairt agus anailís a dhéanamh ar ghnéithe áirithe den pháirt a ghlac Seoirse Mac Tomáis in athbheochan na Gaeilge idir na blianta 1923 go 1934. Léireofar go raibh obair dhúshlánach, éachtach ar bun aige d`fhonn is go bhféadfadh sé pobal agus cultúr na Gaeltachta a chur in oiriúint do shaol agus shibhialtacht an fichiú haois. D`éinne a bhfuil baint aige\aici leis an oideachas in Éirinn, tá ábhar spéise i scéal Mhic Thomáis: a dhearcadh ar thábhacht an oideachais i gcaomhnú cultúir, na hiarrachtaí dár lean, agus an cur ina aghaidh, ó eilimintí sa rialtas agus san eaglais, a dhein deimhin de ná tiocfadh a chuid oibre i réimse an oideachais chun éifeachta. Ba dhuine ar leith é Mac Tomáis i gcomhthéacs gluaiseacht na Gaeilge mar bhí a mheon i leith na hathbheochana múnlaithe ag an sóisialachas Eorpach i gcomórtas leis an náisiúnachas rómánsúil; an meon a bhí ina bhunchloch idé-eolaíochta ag formhór na ndíograiseoirí Gaeilge a bhí chun cinn sna blianta roimh agus díreach i ndiaidh bhunú an Stáit. Cé ná beidh sé faoi chaibidil agam san alt seo, is fiú a lua gurbh é Mac Tomáis a spreag an Blascaodach óg Muiris Ó Súilleabháin chun dul i mbun pinn. B`é toradh na hoibre ná a dhírbheathaisnéis, *Fiche Blian Ag Fás,* leabhar a bhain aitheantas

idirnáisiúnta amach do Mhuiris agus dá eagarthóir, Seoirse Mac
Tomáis.

Rugadh Seoirse Mac Tomáis sa bhliain 1903 in Iarthar Dulwich,
Londain. B`é an mac ba shine ar chúigear clainne a saolaíodh do
William agus Minnie Thomson. Protastúnaigh den dtraidisiún
Ultach ab ea a thuismitheoirí, ach thugadar tacaíocht ó chroí do
ghluaiseacht phoblachtánach na hÉireann, meon a chuaigh i
bhfeidhm ar Sheoirse óg. Ina óige bhí sé mar bhall de Chonradh na
Gaeilge i Londain, agus ina dhiaidh sin bhí sé gníomhach i Sinn
Féin. Sa bhliain 1922 bhain sé scoláireacht amach, a thug deis dó
dul go Coláiste an Rí, Cambridge. Bhí sé i gceist aige staidéar a
dhéanamh ar an Léann Ceilteach ach, toisc ná raibh cúrsa ar bun sa
Choláiste, thug sé faoin Léann Clasaiceach. Sa bhliain 1926 bhain
sé amach céad-onóracha i gCoda 1 agus 2 den Tripos Clasaiceach
agus sna blianta a lean bhain sé aitheantas idirnáisiúnta amach mar
scoláire ar theanga agus ar litríocht na Sean-Ghréige. Le linn dó
bheith ina mhac léinn chuir sé aithne ar an scoláire Robin Flower.
Ar chomhairle Flower, thug sé cuairt ar an mBlascaod Mór leis an
aidhm go bhféadfadh sé feabhas a chur ar a chuid Gaeilge, chun go
mbeadh sé in ann páirt ghníomhach a ghlacadh i ngluaiseacht na
Gaeilge. Míníonn sé sa sliocht seo a leanas an fonn a bhí air:

> During my schooldays in London, which coincided with the
> Black and Tan terror in Ireland, I was an ardent Sinn Féiner and
> a regular attendant of the language classes of the London Branch
> of the Gaelic League. In 1923, armed with an introduction from
> Robin Flower, I paid my first visit to the Blasket Island. My
> object was to perfect my knowledge of the language in order to
> devote myself to the language movement as soon as I had taken
> my degree.[1]

Ina scríbhinní faoin mBlascaod Mór, agus faoi ghluaiseacht na
Gaeilge, deineann Mac Tomáis idirdhealú idir a mheon i leith
phobal na Gaeltachta agus meonta eile a bhí coitianta, i measc
scoláirí agus díograiseoirí eile a chaith sealanna ar an mBlascaod,
agus ceantair Ghaeltachta eile. Nuair a bunaíodh Conradh na
Gaeilge sa bhliain 1893, tosnaíodh ar idéalú a dhéanamh ar phobal

na Gaeltachta. Mheas Dubhghlas de hÍde gur sa Ghaeilgeoir a gheobhfaí:

> everything that is most racial, most smacking of the soil, most Gaelic, most Irish.[2]

Bhí a chomhleacaí Eoin Mac Néill ar aon dul leis nuair a dúirt sé faoin nGaeilgeoir gurbh é:

> the truest and most invincible soldier of his nation"[3].

Cuireadh tús le gluaiseacht liteartha a mhol uaisleacht agus foirfeacht an tsaoil faoin dtuath, gan trácht a dhéanamh ar an mbochtanas a bhí go forleathan. Ag tagairt d'fhilíocht na gluais-eachta, deir Prionsias Ó Conluain agus Donncha Ó Céileachair an méid seo a leanas:

> Is é an teagasc mórálta thar aon rud eile an ghné is suntasaí de litríocht na ré úd, ach níor scaradh an mhorálacht chéanna go hiomlán riamh ó chúrsaí náisiúnta. Ba chuid dhlúth de náisiún-achas cultúrtha na haimsire an t-adhmholadh ar shaol agus ar shaoithiúlacht na tuaithe a fhaighimid i ndánta na tréimhse. Tá áibhéal ag baint le haoibhneas an chineáil a léirítear i ndánta mar seo, go háirithe nuair a smaoinítear ar bhochtanas na tíre ag an am.[4]

Bhí an t-idéalachas céanna le feiscint mar thionchar ar scríbhneoirí Béarla na linne sin. Chaith W.B. Yeats agus Lady Gregory roinnt mhaith ama i gConamara ar thóir ionspráide. Chaith J.M. Synge tréimhsí ar an mBlascaod Mór agus in Árainn; tá cuntais ar na turasanna san sna leabhair *In Wicklow and West Kerry* agus *The Aran Islands*. Cé ná raibh Synge dall ar na fadhbanna sóisialta agus eacnamaíochta a bhí ag goilliúint ar phobal na n-oileán, mheas sé go gcaillfidís gnéithe áirithe dá n-uaisleacht, dá dtiocfadh athrú ar an saol mar a bhí. Athrú ab ea é a bhí ag titim amach sna háiteanna ab iargúlta féin:

> I am in the North Island again, looking out with a singular sensation to the cliffs across the sound. It is hard to believe that those I can just see in the south are filled with people whose lives have the strange quality that is found in the oldest poetry and legend. Compared with them the falling off that has come with the increased prosperity of this Island is full of discouragement. The charm which people over there share with the birds has been replaced here by the anxiety of men who are eager for gain.[5]

Sa bhliain 1906 thug an scoláire meánaoiseach, Robin Flower, cuairt ar an mBlascaod Mór, d`fhonn is go bhféadfadh sé teacht ar Ghaeilge neamh-thruaillithe na Fíor-Ghaeltachta, agus chun léargas a fháil ar chultúr na meán-aoiseanna. Deir Seán Ó Lúing:

> D`aimsigh sé ar an Oileán Tiar, ceann dona loic ba dheireanaí ar domhain ina raibh iarsmaí agus nósanna na meánaoiseanna fágtha slán, cosmas beag inar mhair sibhialtacht ná raibh truaillithe fós ag deascaí na réabhlóide tionscail.[6]

Sna blianta dár lean,chaith Flower tréimhsí fada suaithinseacha ar an oileán ag foghlaim na Gaeilge, ag bailiú béaloidis, agus, fiú, ag sclábhaíocht leis na hoileánaigh. Scríobh sé leabhar faoin oileán, a tháinig amach sna daichidí, dar dteideal *The Western Island.* Cé go raibh tuiscint mhaith aige ar chúrsaí an Oileáin, tá an insint sa leabhar go mór faoi scáth an rómánsachais, agus teipeann air fiorchás sóisialta agus eacnamaíochta na háite a chur ina luí orainn. Sa sliocht seo a leanas, tá sé ag tuirlingt den traen sa Daingean, agus is léir go gceapann sé go bhfuil sé ar tí dul isteach sa tsaol eile, saol a chruthaigh sé i réimse na samhlaíochta. Deir sé:

> You forget London and Dublin, all the cities of the earth, and with Gaelic faces and Gaelic voices about you, stand in the gateway of an older and simpler world.[7]

Sa phíosa seo a leanas, a scríobh Aodh De Blácam, gheibhtear an meon ceannann céanna, meon a bhí an-choitianta i measc díograiseoirí na Gaeilge, dá fhaid ó bhaile iad is ea ba mhó an díograis. Deir De Blácam:

> The Gaeltacht is the place for reading. Your imagination here has calm and contentment, and dwells on tradition or on literature, without that feverishness restlessness that obsesses the city mind.[8]

Ar theacht chuig Seoirse Mac Tomáis, faightear meon nó tuiscint eile ar an nGaeltacht. Ní hí an aisling ba shuim leis ach an rud a chonaic sé lena shúile cinn: bhí fearg agus brón air nuair a chonaic sé drochchás na Gaeltachta:

> I do not believe in Celtic Twilight, or back to the Middle Ages, or anything of that sort, and I have lived long enough on the Blaskets to shed any romantic illusions that may have inspired me at the start...... The poverty of these peasants is appalling. There is no district nurse and the nearest doctor is 12 miles away after you have made the crossing to the mainland.[9]

Cé go raibh an-mheas ag muintir an Bhlascaoid ar na cuairteoirí, thug Mac Tomáis fé ndeara go mbídís, uaireanta:

> a little critical of those friends whose enchantment with the Blasket way of life led them to overlook the lack of essential services which they took for granted in their own lives."[10]

Míníonn an Blascaodach, Seán Ó Criomhthain, gur bhain na cuairteoirí an-sult as an rince, as an gceol agus as an scéalaíocht, rud a chuir ina luí orthu go rabhadar "sna Flaithis."[11] Nocht Blascaodach eile, Eibhlís Ní Shúilleabháin, an tuairim seo a leanas faoi na stráinséirí:

> Visitors going in and coming out of our house talking and talking and they on their holidays and they at home having comfortable homes and no worry during winter or summer, would never believe the misfortune on this Island no school nor comfort, not five hundred of mackeral when last summer it cost £3 a hundred, no lobsters last summer, very very scarce, hard times, everything so dear and so far away. Surely people could not live on air and sunshine. No not at all.[12]

Tuigeadh do Mhac Tomáis nárbh fhéidir leis bheith ag féachaint ar an mBlascaod(nó ar aon cheantar Gaeltachta) mar ríocht a bhí neamhspléach ar an ndomhain mór. Bhí fórsaí eacnamaíochta agus cultúrtha, ón dtaobh amuigh, ag brú isteach ar shaol na Gaeltachta. I gcás an Bhlascaoid, mar shampla, bhí cúrsaí iascaireachta i mbaol toisc go raibh trálaerí ó Shasana, ón bhFrainc, agus ó Mheirice "de shíor ag treabhadh na dtonn mór-thimpeall na mBlascaodaí.... Bhí sé fánach ag fear na naomhóige dul i gcomórtas leis na comhlachtaí móra a bhí ag oibriú na dtrálaerí sin."[13] Bhí, dar le Mac Tomáis, dul amú ar lucht na hathbheochana, nuair a dhein siad neamhní don réabhlóid tionscail i gcomhthéacs shlánú na Gaeltachta. Thuig sé nach ionann buanú cultúir agus cultúr a shlánú, ach a mhalairt, chaithfeadh athrú a bheith i gceist chun freastal ar shíorghluais-eacht na staire. Ghoill sé ar Mhac Tomáis go gcaillfí an teanga agus na luachanna a bhain leis an gcultúr san, mura ndéanfaí rud éigin. Ag tagairt do phobal na Gaeltachta, deir sé go raibh:

> géarchúis acu, buanchuimhne agus dúil i ndíospóireacht, agus fairis sin, ins an iarthar, tá cultúr seanda acu anuas ona sinsir(rud atá caillte i Sasana le fada d`aimsir) a thugann tásta agus tuiscint dóibh i gcúrsaí ealaíne agus i gcúrsaí an tsaoil."[14]

Ach mheas sé ná féadfadh na luachanna sin agus na dea-thréithe sin seasamh in aghaidh sruth na nua-aoise. Deir sé:

> But this standard of values is a fragile thing. It is incapable of surviving except in it's native environment. As soon as it is trans-planted, it withers. The only economic prospect for these people lies in Springfield, Massachusetts, where they walk at one step, as it were, out of the Middle Ages into the lowest class of a modern capitalist industrial city. There, all their culture, all their social and artistic standards, become a positive handicap to them in their struggle to live, and accordingly they are shed. They have no monetary value.[15]

Mheas Mac Tomáis go raibh sé mar dhualgas ag an lucht léinn dul i ngleic leis an bhfadhb seo. D`fhéadfadh an lucht léinn cabhrú leo trí oideachas a sholáthar dóibh, rud thabharfadh deis dóibh dul chun cinn eacnamaíochta agus cultúrtha a dhéanamh, mar nuair:

> a bheidh na daoine sin i gceannas ar a gcúrsaí féin, cuirfear deireadh leis an iargúltacht amach is amach, agus léimfidh an tsibhialtacht ar aghaidh.[16]

Mheas sé gur cheart úsáid a bhaint as an nGaeilge:

> as a means of giving them a modern education so that they could adapt their culture to modern conditions.[17]

Dá mbeadh an Ghaeilge ina huirlis teagaisc, bheadh sí in ann:

> intinn na ndaoine do spriogú ar chuma ná féadfadh an Béarla a dhéanamh, agus is ionann san is a rá go raibh an Ghaolainn níos oiriúnaí dhóibh ná an Béarla mar ghléas oideachais, tráth is gurbh í an Ghaolainn an teanga ba ghaire dá chroí.[18]

Ní oideachas do pháistí amháin atá i gceist aige, ach oideachas iomlán do dhaoine fásta a thabharfadh tuiscint dóibh ar shibialtacht an fichiú haois.

Faoi thosach na dtríochaidí, bhí sé faoi chaibidil ag Mac Tomáis ollscolaíocht a sholáthar do phobal na Gaeltachta, saor in aisce. Bhí sé go mór faoi thionchar James Stuart (scoláire de chuid Choláiste na Tríonóide, Cambridge). B`é Stuart:

> do chuimhnigh ar 'Ollscoil Pheripateticiúil' do bhunú chun na maitheasaí atá le baint as oideachas Ollscoile do chur ar leathadh go fairsing ar fuaid na tíre.[19]

I gcaitheamh na mblianta luatha den naoú céad déag, bhíodh Stuart ag tabhairt léachtaí in aisce do dhaoine sna bailte móra i dTuaisceart Shasana. Deir Mac Tomáis gurbh iad na:

> ceardaithe, lámhoibritheoirí, agus a leithéidí sin is mó a thagadh chun éisteacht leis.[20]

D`éirigh go maith le Stuart agus, le himeacht aimsire, bunaíodh scéimeanna den chineál sin in áiteanna eile sa tír. Fén am a bhí Mac Tomáis ag scríobh, bhí:

> léachtaí á thabhairt don choitiantacht lasmuigh de mhúr an choláiste agus, fairis sin, chun scrúdúchán teastais do chur ar siúil tar éis na léachtaí bheith thart, agus chun scoileanna samhraidh do bhunú istigh ins an choláiste nuair a bhíonn na mic léinn ar a laethanta saoire(agus chun scoláireachtaí Ollscoile do bhronnadh ar dhaoine bochta).[21]

Deir Mac Tomáis gur bhain na mic léinn an-tairbhe as na léachtaí sin agus gur chuir na léachtaí le caighdeán maireachtála na ndaoine:

> Is iad na daoine is mó do bhain taitneamh agus tairbhe as na léachtaí sin i Sasana ná mianadóirí Northumberland; agus is fuirist aithint cad ina thaobh. Sin iad na daoine is beomhaire agus is bríomhaire ins an dúiche ar fad nach mór- géarchúis acu, agus eascúlacht aigne agus íomháineacht as meon.[22]

Chun na scéime a chur ar aghaidh, bheadh, dar leis, gá le léachtóirí ó gach réimse léinn a raghadh ar fud na Gaeltachta ag tabhairt léachtaí. Sa sliocht seo a leanas, míníonn Mac Tomáis conas ba cheart tosnú ar an scéim, agus léiríonn sé na modhanna oibre a bheadh i gceist:

> Ach is minic mé ag cuimhneamh, dá bhféadfadh múinteoir Ollscoile greim a fháil ar mhuintir na Gaeltachta agus gan bunscoil ná meánscoil do bheith ins an tslí eatarthu, agus é ag cur síos dóibh ar gach ábhar eolais is mó tábhacht lenár linn, ar na healaíona agus ar na heolaíochtaí mar an gcéanna, gurbh éachtach an fhuascailt intinne do sna daoine sin an saol nua-aimseartha so againn do bheith dá nochtadh dhóibh tríd an dteangain a labhrann lena gcroí.
> Ceathar nó cúigear do bhailiú ins na hOllscoileanna chun léachtaí do leagadh amach iad ullamh chun iad do thabhairt uatha uair éigin i rith an tsamhraidh. Ansan, fógra do chur suas i nDún Chaoin, fógra eile sa Cheathrú Rua, fógra eile fós i Rann na

Feirste. Cuimsímís ar Dhún Chaoin mar shampla. Tá sean-obair ins an pharóiste ar a dtugtar Tigh Mhóire; tá ainm Phiarais Fheirtéir rite tríd an gceantar; agus is minic na fir ag iascach mhacrael. Tugaimís léacht dóibh, mar sin ar Thigh Mhóire, cathain a tógadh é dar leis an lucht léinn, conas a tógadh é agus cad ina thaobh: do mhúsclódh sin a suim ins an réamhstair. Tugaimís léacht eile dhóibh ar Phiaras Feirtéar, ar na dánta do cheap sé agus ar chúrsaí a shaoil: do mhúsclódh san a suim ins an stair agus ins an litríocht. Tugaimís léacht eile dhóibh ar conas mar síolraítear an macrael, conas a gintear é, gach aon rud a bhaineann lena nósa is lena imeachtaí fé mhuir: do mhúsclódh san a suim ins an bheatheolas. D'fhéadfaimís cur síos dóibh ar an aimsir agus mar sin siar go dtí cúrasaí meteorloige agus réalteolais. D'fhéadfaimís cur síos dóibh ar an gcuma go ndeintear biotáille agus mar sin siar go dtí an cheimíocht.

Dá dtosnóimós ag cur síos mar sin ar chúrsaí a bhaineann go dlúth le saol na ndaoine, níl aon bhaol ná go bhféadfaimís a suim do tharrac siar go dtí préamh an chúrsa ar an gcuma san; óir is beag duine le fáil, nuair a músclaítear ceist éigin mar iad san thuas, atá comh héascúil chun taighde síos go bun uirthi agus tá Gael an iarthair; agus is maith an comhartha é sin go n-éireodh leis na léachtaí ins an Ghaeltacht ach amháin iad do chur ar bun.

Ní leor don léachtóir an léacht do thabhairt uaidh agus ansan dul abhaile. Ní bheidh aon rath ar an obair mura bhfaighidh sé aithne phearsanta ar an lucht éisteachta ins an tslí go bhféadfadh siad go léir an t-eolas do bhaint amach agus do chur fé scrúdú as chomhairle a chéile. Caithfidh sé iad do spriogú chun ceisteanna do ropadh chuige i ndeireadh gach léachta agus díospóireacht do chur ar bun, agus caithfidh sé iad do mhealladh chun Coiste Áitiúil do dhéanamh díobh féin ins an tslí go bhféadfaidh siad leanúint ar an obair nuair bheidh na léachtaí ar leataoibh.

Ansan, nuair bheadh an obair ar a bonna ins an Ghaeltacht, ní bheadh a bhac orainn druideam aniar tamall agus na léachtaí céanna do thabhairt i dTrá Lí agus i mBaile Átha Cliath agus ins na bailte beaga mórdtimpeall. Dá bhféadfaimís gluaiseacht oideachais mar sin do chur ar bun ar fuaid na hÉireann agus í trí Ghaolainn, do bheimis ag dul i bhfad ar an nGaeltachrt do shábháil agus ar an nGalltacht do Ghaelú, agus gan trácht ar an rath a bheadh ag teacht ar mhuintir na tíre i gcúrsaí oideachais.[23]

Sa bhliain 1929, tosnaíodh ar phlean chun Coláiste na hOllscoile i nGaillimh do Ghaelú. Chuir an tAire Airgeadais, Earnán de Blaghd, spéis i gCathair na Gaillimhe; agus bhí sé mar aidhm aige an chathair ar fad a Ghaelú. Thug sé lántacaíocht don choláiste maidir le hábhair a chur ar fáil trí Ghaeilge. Deir Criostóir Mac Aonghusa go raibh sé:

> faoi réir a ndíol airgid a thabhairt do lucht ceannais an choláiste leis an obair a dhéanamh[24]

I gcaitheamh na bliana cuireadh reacht ("1929 Act") ar bun a thug cead don choláiste ábhair léinn a mhúineadh trí Ghaeilge. Sa bhliain 1931, d'fhógair an coláiste ceithre phost léachtóireachta: ceann sa bhFisic Thurgnamhach, dhá cheann sna Teangacha Clasaiceacha, gus ceann san Oideachas. Ceapadh Seoirse Mac Tomáis agus Maighréad Ní Éimhthigh i Roinn na dTeangacha Clasaiceacha. Bhí Mac Tomáis freagrach as teagasc na Gréigise, trí Ghaeilge, agus fágadh an Laidin faoi Mhaighréad Ní Éimhthigh. Adhmhaíonn Seoirse Mac Tomáis gur bhain sé amach an post le cabhair agus tacaíocht ó Earnán de Blaghd:

> with his support I secured the lectureship.[25]

Cháin roinnt dá chomrádaithe Mac Tomáis nuair a chuir sé faoi i nGaillimh. Scríobh an tOllamh E.R. Dodds, go raibh dul amú air nuair a d'fhág sé Cambridge:

> to bury his talents in Galway as a lecturer at a small and remote University College.[26]

D'fhéach Mac Tomáis ar an bpost mar dheis iontach chun a n-aidhmeanna a chur i bhfeidhm.

Sa bhliain 1930, sula bhfuair sé an post, bhí sé féin agus Earnán de Blaghd ag comhoibriú le chéile d'fhonn is go bhféadfaidís an scéim thuasluaite a chur ar bun. Deir Mac Tomáis:

I had been laying plans together with Ernst Blythe, who was the Minister for Finance, for starting a scheme of University extension lectures in Connemara.[27]

Faoi dheireadh, chuaigh Mac Tomáis siar go Conamara chun na scéime a chur ar bun. Ar an gcéad dul síos bhí foirgneamh ag teastáil a bheadh oiriúnach do shéisiúin léachtóireachta, an scoil náisiúnta mar a tharla. Bhí cead ag teastáil óna sagairt pharóiste, a bhí ina mbainisteoirí scoile, ach ní bhfuair sé ach an chluas bhodhar agus léasadh binbeach a d`fhág é lena eireaball idir a dhá chois.

I had not proceeded far with my arrangements when it was made plain to me that there was not a priest throughout the length and breadth of Connemara who would dream of permitting his school to be used for anything so subversive as a University extension lecture in Irish or any other medium; nor was any support forthcoming from the National University or the Ministry of Education to induce a change of mind. So that was that.[28]

Nach ait an meon san. Tá fuílleach fianaise againn go raibh an Stát agus an Eaglais i bhfabhar cur chun cinn na Gaeilge agus an Ghaelachais. Bhí stádas oifigiúil ag an teanga i nDáil Éireann. Bhí sé riachtanach do gach mac máthar Gaeilge a fhoghluim ar scoil. Ní fhéadfadh duine post a aimsiú sa státsheirbhís gan Ghaeilge a bheith aige. Nach raibh siad "ar son na Gaeilge." De réir taithí Mhic Thomáis, ní raibh. Mheas sé go raibh an ghluaiseacht, ar leibhéil áirithe, ag iarraidh na Gaeilge a úsáid mar fhalla cosanta in aghaidh an nua-aoiseachais. Deir sé:

The authorities did not want the peasants to be educated. It might put ideas in their head. It might inspire them to demand an improvement in their lot. The authorities saw this more clearly even than I did. As the teaching of Irish spread in the schools, they formulated more and more openly the aim which under their direction the revival of the language was intended to serve. The language was to be used not as a means of introducing modern European culture, but as a means of keeping it out. For the Cosgrave administration the national movement had proceeded far enough. They had got what they wanted, so they set their faces against further change. In particular they had no intention of making any large-scale improvement in the social services. This attitude was inevitably reflected in their educational policy, and in the Irish language, untouched as it was by influences from contemporary Europe, they found a useful instrument. The Irish language and literature became a means of turning the eyes of the people away from their future to their past, and consequently the very energy and efficiency with which they promoted it, only served to weaken it as a progressive force.[29]

B`fhiú, anois, féachaint ar an meon a bhí ag lucht an choláiste i leith Shoisíalachais Mhic Thomáis. Cé ná raibh tacaíocht á thabhairt do phlean Sheoirse, bhí an coláiste sásta iarrachtaí níos mó a dhéanamh chun an coláiste a Ghaelú. Bhí roinnt mhaith sásta athlonnú sa bhFíor-Ghaeltacht ach gan oideachais a sholáthar saor in aisce do mhuintir na háite sin. Bhí cuimhneamh ag Eric Mac Fhinn ar chruinniú a tionóladh chun todhchaí an choláiste mar institiúid Ghaelach a phlé:

> Bhí Seoirse ar thaobh cruinniú mar sin a bheith ann, ar ndó, agus tháinig sé. Ach b`é Liam Ó Buachalla a mhol an cruinniú a bheith ann, agus a thug an cruinniú le chéile. Tháinig Seoirse Mac Tomáis agus Síghle ní Chinnéide agus Eoghan Mac Cionnaith agus mé fhéin agus, ar ndó Liam Ó Buachalla freisin, agus sílim Maighréad Ní Éimhthigh (nílim cinnte amach is amach faoi sin - ach sílim go dtáinig). Cuireadh ráiteas chuig Tomás Ó Deirg (mar Aire Oideachais). Is dóigh go bhfuil an ráiteas - sa gcartlann - an t-am ar fad. Moladh amháin a rinneadh, go n-iarrfadh muid bheith neamhspleadhach agus muid a imtheacht ón mbaile mór, áit a bheith againn féin sa nGaeltacht agus cumhacht againn céimeanna agus cáilídheachtaí mar sin a bhronnadh. Chuir Síghla Ní Chinnéide, amhthach, go láidir i gcoinne an mholadh imtheacht amach faoi`n tuaith agus níor moladh é.[30]

Sa bhliain 1934, gan rabhadh ceart a thabhairt d`údaráis an choláiste, d`éirigh Mac Tomáis as a phost sa choláiste agus d`fhill sé ar Shasana. Is deacair teacht ar eolas cruinn fé na cúiseanna a bhí aige (mar níl aon chur síos déanta aige féin ar an scéal), ach creidtear go raibh feachtas ar bun ina choinne sa choláiste agus in áiteanna eile i nGaillimh. Ní foláir ná go raibh a aidhmeanna réabhlóideacha ina n-ábhair imní don lucht ceannais i ngach réimse cumhachta. Deir Ristéard Ó Glaisne:

> gur ghlac cuid den chléir suas go dtí leibhéal na nEaspag féin
> páirt ghníomhach san fheachtas sin.[31]

Deineann Mac Fhinn tagairt do Ridirí Naomh Columbanus, á rá go raibh Mac Tomáis fá chaibidil acu:

> ach níl féith ar bith agam go raibh siad ar thaoibh Sheoirse ná in
> a choinne.[32]

Luann Ó Glaisne Liam Ó Briain (Ollamh le Teangacha Rómán-sacha):

> fear nach mbeadh aon ghlacadh aige ar leagan amach shóisialta
> Mhic Thomáis.[33]

Is dócha, dar le Ó Glaisne, gurbh é Ceann na Roinne, An tAthair Ó Fathaigh, a bhí "ar thús cadhnaíochta"[34] sa bhfeachtas ina choinne. Duine a sheas go láidir le lucht an tSaorstáit ab ea Ó Fathaigh agus bhí sé ina bhall tábhachtach de Chumann na nGaedhal. Sa bhliain 1979 foilsíodh an t-alt seo sa *Sunday Press* fé Sheoirse:

> A number of distinguished scholars received honary degrees at
> University College Galway.. Sadly ill-health prevented Professor
> George Thomson from accepting an Honary Doctorate. His
> health would not allow him to travel to Galway and he believes
> honary degrees should be accepted in person and not in abstentia.
> Had he been honoured in Galway, as the U.C.G. authorities
> wanted him to be, it would have been an ironic moment in
> history. For Professor Thomson,an Englishman, lectured in
> Greek through the medium of Irish at U.C.G. in the thirties,
> something which the Irish Greek scholar, Professor Michael
> Tierney, said could not be done. George Thomson met with
> considerable resistance and some hostility in Galway, not least
> from clerical members of the University staff. After a time, he

felt it wise to leave Galway University, and his reputation as a Greek scholar came later from his work in an English University.[35]

Sna blianta dár lean, bhain sé amach aitheantas idirnáisiúnta mar Mharxach díograiseach. Chaith sé tréimhse ar choiste an Pháirtí Chumannaigh sa Bhreatain. Chaith sé an chuid eile dá shaol mar Ollamh le Gréigis in Ollscoil Birmingham.I mBirmingham beidh cuimhne buan air mar dhuine a d'oibrigh gan stad ar mhaithe le coitiantacht na cathrach. Deir Tim Enright:

> He taught Marxist classes where he was noted for the clarity of his exposition of the subject, just as at Galway it was said he never had to fumble for the right word in Irish. This made him popular as a teacher in factory branches in Birmingham. On Sundays, with the men left at home, he taught the wives of factory workers about the role of women in society, long before the modern feminist movement arose.[36]

Níor leag sé a chos arís ar thalamh Éireann go 1976 nuair a tháinig an dara eagrán de *Fiche Blian ag Fás* amach. I samhradh na bliana 1979, dhein Proinsias Mac Aonghusa tagairt do Sheoirse: "fear é nach bhfuair a cheart riamh, feicthear dhom".

Sa bhliain chéiliúraidh seo is gá, dar liom, cuimhneamh ar a leithéid de dhuine, a d'oibrigh ar son na ndaoine in Éirinn, a bhí brúite faoi chois ag dream polaiteoirí agus cléireach a chruthaigh córas oideachais (go háirithe i réimse na meánscolaíochta agus na hollscolaíochta) nár chothaigh ach an duine a raibh airgead agus ór sna pócaí aige. Glacaim go raibh bunscolaíocht curtha ar fáil don daonra, ach is fiú cuimhneamh, nach ionann maitheasaí bun-scolaíochta agus riachtanais an oideachais.

330

NÓTAÍ

[1] George Thomson, 'The Irish Language Revival', *Yorkshire Celtic Studies* 3, 1946, lch. 7.

[2] Douglas Hyde, 'The Necessity for De-Anglicising Ireland', in Douglas Hyde, *Language, Lore and Lyrics (Essays and Lectures)*, Brendan Ó Conaire, eag., Dublin, 1986, lch. 155.

[3] Luaite ag Máirín Nic Eoin, *An Litríocht Réigiúnach*, Baile Átha Cliath, 1982, lch. 15.

[4] Proinsias Ó Conluain agus Donncha Ó Céileachair, *An Duinníneach*, Baile Átha Cliath, 1958, lch. 39.

[5] Synge, *The Aran Islands*, with an introduction by Tim Robinson London, 1992, lch. 39.

[6] Seán Ó Lúing, 'Robin Flower: Oileánach agus Máistir Léinn', *Journal of the Kerry Archaeological Society*, 10 1977, lch. 111.

[7] Robin Flower, *The Western Island*, Oxford, 1985, lch.1.

[8] Aodh De Blacam, *From A Gaelic Outpost*, Dublin, 1921, lch. 43.

[9] Thomson, *'The Irish Language Revival'*, lch. 43.

[10] George Thomson, *The Blasket That Was*, Maigh Nuad, 1982 lch. 55.

[11] *Leoithne Aniar*, Pádraig Tyers, eag., Baile an Fheirtéaraigh, 1982, lch. 83.

[12] Eibhlís Ní Shúilleabháin, *Letters from The Great Blasket*, Seán Ó Coileáin, eag., Cork, 1992, lch.88.

[13] Seoirse Mac Tomáis, *An Blascaod A Bhí*, Maigh Nuad, 1977, lgh. 4-5.

[14] Seoirse Mac Tomáis, 'Oideachas Ollscoile ins an Ghaeltacht', in *Seoirse Tomáis: Gach Órlach De Mo Chroí* Mac, Seán Ó Lúing, eag., Baile Átha Cliath, 1988 lgh. 15-19 .(foilsithe den chéad uair in *The Star*, 24 Bealtaine, 1930).

[15] Thomson, *'The Irish Language Revival'*, lch.8

[16] Mac Tomáis, *An Blascaod A Bhí*, lch. 26

[17] Thomson, *'The Irish Language Revival'*, lch. 8

[18] Seoirse Mac Tomáis, 'Ceann Caol na hAoise',in *Seoirse Mac Tomáis: Gach Órlach De Mo Chroí*, Seán Ó Lúing, eag., lch. 22, (foilsithe den chéad uair in *The Star*, 12 Iúil, 1930).

[19] Mac Tomáis, *'Oideachas Ollscoile ins an Ghaeltacht'*, lch. 15.

[20] *Ibid.*

[21] *Ibid.*, lgh. 15-6.

[22] *Ibid.*, lch. 16.

[23] *Ibid.*, lgh. 17-8.

[24] Criostóir Mac Aonghusa, 'Cathair na Gaillimhe sna Tríochaidí', in *Scríobh* 5, Seán Ó Mordha, eag., Baile Átha Cliath, 1981, lch. 211.

[25] Réamhnóta a chuir Seoirse Mac Tomáis leis an lámhscríbhinn de *Fiche Blian Ag Fás*

[26] Journal and Letters of Stephen MacKenna, E.R. Dodds, eag., London, 1936, lch. 130.

[27] Thomson, 'The Irish Language Revival', lch. 9.

[28] Ibid.

[29] Ibid.

[30] Luaite ag Risteárd Ó Glaisne, 'An Moinsineoir Pádraig Eric Mac Fhinn', Irisleabhar Mhá Nuad, Pádraig Ó Fiannachta, eag., Má Nuad, 1988, lgh. 134-5.

[31] Risteárd Ó Glaisne, 'Seoirse Mac Tomáis', Inniu, 16 Eanáir 1981, lch.11.

[32] Ó Glaisne, 'An Moinsineoir Pádraig Eric Mac Fhinn', lch. 129.

[33] Ó Glaisne, 'Seoirse Mac Tomáis' lch.11

[34] Ibid.

[35] The Sunday Press, 15 Iúil 1979, lch.7.

[36] George Thomson, Island Home: The Blasket Heritage, with a memoir by Tim Enright, Dingle, 1988, lch. 139.

MEDIA & COMMUNICATION STUDIES

22

BEYOND THE PALE:THE CASE
FOR REGIONAL BROADCASTING

DÍÓG O'CONNELL

Introduction

> The private citizen today has cause to feel rather like a deaf
> spectator in the back row......He knows he is somehow affected
> by what is going on. Rules and regulations continually, taxes
> annually and wars occasionally remind him that he is being swept
> along by great drifts of circumstance....As a private person he
> does not know for certain what is going on, or who is doing it, or
> where he is being carried. No newspaper reports his environment
> so that he can grasp it; no school has taught him how to imagine
> it; his ideals, often, do not fit with it; listening to speeches,
> uttering opinions and voting do not, he finds, enable him to
> govern it. He lives in a world he cannot see, does not understand
> and is unable to direct.[1]

This article is an attempt to examine the case for regional broadcasting in Ireland, prompted by the 1995 Green Paper for Broadcasting.[2] The success of local radio is testimony to the popularity
among audiences of regional broadcasting. Local radio generally
achieves higher listenership ratings and market share than RTE, in

its own catchment area. Although both figures, on average, are close to 50%, the further from Dublin a radio station is located, the higher its ratings, for example, Highland Radio in north-west Donegal achieves over 70% listenership ratings. While these figures suggest a case for regional broadcasting, the issue is not simply one of ratings. This paper will examine whether regional broadcasting is an economic, cultural or political decision. To answer this question, the current debate between public service broadcasting and the market needs to be examined as do questions surrounding public opinion and consensus. The implications of developing and new technologies will inevitably influence regional broadcasting in the future. Because we allegedly acquire 80% of our political knowledge by means of the mass media, regional broadcasting is necessary, in order to cater for diversity and debate. There is a feeling abroad, and suggested in the Green Paper, that a particular view of Ireland and Irish society is dominant in our Dublin-based mass media. An examination of current programming policy will suggest at what level a decision regarding regional broadcasting ought to be taken - economic, cultural, or political.

Changing Structures

The public service model, as inherited by Ireland, developed in Britain in the 1920's on the basis of experience garnered during World War 1. At this time British society was managing on scarce resources while attempting to give what was regarded as essential services in certain sectors, for example, the Forestry Commission and the Central Electricity Board. The British Broadcasting Company was transformed into a public service organisation in 1926, the British Broadcasting Corporation, suggesting that broadcasting was an essential service and, therefore, needed to be controlled by government. Broadcasting was regarded as a natural monopoly on two accounts, firstly because of its 'outstanding contribution to the community', in the form of public service and secondly, because of the limited access of frequencies. United States legislation followed suit in 1927, treating broadcasting as a public service although commercialism was already firmly established. Hood[3] suggests that this was a 'coincidence of concepts'. Despite the differences of control in the US and Britain, the 'politicians of consensus' sought to adopt this highly regulated form of 'public control'.

The idea of public control or trusteeship is in conflict with the notion of public accountability. It denies the role of the media as manager of news and political mediator. It is assumed that the neutrality of the broadcasting institutions is assured because it is managed by a governing body. In this form, supposedly, the public are in control. However, a governing body is government appointed and generally reflects, in its make-up, the government of the day. Ireland is no exception. Most governing bodies are made up of people from similar class, outlook and political belief. While a particular government can award people on merit, often appointment is by means of compliment or political favour, thus raising questions of control.

The public service model has been under attack for a decade or so. The 'natural monopoly' theory is no longer sustainable. Challenges to the model are coming from both the left and the right. The former argue for greater degrees of access while the latter see developing technologies opening a whole range of economic opportunities. Should economic or political decisions determine which direction to take? The cultural terms of public service broadcasting - to educate, inform and entertain - do not justify clinging on to this model in light of economic changes. Broadcasting institutions are operating in an increasingly competitive world. On the other hand, one must ask, does deregulation offer freedom, to whom does it offer it and on what terms? It is becoming more evident that neither model can embrace all aspects of broadcasting in the twenty-first century. The time has come for a new model embracing the ideals of public service alongside the practicalities of the market. This is not a new idea[4] yet an alternative somewhere between the two poles has yet to be conceived. The only response to a changing broadcasting environment, until very recently, has been as a reaction to the market, which has led to unsatisfactory and unworkable solutions.

The current broadcasting developments are characterised by pay service and corporate expansion. The televising of sport is no longer a public service but in the domain of the highest bidder, albeit catering to audience demands. It is therefore difficult to sustain the notion of regional broadcasting on any other level than that of economics if we are to respond to the market, that is, a commercial dimension to regional broadcasting policy needs to be fostered. Public service broadcasting, it would appear, is in conflict with such developments.

However the virtue of public service broadcasting is that it provides a service to all, regardless of economic or geographical location and it provides equal access to a wide range of services. It sets out to ensure that the aim of the programme producer is to satisfy a range of tastes rather than just those tastes that show largest profit. On the other hand, critics of the public service model have suggested that instead of catering for a variety of tastes, the public service broadcaster gives the public what the broadcaster thinks the audience wants, rather than what the audience actually wants. Regional broadcasting is an arguable case under the public service model. Culturally, regional broadcasting is a service that ought be provided irrespective of the market. The public service broadcasting model ensures a technical service regardless of economic or geographical location. Without the political will, the programming service cannot be guaranteed.

Garnham argues that within the public service model there lies a crisis of imagination,

> an inability to conceive of an alternative to broadcasting control-led by profit-seeking private capital other than as centralised, bureaucratic, inefficient, arrogantly insensitive to the people's needs, politically subservient to the holders of state power and so on.[5]

Recent legislative changes in Ireland cater for the independent production sector (1988 and 1990 Broadcasting Acts) and the commissioning of programmes from this sector by RTE has meant changes within the public service model as it works in Ireland. Radio Teilifis Eireann, the national broadcaster, has always been in an unusual position. While entrusted with the public service mandate, it is a commercial entity, drawing revenue simultaneously through advertising and a licence fee. Many have seen this, particularly in the independent sector, as an unfair advantage. Straddling the divide, somewhere between public service and de-regulation, will allow greater flexibility in change. The new information technologies have pre-empted a battle between the public service and the market models of cultural production and consumption. If this is not acknowledged, and policy developed in response,

> the dispersed corporation will create a dispersed culture of its own image. Within it a certain local autonomy will perhaps be tolerated, but the centres of strategic intelligence and cultural power will be elsewhere.[6]

Protection ought to be afforded to the public service broadcasting model while simultaneously allowing the service the independence to compete in the new broadcasting environment. The values attached to public service broadcasting are indeed laudable, in many respects. Public service broadcasting is duty bound to society, as governed by legislation, to educate, inform and entertain. Many political scandals, corruption and abuses in our society have come to light through the work of broadcasters. However, the face of broadcasting is changing, with the advance of digital technology and as national broadcasting boundaries become obsolete. A model which embraces the ideals of public service while facilitating competitiveness in the changing environment has yet to emerge. Before this can happen, many of the accepted notions of broadcasting need to be challenged.

Public Or Political Opinion

Looking at regional broadcasting as a cultural, political or economic phenomenon raises the issue of public opinion and its formation. In the seventeenth and eighteenth centuries the coffee-houses in Britain and the salon in France were the places for developing and fostering public opinion. The coffee-house in Europe were important for news gathering and dissemination, political debate and literary criticism.[7] Public opinion is formed in the public sphere, a 'space for a rational and universalistic politics distinct from both the economy and the state.' The mass media today is, arguably, synonymous with the public sphere. Garnham sees the function of the public sphere as two-fold - the collection and dissemination of information and the provision of a forum for debate. The public service model of broadcasting, therefore, 'presupposes and then develops in its practice a set of social relations which are distinctly political rather than economic',[8] so while in theory it allows debate, in practice it insulates from debate. Thus, its role in the formation of public opinion is on a par with the coffee-house and salon of previous centuries.

John Locke wrote that man judges the rectitude of his actions according to three laws, the divine law, the civil law and the law of opinion and reputation. He described the law of opinion:

> to be nothing else but the consent of private men, *who have not authority enough to make a law*[9]

Access to information is a pre-requisite of public opinion. In nineteenth century Europe, public opinion was similar to opinion expressed by the political representatives of the electorate, by newspapers and by prominent members of organisations of the middle class.[10] Access to public opinion was seen in the nineteenth century as a threat to public opinion itself. Many writers believed that class distinction should limit participation in public debate. Some feared the power one person, such as a journalist, had in accessing thousands of readers and influencing them. However, this assumes that the human mind is a sponge and without critical faculties. Research has found that the media does not create opinion or thought but rather 'agenda-sets', that is, it decides what topics or issues get priority, hence introducing subjects to the public mind. Many Irish commentators in recent times have pointed the finger at the 'Dublin media', as setting the agenda for the rest of the country, an opinion held by people from diverse sections within society and not just by reactionaries to the 'liberal agenda'. This agenda, it is argued, is not representative of the diversity of opinion in Ireland. Such diversity is particularly evident in broadcasts coming from beyond Dublin whether in the form of local/community radio or outside broadcasts by RTE. To open up the public sphere and widen public opinion a structured regional policy for broadcasting, it seems, is necessary.

The 1995 divorce referendum is one example where public opinion can be miscalculated. The figures in support of removing the prohibition on divorce from the constitution fluctuated significantly in the months prior to the referendum. In February 1995 there was a comfortable majority in favour of the referendum. This declined slightly to 61% by September. Two months later support was down to 45%, a figure that surprised many, notably the national media. Because the messages coming from the mass media are centralised and Dublin oriented, the decline in support for divorce was not predicted. People responded as the campaign progressed in two ways. Part of the final *No* vote was an expression of anti-government feeling while another section was swayed by the campaign strategy. The government, who in its entirety supported a *Yes* vote, did not see the need to campaign until it was too late. In this case, 'public opinion' and 'consensus' proved to be out of touch.

According to Michael Foley, Media Correspondent of The Irish Times, journalists and broadcasters, outside of Dublin, all felt that the *No* campaign was more focused and far more organised than the *Yes* campaign.[11] The *Yes* campaign appeared not to understand the huge influence local radio has and the importance of accessing its audience which comprises half of the State's radio audience. It was felt that a more concerted campaign outside Dublin could have achieved a comfortable *Yes* win, instead of the very tight margin.

Public policy, should, if democracy is to be taken seriously, favour citizen participation in debate. If that is the case debate must include as many of the existing views in a society on the relevant issues as possible. This cannot, by definition, be provided by sectionalised, ghettoised media talking only to a particular interest group or the party faithful.[12] Garnham argues that in order to defend and expand the public sphere, we need to hang on to aspects of the public service model, to defend it in light of growing threats and adopt it to the needs of a modern democratic society. A regional policy, it can be concluded, will only fit in a variation of the public service model. This variation ought to emerge according to the changing broadcasting environment.

Developing Technologies

The task of providing a full television service regardless of geographical location is both difficult and expensive, particularly for a country like Ireland and its topography. The central plain is flat while the terrain is hilly and mountainous towards the coast, where a high percentage of the population live. Providing the service is expensive because Ireland's population density is low, by European standards. This necessitates a greater number of transmitters to provide television coverage over the national territory. In the Spring of 1994 RTE ran a pilot news scheme five nights a week for six weeks in eight regions. This enabled eight regions to 'opt-out' from the national news, cover regional issues, and then 'opt-in' again. The pilot scheme was well received locally and in RTE, however it was discontinued at the end of the six week period.

One of the main obstacles to continuing the 1994 pilot regional news project is the nature of the technical foot-print in Ireland. Radio signals have no boundaries. Depending on the location of the transmitters, a region can receive another region's news. For example, parts of Co. Clare received Cork regional news because their sets were being fed from the Mullaghanish transmitter in Co. Kerry. Other parts of Clare, such as the Killaloe area, receive their signals from the Cairn Hill transmitter in the midlands. In Mayo, due to its mountainous topography, regional news came from up to five different transmitters from different parts of the country. Due to the lie of the land, in places, the whole purpose of regional news was defeated. News from Athlone is not appropriate to a Killaloe audience. Short of installing a transmitter in each county this opt-out system characteristic of broadcasting in Britain does not appear feasible at present. Unless a way around the technical foot-print problem is found the 'opt-out' system will not work. It is not cost-effective due to the low population density in many parts nor possible with regard to frequency allocation. Increasing the number of transmitters around the country would be costly and cumbersome, and not practical in the digital age.

Another recent technological development is the satellite van, based in Limerick, which allows more flexibility and diversity in regional broadcasting. By using satellite, a message can be sent live on air from anywhere in the country to Dublin and then transmitted around the country. News stories can be covered as they break from anywhere in the country, thus increasing access to and representation on the airwaves. The drawback to this process is that all correspondence and packages must go through RTE in Dublin for transmission, which in turn means a centralised editorial control, which by its nature will lead to a dilution of the concept of regional broadcasting.

Decentralise and Diversify

Recent legislation in the form of the 1988 and 1990 Broadcasting Acts has changed the face of broadcasting in Ireland. These acts set in train the procedure for the independent production sector to grow. Provisions were made for the setting up of an independent national radio broadcasting service and for a private TV channel and for the regulation of local radio.[13] Developments in communications in Ireland since the late 1980's have been determined by industrial decisions, little examination of the model for public service broadcasting has taken place, nor have cultural implications been considered.[14] Until the publication of the 1995 Green Paper discussions about broadcasting in Ireland which traditionally focused on the key concerns of defending Irish sovereignty and cultural identity had given way to questions of commercial strategy and consumer preference. It appears there has been a return to concerns of cultural and national implications. It is timely then (for cultural and political reasons) to devise a regional broadcasting policy.

According to Bell and Meehan 'an identifiable *public interest* in communication provision is being sacrificed to the profit imperatives of private investors, particularly large multi-national ones.'[15] In light of this a more structured approach to regional broadcasting as a public service in the public interest is required. It is possible for regional broadcasting to operate in an environment that incorporates the commercial factors of today's broadcasting world. At present there are RTE studios dotted around the country in Cork, Limerick, Waterford, Galway, Athlone, Drogheda, Belfast and Sligo. These centres contribute to RTE news programmes but are often in competition with each other to get their stories on air. There have been moves by RTE in recent years to develop regional programming, but primarily in the news department. As mentioned above, overcoming the technical difficulties appears to be the only tangible barrier to developing this service.

Current Programming

In the autumn of 1994 'regional programming' consisted of *Nationwide* once a week; the occasional outside broadcast (including Sunday mass); *12.2.1* with links to regional studios; *Our House,* an independent production from Cork, and programmes like *Ear to the Ground* and *Cúrsaí* covering issues of a local and/or regional nature. Under 'Broadcasting Structures' in the Green Paper, the criticism of the national broadcaster being 'primarily oriented towards its Dublin audience' is acknowledged. However the questions raised concern regional representation on the RTE Authority rather than developing a coherent regional programming policy.

Five of the thirteen *Questions and Answers* between September and December 1995 were outside-broadcasts, that is the programme was broadcast from outside the studio in Montrose. Some of the highest TAM[16] ratings for this show were achieved from outside-broadcasts. On 20 November 1995 the programme was transmitted from Mallow, Co. Cork and reached a TAM rating of 617,000 (the highest ever in the history of the programme). When the programme comes from outside Dublin there is a marked increase in requests for tickets. In fact, while there can be difficulties filling the audience seats during a Dublin broadcast, demand far exceeds supply for an outside broadcast. One can argue that Dublin audiences are used to the programme being based in Dublin, therefore they would not be as eager to participate. However, 29% of the population lives in Dublin and the population density is greater than many of the outside broadcast locations. Therefore, there is a greater pool to choose from. Bar the week prior to polling day on divorce, an outside broadcast recorded the highest number of contributions, in the form of questions and comments, from the audience during this season.

In every *Questions & Answers* recorded in Dublin between September and the beginning of December 1995, questions on two of the following three issues were always posed, the Catholic Church, Northern Ireland / peace process and divorce (in some cases these issues were the only ones covered). On October 9 and 16, questions on the following issues were asked - sex abuse scandals, the famine, the Lowry affair, Seamus Heaney, ecstasy tablets, Liz Hurley moving to Cork, professional boxing, divorce, Sean Duignan's book *One Spin on the Merry-go-round,* and the United Nations. Both these programmes were outside broadcasts. The period between September and December 1995 illustrates that outside broadcasts provide a wider range of questions from the audience and therefore add an exciting dimension to a programme that, because of its structure, can become quite flat and pre-dictable. It also allows for diverse views to be expressed on issues of public concern and indicates how people feel on these issues around the country.

Nationwide is the only programme in the current schedule with a deliberate regional approach. It started in 1992 going out once a fortnight. It then progressed to once a week and now it broadcasts three times a week, growing steadily in accordance with its audience ratings. Previous to *Nationwide* the only commitment to regional broadcasting, other than outside broadcasts, was a twelve minute regional report on Sundays. Although produced by the News Department, *Nationwide* is not a news programme; it sits more comfortably in the features/magazine programme depart-ment. It is anchored in the Cork studio with brief slots that last anywhere between forty seconds and six minutes. These can be contributed by the regional studios around the country. Material produced from the Cork studio and that coming from regional correspondents pans out on roughly a 50/50 basis.[17]

345

In some cases the regional correspondents would pitch their idea to the editor of *Nationwide*, other times they are commissioned to cover an item. However, the duty of the regional correspondents lies primarily with news, any thing else is additional. By their very nature, feature items allow for more scope averaging out at three minutes duration whereas news items tend to last one and a half minutes. From this point of view, *Nationwide* is attractive to correspondents with no outlet other than news.

In the three week period between 13 November and 1 December 1995 *Nationwide* achieved audience figures between 15% and 17%. On 22 November 549,000 viewers aged four and over watched *Nationwide*. It appeared at number eighteen in the top twenty programmes of that week as measured by TAM. This exceeded the objectives of the programme's editor thus indicating its popularity and suggesting a case for regional programmes.

Nationwide's present structure within the overall schedule is problematic. By giving over one programme to 'popular regional news', there is the tendency to ghettoise regional programming. Without a coherent policy towards regional broadcasting, such endeavours have the danger of being read as token gestures.

Structuring Regional Broadcasting

Local radio and the response to outside broadcasts of *Questions and Answers* illustrates that regional programming, when tried, has been successful. The difficulty now lies in finding a structure appropriate to our unique position as an island culture, both rural and urban, with a minority language. Zimmermann lists five types of regional television as follows:

> 1. Regional production centres that work for a national television corporation or regional news correspondents e.g. Ireland & Greece.

> 2. Regional production centres which have the exclusive rights to distribute or broadcast local news independently in their own region e.g. France, Denmark, Italy.

> 3. Regional broadcasting centres which have more than one hour of broadcasting time and which have a 'job description' extending

beyond news reporting e.g. cultural / entertainment, advertising e.g. BBC.

4. Regional production centres which broadcast a full range of programmes, but within the frame of an organisation covering a larger territory e.g. Germany - where each Lander has its own regional broadcasting system but all the Lander broadcast under the umbrella of the federalised public broadcasting system (ARD).

5. Fully independent regional broadcasting services are provided by autonomous public corporations which cover their own territory e.g. Spain and Belgium.

Regional broadcasting in Europe has emerged and developed as a result of strong political and cultural pressure. Blancon and van den Bulck argue that the discussion about broadcasting and culture in the European community has been centred too much around economic and cultural arguments. According to them, problems surrounding questions of regional broadcasting are not cultural or economic but political (Spain and Portugal). Blancon and van den Bulck describe a region as a *'distinctive culture within a nation-state separated from the rest of that state by a common language'.*[18] In terms of regional broadcasting in Ireland this definition is difficult to apply. The Belgian and Spanish cases show that regional television is a result of a long political process. Teilifís na Gaeilge is the result of an extensive political lobbying programme but serves a geographically dispersed audience united only through a common minority language.

Blancon and van den Bulck argue that:

> the claims of regional television in Europe are....legitimate only.......to the extent to which the claims of the political entities ('cultures') they reflect are legitimate'

and that legitimate political entities are determined by minority language.[19] This would argue against the claim for developing regional broadcasting in Ireland. However it would strongly support the case for Teilifís na Gaeilge and while it has been argued for on the basis of culture rather than economics, its setting up, and the decisions taken to allow same, was a political one.

Blancon and van den Bulck's definition of regional broadcasting appears to apply to larger states with minority languages such as Belgium and Spain. Ireland, on the other hand, is a small state with a minority language. As already suggested Blancon and Van den Bulck's theory of the political process and regional broadcasting does not lend itself to countries like Ireland even though their conclusions are predominantly drawn from European examples of broadcasting structures and society make-up. It is more appropriate, in this context, to draw comparisons between Ireland and New Zealand.

In New Zealand regional broadcasting emerged as a result of economic necessity. Television in New Zealand has always been regulated by the needs of advertisers and the state due to a small population spread over a hilly terrain. New Zealand moved very fast in de-regulating national television, private production now accounts for the majority of local programming. The two television channels, TV3 (Canadian owned) and TVNZ found that local programming is the key to the ratings war. In New Zealand there is no public service remit, no local content quota, or requirements for news, information and education programmes. Bell argues that both networks (TV3 & TVNZ) regard local content as the key to the ratings war as well as allowing the broadcasters fulfil their role; as 'good (and patriotic) citizens'.[20] However by local she appears to mean national and goes on to say that figures for local programming are boosted by the prevalence of 'cheap programming genres such as game shows and magazine and lifestyle programmes'. This suggests that economic determinants should not be the only guiding force in regional broadcasting policy. However, it can support the case.

Conclusion

In 1959 with the introduction of independent television in Britain, the local service of ITN in Northern Ireland, Ulster Television, found that in order to achieve viewers and increase ratings they had to expand content and include the Catholic minority population as part of the projected audience. This is in contrast to the Unionist-dominated BBC who as a public service broadcaster, was not obliged to incorporate the Catholic viewer as a significant consumer but could relegate them to the status of minority interest.[21]

There are cases where the audience can influence and have an effect on programme content and broadcasting policy. But in order to avoid a plethora of cheap programming some guidelines are necessary. It is from this position that regional broadcasting can develop in Ireland. Organised on a provincial basis, with four regional offices in Donegal, Galway, Limerick and Waterford, the existing system can be nurtured to create a more structured regional policy. Existing facilities at present fulfil requirements as news correspondents and produce material of a regional nature in other genres. As Channel 4 did in the 1980s, overheads and administration costs can be kept at a minimum by commissioning the independent sector country-wide to contribute to this sector. The time has come to create a new approach incorporating the virtues of public service broadcasting alongside the practicalities of the market.

The technological difficulties remain. Without an increase in transmitter locations, opt-outs do not guarantee a service to everyone regardless of geographical location. It seems that low population density does not justify a transmitter in each county. Given this scenario the alternative is regional broadcasting on a national level, that is, all viewers of a programme such as *Nationwide* would receive the same broadcast. On the other hand, could the regions be re-defined according to transmitter location? This is not an unknown scenario in other countries. After all, the existing regions are a construction that has no basis in reality other than geography.

Regional broadcasting requires a combined economic, cultural and political support. Developing technologies allow for progression economically. The exposure of Irish society during the 1995 divorce referendum illustrates the diversity and division that exists. While regional broadcasting is not about access to the extremes in our society at vulnerable times, a policy that allows an outlet for the representation of diverse opinion, at all times, is required. The pilot regional news of 1994 illustrated how a local point of view can give a whole new structure to what has become a platitudinous format. While there is a strong case for regional broadcasting at the level of culture and economics, as long as broadcasting is governed by legislation, there will always be a need for political will as well.

NOTES

[1] Walter Lippmann, *The Public Phantom,* London, 1925.

[2] Green Paper on Broadcasting: *Active or Passive? Broadcasting in the Future Tense.* Dept. of Arts, Culture and the Gaeltacht, 1995.

[3] Stuart Hood, *The Mass Media,* London, 1972.

[4] See N. Garnham, *Capitalism and Communication, London, 1990.*

[5] *Ibid.*

[6] *Ibid.*

[7] H. Speier, in H.D. Lasswell D. Lerner & H. Speier, *Propaganda & Communication in World History, vol. 2,* Hawaii, 1980.

[8] Garnham, *op.cit.*

[9] See Speier, *op.cit.*

[10] *Ibid.*

[11] *Irish Times, 27 November 1995.*

[12] Garnham, *op. cit.*

[13] Wolfgang Treutzschler, 'Broadcasting Law and Broadcasting Policy in Ireland' in *Irish Communications Review,* vol. 1, 1991.

[14] See D. Bell & N. Meehan 'Cable, Satellite and the emergence of Private TV in Ireland: from Public Service to Managed Monopoly' in *Media, Culture & Society,* vol. 2, 1989.

[15] *Ibid.*

[16] Audience measurement device.

[17] Conversation with Michael Ryan, editor of *Nationwide.*

[18] V. Blanco, & J, van den Bulck, 'Regions versus States and Cultures in the EC Media Policy Debate: Regional Broadcasting in Belgium and Spain' in *Media, Culture & Society,* vol. 17, no. 2, April 1995.

[19] *Ibid.*

[20] A. Bell, 'An Endangered Species: Local Programming in the New Zealand Television Market' in *Media, Culture & Society,* vol. 17, no. 2, April 1995.

[21] P. Schlesinger, *Putting 'Reality' Together - BBC News,* London, 1987.

23

FEATURE WRITING IN WOMEN'S MAGAZINES: A LIMITED IDEOLOGICAL CHALLENGE

SUSAN LIDDY

Introduction

Since the emergence of the international women's movement in the early 1970s women's magazines have increasingly popularised feminist ideas. The fragmented format of the genre ensures that a debate on feminist issues can surface in features side by side such old reliables as beauty tips. recipes or advice on how to attract and keep a man. In 1991 over one third of feature writing in *Woman's Way* and three quarters in *U* reflected items from the Irish feminist agenda. Issues like the wage gap, the absence of state funded child care, the need for equal status legislation. rape and domestic violence were all debated on the feature pages of these magazines, though considerable differences did emerge between the two publications.

Under discussion here is the extent to which such features remain within the parameters of patriarchal ideology, even when influenced by feminism, and how this can vary according to the readership of each magazine. However, before undertaking such an analysis, it is necessary, in the first instance, to legitimate the study of a genre frequently dismissed as unworthy of serious attention, to clarify the concepts of ideology, patriarchy and feminism, and to offer an outline of the methodological approach adopted.

The Nature of The Genre

Throughout the history of the women's press, the social condition and social role of women has been associated with the content of women's magazines. They are reliable indicators of prevailing attitudes to women and a reflection of the lives of many of the women who read them. White's historical work highlights how magazines are:

> imbued with the spirit of the age in which they appear and each period has a character of its own. [1]

As a genre, they are unique to the female sex, they provide a long-standing commentary on women's lives and experiences in a male dominated society and are read regularly by a great number of women. They are, what Ferguson has termed, 'a gender genre'. [2] They have been likened to a club; a club with only one entry requirement, membership of the female sex. Specialist and generalist, women's magazines cater simultaneously for a single sex and deal with a wide spectrum of traditionally perceived "feminine concerns", such as beauty, fashion, cookery and romance.

This sets them firmly apart from other media which seek a male and female audience. There is not male equivalent of the women's magazine. A variety of special interest magazines are available which are aimed primarily at men and encompass subjects such as D.I.Y. or fishing. Unlike women's magazines, however, they make no attempt to cater for masculinity as a whole, the implication being that the male sex already know everything there is to know about masculinity. Winship has identified what is termed the "consciously classless" element in this genre. [3] In women's magazines, all women are united in their capacity to be mothers, housewives or sex objects, and, in the assumptions that women share the same goals, interests, outlook and activities. Effectively, "women are women the world over."

Women's magazines are comprised of separate elements; designed to be 'dipped into'. Each section stands alone and can be read as an individual entity. The magazine is an amalgamation of such entities. Because of this, contradiction is not anathema to the genre. Recipes for cream cakes can sit happily beside articles on weight loss or exercise routines. Advice on how to keep marriages romantic and exciting can co-exist with experiences of real-life marriages, as recounted in the agony columns. Ballaster et al. recognise that:

> Anything can co-exist with anything on the pages of the magazine, (and does). The identification of 'contradiction', therefore, fails to embarrass either editors, writers or readers.[4]

Because of the fragmented format, a debate on feminist issues can surface side by side the beauty tips and the recipes which remain, of course, the main-stay of the magazine.

It was decided that features would be the exclusive focus of this piece of work because unlike the advice columns, or the beauty pages, they deal with a wide variety of issues beyond the domestic. They can include, for instance, interviews with celebrities like chat show host Jonathan Ross, 'I love the sound of my own voice'[5] or general articles like 'Data-Chase what do the computers know about you and how can you find out?'.[6] However, more importantly, it was feature writing that first reflected the genre's growing concern with 'social issues' and which first tackled so called hard subjects like 'living together' and equal pay. Thus, a debate on current feminist concerns seemed more likely to emerge in this part of the magazine. For a variety of reasons, then, it is argued that the study of women's magazines is an appropriate focus

Ideology, Patriarchy and Feminism

Ideology defines and explains the social world and our place within it, moreover, our everyday feelings, thoughts and actions are shaped by it. Ideologies construct aspects of the social world as 'natural' and 'universal' though they are, essentially social constructions. What it means to be a man or a woman, for instance, often seems rooted in 'common sense'. This is particularly true of the dominant ideology in any culture. A dominant ideology is produced and reproduced by those in positions of power and its ideas are thus more easily able to be presented as 'natural'. The dominant beliefs of a society can be found in what Lowe and Hubbard have termed "the ordinary truths and realities" of that society and are widely accepted.[7]

The dominant ideology in a patriarchy. which Rich has described as a familial. social. ideological and political system in which men, and not women, wield power. incorporates notions about a woman's place and the conduct and demeanour deemed appropriate to the female sex.[8] Patriarchal ideology refers to "the particular set of linked ideas that seem to support female subordination and make it seem natural".[9] The assumption that patriarchal institutions and practices are 'natural' or of purely individual concern can be viewed as 'an ideological curtain' that conceals the reality of women's systematic oppression.[10]

Within a society at any given time, there may be a variety of ideologies competing for hegemony or widespread acceptance. The concept of hegemony was the central idea in Gramsci's social theory and moral philosophy. For him, hegemonic leadership involved:

> producing a world view, a philosophy and moral outlook, which other subordinate and allied classes and groups in a society accepted.[11]

In a patriarchal society, for example, women are often encouraged to develop characteristics of restraint and complacency. to think of themselves primarily as wives and mothers, to accept that housework and child care are innately 'women's work' and to express a sexuality which affirms the centrality of the male. Patriarchal hegemony ensures that many women, and men, internalise these beliefs and expectations and, despite their restrictive nature, do not view them as a sign of subordination.

Feminism. as defined by Dahlerup and endorsed in this piece of work is:

an ideology whose basic goal is to remove the discrimination and degradation of women and to break down the male dominance of society. It is the ideology behind the women's movement which comprises 'the conscious, collective activity of women fighting for feminist goals'.[12]

Feminism is not a unitary ideology, however, and different strands of feminist thought exist proffering different explanations both for the existence of a male dominated society and the measures that should be taken to combat it. An examination of the then Council for the Status of Women's (now renamed The National Women's Council of Ireland which is an umbrella organisation for women's groups, both feminist and non feminist,) 1990 Annual Report, and a review of the development of feminism in this country, identified welfare liberal and radical feminist agendas which were used as a framework for the analysis of features.

Liberal feminism promotes equal rights for women and calls for the incorporation of women into the public sphere, side by side, and on an equal footing with men. Its focus is on legislative reform, the removal of discriminatory laws and procedures which restrict women's entry into, and success within, the public sphere. Among the issues prioritised are equal status legislation, inadequate child care provision and gender equality in education and unfair social expectations which are all deemed to be limitations on women's opportunities.

Liberal feminists divide into two categories, classical and welfare liberals. Classical liberal feminists believe that once discriminatory laws and policies are removed, women have exactly the same opportunities as men. If they fail to avail of these, there is little else to be done. Welfare liberal feminists, on the other hand, as characterised by liberal feminism in Ireland, argue that it is the responsibility of government to actively break down existing bias by direct intervention.

Radical feminists reject the concept of inequality and argue that law reform is not sufficient to eradicate the male domination of society. Women are an oppressed group and this oppression is rooted in the way in which a patriarchal society has constructed female sexuality. Issues such as pornography. rape and sexual

355

harassment are highlighted as important because these are manifestations of male control over female sexuality. Women are exhorted to take control of their own sexuality. Revolution, rather than reform, is promoted and nothing less than the creation of a new society demanded.

Methodology

Two magazines, *Woman's Way* and *U* were selected for analysis for a number of reasons. These are the two most popular Irish produced women's magazines in terms of circulation and reader-ship (see Table 1). The former refers to the number who actually purchase the magazine and the latter to the many more who read it *i.e.* the secondary readership. *Woman's Way* is an example of a weekly publication and *U* an example of a monthly; each of the magazines is targeted at a different audience and age group. This facilitated a comparative analysis of the impact of feminism on the coverage and treatment of the welfare liberal and radical feminist agendas within features in these magazines.

Table 1

MAGAZINE CIRCULATION AND READERSHIP, 1990[13]

MAGAZINE	CIRCULATION	READERSHIP
Woman's Way	72.350	407,000
U	23.732	160,000

A 'typical' *Woman's Way* reader is seen to be between 16 and 70 years old with. the majority readership In the 20-40 age bracket. Most readers are married with children and belong to a one income family. Effectively. the reader of *Woman's Way* is the Irish home-maker. In contrast. the *U* reader is between 18 and 26 years old, Dublin based and economically independent. She is single, or if involved in a relationship, is co-habiting with a partner.

The election of Mary Robinson as President of Ireland in 1990 influenced the selection of one specific year viz. 1991. Her election was accompanied by intense media interest in her status as a woman and a feminist. It was decided to focus on magazine features in the following year in order to explore whether issues from the feminist agenda in Ireland had found their way into features in women's magazines in this more positive climate for Irish feminism.

Corcoran's observations on research into television acknowledge a shift from empiricism to the underlying media messages. Of interest here is:

> how mediated messages are structured...how they function in the circulation and securing of hegemonic social definitions and how communication can be analysed as a process through which a particular world-view can be represented and maintained. [14]

Within the magazines. attention was directed specifically to the category of *Features*. It was decided that only here could a debate on feminist issues surface. Following a process of 'qualitative mining'[15] which involved a close textual examination of features in these magazines, key themes were identified, viz. femininity, the division of domestic labour and sexuality (including restrictive contraception and abortion facilities and the sexual double standard). These were subsequently analyzed in detail to assess the extent to which they posed an ideological challenge.

This piece of work relates to feature content and makes no claims as to how individual readers might negotiate with the text. Readers, like all audiences, are socially positioned prior to inter-acting with any text and this can influence interpretation.[16] Nonetheless, the focus on content stems from a long tradition in examining media messages. A content-based approach provides an opportunity to identify and explore the issues which are central to feminism in Ireland and the extent to which these issues have been absorbed by a popular genre like the woman's magazine. An exploration of the extent to which features pose an ideological challenge to patriarchy, by debating issues from the feminist agenda, would seem to be an interesting and relevant undertaking.

Femininity

In this context, femininity refers to socially constructed aspects of temperament involving, for instance, non-confrontational interaction and docility. It is. effectively. a 'grand collection of compromises' that each woman is expected to make if she is to be a successful example of her sex.[17] There is agreement among welfare liberal feminists and many radical feminists that femininity, as opposed to femaleness, is a patriarchal construct and serves to restrict women. There is nothing random about the social constr- uction of femininity, it is argued. In a patriarchal society, girls are socialised to acquire a 'feminine' temperament; the characteristics of which are designed to be both pleasing and non-threatening to men.

Welfare liberals contend that feminine and masculine identities are the near exclusive product of socialisation, and males and females are moulded according to sexual stereotypes which reflect the values and needs of the dominant group. Some radical feminists agree that the socialisation process creates femininity. Thus. they argue, many characteristics that patriarchy actively encourages in women are deemed inappropriate and undesirable in the male. Even those radical feminists who valorise biological femaleness recognise that many aspects of femininity effectively contribute to female subordination. Femininity, then. is viewed as one aspect of a 'double-bind' process which is a daily reality for women. Women are damned if they do not become 'feminine' but they are no less damned if they follow the precepts of femininity, for this disqualifies them from participation in high status, male activities.[18]

An examination of *Woman's Way*, during 1991, indicates that certain traits traditionally perceived as feminine, viz. patience and confrontation avoidance, are still posited as an appropriate female response. An attempt is made to dissipate anger by focusing on minor successes rather than major grievances. Thus, a feature on sexism in primary schools exaggerates the significance of limited achievements. 'Breaking barriers: does school really promote equality?' comments:

> at the All-Ireland football final this year primary school girls played football in Croke Park in the interval. Five years ago such an idea would have been unthinkable. [19]

Similarly, while drawing attention to the continuing discrimination facing women in golf clubs around the country, 'Golf and the

Gender Game', displays little anger and urges passivity and restraint. The secretary of the Irish Ladies Golf Union contends that "aggression isn't going to get us anywhere". A spokesman for the Golfing Union of Ireland cautions against a 'militant' attitude and observes:

> the ladies are very good at getting good conditions for themselves by using subtle, non-confrontational methods... they set their cause right back by being so aggressive.[20]

In the same way, 'Why sport is a different ball game for women' condemns the lack of media coverage for women's sports but endorses patience as the preferred strategy:

> What I would hope Is that the coverage of women's sports will grow as a natural progression. rather than exercise in positive discrimination.[21]

'They're in the Army Now' celebrates what is represented as huge strides in equality in the Irish Army by noting that there are one hundred women in an army of 13,000. It is an 'extraordinary imbalance', the feature, acknowledges. However, the female soldier who is interviewed exhibits typical 'feminine' qualities of resignation and docility.

> When we first came. there weren't many appointments open to us. Now there are. and I suppose in another ten years everything will be open to us.[22]

In this way, even in features where discrimination is acknowledged and condemned. the countenance of this 'feminine' behaviour serves to diffuse anger and curtail action. Ideological hegemony ensures that fundamental assumptions relating to women, as defused by a patriarchal society, are internalised as norms by a majority of women and men. Features are written within and reflect this context. In effect. many women collude with patriarchal ideology. In 'Golf and the Gender Game', the 'lady captain' of one golf club illustrates such a collusion. "Many ladies," she comments, "are motivated by a love of sport and when it comes to the question of full membership of golf clubs they demur. Maintaining the condition of the golf course must be the top priority: if everyone was able to go out and play at weekends. it would soon deteriorate." [23] There is no question that male members might forego play in order to maintain the condition of the course. Effectively. this stance accords a very decisive second class status to women by a woman. This illustrates the way women can internalise the values and norms established by the patriarchy and very often do not, or will not, perceive them as strategies devised to exclude them from the public sphere or to limit their involvement in that sphere.

The vision of femininity reflected in *U* is less submissive and accommodating. than that in *Woman's Way*. Restraint, calmness and patience are not called upon; instead, women are encouraged to reconsider feminine virtues of 'niceness' and submissiveness. 'Sexual Violence' urges women to fight this 'niceness', and a socialisation that gives them 'very little permission to be angry', to stand up and be heard: 'Once we start to talk to each other more openly, we might be surprised by what comes out.'[24] Similarly, 'The Sounds of Silence' contests feminine conditioning and the approved ways of dealing with men in a pleasant, supportive, unassertive way.

> In our efforts to be affiliative, co-operative and self-sacrificing we have often unwittingly been shoring up institutions that are basically destructive, exploitative and manipulative.[25]

'I'm Just a Girl Who Can't Say No' highlights how hard it is for women to break free from the feminine stereotype. We are brought up to be polite, helpful and to follow the rules. The feature asks: "How on earth can she assert her rights and choices without being seen as an inflexible hard bitch?" [26]

'Femininity', as constructed in patriarchy, encourages submissiveness and functions to maintain the status quo. As the examples have illustrated, *Woman's Way* endorses many traditional elements of femininity and does not perceive this as being another aspect of oppression. *U*, on the other hand, challenges them as ploys designed to contain women and, effectively, calls for the rejection of many of the 'feminine' traits fostered in women by a patriarchal society. This is perhaps explained by the fact that the majority of *Woman's Way* readers are older are married with children and are financially dependent on men. *U* readers are financially independent and primarily single which may account for the readiness of that magazine to confront many patriarchal procedures for keep women in line. Magazines, of course, exist first and foremost as commodities, i.e. as a window for the advertising industry, so the maintenance of sales is obviously of primary importance. Essentially readers must be kept happy. Therefore, to some extent. features must reflect the reader's pre-occupations, concerns and lifestyles.

Division Of Domestic Labour

Patriarchal ideology asserts that the division of labour in the home is natural and universal rather than historical and social. It promulgates the notion that taking primary responsibility for housework and child care is 'natural' for women. In Ireland today, it is a notion that still takes priority, even if women also engage in paid labour outside the home. Neither *Woman's Way* nor *U* contest the status quo in this area, though there is a suggestion that it is not the ideal situation for women.

Both welfare liberal and radical feminism stress the importance of escaping economic dependency through employment, from this women gain "a measure of. that economic. social and psychological independence which is the *sine qua non* of freedom".[27] Women have always worked, so the issue is economic reward not labour. Yet. housework, which is overwhelmingly carried out by women in Western society, is unpaid labour.[28] Moreover. in the work-force, women still earn substantially less than men.[29] Within features in *Woman's Way*, the success of welfare liberal feminism manifests itself in an acknowledgment of the need and right of all women to paid employment. However. the primacy of marriage and motherhood. with its assumption of economic dependence, results, in the main, in the promotion of low pay, low status work viz. small home based businesses. part-time jobs or job sharing, as an intermediate measure.

Woman's Way's treatment of paid employment for women mirrors the trends emerging in studies carried out in Britain[30] and in the United States.[31] In portraying paid employment as secondary to the career of wife and mother. This has considerable impact on the type of employment strategies discussed and the extent to which women are portrayed as free to pursue a full time career outside the home. Full time work outside the home is acceptable only insofar as women are prepared to work the 'double day' as a 'natural' consequence. It is acknowledged that the employed woman is responsible for more than her fair share of menial household tasks but the question of why women should shoulder this responsibility remains unasked. It is observed in 'Job-sharing - the best of both worlds' that:

> I think the mother is still responsible for picking up all the pieces and organising all the washing, getting it out on the line and then in before it rains and so on, no matter how supportive the partner is.[32]

In the same feature, it is stressed that job sharing may damage one's profile in the workplace: you may not be taken as seriously as you might if you were in the position full time. Nonetheless, it is presented as an ideal strategy for women who are reluctant to ask for time off to attend school, sports days and so on, and who are concerned about not being 'the perfect mother'. There is no assumption that the father who misses school events might experience the same concern. Inadequate child care is cited as a prohibitive factor for many career-minded women in *Woman's Way*. What is not discussed is that the lack of child care facilities has not hindered career-minded men. Even the term 'career man' is an unfamiliar one: women are, unquestionably, assumed to be the natural carers.

In contrast to *Woman's Way*, *U*'s treatment of paid work does not revolve around traditional marital responsibilities and the emphasis is firmly on the establishment of a full-time career. Nonetheless. there is also recognition in both *Woman's Way* and *U* that exclusion from the workforce has been replaced by subordination of women in terms of horizontal and vertical segregation. Horizontal segregation refers to the tendency for women's employment to be segregated into a narrow range of occupations and sectors of industry. Vertical segregation relates to the fact that:

> in every sector of the economy, women are relegated to the lowest levels of the job hierarchy and grossly under-represented in top jobs.[33]

Women are encouraged to devise individual strategies such as buying the services of other women, depending on a co-operative relative or managing their own time in such a way as to accommodate the demands made of them in the public and private sphere. Ideally, relationships should be egalitarian, it is implied, but the reality is, they are not. Instead of developing the argument to investigate why this is so and how the situation could be altered, strategies are sought to circumvent a confrontational look at the unequal balance of responsibility in the home.

The 'Sponge Woman' and 'Deputy Woman' models surface in features in *Woman's Way* illustrating one way of diffusing potential conflict.[34] The 'Sponge Woman' absorbs new responsibilities again and again in order to retain the option of remaining in the labour force. Sponge women take on paid work while continuing to carry out all the domestic tasks in the home, by being determined, efficient and well organised. The 'Deputy Woman' delegates responsibility to others in order to facilitate participation in the labour force. *Woman's Way* has not identified the centrality of motherhood as being a factor in the consignment of women to a different category of (low paid) work or in the off-putting prospect of the 'double day'. On the contrary, to be permitted to earn a wage while engaging in obligatory home duties is presented as something of a 'perk'.

The majority of Woman's Way readers are married with a family and the majority of part-time workers in Ireland (seventy per cent) are married women.[35] Moreover, in a Woman's Way survey carried out in conjunction with the then Council for the Status of Women, it emerged that the availability of part-time work and more flexible working arrangements were important issues for women themselves. In its promotion of paid employment, then, *Woman's Way* must bear the reality of readers lives in mind. *U* recognises the inequality inherent in the division of domestic labour both in the home and the workplace. Unlike *Woman's Way*, it makes no attempt to valorise part-time work, for example, simply because this is the type of work that suits housewives who want a little financial independence. Instead, it focuses on career opportunities like airline pilot, costume designer, camera woman etc. Neither does *U* engage in a discussion on how to confront the inequalities in the private arena. This is likely to be related to its readership. Primarily young, single, working women can afford to look at the harsh realities of women's status in the labour market. Moreover, they can acknowledge structural inhibitors like the unequal division of labour without concerning themselves with a search for a strategy to combat the problem.

Female Sexuality

Radical feminists argue that sexuality is not a private matter to be explained in terms of sexual preference or psychological processes fixed in infancy "but rather that it is socially organised and critically structured by gender inequality".[36] Patriarchy, they insist, has fashioned female sexuality to be passive, submissive and male-centred as a means of retaining control over the activities of a subordinate group. A patriarchal society controls women's sexuality not only by means of 'compulsory' heterosexuality but by the institution of marriage, pornography, rape and other forms of violence and coercion. While neither magazine rejects outright the patriarchal model of female sexuality, considerable differences in awareness do emerge between *Woman's Way* and *U*.

Features in *Woman's Way* and *U* endorse patriarchal ideology pertaining to a number of issues around the area of sexuality. Heterosexuality is presented as 'natural' and men are inevitably depicted as the prime focus of female desire and attention. In the main, both magazines are concerned with heterosexual relations, which are represented as the normal expression of female sexuality.

364

While *U* does acknowledge lesbianism and, moreover, does attempt to break down ignorance and misconceptions relating to lesbians, nonetheless, it stops short of embracing it as either a political statement or a valid sexual option for all women. Lesbianism is viewed with tolerance and understanding but from a safe distance. It is a practice engaged in by other women, not 'us', the readers of *U*.

The institution of marriage is never brought into question by *Woman's Way*. In 1991, the year of this study, 'Single Mums in the 90's' suggests that Irish society has become more accepting of the single woman who has a child outside marriage.[37] However, there is no suggestion that the institution of marriage, itself may be flawed. While marriage is not rejected outright by *U* neither is it presented as wholly unproblematic. 'Love. Marriage and Problems' highlights the difficulties which can arise in marriage viz. alcohol abuse and domestic violence. De Valera's 'fairy-tale vision' of marriage is rebuked. *U* introduces the possibility of choice in relation to marriage and suggests that a woman could opt to have a child outside marriage, if she so wished.[38]

This is not a necessarily surprising stance, however, if one considers the marital status of the reader. The typical *Women's Way* reader is married with a family and is arguably, less likely to condemn an institution which is an integral part of her life and experience. In contrast, the *U* reader is more likely to be cohabiting than married, if indeed, she is involved in a heterosexual relationship at all. This allows for a more dispassionate appraisal of the institution of marriage. *U* recognises that domestic and sexual violence are the means by which a patriarchal society maintains the status quo both at an individual and collective level. Features explore the way in which male power is exercised and reinforced by domestic violence, sexual harassment pornography and rape. In 'The Politics of Seduction', it is declared that: "Through sexuality, the fundamental aggression, that of men over women, is maintained". [39]

U points out that women keep silent about domestic violence to protect their husband's job or to save face with the neighbours. They also keep silent about sexual abuse because of uncertainty about society's response. However, despite confronting many of the ways that patriarchy oppresses women, there is never a suggestion that women might possibly be better off without men in their lives.

Patriarchal ideology in relation to female sexuality is not questioned to any great extent in *Women's Way*. However much of it is comprehensively rejected by *U*. Women in *U* are encouraged to empower themselves, to express and enjoy their sexuality and to shake off many patriarchal shackles. Despite very great differences in *U*'s treatment of female sexuality. the dominant ideology underlying features in both magazines is nonetheless predominately patriarchal. *Women's Way* seems not yet comfortable with female sexuality outside the confines of marriage. It is discussed only in a problematic context viz. the plight of single motherhood and the dangers of contracting Aids from one night stands. *U*'s rally cry for assertiveness and sexual confidence is underpinned by the assumption that heterosexuality. and male approval is central and desirable in all women's lives.

Radical feminists contend that in a patriarchal society a number of mechanisms serve to maintain male control over women's sexuality. These include restrictive contraception, abortion. and the sexual double standard. A patriarchal society, it is argued, withholds contraceptive information and either limits abortion or seeks to outlaw it completely. Effectively, radical feminists believe that men restrict female sexual expression and restrict the availability of contraception and abortion in order to maintain power. Welfare liberal feminists contend that because it is women who become pregnant and who are expected to care for the young, restrictive contraception and abortion facilities are discriminatory. Moreover, as sex is a private matter between consenting individuals, such restrictions are a violation of the individuals right to privacy.

The 'sexual double standard' refers to the sexual morality which dictates that men can enjoy sexual freedom and 'good' women cannot. It condemns women who wish to engage in sexual activity with a variety of partners while admiring men who do likewise. Patriarchal ideology stresses the greater sexual urge of the male thereby sanctioning the double standard. Unlike the male, the female is groomed to become a sexual object not a sexual subject. Women are considered to be sexual objects for use and appreciation by other sexual beings, men. They have been socialised to view an active sexuality as 'unfeminine' and must resort to exercising their 'feminine wiles' and hope for success. The calibre of the man they eventually 'catch' will often determine their own status.[40]

Both magazines identify the sexual double standard. However, while *Women's Way* does not endorse this, neither does it reject it. In 'the one night stand goes on', it is acknowledged that men can "sow the wild oats but women who express their sexuality outside the confines of marriage are labelled tarts" Nonetheless, sexual restraint is prescribed for its readers; "our bodies should not be passed around like a tray of hors d'oeuvres."[41] *U*, on the other hand, comprehensively rejects the cult of virginity and defines female sexuality as heterosexual and active. Moreover, women are called upon to rebel against the sexual double standard. to defy the passive role society has forced upon them. In 'The Politics of Seduction' it is suggested that: "More women are making the first move and this is actually happening more often."[42]

Despite the inclusion of, items relating to the welfare liberal and radical agenda, neither magazine makes any connection between the patriarchal control exerted on women in relation to sexuality viz. sexual harassment and rape, for example, and women's lack of autonomy as regards their reproduction. Abortion on demand, as a women's right to control her own fertility, is not advocated. The question of power, about who precisely controls reproduction in our society, is not confronted. *Women's Way* tries to understand why so many abortions occur each year but does not call for any change in the legal position of abortion. *U*, however, does advocate access to information and implies that individual women must then decide what choice they wish to make. 'Home Truths' argues that:

> If you're having sex. you must take responsibility, you must understand what's happening.[43]

Summary

In 1991, features in *Women's Way* and *U* have debated issues on the welfare liberal and radical feminist agenda. Of those features which did reflect feminist concerns, coverage was primarily welfare liberal in the case of *Women's Way* and radical, in the case of *U*. Coverage occurs predominantly within the parameters of patriarchal ideology, though this did vary between the two magazines. Features continue to reflect a number of patriarchal notions relating to women and women's place in the family and the wider society. This may be indicative of the fact that women's magazines just cannot afford to fully recognize and acknowledge the extent to which a patriarchal society oppresses women; the woman's magazine is itself a product of such a society. Moreover, to identify the existence of patriarchy is synonymous with the possibility of identifying a world in which the plight of many readers is bleak and the prospect of change remote.

Because magazines are part of an economic as well as an ideological system, features must, to some extent, be mindful of the lives and experiences of the majority of their readers. In the case of *Woman's Way* most readers are married and financially dependent on men, though part-time work offers a measure of financial independence. The implied reader may not wield sufficient personal power to challenge the system and this is implicitly recognised in features in 1991. Arguably. this has a bearing on the issues which arise for discussion. Discrimination occurs 'out there' in faceless institutions like golf clubs or the education system or politics but not in the home or in personal relationships. What emerges is an understanding that if women's lives are ever to change, the key lies in altering many of society's structures and practices which will open up greater choices for future generations.

In contrast, the majority of *U* readers are younger, financially independent and primarily single which may account for the magazine's greater readiness to confront unpleasant truths about the lives and experiences of women in contemporary society. The *U* reader is embarking on a different life with different expectations and aspirations than the implied *Woman's Way* reader. These women are assumed to be outspoken, less fearful of upsetting the status quo and almost jubilant about the expression of their own sexuality. While *Woman's Way* leaves many patriarchal power structures unchallenged, coverage in *U* illustrates how a younger generation of women have rejected many aspects of patriarchal ideology. Features assume that readers are ready to engage in another level of debate by recognizing the existence of a struggle of power between men and women.

It would appear that many feminist issues have gained popular currency. Feminism is engaged in challenging patriarchal hegemony and the inclusion of features promoting items from the welfare liberal and radical feminist agenda is testament to some measure of its success. Both magazines present women as having a right to work outside the home, for instance, a right to representation in public life and so on. Ultimately, however, many of the features reproduce patriarchal ideology and diffuse anger and resentment at women's second class status. The ideological challenge of these features is, therefore, ultimately a rather limited one.

NOTES

[1] Cynthia White, *Womens's Magazines 1963-1968,* London, 1970, p. 278.

[2] Marjorie Ferguson, *Forever Feminine,* London, 1983, p. 183.

[3] Janice Winship, *Inside Women's Magazines* London, 1987, p. 54.

[4] Ros Ballaster, M. Beethan, E.Frazer and S.Hebron, *Women's Worlds: Ideology, Femininity and the Woman's Magazine,* London, 1991 p. 7.

[5] *Woman's Way,* 20 December, 1991.

[6] *U,* October, 1991.

[7] Marian Lowe and Ruth Hubbard, *Women's Nature: Rationalisations of Inequality* New York, 1986, p. 1.

[8] Adrienne Rich, *Of Woman Born: Motherhood as Experience and Institution,* London, 1986, p. 57.

[9] Helen Crowley, and Susan Himmelweit (eds.), *Knowing Women: Feminism and Knowledge,* Cambridge, 1992, p. 18.

[10] Alison M Jagger, *Feminist Politics and Human Nature,* Sussex, 1983 p. 101.

[11] Robert Bocock, *Hegemony,* London, 1986, p. 46.

[12] Drude Dahlerup, (ed.), *The New Women's Movement* London, 1986, p. 6.

[13] Audit Bureau of Circulation (JNRR). 1990

[14] Farrel Corcoran, "Television as Ideological Apparatus: the Power and the Pleasure" in *Critical Studies in Mass Communications,* no 1, 1984, pp 131-45.

[15] G. McCracken, *The Long Interview*, London, 1988, p. 11.

[16] David Morley, *Television, Audiences and Cultural Studies*, London, 1991; Liesbet Van Zoonen, "Feminist Perspectives on the Media" in James Curran, and Michael Gurevitch, *Mass Media and Society*, London, 1991.

[17] Susan Brownmiller, *Femininity*, New York, 1984, p. 16.

[18] Dale Spender, *For the Record. the Making and Meaning of Feminist Knowledge*, London, 1988, p. 38.

[19] *Woman's Way*, 11 October, 1991, p. 15.

[20] *Woman's Way*, 29 March, 1991, p. 21.

[21] *Woman's Way*, 4 October, 1991, p. 23.

[22] *Woman's Way*, 1 November, 1991, p. 20.

[23] *Woman's Way*, 29 March, 1991, p. 21.

[24] *U*, May. 1991, p. 70.

[25] *U*, May, 1991, p. 78.

[26] *U*, March, 1991, p.54.

[27] Kate Millett, *Sexual Politics*, London, 1970, p 88.

[28] Pamela Abbott and Clair Wallace, *An Introduction to Sociology: Feminist Perspectives*, London, 1990, pp 121-45.

[29] Harriet Bradley, *Men's Work, Women's Work: A Sociological History of the Sexual Division of Labour*, Cambridge, 1989; John Blackwell, *Women in the Labour Force Dublin*, 1990.

[30] Winship, *op. cit.*; Ballaster et al., *op. cit.*

[31] G. Tuchman, (ed.), *Hearth and Home: Images of Women in the Mass Media*, New York, 1978; Nona Glazer, "Overworking the Working Woman: the Double Day in a Mass Magazine", *Women's Studies International Quarterly*, 1980, pp 74-83.

[32] *Woman's Way*, 31 May, 1991, p. 18.

[33] Bradley, *Men's Work, Women's Work*, p. 12.

[34] Glazer, *Working Woman*, p. 90.

[35] Blackwell, *Women in the Labour Force*, p. 33.

[36] Sylvia Walby, *Theorizing Patriarchy, Oxford*, 1990, p. 121.

[37] *Woman's Way*, 6 September, 1991.

[38] *U*, February, 1991.

[39] *U*, June, 1991.

[40] Germaine Greer, *The Female Eunuch*, London, 1971, p. 19.

[41] *Woman's Way*, 20 September, 1991.

[42] *U*, June, 1991, p. 32.

[43] *U*, July, 1991, p. 87.